Violence and Community

Violence and community were intimately linked in the ancient world. While various aspects of violence have been long studied on their own (warfare, revolution, murder, theft, piracy), there has been little effort so far to study violence as a unified field and explore its role in community formation. This volume aims to construct such an agenda by exploring the historiography of the study of violence in antiquity, and highlighting a number of important paradoxes of ancient violence. It explores the forceful nexus between wealth, power and the passions by focusing on three major aspects that link violence and community: the attempts of communities to regulate and canalise violence through law, the constitutive role of violence in communal identities, and the ways in which communities dealt with violence in regard to private and public space, landscapes and territories. The contributions to this volume range widely in both time and space: temporally, they cover the full span from the archaic to the Roman imperial period, while spatially they extend from Athens and Sparta through Crete, Arcadia and Macedonia to Egypt and Israel.

Ioannis K. Xydopoulos is Assistant Professor of Ancient Greek History at the Aristotle University of Thessaloniki. He is the author of *Social and Cultural Relations between the Macedonians and the Other Greeks* (2006) and *The Image of the Thracians in Classical Historiography* (2007).

Kostas Vlassopoulos is Assistant Professor of Ancient Greek History at the University of Crete. He is the author of *Unthinking the Greek Polis: Ancient Greek History beyond Eurocentrism* (2007), *Politics: Antiquity and its Legacy* (2010) and *Greeks and Barbarians* (2013).

Eleni Tounta is Assistant Professor of Medieval History at the Aristotle University of Thessaloniki. She is the author of *Medieval Mirrors for Princes: Histories and Narratives in the Norman South of Italy* (2012) and co-editor of *Usurping Ritual Volume III: State, Power and Violence* (2010).

Violence and Community

Law, Space and Identity in the
Ancient Eastern Mediterranean World

**Edited by
Ioannis K. Xydopoulos,
Kostas Vlassopoulos
and Eleni Tounta**

Routledge
Taylor & Francis Group

LONDON AND NEW YORK

First published 2017
by Routledge

2 Park Square, Milton Park, Abingdon, Oxfordshire OX14 4RN
52 Vanderbilt Avenue, New York, NY 10017

Routledge is an imprint of the Taylor & Francis Group, an informa business

First issued in paperback 2020

British Library Cataloguing-in-Publication Data
A catalogue record for this book is available from the British Library

Library of Congress Cataloguing-in-Publication Data
Names: Xydopoulos, I. K., editor. | Vlassopoulos, Kostas, 1977– editor. |
    Tounta, Eleni, 1973– editor.
Title: Violence and community : law, space and identity in the ancient
    Eastern Mediterranean world / edited by Ioannis K. Xydopoulos, Kostas
    Vlassopoulos, and Eleni Tounta.
Description: Abingdon, Oxon ; New York, NY : Routledge, 2017. |
    Includes bibliographical references and index.
Identifiers: LCCN 2016047497 | ISBN 9781472448323
    (hardback : alk. paper) | ISBN 9781315548159 (ebook)
Subjects: LCSH: Violence—Greece—History. | Communities—Greece—
    History. | Law, Greek—History. | Greece—History. |
    Greece—Civilization—To 146 B.C.
Classification: LCC HN10.G7 V56 2017 | DDC 303.609495—dc23
LC record available at https://lccn.loc.gov/2016047497

ISBN: 978-1-4724-4832-3 (hbk)
ISBN: 978-0-367-59518-0 (pbk)

Typeset in Times New Roman
by Apex CoVantage, LLC

Contents

Abbreviations

Αρχαία Μακεδονία IV:	*Αρχαία Μακεδονία, IV: ανακοινώσεις κατά το τέταρτο διεθνές συμπόσιο, Θεσσαλονίκη, 21–5 Σεπτεμβρίου 1983*, Thessaloniki, Greece, 1986
Αρχαία Μακεδονία VI:	*Αρχαία Μακεδονία VI: ανακοινώσεις κατά το έκτο διεθνές συμπόσιο Θεσσαλονίκη, 15–19 Οκτωβρίου 1996*, Thessaloniki, Greece, 1999
Αρχαία Μακεδονία VII:	*Αρχαία Μακεδονία VII: Η Μακεδονία από την εποχή του σιδήρου έως το θάνατο του Φιλίππου Β΄: Έβδομο Διεθνές Συμπόσιο, Θεσσαλονίκη, 14–18 Οκτωβρίου 2002*, Thessaloniki, Greece, 2007
AErgMak:	*Το αρχαιολογικό έργο στη Μακεδονία και τη Θράκη*
AHB:	*Ancient History Bulletin*
AION:	*Annali dell'Istituto universitario orientale di Napoli*
AJA:	*American Journal of Archaeology*
AJP:	*American Journal of Philology*
AWE:	*Ancient West and East*
BCH:	*Bulletin de Correspondance Hellénique*
BSA:	*Annual of the British School at Athens*
BMCR:	*Bryn Mawr Classical Review*
CA:	*Classical Antiquity*
CP:	*Classical Philology*
CQ:	*Classical Quarterly*
DT:	A. Audollent, *Defixionum tabellae*, Paris, 1904
DTA:	R. Wünsch, *Defixionum Tabellae Atticae* (= *IG* III.3 Appendix), Berlin, 1897
FGrHist:	F. Jacoby, *Die Fragmente der Griechischen Historiker, I-III*, Leiden, Netherlands, 1923–58
G&R:	*Greece and Rome*
GDI:	H. Collitz and F. Bechtel, eds., *Sammlung der griechischen Dialekt-Inschriften, I-IV*, Göttingen, 1884–1915
GRBS:	*Greek, Roman and Byzantine Studies*

Heracles to Alexander:	*Heracles to Alexander the Great: Treasures from the Royal Capital of Macedon, a Hellenic Kingdom in the Age of Democracy*, Oxford, UK, 2011
IJG:	R. Dreste, B. Haussoullier and T. Reinach, *Recueil des inscriptions juridiques grecques*, I-II, Paris, 1898
IPArk:	G. Thür and H. Taeuber, *Prozessrechtliche Inschriften der griechischen Poleis: Arkadien*, Vienna, 1994
JHS:	*Journal of Hellenic Studies*
JRA:	*Journal of Roman Archaeology*
JRS:	*Journal of Roman Studies*
LGPN:	P.M. Fraser and E. Matthews, *A Lexicon of Greek Personal Names*, Oxford, UK, 1987–2013
LSJ:	H. G. Liddel, R. Scott and H. S. Jones, *Greek-English Lexicon, with a Revised Supplement*, Oxford, UK, 1996
MDAI:	*Mitteilungen des Deutschen Archäologischen Instituts*
MEP:	*Minima epigraphica et papyrologica*
MHR:	*Mediterranean Historical Review*
Michel:	C. Michel, *Recueil d'inscriptions grecques*, Brussels, 1900
NGCT:	D. R. Jordan, 'New Greek curse rablets (1985–2000)', *GRBS* 41, 2000, 5–46
Nomima I & II:	H. van Effenterre and F. Ruzé, *Nomima. Recueil d'inscriptions politiques et juridiques de l'archaïsme grec*, I-II, Rome, 1994–5
PAA:	J. H. Traill, *Persons of Ancient Athens*, Toronto, 1994–
PCPS:	*Proceedings of the Cambridge Philological Society*
PMG:	D. L. Page, *Poetae Melici Graeci*, Oxford, UK, 1962
P&P:	*Past & Present*
QUCC:	*Quaderni urbinati di cultura classica*
REG:	*Revue des Études Grecques*
RhM:	*Rheinisches Museum*
SEG:	*Supplementum Epigraphicum Graecum*
SGD:	D. R. Jordan, 'A Survey of Greek Defixiones Not Included in the Special Corpora', GRBS 26, 1985, 151–197 EG: Supplementum Epigraphicum Graecum
Syll²:	W. Dittenberger, *Sylloge Inscriptionum Graecarum*, 2nd ed., Leipzig, Germany, 1898–1901
TAPA:	*Transactions of the American Philological Association*
ZPE:	*Zeitschrift für Papyrologie und Epigraphik*

Notes on contributors

Mirko Canevaro is Chancellor's Fellow in Classics at the University of Edinburgh. He is the author of *The Documents in the Attic Orators: Laws and Decrees in the Public Speeches of the Demosthenic Corpus* (2013) and co-editor of *Oxford Handbook of Ancient Greek Law* (forthcoming).

Nick Fisher was for many years Professor of Ancient History at Cardiff University. He is the author of *Hybris: A Study in the Values of Honour and Shame in Ancient Greece* (1992), and co-editor of numerous volumes, including most recently *'Aristocracy' in Antiquity: Redefining Greek and Roman Elites* (2015).

Nikolaos Giannakopoulos is Assistant Professor of Ancient Greek History at the Aristotle University of Thessaloniki. He is the author of *The Institution of the Gerousia in the Greek Cities of the Roman Period* (2008) and *Institutions and Function of the Cities of Hellenistic and Roman Euboea* (2012).

Elias Koulakiotis is Assistant Professor in Ancient Greek History at the University of Ioannina. He is the author of *Genese und Metamorphosen des Alexandermythos im Spiegel der griechischen nichthistoriographischen Überlieferung bis zum 3. Jh. n. Chr* (2006) and co-editor of *Marathon: The Day After* (2013).

David Lewis is Assistant Professor of Ancient History at the University of Nottingham. He is the author of *Greek Slave Systems and their Eastern Neighbours: A Comparative Study* (forthcoming) and co-editor of *The Ancient Greek Economy: Markets, Households and City-States* (2015).

Zinon Papakonstantinou is Associate Professor of History and Classics at the University of Illinois at Chicago. He is the author of *Lawmaking and Adjudication in Archaic Greece* (2008) and editor of *Sport in the Cultures of the Ancient World: New Perspectives* (2010).

Eleni Tounta is Assistant Professor of Medieval History at the Aristotle University of Thessaloniki. She is the author of *Medieval Mirrors for Princes. Histories and Narratives in the Norman South of Italy* (2012) and co-editor of *Usurping Ritual Volume III: State, Power and Violence* (2010).

Kostas Vlassopoulos is Assistant Professor of Ancient Greek History at the University of Crete. He is the author of *Unthinking the Greek Polis: Ancient Greek History beyond Eurocentrism* (2007), *Politics: Antiquity and its Legacy* (2010) and *Greeks and Barbarians* (2013).

Ioannis K. Xydopoulos is Assistant Professor of Ancient Greek History at the Aristotle University of Thessaloniki. He is the author of *Social and Cultural Relations between the Macedonians and the Other Greeks* (2006) and *The Image of the Thracians in Classical Historiography* (2007).

1 Introduction

The study of violence and community in ancient Greek history

Kostas Vlassopoulos and Ioannis K. Xydopoulos

The inseparable link between violence and community makes its appearance at the beginning of classical literature. Given that the *Iliad* and the *Odyssey* are framed around the theme of the Trojan War, this is hardly surprising. A significant part of the *Iliad* consists of graphic descriptions of battles between Achaeans and Trojans, and the ways in which intercommunal violence affects all aspects of the Trojan city and the Achaean camp. But equally significant is the fact that both epics are dominated by a different kind of violence, which takes place within a particular community. The first scene of the *Iliad* narrates how a violent confrontation between Agamemnon and Achilles was barely averted, and the rest of the work follows the fatal consequences of this initial conflict. Intracommunal violence is at the heart of the *Odyssey*, which focuses on the conflict between Odysseus' household and the Suitors, the violent settling of this conflict and the peaceful avoidance of further bloodshed through divine intervention.[1]

It is thus hardly surprising that violence, in its various manifestations, has been at the forefront of the research interests of ancient historians for a very long time. What is more surprising is the peculiar way in which violence in the ancient Greek world has been studied until very recently.[2] Scholars have not approached violence as a unified field of study; instead, different facets of violence have formed independent fields, which tend to be examined by different kinds of scholars with distinct research agendas and research traditions. The study of Greek warfare has obviously a very long pedigree, and has in recent decades experienced a major transformation through the application of novel approaches and the broadening of perspectives; but it remains the case that the intercommunal violence which constitutes warfare tends to be examined separately from the various forms of intracommunal violence.[3] If in the case of intercommunal violence there is at least a unified field of study, in the case of intracommunal violence even this is largely missing. The diverse aspects of violence within Greek communities tend to be examined in different contexts and by different scholars: the study of *stasis*, the various forms of political conflict and violence that were a characteristic feature of Greek history, has hardly developed any links with the study of assault and homicide.[4] To give another example, the debates on the extent to which Greek communities were states which monopolised the legitimate exercise of violence are not connected with the study of the violence that Greek masters habitually exercised over their slaves.[5]

This volume aims to make a contribution towards the study of violence in ancient Greek communities as a unified field of study by tracing an agenda of interconnected themes. But in order to frame such an agenda it is essential first to explore the wider scholarly approaches that have shaped how aspects of violence and community have been perceived.

Narratives and scholarly traditions

Most approaches to violence and community in ancient Greece have been influenced, in one way or another, by the tradition which is usually associated with Thomas Hobbes. This is a tradition which has its origins already in fifth-century Greece, and Hobbes built his edifice with ancient materials.[6] His *Leviathan* has drawn a vivid image of the violent world of pre-political society and the order created by the social contract that led to the creation of the state and its monopoly of violence. In the Hobbesian narrative the state is the undoubted hero. Societies without states are characterised by eternal feuding and vendettas; self-help is the only means of achieving results in the face of conflict, and this unsurprisingly generates recurring or escalating circles of violence. The emergence of the state presents a radical break: states create laws and institutions which provide alternative, non-violent ways of achieving results.

The impact of this narrative on the study of violence and community in ancient Greece cannot be doubted. 'The rise of the polis' is the standard account of the Hobbesian narrative in Greek history. In the Dark Ages and the early archaic period, so the story goes, the absence of formal institutions and laws meant that the punishment of violence could only be achieved through feuding and self-help. In an early stage of development the polis tried primarily to limit the forms that feuding and self-help could take by devising regulations like Draco's famous homicide law, whose provisions are examined by Mirko Canevaro in this volume (pp. 52–63). But by the classical period the polis had managed to take over and control the whole process of punishing violence: by now, the only legitimate recourse for punishing violence consisted in prosecuting offenders in communal law courts on the basis of the explicitly formulated laws of the polis. According to this approach, the citizens of a classical Greek polis lived in a world that was incomparably less violent compared to the world of their ancestors in Homeric Greece.[7] It is telling that a recent global account that presents the paradoxical claim that the escalation of warfare has created stronger states, which have managed to create a far less violent world, has been written by a scholar who started his career with a book on the transition from the Dark Ages to the emergence of the polis in the course of the archaic period.[8]

If the Hobbesian narrative features the state as the main hero, an alternative tradition focuses instead on economy and culture. If the first tradition found its most influential formulation with Hobbes in the seventeenth century, the latter was primarily shaped in the course of the eighteenth-century Enlightenment and its debates. At the centre of the 'Enlightened narrative' is a fundamental distinction between ancient and modern societies.[9] In ancient societies, which were primarily agricultural and pastoral, predation played a fundamental social and economic role. Given the limits of agricultural growth in pre-industrial societies, violent extortion and warfare constituted the most efficient ways of amassing wealth and power. Consequently, ancient societies were warrior cultures that put a premium on successful violence; but they were also slave societies, because the violent subordination of labourers was the only means of procuring wealth on a large scale. A further consequence concerned the limited 'moral circle' of ancient societies. Protection from violence was restricted to full members of the community (citizens); all outsiders were fair game to unmitigated private and collective violence.[10]

Modern societies were radically different, the 'Enlightened narrative' posited. On the one hand, they were based on commerce: commerce requires peaceful exchanges, and therefore tends to strongly limit the utility of recourse to warfare. The novel significance of the market meant that free labour was the modern alternative to the violent domination of slaves and serfs that characterised pre-modern societies.[11] Furthermore, as a result of the impact of Christianity and the Enlightenment, modern societies had undergone a transformation in terms of sensibility and morality. Christianity and the Enlightenment had widened the moral circle by recognising the natural rights of all human beings, even if they were outsiders to the community. The abolition of slavery, which started in the late eighteenth century and was largely accomplished in the course of the nineteenth, at least for the Western world, was a major consequence of this revolution in morality. Equally significant was a revolution in sensibility that made modern people abhor violence as a means of achieving order: violent punishment, whether for children or convicted felons, was widely criticised and ultimately abolished from the late eighteenth century onwards.[12]

These themes have been explored in a range of highly influential modern works from a variety of perspectives. Norbert Elias has examined what he famously described as 'the civilising process': the process through which European societies from the Middle Ages onwards came to radically transform their standards of acceptable violence through the gradual diffusion of courtly etiquettes that created new understandings of shame and repugnance.[13] Michel Foucault explored the break between early modern forms of punishment that were based on the public spectacle of inflicted violence and the modern form of punishment which emerged from the nineteenth century onwards and was organised on the basis of new forms of discipline based on incarceration. Foucault challenged the traditional description that presented the abolition of corporal punishment as a progressive result of humanitarian concerns; but his memorable descriptions of the employment of spectacles of violence by early modern states had a major impact on scholarship.[14] To give a final example, Steven Pinker has presented an influential account which argues that in the course of human history the frequency and impact of violence has declined as a result of five interrelated processes: the growth of modern states with their monopoly of legitimate violence, the impact of *doux commerce* in regulating human affairs peacefully, the increasing influence of cosmopolitan perspectives, the 'feminisation' resulting from a growing respect for female interests, and the intensified application of knowledge and reason to human affairs.[15]

These approaches have had their impact on the study of ancient Greece. Danielle Allen has taken her cue from Foucault's study of punishment and the spectacle of public violence in order to provide a comprehensive examination of the politics of punishment in classical Athens and the interconnections and contradictions between Athenian democracy and its critics.[16] Jon Ploug Jørgensen has applied Elias' approach to archaic Greece, by exploring the civilising process through which Greek elites came to abandon the everyday carrying of arms and the violent settling of disputes.[17] In his contribution to this volume, Nick Fisher explores the extent to which Pinker's account of how interrelated processes led to the limitation of violence can be applied to ancient Greece, by focusing in particular on the rituals and institutions of educating and socialising the young in Sparta, Crete and Athens.

A third narrative, related to but distinct from the other two, can be described as 'the rise of representative government'. Its origins can be found among the Enlightenment discourses on politics, but its clearest formulation emerged in the course of the debates engendered by the American and French revolutions. The major question for these revolutions was whether there existed an alternative to the royal absolutisms that dominated Western politics, and whether modern polities could be governed by their own citizens. For thinkers like David Hume, the authors of the *Federalist Papers* and Benjamin Constant this was possible, because of a fundamental difference between ancient and modern politics. Ancient politics meant the direct participation of citizens in the government of small-scale communities, usually city-states. Direct participation exacerbated the combustible potential of class divisions and the passions enflamed by personal animosities. The result was that ancient polities were dominated by political violence: civil wars, revolutions, massacres and masses of political exiles filled the annals of ancient history. Modern politics could employ a novel kind of republicanism based on representation: by eliminating direct participation and by diluting the passions and interests of small-scale communities into the large-scale politics of modern states, representative government could achieve the advantages of republics, while avoiding the political violence that characterised ancient politics.[18]

The critique of Athenian democracy as a violent version of mob rule has a long pedigree in the Western discourses of the last few centuries; among many recent examples, particularly interesting are studies exploring the commonality with which Athenian democracy inflicted the death penalty on politicians whom it deemed that they had failed in protecting its interests, or the violent effects of mass paranoia in a system of direct democracy.[19] Numerous studies have been devoted to *stasis*, the peculiar form of political conflict and violence which is such a dominant theme in Greek history and political thought.[20]

A final narrative focused more specifically on intercommunal violence and warfare. This narrative had an equally long tradition, but its most influential formulation emerged in the early twentieth century within the fields of anthropology and military studies. If Hobbes had mobilised a long tradition depicting pre-state societies as brutish, violent and anarchic, Rousseau could mobilise the equally long tradition of the Noble Savage, in order to argue that societies without inequality were fundamentally peaceful and compassionate. The growth in anthropological knowledge in the course of the nineteenth century seemed to challenge both Rousseau's image of peaceful natives, as well as Hobbes' account of 'primitive' societies as brutish and anarchic. These paradoxical findings led to the formulation of a new narrative that was based on a distinction between 'primitive' and 'civilised' (or 'real') warfare.[21] If 'civilised' or 'real' warfare had economic and political motives that led to the conquest of territory and the exaction of tribute, 'primitive' warfare had primarily psychological and social motives whose aim was honour and prestige. The highly ritualised form of 'primitive' warfare was a telling sign that the end was less important than the means: ritualised forms of warfare minimised casualties and fulfilled the requirements of codes of honour that were its main motives.[22]

This narrative has exercised a deep impact on the study of ancient Greek warfare. The style of warfare depicted in the Homeric epics has been one of the major inspirations for the construction of the model of 'primitive' warfare; from the opposite direction, the 'primitive' warfare of the inhabitants of the highlands of Papua New Guinea has been employed as a source for understanding Homeric warriors and their battles.[23] But similar concerns have characterised the attempts of ancient historians to understand the highly ritualised form of the hoplite battle, a style of warfare that appears largely unsuitable to Greek topographies. It has been quite common to project a transition between an original era, in which the ritualised hoplite battle dominated Greek warfare, and later periods, usually from the Peloponnesian War onwards, when the emergence of 'real' or 'civilised' warfare changed the nature and aims of Greek intercommunal violence.[24]

Modern narratives and ancient paradoxes

The modern narratives we explored previously have had a deep impact on the study of violence and community in the Greek world, as the examples we have mentioned indicate. Nevertheless, the study of Greek history has revealed a number of important paradoxes, which create major challenges for the frame of reference of these narratives. The study of violence and community in the Greek world can consequently play a major role in rethinking assumptions about violence in other fields of history, politics and anthropology.

The first paradox concerns the narrative that focuses on the state. Greek communities raise major conceptual problems for modern theories of the state. These theories tend to assume that states have apparatuses, like the police, armies and bureaucracies, which curtail violence and maintain order. But Greek communities do not fit very well into this description. As Hans van Wees has shown, in the Dark Ages and the early archaic period carrying arms on an everyday basis was a widespread custom; as Thucydides famously pointed out, the custom still existed among various Greek communities in mainland Greece (Thuc. 1.5.3). But in the course of the archaic period, most Greek communities came to abandon the custom of habitually carrying arms on an everyday basis (see the relevant discussion of Xydopoulos in this volume, pp. 77–81).[25] In contrast to the Hobbesian narrative, this development cannot be attributed to the emergence of a strong state apparatus that managed to monopolise the use of legitimate force.

Greek communities usually lacked standing armies; their military forces consisted of amateur armed citizens and were ready for use only when specifically mobilised for a particular purpose. Their police forces and bureaucratic apparatuses, where they existed at all, were embryonic and generally functioned reactively, rather than proactively. This meant that self-help was an essential aspect of dealing with violence and dispute settlement. It was not the few policemen who dealt with arresting criminals; people largely relied on self-help for this.[26] There was no public prosecution of theft, assault or homicide: such violent acts could be punished only if the victims, or other private citizens on their behalf, were willing and able to undertake prosecuting the culprits.

There are of course many societies that lack state apparatuses and rely on self-help for settling disputes and dealing with violence. A significant part of the population in such societies carries arms, both for protection as well as for avenging crimes; the ensuing high level of violence in such societies was one of the major themes of the Hobbesian narrative.[27] The Greek paradox lies in the combination of crucial elements from both non-state and state societies: the dominance of self-help and lack of bureaucratic apparatuses on the one hand, and the communal monopoly of legitimate force and the dominance of institutionalised procedures for dealing with violence on the other. Greek communities lacked standing armies and had embryonic police forces, but the only legitimate forms of violence were those undertaken in the name of and with the authorisation of the community; violence perpetrated by individuals was a punishable offence.[28] The arrest and prosecution of violent offenders depended often on self-help: the punishment of offenders could not be legitimately undertaken by private citizens, but could only come through trial in communal institutions.[29] Despite the significance of self-help, the practice of vendetta, so widespread in periods of Mediterranean history with weak or limited state mechanisms, was largely unknown in Greek communities, wherever we have sufficient evidence to judge, like ancient Athens.

In other words, many elements which are traditionally associated with the emergence of the state in the Hobbesian narrative can be observed in ancient Greece; but while in the case of late mediaeval, early modern and modern Europe we can perceive monarchies and state apparatuses as independent agents that sought for their own purposes to monopolise the legitimate use of violence, in the case of ancient Greece there are simply no such independent agents to be seen.[30] In terms of the *imaginaire*, the Greeks were able to create an abstract conception of the polis as the only agent of legitimate violence; but it would be a grave mistake to hypostatise the polis, as if it was an agent with a volition of its own (as one can do with a certain plausibility as regards e.g. late mediaeval monarchies).[31] The Hobbesian narrative needs a different hero when it comes to ancient Greece.

If major changes in the relationship between violence and community cannot be attributed to the state, perhaps we should turn to the second narrative of the economics and culture of violence. And this constitutes our second paradox. As before, many aspects in the traditional depiction of ancient societies as violent, predatory and with a limited moral circle can be accepted without debate; but at the same time, many elements that in the traditional narrative should appear only after the modern revolution in sensibility and morality can already be observed in the ancient Greek world. There is no doubt that Greek communities can be described as honour cultures. The 'moral circle' of ancient Greeks was undoubtedly limited: the ideological imperative of 'helping friends and harming enemies' expressed clearly the limits of the dominant morality. Revenge on one's enemies was not only unapologetically asserted, but a failure to pursue this end could lead to a damaging loss of face and honour.[32]

It is quite remarkable that ancient thinkers explicitly posit the existence of a 'civilising process' that had changed the level of violence in Greek societies from the archaic period to the classical. Thucydides describes a transition from an early period in which Greek communities accepted and applauded the predatory habits of raiding and piracy to a current stage in which such practices are shunned; a similar transition has seen the abandonment of the habit of carrying arms on an everyday basis. Thucydides offers an economic and cultural explanation for these transitions: the emergence of alternative forms of wealth made predation less appealing, and the adoption of a more luxurious lifestyle was linked to the abandonment of carrying arms by the Athenians (Thuc. 1.4–6).[33] Equally, Aristotle condemns the primitive and barbaric customs that Greeks followed in early times, like carrying arms and buying wives: since sciences tend to accumulate knowledge and progress, Aristotle argues, it is unsurprising that political science has managed to eliminate such practices (*Pol.* 1268b32–1269a4).

To date, the most ambitious and controversial work on the diminishing significance of violence in ancient Greece is Gabriel Herman's study of morality and behaviour in classical Athens.[34] Herman's views are in direct confrontation with another approach, most clearly formulated by David Cohen, which employs anthropological work on shame and honour in modern Mediterranean societies, in order to depict classical Athens as a feuding culture in which revenge in defence of one's honour was a paramount value and laws and institutions were merely means employed to further such aims.[35] Herman has presented a diametrically different image of classical Athens, in which, in contrast to most Mediterranean societies, violence was very successfully limited and the culture of honour and revenge was substituted by an alternative moral code, based on altruism and cooperation, which abhorred aggression and retaliation.[36] Herman's work has generated wider debates about the extent to which pity for the victims of violence and misfortune was a significant value in classical Athens, and concerning the links among altruism, revenge and the Athenian legal system.[37]

The third paradox concerns the narrative of 'the rise of representative government'. There is no doubt that *stasis* was a perennial feature of the history of ancient Greek communities; the political exiles from Tegea, and the complex problems of re-incorporating them into the citizen body, which are studied in this volume by Elias Koulakiotis (pp. 159–64) is merely one example among many.[38] But, paradoxically, Athens and Sparta, the two most important classical Greek communities, and the ones we know most about, had very low levels of *stasis* and political violence, which can be compared with most modern liberal democracies. As Nick Fisher comments in his contribution (p. 123), Athens experienced a brief period of limited political violence in the late 460s BCE, as well as two brief, but intense, moments of violence during the oligarchic counterrevolutions of 411/10 and 404/3 BCE. But for most of the almost two centuries between 508–323 BCE Athens was remarkably free of political violence; the same is largely true of classical Sparta, even if our knowledge is less detailed. How can we square the coexistence of recurrent political violence in most Greek communities with its emphatic absence in the two most important Greek poleis? Do we need to posit explanations which depend on factors which are specific to Athens and Sparta, like Josiah Ober's argument that Athenian stability depended on the domination of public rhetoric and ideology by the Athenian masses?[39] Now that we know much more about Greek democracies apart from Athens, can we attribute the peculiar lack of political violence in Athens to democracy per se?[40] Or do we need to rethink our framework of analysing Greek politics in order to account for the differential role of violence within it?

The nexus of violence: wealth, power and the passions

In the Mytilenean debate, Thucydides presents Diodotos offering a sophisticated argument about the causes of conflict and violence and the inability of the death penalty to provide an adequate deterrent:

> It is probable that in early times the penalties for the greatest offences were less severe, and that, as these were disregarded, the penalty of death has been by degrees in most cases arrived at, which is itself disregarded in like manner. Either then some means of terror more terrible than this must be discovered, or it must be owned that this restraint is useless; and that as long as poverty gives men the courage of necessity, or plenty fills them with the ambition which belongs to insolence and pride, and the other conditions of life remain each under the thraldom of some fatal and master passion, so long will the impulse never be wanting to drive men into danger.[41]

Diodotos suggests various causes of conflict and violence. The first concerns wealth and its absence, poverty. In his analysis of the various lifeways and forms of acquiring wealth, Aristotle mentions, alongside pastoralism, agriculture and trade, that of hunting: the application of violence in order to procure sustenance and even wealth, whether it applied to wild animals and fish, or to human beings.[42] Many excellent studies have been devoted to brigandage and piracy in classical antiquity and there is no need to rehearse their conclusions extensively here.[43]

It is sufficient to stress that brigandage and piracy reveal the strong links between intercommunal and intracommunal violence, between violence and communal identity, between violence and space. It is a well-known phenomenon that brigands and pirates, while usually inflicting their violence indiscriminately, could be enlisted by communities as privateers in more targeted operations in the course of intercommunal violence. If brigandage and piracy were universal phenomena, they were also strongly linked to the formation of communal identities. Some communities were seen by outsiders, and occasionally presented themselves in such a light, as practitioners of brigandage and piracy par excellence: the pirate reputation of the communities of Crete and Cilicia and the bandit reputation of the highlander communities of Isauria are telling examples in this respect.[44] But equally significant is how many communities constructed their identity in explicit link to the suppression of piracy and brigandage and the safeguarding of public and even international peace, whether we think of classical Athens, Hellenistic Rhodes or the Roman Empire.[45] This last aspect points to the link between violence and space: suppressing piracy and brigandage is necessarily connected to control over territory and routes, whether the mountainous hinterland of a community, the no-man's-land between communal territories, or the seaways, islets and promontories often used by pirates.

If we are relatively well-informed concerning brigandage and piracy in antiquity, our knowledge of other forms of violent acquisition of wealth, such as theft and burglary, is much more limited. The reason for this difference is primarily due to the nature of our sources. Brigandage and piracy, which are often on a large scale, can easily impinge on the big events of political and military history that are the focus of ancient sources like historiography; petty acts of burglary are less likely to have major consequences and are rarely mentioned in literary sources, except as background noise. The same applies to sources like the forensic speeches from classical Athens: cases of petty theft would involve relatively limited amounts of money and would thus be unlikely to reach a trial requiring the expensive services of a professional speech-writer who created our surviving law-court speeches. Nick Fisher's detailed examination of the evidence for organised crime in classical Athens provides an exemplary analysis both of the nature of our sources and of the conclusions we can draw on their basis.[46] It is primarily in the Hellenistic and Roman periods when the expansion in the form and nature of our sources allows us to form a more detailed image. It is in particular the papyrological evidence from Hellenistic and Roman Egypt that allows us to come face to face with how violent acts related to property affected the lives of ordinary inhabitants in Egypt. In his contribution to this volume, Nikolaos Giannakopoulos employs papyrological and epigraphic sources in order to explore a particular aspect of this wider phenomenon: the violation of the private space of the household by acts of burglary and the ways in which individuals, groups and communities tried to deal with the problem and face the dilemmas that it raised.

But it would be grossly misleading to limit the link between violence and wealth in antiquity to brigandage, piracy and theft. If Aristotle implied that the violent lifeway of the hunter of men and animals is firmly distinguished from the peaceful lifeway of agriculture, the famous song of the Cretan Hybrias offers a very different link between violence and wealth:

> I have great wealth – a spear and a sword
> and the good shield of animal hide which protects the body;
> with this I plough, with this I reap,

with this I tread the sweet wine from the vine,
with this I am called master of the slaves.
Those who do not dare wield a spear and sword
and the good hide-bound shield, the body's protector,
all of them, falling around my knee
worship me, and call me
master and great king.[47]

Hybrias' song might be the most unashamed proclamation from antiquity that violence is at the root of social inequality; but the idea that violence enables the wealthy to control the land and the people who cultivate it and generate wealth is by no means rare in ancient sources. The Digest's attempt to derive the etymology of the Latin words for slaves from acts of violence is eloquent testimony:

> Slaves *(servi)* are so called because commanders generally sell the people they capture and thereby save *(servare)* them instead of killing them. The word for property in slaves *(mancipia)* is derived from the fact that they are captured from the enemy by force of arms *(manu capiantur)*.[48]

There is of course an enormous literature on ancient slavery and the intimate link between slavery and violence;[49] there is equally no need to rehearse this literature here, apart from noting the sad fact that this literature tends to dissociate the violence of slavery from the wider issue of the link between violence and wealth in ancient societies.

This brings us to the wider issue of the violent consequences of the unequal distribution of wealth in ancient societies; for Diodotos' first comment above on the causes of violence concerned the consequences of poverty. The unequal distribution of wealth that causes poverty created deep fissures within Greek communities, which often took the form of collective conflict and violence. Theognis, Aristophanes, Plato and Aristotle paid particular attention in their works to the violent conflicts between wealthy and poor and looked to solutions that could avoid or eschew such conflicts by alleviating poverty or mitigating its effects.[50] In his contribution to this volume, David Lewis examines how communities in archaic Athens and Israel tried to deal with the forms of violence that were engendered by the inequalities of wealth and the attempts of rich and poor to redress the balance in their interest.

Apart from its link to wealth, violence forms a strong nexus with power. The song of Hybrias should have made obvious that violence is not merely a means of acquiring wealth; it is also a means of exercising power over those who address Hybrias as 'great king', as well as the foundation of a distinction between the brave overlords who can successfully yield shield and spear and the cowards who acquiesce to their overlords' superior force and courage. Violence and power are of course intimately linked. Not all forms of violence constitute power, and power is by no means tantamount to violence; but if Hobbes is at the origins of a modern narrative that put violence at the constitutive point of power and the state, the ancient Greeks offered themselves a long and complex tradition of reflections on the link between power and violence. Thucydides' Melian dialogue is a famous exploration of the nexus, as is Aeschylus' *Prometheus Bound*, or most of the Platonic corpus.

If the nexus between power and violence is universal, the specifics of the Greek case can be better understood by taking into account some of the peculiarities of the Greek world. In contrast to many other societies in world history, the Greeks inhabited an intracommunal and intercommunal environment in which the locus of power was particularly inchoate and unstable. We have already mentioned the paradox of the 'statelessness' of the Greek polis and the absence of a clear locus of power usually associated with kings and state apparatuses in most of world history. In the case of Rome, the link between violence and power was visually and ritually represented by the fasces carried by the lictors who accompanied the two consuls, the chief magistrates of the community; it is probably not accidental that such a visual representation of power is generally absent from the Greek world.[51]

If Greek discourses on violence and power within a community tended to focus on the image of the tyrant, this is partly because tyrants made much clearer and more visible where the locus of power and violence was.[52] One result of this was the remarkable phenomenon of the employment of public slaves, such as the Scythian archers in Athens, as key agents in exercising violence on behalf of the community towards its members. When Lysistrata expresses outrage that a Scythian slave, following the magistrate's order, could exercise violence over a free Athenian woman, the paradox becomes particularly prominent.[53] As Paulin Ismard has persuasively argued, the employment of public slaves was a means of limiting the ability of the state apparatus to exercise a volition of its own and employ violence in order to further its own interests, rather than the interests of the community as a whole.[54]

On the other hand, the absence of a clear locus of power could make Greek politics much more violent than other societies in world history. Conflicts and disputes could escalate into violence much more readily than in societies in which rulers had long-term and institutionalised access to the means of violence. This feature was further exacerbated by the anarchic nature of Greek interstate politics.[55] In the absence of an unchallenged centre or regulative force, international relations in the Greek world were characterised by an anarchic and easily destabilised balance of power, in which bouts of violence could be a recurrent phenomenon. Thucydides' description of civil war in Corcyra is an illuminating example of the interlinking between intracommunal conflict and intercommunal anarchy.[56]

Greek discourses on violence and power/wealth tend to be couched in the language of passions, a third major factor: it is interesting that in the passage of Thucydides mentioned previously (p. 8), Diodotos connects the possession of wealth with ambition, pride and insolence as causes of violence. Greek discussions of civil strife (*stasis*) illustrate its links with disputes between rich and poor about wealth and between mass and elite or democrats and oligarchs about the distribution of power and political rights; but equally important is the significance they attribute to passions like greed, ambition and shame in explaining the causes of strife.[57] Equally telling is J. E. Lendon's exploration of vengeance as a cause explaining the outbreak of ancient Greek wars.[58] Of particular significance in this respect is the Greek concept of *hybris*: the violent assault against an individual which particularly affects the attacked person's honour.[59] There is an enormous literature on the constitutive role of honour and shame in Mediterranean societies from antiquity through the present and how they generated emotions and passions which were prone to violent reactions. We have already mentioned the work of Gabriel Herman, who has argued that Athenian democracy maintained a particularly low level of violence because it shaped its citizens in abhorring the violent retaliation demanded by honour cultures and in espousing altruism and collaboration. The growing body of work on ancient Greek emotions and passions is increasingly throwing light on the nexus with violence. Balot's study of greed and Sanders' study of envy and jealousy show that it is impossible to understand Athenian society without paying sufficient attention to how these emotions shaped most facets of Athenian life, including Athenian reactions to violence.[60] Furthermore, as Balot's more recent work on courage shows, Athenians conceived courage as a specifically democratic emotion that helped them both face as well as perpetrate violence on behalf of their community.[61]

Dealing with conflict: law, civic identity and space

Having analysed the historiographies of studying ancient Greek violence, the paradoxes that face the major lines of interpretation, and the nexus that links violence to wealth, power and the passions, we now come to the nucleus of this book: the ways in which ancient Greek communities attempted to deal with violence and the ways in which violence shaped ancient Greek communities and their institutions, territories and identities. This volume focuses on three main areas of interconnection between violence and community. The first concerns the ways in which Greek communities employed law and devised procedures in order to contain the violence that was inherent in conflicts between members of the community, regulate its application, settle disputes and punish violent transgressions; the second explores the constitutive role of violence in shaping the identity of Greek communities and their members; finally, the third relates to the role of space as the framework within which violence is exercised within and between communities and the effects of violence on the shaping of communal space and territories.

While all communities have norms concerning violence, the fact that certain communities come to regulate violence through explicitly defined rules and laws is of major consequence. Many communities in world history consider the violence that results from disputes concerning wealth, power and the passions as essentially private matters involving individuals and groups; the role of the community in dealing with violence is circumscribed, often limited to providing arbitrators or setting down compensation payments for perpetrators of violent acts.[62] The decision of the community to become directly involved in dealing with acts of violence might take a variety of forms. One set involved the creation of institutionalised responses to the causes of violence and to violent acts. In his contribution to this volume, David Lewis offers a stimulating comparative examination of how communities in archaic Athens and Israel endeavoured to find institutional answers to the violence caused by inequalities in wealth and power. In both communities individuals and groups amassed wealth and power over other individuals and groups by a variety of means, which included violence; furthermore, wealth and power inequalities created social and political turmoil which could result in large-scale violence. Solon's law on violent assault (*hybris*) in Athens, or the reform of judicial institutions in both communities, were attempts to employ law and legal procedure in order to find long-term solutions to the causes and effects of violence.

The means through which communities chose to use law and legal procedure in order to intervene in acts of violence could vary considerably. Draco's law on homicide in the late seventh century BCE, examined by Mirko Canevaro in this volume (pp. 52–63), attempted to deal with violence by defining the choices open to the relatives of the victim for punishing the perpetrator and the contexts in which violent retribution was legitimate; by the time we reach the fifth century BCE, Athenian law had largely made the legitimate punishment of violent acts only available through public institutions. It is quite interesting that violent retribution was limited to a few cases of self-help, which raised legal problems of their own: the attempt of the speaker in Lysias 1 to justify killing the lover of his wife caught in the act inside his house is a characteristic example of how violent responses had developed in the context of changing communal interventions.[63]

But communal attempts to affect the causes of violence and canalise responses to it through carefully crafted legal procedures had their own distinct limits. In certain cases the limits of governmental infrastructure proved decisive for the extent to which laws and procedures could prove effective. As it has been observed in relation to mediaeval Europe, while Carolingian kings legislated to turn violent acts into offences punishable by the authorities, the limits of the infrastructure available created a significant gap between theory and practice.[64] While Carolingian kings considered violent acts like murder public offences to be punished in theory by civil authorities, ancient Greek communities like classical Athens had a more ambivalent response: while punishment of violent acts could only legitimately take place through public procedures; punishment was not the responsibility of civil authorities, but depended on the initiative of volunteer prosecutors. This meant that Greek communities spent less effort in developing institutions that punished violence and more in providing a public arena in which disputes involving violence could be settled.[65] As it has been observed in relation to the emergence of public procedures dealing with violence in late mediaeval Europe, the employment of courts instead of vendettas originally largely provided an alternative arena for exercising the passions that had led to the disputes and the violent acts.[66] Zinon Papakonstantinou's contribution illuminates this issue through a particularly challenging source: the curse tablets through which Athenian litigants attempted to register supernatural agents in order to inflict violence of various forms to their court adversaries. The existence of public procedures was not the end point of conflict and violence: it merely provided a new arena for disputes, and even within that arena, recourse to extra-institutional agents for defeating an enemy was not shunned by those Athenians who left the curse tablets recovered by modern scholars.

Given these factors, Greek communities did not limit themselves to institutions and laws punishing violent acts. They equally tried to use a variety of means in order to prevent violence, by moulding their citizens in such a way that recourse to violence was avoided or canalised to the proper forms and targets. This attitude could take a variety of forms; as has been shown in a seminal study by Virginia Hunter, in the absence of substantial and effective policing and bureaucratic mechanisms, classical Athens developed alternative forms of social control, in which practices like gossiping played a major role in stopping people from transgressing communal norms.[67] If practices of gossiping were largely informal, other practices became more or less institutionalised. In his contribution to this volume, Nick Fisher examines a range of practices, including banqueting and civil and military education, through which Greek communities attempted to teach their young about the proper use of violence.[68] In a similar vein, Jason Crowley has explored how an army consisting of amateurs, like the Athenian hoplites, could be accustomed to facing and inflicting violence in the absence of the standardised training offered to modern soldiers, whether conscripts or professionals.[69]

This means that it is essential to examine violence in relation to the articulation of communal identities in the ancient Greek world: access to and protection from violence were determined by civic identity, but at the same time violence played an important role in shaping communal identities. Law and civic identity were closely linked in their connection to violence.[70] Greek laws accepted legal status as a major determinant of how violence could or could not be employed within a community.[71] Status determined who could legitimately be subjected to violence. A master had effectively unlimited licence to inflict violence on his slaves; but while lashing was the quintessential form of punishing slaves, lashing a free citizen could carry the death penalty. Status determined whether an individual was liable to torture: while citizens were exempted from torture unless under exceptional circumstances, torture could be inflicted on metics much more easily, and slave evidence was usually inadmissible in court unless exacted through torture.[72] Status determined whether an individual was subject to violent punishment by the community, as Demosthenes clearly stated:

> Indeed, if you wanted to contrast the slave and the freeman, you would find the most important distinction in the fact that slaves pay for all offences with their body, while freemen, even in the most unfortunate circumstances, can protect their persons. For it is in the shape of money that in the majority of cases the law must obtain satisfaction from them.[73]

Punishment for violence was also related to status. The deliberate murder of a citizen carried the death penalty, while the non-deliberate killing carried the penalty of exile; but the killing of a metic, whether deliberate or not, could only be punished by exile; violence against metics came clearly much cheaper.[74] David

Lewis' contribution examines in detail the process through which in archaic Athens and Israel communities came to define more clearly the status barriers of identity as a response to the multiple conflicts that affected them. But it would of course be misleading to think that status boundaries always determined how violence functioned: as Zinon Papakonstantinou shows in his contribution, many conflicts reached beyond status boundaries to include citizens, metics and slaves indiscriminately, as one would have expected in the complex socio-economic world of classical Athens.[75]

But equally significant is the constituent role of violence in shaping communal identities. We can start with the issue of how the ruling class of a particular community seeks to justify its dominant position and broadcast its superior identity. The anthropologist Alain Testart has written a magisterial study of the global phenomenon of the large-scale ritual slaughter of animals and human beings in sacrifices and funerals and the strong link between ritualised violence and processes of state formation and elite consolidation.[76] Herodotus might have discussed the ritual slaughter of human beings for the funerals of Scythian kings (4.71), but such forms of violence are generally absent in processes of state- and elite-formation in the ancient Greek world and the wider Mediterranean area.[77]

Instead, it is violence in the form of weapon-carrying which is particularly prominent in various areas of the Mediterranean world in the first millennium BCE. This is a practice which can be traced through a variety of sources: apart from written sources, it also makes its appearance in the archaeological remains of burials and in the iconography of vases, monuments and other forms of material culture. While warriors were exclusively male in most ancient societies, weapons as a status symbol of power and identity were not always restricted to adult males. An influential study of Anglo-Saxon burials from the first millennium CE has revealed that weapon burials were also accorded to women and children: this is a striking example of the potential of violence to shape the most diverse identities and forms of power.[78]

Nevertheless, what is striking about the history of the Greek world in the archaic and classical periods is the process through which weapon-carrying became gradually redundant both in everyday life and in ritual manifestations of identity. We have already commented on the fact that in the course of the archaic period in most Greek communities elites and ordinary people stopped carrying weapons as a standard everyday accessory; but equally significant is the fact that weapon burials, which were relatively common during the Early Iron Age, became gradually extinct from most parts of the Greek world.[79] How to interpret this changing role of violence in processes of identity- and power-formation is still an open question; but equally significant is how to explain the continuation, and renewed prominence, of this phenomenon in certain areas of the Greek world. In his contribution to the volume, Ioannis Xydopoulos examines the fascinating case of the long tradition of weapon burials in Macedonia, in the context of the formation of local identities and the expansion of the Macedonian kingdom.

But the link between violence and identity was not restricted to the archaic period. In fact, one of the deepest controversies, both in antiquity as well as in modern times, debates the extent to which a focus on violence was a peculiar characteristic of ancient Sparta that distinguished it sharply from Athens, or more generally the average Greek community.[80] In a famous anecdote, Plutarch narrates how Agesilaus dealt with the complaint of the Spartan allies that they faced constant military dangers, although they contributed many more troops than the Spartans:

> He ordered all the allies to sit down by themselves mixed up, and the Lacedaemonians apart by themselves. Then his herald called upon the potters to stand up first, and after them the smiths, next, the carpenters in their turn, and the builders, and so on through all the handicrafts. In response, almost all the allies rose up, but not a man of the Lacedaemonians; for they were forbidden to learn or practise a manual art. Then Agesilaus said with a laugh: 'You see, O men, how many more soldiers than you we are sending out'.[81]

Thucydides, Plato and Aristotle commented in a number of contexts on what they considered a peculiar Spartan fixation with war as the factor that deeply shaped their society and contrasted them, in both positive and negative ways, with Athens and the rest of the Greek world.[82] That Spartan commanders and officials were prone to exercise violence against their inferiors and collaborators was a factor which had a significant impact on the relationship between Sparta and its allies and the long-term success of Spartan empire-building.[83] But whether we can generalise from such examples to argue that Sparta was a militaristic society in which the exercise of violence and the preparation for the successful application of violence penetrated and shaped every aspect of Spartan society is more debatable.[84] If Spartan identity eschewed the practice of farming and crafts in favour of warfare, this leaves it open whether this is because the Spartans were peculiarly militaristic, or whether Spartan identity was an extreme (because it applied to all citizens, rather than solely to the elite) version of the Greek ideal of the leisured gentleman, who abstained from demeaning labour in order to focus on the noble pursuits of war and politics. As Nick Fisher shows in his contribution to this volume, while a circumscribed use of violence was an essential aspect of the education of Spartan youths, there is very little evidence that violence spilled over these carefully circumscribed limits: in contrast to many other Greek communities, where violent conflicts of various sorts were relatively common, Sparta does not appear to be a particularly violent society.

Violence does not happen in a void: if it is rather obvious that it takes place in specific spatial contexts, it is even more important to examine how communities attempt to construct and define space in relation to violence. No better way can be found to express this, than the words that Aeschylus puts at the mouth of Athena in her effort to convince the blood-stained Furies to accept a new position within the Athenian community:

> In my territories please do not hurl
> blood-stained whetstones, damaging to the passions
> of the young, making them mad with rage not fuelled by wine,

Neither should you, making their hearts seethe like fighting cocks,
establish the god of War among my citizens
internal and savage against each other.
Let war be beyond the gates, present in abundance,
for the man in whom there will be a dread love for glory.
I do not value the fight of a bird inside its home.
These are the things which are there for you to choose from me,
doing good, receiving good, being well honoured,
to have your share in this land most loved by gods.[85]

Violence serves as a fundamental way of dividing insiders from outsiders in ancient communities: violence against outsiders is a laudable aim, but violence inflicted by members of the community against each other is a horrific problem. Communities sought to deal with this challenge by territorialising violence: by creating a territory beyond which violent acts against outsiders were welcome, but within which were to be controlled by the community. As Mirko Canevaro shows in his contribution to this volume, the spatial definition of Attica as the territory of the Athenian community was intimately linked with communal processes that sought to restrict violence, punish violent acts and define spaces free from violence. In his contribution, Nick Fisher explores a similar theme in relation to the ephebes: communities all over the Greek world, from Sparta and Athens to Crete, created institutions and practices for educating young warriors, which involved guarding the borders, touring the communal territory and committing various ritual and practical acts in the liminality of the no-man's-land, or the *eschatiai*. In his turn, Ioannis Xydopoulos examines how the warrior burials and the death rituals and tumuli they were associated with created landscapes of memory that were closely connected with the formation of communal identities.

But equally important is the location of violence within spaces controlled by the community. The community vouched to protect from violence certain spaces within its territory: Nikolaos Giannakopoulos examines the case of the inviolability of the household and the ways in which communities in the Greco-Roman Eastern Mediterranean tried to deal with the challenges that burglary created. But Giannakopoulos' chapter raises also the problem of the qualitative difference of spaces as they related to violence. The violence of burglary and theft had different implications when it occurred in the small face-to-face societies of villages in the Egyptian countryside or in a large city like Athens or Ephesos: Giannakopoulos explores in some detail the consequences of violent acts when the perpetrators are known or easily suspected in a tightly-knit community. In a different manner, Elias Koulakiotis examines the consequences of the redistribution of space in the aftermath of a violent civil conflict: the community of Tegea, bowing to Alexander's decree about the return of the exiles, had to deal with the problem of restoring the exiles' property, including the houses and in particular the gardens, that seem to constitute such an important aspect of the Tegean urban landscape.

Summary of the chapters

This volume aims to bring out the need to study violence in the ancient Greek world as a unified field of study, and to explore the complex links between violence and community in the cases of law, identity and space. The chapters summarised range widely in both time and space: temporally, they cover the full span from the archaic to the Roman imperial period, while spatially they extend from Athens and Sparta through Crete, Arcadia and Macedonia to Egypt and Israel.

According to Bourdieu 'symbolic' violence is 'the capacity to secure a lasting hold over someone through economic means or through the manipulation of affective obligations'.[86] This kind of symbolic violence is as the centre of David Lewis' opening chapter. Violence in general was present in Attica as well as in Israel; the pursuit of wealth by the rich at the expense of others, abuses (crooked legal judgements), justice sold for money to the rich and powerful citizens, and generally a despotic authority over the dependants were the rule. Solon's reform in Attica achieved its aim thanks to the reorganisation of the judicial system. The Athenian community was now depending on multiple persons for justice, instead of untrustworthy wealthy individuals. In Lewis' chapter, symbolic violence should be closely connected with the notion of identity, since members of the same political community were forced into slavery. Therefore the question arises if a new concept of identity emerges from the new legal institutions. In the Greek case, Solon's decision to apply his laws to all free residents of Attica and not only to the Athenian citizens contributed to a different perception of the boundaries of the *polis*. This territorial reform should have influenced the way that residents of Attica came to identify themselves.

The link between space and violence is the focal point in Mirko Canevaro's chapter about the process of casting criminals outside Athenian territory. According to Canevaro, the criminal was a full outlaw (*atimos*), but whoever had committed an unintentional homicide was not to be killed freely, unless he was found in specific places, from where the law was forbidding him to be. These were legal spaces, which had to be unpolluted, and the lawgiver marked as such specific areas, connected with the city's political and social life. The criminal was not going into exile; he was merely within the city until his trial. Although the territorial borders of the political community were not part of the process of casting out criminals, the community did define particular spaces as inaccessible to the criminal. The growth of the city's borders, including the *chora*, was parallel to the development of these legal spaces.

There is, however, another aspect of how violence was perceived or exercised in communities that were outside the *polis* world. Ioannis Xydopoulos focuses specifically on questions of local identities during the period of Macedonian expansion from the mid-seventh century BCE onwards. Here contemporary literary sources simply do not exist and the later ones present a largely unclear picture regarding this expansion. Xydopoulos' chapter is based on the archaeological data available and engages more directly the issues of both the Bottiaean and Macedonian identities, as well as tracing these identities via the archaeologically visible remains at the cemeteries of Archontiko, near Pella. He concludes that in Macedonia the problem the Macedonians were facing was to impose their authority upon all other tribes located in the region, an aim achieved by expelling all of them from the area and that the Macedonians who had conquered Bottiaea and belonged to the elite were thus 'compelled' in a way to demonstrate their status in the 'new lands' and to ensure their prominence in them, after the violent expulsions they had conducted. On the other hand, the expelled Bottiaeans in Chalcidice developed a new, different identity: except for the name of their new dwellings (Bottike), they seem to have accepted the *polis* culture, in which the role of violence in the construction of identity at death was radically different.

The volume continues with Nick Fisher's effort to show how the role of education and military training in Greek cities was a means of restraining violence within their societies, legitimising violence against enemies and defending the boundaries of the community. He deals with evidence from Sparta, Crete, and Athens, where he presents a detailed account of the development of the *ephebeia*, from the archaic period to the reform of Epicrates in the late fourth century BCE. He concludes that not only the aforementioned cities, but probably all other Greek cities, sought to generate patriotic feelings in their new citizens, thus creating a link with the past and a sharing of the '*hiera* and *hosia*'. Myths and rituals, shared religious practices and collective training, physical exercise and choral song and dance were the means to achieve this aim. Despite the differences between the approaches employed at Sparta, in the Cretan cities and those used at Athens (perhaps an indication of 'radically different civic ideologies'), all cities seem to have made use of the collective imaginaries that were located in myth, in order to construct their own versions of communal identity.

Zinon Papakonstantinou draws on the evidence of curse tablets to offer a novel perspective on social interaction and conflict management in the Athenian context of the classical period. He employs the corpus of curse tablets from the fifth and fourth centuries BCE as evidence for conflict management and dispute resolution strategies. Papakonstantinou argues that the institutional setting of Athenian democracy had a deep impact on these strategies, which need to be explored in detail. He focuses on two main factors: on the one hand the wide range of decision-making institutions (assembly, law courts, Boule) and the open access to them enjoyed by Athenian citizens, and on the other the intermingling of individuals of various statuses in the complex socio-economic environment of classical Athens. Papakonstantinou argues that a major consequence of these factors was the development of new forms of individual and collective agency, employed in the most diverse contexts. If we want to understand the link between violence and community, the formation and construction of agency as shaped by both factors will be a crucial parameter.

The final two chapters deal with territorial borders and urban spaces that certainly played a vital role in the definition of citizen identity. Elias Koulakiotis deals with the reintegration of the Tegean exiles, an action that was inevitably linked with perceptions of land property and urban landscape. Since, as it was shown by Canevaro's chapter, the exiled persons were banned from the city's territory, getting back their social and political rights must have caused serious social problems regarding spatial arrangements. This is especially true for a late classical city, where the house and its garden, i.e. an enclosed cultivated land, formed the entity of the *oikos*. The importance attached to the private urban land-scape in regards to the regaining of civic identity is equal to that acknowledged to the public spaces and their re-appropriation by the former exiles.

In the same Hellenistic, as well as Roman imperial context, Nikolaos Gian-nakopoulos deals with an interesting aspect of urban violence that seems to have defined social relations, that is to say the structures of the political community itself. As Giannakopoulos shows on the basis of a corpus of sources depicting everyday life, housebreaking was committed by poor but ordinary city dwellers, whose identity was not unknown to their victims. The question therefore arises: what was the role of violence in constructing the urban community's identity and if in these cases a strong performative, that is to say symbolic, aspect, should be investigated. He concludes that space was also allowed for the emergence of a more elaborate form of civic identity which embraced not the totality of the citizens, but only those respectful of the private *oikia*, private property and ultimately the *Pax Augusta*.

We finish where we started – with the Homeric epics. The cover image for this volume is a nineteenth-century reconstruction of the famous shield of Achilles described in the *Iliad* (18.478–608). In juxtaposing the city in war, facing a siege, and the city in peace, dealing with a trial concerning a murder case, it is an excel-lent illustration of the relationship between violence and community and the three aspects that link them together: law, identity and space.

Notes

1 Van Wees 1992.
2 The papers in van Wees 2000 constituted a pioneering contribution to studying vio-lence as a unified field; see also Bertrand 2005.
3 Van Wees 2004; Low 2007; Crowley 2012.
4 On stasis, see Lintott 1982; Gehrke 1985; Manolopoulos 1991, 1995; Wolpert 2001; Forsdyke 2009. On assault and homicide, see Fisher 1992; Cohen 1995; Carawan 1998; Phillips 2008.
5 On the state-ness of Greek communities and the monopoly of violence, see Hansen 2002; Berent 2004, 2005, 2006; Anderson 2009. On violence and slavery, see Klees 1998: 176–217; Wrenhaven 2012: 63–74.
6 Diesner 1980; Brown 1987; Scott 2000.
7 See, e.g. Hall 2013.
8 Morris 2014; for the early book, see Morris 1987.
9 Schneider 1988; Pocock 1999.
10 Rahe 1992.
11 Rosanvallon 1979.
12 Rahe 1994.
13 Elias 1978–82.
14 Foucault 1977.
15 Pinker 2011.

16 Allen 2000.
17 Jørgensen 2014.
18 Kalyvas and Katznelson 2008: 88–117; Vlassopoulos 2010: 102–5.
19 Knox 1985; Sagan 1991.
20 Lintott 1982; Gehrke 1985; Manolopoulos 1991, 1995; Wolpert 2001; Forsdyke 2009.
21 Turney-High 1949.
22 Keeley 1996 provides a historiography of 'primitive' warfare and a trenchant critique of the concept; see also Gat 2006.
23 For an analysis, see van Wees 2004: 153–65.
24 For a critique of such approaches, see van Wees 2004: 115–50.
25 Van Wees 1998.
26 Hansen 1976.
27 Roberts 1979.
28 Harris 2013: 50–9; Alwine 2015: 145–50.
29 Allen 2000.
30 For mediaeval and later developments, see Strayer 1970; Ertman 1997; Brown and Górecki 2003; Bisson 2009; Watts 2009; Brown 2011.
31 See the stimulating discussion of Anderson 2009.
32 Roisman 2005; McHardy 2008; Alwine 2015: 23–54.
33 For similar processes in mediaeval Europe, see Bartlett 1993: 300–6; Davies 2000: 113–41.
34 Herman 2006; for reviews and critical reactions, see Christ 2007; Balot 2008; Kucharski 2008; van Wees 2008.
35 Cohen 1995, 2005.
36 See also his early studies (Herman 1994, 1996), where the case is made more succinctly, and the detailed reaction of Fisher 1998.
37 Hall Sternberg 2006; Lanni 2009; Christ 2012; Harris 2013; Alwine 2015.
38 For a full register of forms of *stasis* in archaic and classical Greece, see Gehrke 1985. For political exiles, see Balogh 1943; McKechnie 1989.
39 Ober 1989: 17–35, 332–9.
40 For Greek democracies outside Athens, see Robinson 2011.
41 Thuc. 3.45.
42 *Pol.* 1256a30–40.
43 Shaw 1984; Riess 2001; de Souza 2002; Wolff 2003; Grünewald 2004.
44 Brulé 1978; Shaw 1990; Avidov 1997.
45 Braund 1993; de Souza 2002; Brélaz 2005.
46 Fisher 1999.
47 *PMG* 909 Page.
48 Digest, 1.5.2–3.
49 Klees 1975, 1998; Bradley 1984: 113–38, 2000; Clark 1998; Wrenhaven 2012.
50 Ste. Croix 1981; Fuks 1984.
51 Bell 2004.
52 Morgan 2003.
53 Ar. *Lys.* 433–6.
54 Ismard 2015. Ismard is influenced by the work of Pierre Clastres, the prominent anthropologist of violence and the state: see Clastres 1987, 2010.
55 Eckstein 2007: 37–78.
56 Price 2004.
57 Fisher 2000.
58 Lendon 2000.
59 See the exhaustive discussion of Fisher 1992.
60 Balot 2001; Sanders 2013.

61 Balot 2014.
62 Cf. Miller 1990.
63 Harris 2013: 21–59.
64 Brown 2011: 69–91.
65 Riess 2008.
66 Smail 2003.
67 Hunter 1994.
68 See also Fisher 1989, 2010.
69 Crowley 2012; see also Burckhardt 1996; Pritchard 2010.
70 Hunter and Edmondson 2000.
71 Alwine 2015: 136–45.
72 Allen 2000: 102–7.
73 Dem. 22.55.
74 Todd 1993: 169.
75 Fisher 1995.
76 Testart 2004.
77 For a comparative perspective, see Ruby 1999.
78 Härke 1990.
79 Van Wees 1999.
80 Hornblower 2000; Hodkinson and Powell 2006; for the case of Athens, see Sagan 1991; Pritchard 2010.
81 Plu. *Ages.* 26.4–5.
82 Thuc. 1.84, 2.39; Plt. *Lg.* 666e-667a; Arist. *Pol.* 1271b2–6, 1324b7–9.
83 Hornblower 2000.
84 Hodkinson 2006.
85 *Eum.* 858–69.
86 Bourdieu 1977: 191.

Bibliography

Allen, D. (2000) *The World of Prometheus: The Politics of Punishing in Democratic Athens*, Princeton, NJ.

Alwine, A. T. (2015) *Enmity and Feuding in Classical Athens*, Austin, TX.

Anderson, G. (2009) 'The personality of the Greek state', *Journal of Hellenic Studies* 129, 1–22.

Avidov, A. (1997) 'Were the Cilicians a nation of pirates?', *Mediterranean Historical Review* 12, 5–55.

Balogh, E. (1943) *Political Refugees in Ancient Greece*, Johannesburg.

Balot, R. K. (2001) *Greed and Injustice in Classical Athens*, Princeton, NJ.

Balot, R. K. (2008) 'Review of Herman 2006', *Classical Philology* 103, 320–5.

Balot, R. K. (2014) *Courage in the Democratic Polis: Ideology and Critique in Classical Athens*, Oxford, UK and New York.

Bartlett, R. (1993) *The Making of Europe: Conquest, Colonisation and Cultural Change 950–1350*, London.

Beck, H. (ed.) (2013) *A Companion to Ancient Greek Government*, Oxford, UK.

Bell, A. (2004) *Spectacular Power in the Greek and Roman City*, Oxford, UK.

Berent, M. (2004) 'In search of the Greek state: a rejoinder to M. H. Hansen', *Polis* 21, 107–46.

Berent, M. (2005) 'Anthropology and the classics: war, violence, and the stateless polis', *Classical Quarterly* 50, 257–89.

Berent, M. (2006) 'The stateless polis: a reply to critics', *Social Evolution & History* 5.1, 141–63.

Bertrand, J.-M. (ed.) (2005) *La violence dans les mondes grec et romain*, Paris.

Bisson, T. N. (2009) *The Crisis of the Twelfth Century: Power, Lordship and the Origins of European Government*, Princeton, NJ and Oxford, UK.

Bourdieu, P. (1977) *Outline of a Theory of Practice*, Cambridge and New York.

Bradley, K. R. (1984) *Slaves and Masters in the Roman Empire: A Study in Social Control*, Tournai, Belgium.

Bradley, K. R. (2000) 'Animalizing the slave: the truth of fiction', *Journal of Roman Studies* 90, 110–25.

Braund, D. (1993) 'Piracy under the principate and the ideology of imperial eradication' in J. Rich and G. Shipley (eds.), *War and Society in the Roman World*, London and New York, 195–212.

Brélaz, C. (2005) *La sécurité publique en Asie Mineure sous le Principat (Ier-IIIe s. ap. J.-C.)*, Basel, Switzerland.

Brown, C. Jr. (1987) 'Thucydides, Hobbes and the derivation of anarchy', *History of Political Thought* 8, 33–62.

Brown, W. C. (2011) *Violence in Medieval Europe*, Abington, UK and New York.

Brown, W. C. and Górecki, P. (eds.) (2003) *Conflict in Medieval Europe*, Aldershot, UK.

Brulé, P. (1978) *La piraterie crétoise hellénistique*, Besançon, France.

Burckhardt, L. A. (1996) *Bürger und Soldaten: Aspekte der politischen und militärischen Rolle athenischer Bürger im Kriegswesen des 4. v. Chr.*, Stuttgart, Germany.

Carawan, E. (1998) *Rhetoric and the Law of Draco*, Oxford, UK.

Christ, M. (2007) 'Review of Herman 2006', *Bryn Mawr Classical Review* 2007.07.37, available at http://bmcr.brynmawr.edu/2007/2007-07-37.html.

Christ, M. (2012) *The Limits of Altruism in Democratic Athens*, Cambridge, UK.

Clark, P. (1998) 'Women, slaves, and the hierarchies of domestic violence: the family of St. Augustine' in S. R. Joshel and S. Murnaghan (eds.), *Women and Slaves in Greco-Roman Culture: Differential Equations*, London and New York, 109–29.

Clastres, P. (1987) *Society against the State: Essays in Political Anthropology*, New York and Cambridge, MA.

Clastres, P. (2010) *Archaeology of Violence*, Cambridge, MA and London.

Cohen, D. (1995) *Law, Violence and Community in Classical Athens*, Cambridge, UK.

Cohen, D. (2005) 'Crime, punishment, and the rule of law in classical Athens' in M. Gagarin and D. Cohen (eds.), *The Cambridge Companion to Ancient Greek Law*, Cambridge, UK, 211 35.

Crowley, J. (2012) *The Psychology of the Athenian Hoplite: The Culture of Combat in Classical Athens*, Cambridge, UK.

Davies, R. R. (2000) *The First English Empire: Power and Identities in the British Isles 1093–1343*, Oxford, UK.

de Souza, P. (2002) *Piracy in the Graeco-Roman World*, Cambridge, UK.

Diesner, H.-J. (1980) 'Thukydides und Thomas Hobbes: zur Strukturanalyse der Macht', *Historia* 29, 1–16.

Eckstein, A. M. (2007) *Mediterranean Anarchy, Interstate War and the Rise of Rome*, Berkeley, CA, Los Angeles and London.

Elias, N. (1978–82) *The Civilising Process*, I-II, Oxford, UK.

Ertman, T. (1997) *Birth of the Leviathan: Building States and Regimes in Medieval and Early Modern Europe*, Cambridge, UK.

Fisher, N. (1989) 'Drink, *hybris* and the promotion of harmony at Sparta' in A. Powell (ed.), *Classical Sparta: Techniques behind her Success*, London, 26–50.

Fisher, N. (1992) *Hybris: A Study in the Values of Honour and Shame in Ancient Greece*, Warminster, UK.

Fisher, N. (1995) 'Hybris, status and slavery' in A. Powell (ed.), *The Greek World*, London, 44–84.

Fisher, N. (1998) 'Violence, masculinity and the law in classical Athens' in L. Foxhall and J. Salmon (eds.), *When Men Were Men: Masculinity, Power and Identity in Classical Antiquity*, London and New York, 68–97.

Fisher, N. (1999) '"Workshops of villains": was there much organised crime in classical Athens?' in Hopwood (1999), 53–96.

Fisher, N. (2000) 'Hybris, revenge and stasis in the Greek city-states' in van Wees (2000b), 83–123.

Fisher, N. (2010) '*Charis, Charites,* festivals and social peace in the classical Greek city' in I. Sluiter and R. Rosen (eds.), *Valuing Others in Classical Antiquity*, Leiden, Netherlands, 71–112.

Forsdyke, S. (2009) *Exile, Ostracism and Democracy: The Politics of Expulsion in Ancient Greece*, Princeton, NJ.

Foucault, M. (1977) *Discipline and Punish: The Birth of the Prison*, London.

Fuks, A. (1984) *Social Conflict in Ancient Greece*, Jerusalem and Leiden, Netherlands.

Gat, A. (2006) *War in Human Civilisation*, Oxford, UK and New York.

Gehrke, H.-J. (1985) *Stasis. Untersuchungen zu den inneren Kriegen in den griechischen Staaten des 5. und 4. Jahrhunderts v. Chr.*, Munich.

Grünewald, T. (2004) *Bandits in the Roman Empire: Myth and Reality*, London and New York.

Guerci, L. (1979) *Liberta degli antichi e liberta dei moderni. Sparta, Atene e i 'philosophes' nella Francia del 700*, Naples.

Hall, J. M. (2013) 'The rise of state action in the archaic age' in H. Beck (ed.) (2013) *A Companion to Ancient Greek Government*, Oxford, UK, 7–21.

Hall Sternberg, R. (2006) *Tragedy Offstage: Suffering and Sympathy in Ancient Athens*, Austin, TX.

Hansen, M. H. (1976) *Apagoge, Endeixis and Ephegesis against Kakourgoi, Atimoi and Pheugontes: A Study in Athenian Administration of Justice in the Fourth Century BC*, Odense, Denmark.

Hansen, M. H. (2002) 'Was the polis a state or a stateless society?' in T. H. Nielsen (ed.), *Even More Studies in the Ancient Greek Polis*, Stuttgart, 17–47.

Härke, H. (1990) '"Warrior graves"? The background of the Anglo-Saxon weapon burial rite', *Past & Present* 126, 22–43.

Harris, E. M. (2013) *The Rule of Law in Action in Democratic Athens*, Oxford, UK.

Herman, G. (1994) 'How violent was Athenian society?' in R. Osborne and S. Hornblower (eds.), *Ritual, Finance, Politics: Athenian Democratic Accounts Presented to David Lewis*, Oxford, UK, 99–117.

Herman, G. (1996) 'Ancient Athens and the values of Mediterranean society', *Mediterranean Historical Review* 11, 5–36.

Herman, G. (2006) *Morality and Behaviour in Democratic Athens: A Social History*, Cambridge, UK.

Hodkinson, S. (2006) 'Was classical Sparta a military society?' in S. Hodkinson and A. Powell (eds.) (2006) *Sparta and War*, Swansea, UK, 111–62.

Hodkinson, S. and Powell, A. (eds.) (2006) *Sparta and War*, Swansea, UK.

Hopwood, K. (ed.) (1999) *Organized Crime in Antiquity*, London and Swansea, UK.

Hornblower, S. (2000) 'Sticks, stones and Spartans: the sociology of Spartan violence' in H. van Wees (ed.) (2000) *War and Violence in Ancient Greece*, London and Swansea, UK, 57–82.

Hunter, V. (1994) *Policing Athens: Social Control in the Attic Lawsuits, 420–320 B.C.*, Princeton, NJ.

Hunter, V. and Edmondson, J. (eds.) (2000) *Law and Social Status in Classical Athens*, Oxford, UK.

Ismard, P. (2015) *La démocratie contre les experts: les esclaves publics en Grèce ancienne*, Paris.

Jørgensen, J. P. (2014) 'The taming of the aristoi – an ancient Greek civilizing process?', *History of the Human Sciences* 27.3, 38–54.

Kalyvas, A. and Katznelson, I. (2008) *Liberal Beginnings: Making a Republic for the Moderns*, Cambridge, UK.

Keeley, L. H. (1996) *War before Civilisation*, Oxford, UK and New York.

Klees, H. (1975) *Herren und Sklaven: die Sklaverei im oikonomischen und politischen Schrifttum der Griechen in klassischer Zeit*, Stuttgart.

Klees, H. (1998) *Sklavenleben im klassischen Griechenland*, Stuttgart.

Knox, R. A. (1985) ' "So mischievous a beaste"? The Athenian demos and its treatment of its politicians', *Greece & Rome* 32, 132–61.

Kucharski, J. (2008) 'Review of Herman 2006', *Ancient History Bulletin* 22, 89–95.

Lanni, A. (2009) 'Social norms in the courts of ancient Athens', *Journal of Legal Analysis* 1.2, 691–736.

Lendon, J. E. (2000) 'Homeric vengeance and the outbreak of Greek wars' in van Wees (2000b), 1–30.

Lintott, A. (1982) *Violence, Civil Strife and Revolution in the Classical City, 750–330 BC*, London.

Low, P. (2007) *Interstate Relations in Classical Greece: Morality and Power*, Cambridge, UK.

Manolopoulos, L. (1991) *Στάσις-επανάστασις, νεωτερισμός-κίνησις: συμβολή στην έρευνα της πολιτικής ορολογίας των αρχαίων Ελλήνων*, Thessaloniki, Greece.

Manolopoulos, L. (1995) *Πόλις φλεγμαίνουσα και πόλις υγιής: οι εμφύλιοι πόλεμοι στις αρχαίες ελληνικές πόλεις και ο πολιτικός στοχασμός*, Thessaloniki, Greece.

McHardy, F. (2008) *Revenge in Athenian Culture*, London and New York.

McKechnie, P. (1989) *Outsiders in the Greek Cities in the Fourth Century BC*, London.

Miller, W. I. (1990) *Bloodtaking and Peacemaking: Feud, Law and Society in Saga Iceland*, Chicago and London.

Morgan, K. A. (ed.) (2003) *Popular Tyranny: Sovereignty and Its Discontents in Ancient Greece*, Austin, TX.

Morris, I. (1987) *Burial and Ancient Society: The Rise of the Greek City-State*, Cambridge, UK.

Morris, I. (2014) *War! What Is It Good for? Conflict and the Progress of Civilisation from Primates to Robots*, London.

Ober, J. (1989) *Mass and Elite in Democratic Athens: Rhetoric, Ideology, and the Power of the People*, Princeton, NJ.

Phillips, D. D. (2008) *Avengers of Blood: Homicide in Athenian Law and Custom from Draco to Demosthenes*, Wiesbaden, Germany.

Pinker, S. (2011) *The Better Angels of our Nature*, London.

Pocock, J.G.A. (1999) *Barbarism and Religion. II: Narratives of Civil Government*, Cambridge, UK.

Price, J. J. (2004) *Thucydides and Internal War*, Cambridge, UK.

Pritchard, D. M. (ed.) (2010) *War, Democracy and Culture in Classical Athens*, Cambridge, UK.

Rahe, P. A. (1992) *Republics, Ancient and Modern I: The Ancien Régime in Ancient Greece*, Chapel Hill, NC and London.

Rahe, P. A. (1994) *Republics, Ancient and Modern II: New Modes and Orders in Early Modern Political Thought*, Chapel Hill, NC and London.

Riess, W. (2001) *Apuleius und die Räuber: Ein Beitrag zur historischen Kriminalitäts-forschung*, Stuttgart.

Riess, W. (2008) 'Private violence and state control: the prosecution of homicide and its symbolical meanings in fourth-century BC Athens' in C. Brélaz and P. Ducrey (eds.), *Sécurité collective et ordre public dans les sociétés anciennes*, Geneva, 49–94.

Roberts, J. T. (1997) *Athens on Trial: The Antidemocratic Tradition in Western Thought*, Princeton, NJ.

Roberts, S. (1979) *Order and Dispute: An Introduction to Legal Anthropology*, New York.

Robinson, E. W. (2011) *Democracy beyond Athens: Popular Government in the Greek Classical Age*, Cambridge, UK.

Roisman, J. (2005) *The Rhetoric of Manhood: Masculinity in the Attic Orators*, Berkeley, CA, Los Angeles and London.

Rosanvallon, P. (1979) *Le capitalisme utopique: critique de l'idéologie économique*, Paris.

Ruby, P. (ed.) (1999) *Les princes de la protohistoire et l'émergence de l'état*, Naples.

Sagan, E. (1991) *The Honey and the Hemlock: Democracy and Paranoia in Ancient Athens and Modern America*, Princeton, NJ.

Sanders, E. (2013) *Envy and Jealousy in Classical Athens: A Socio-Psychological Approach*, Oxford, UK.

Schneider, H. (1988) 'Schottische Aufklärung und antike Gesellschaft' in P. Kneissl and V. Losemann (eds.), *Alte Geschichte und Wissenschaftsgeschichte: Festschrift für Karl Christ zum 65. Geburtstag*, Darmstadt, Germany, 431–64.

Scott, J. (2000) 'The peace of silence: Thucydides and the English Civil War' in G. A. J. Roberts and T. Sorell (eds.), *Hobbes and History*, London and New York, 112–36.

Shaw, B. D. (1984) 'Bandits in the Roman Empire', *Past & Present* 10, 3–52.

Shaw, B. D. (1990) 'Bandit highlands and lowland peace: the mountains of Isauria-Cilicia', *Journal of the Economic and Social History of the Orient* 33, 199–233.

Smail, D. L. (2003) *The Consumption of Justice: Emotions, Publicity and Legal Culture in Marseille, 1264–1423*, Ithaca, NY and London.

Ste. Croix, G. E. M. (1981) *The Class Struggle in the Ancient Greek World*, London.

Strayer, J. R. (1970) *On the Medieval Origins of the Modern State*, Princeton, NJ.

Testart, A. (2004) *La servitude volontaire*, I-II, Paris.

Todd, S. C. (1993) *The Shape of Athenian Law*, Oxford, UK.

Turney-High, H. (1949) *Primitive War: Its Practice and Concepts*, Columbia, SC.

van Wees, H. (1992) *Status Warriors: War, Violence and Society in Homer and History*, Amsterdam.

van Wees, H. (1998) 'Greeks bearing arms: the state, the leisure class and the display of weapons in Archaic Greece' in H. van Wees and N. Fisher (eds.), *Archaic Greece: New Approaches and New Evidence*, London, 333–78.

van Wees, H. (1999) 'The mafia of early Greece: violent exploitation in the seventh and sixth centuries BC' in Hopwood (1999), 1–51.

van Wees, H. (ed.) (2000) *War and Violence in Ancient Greece*, London and Swansea, UK.

van Wees, H. (2004) *Greek Warfare: Myths and Realities*, London.

van Wees, H. (2008) 'Review article: violence', *Journal of Hellenic Studies* 128, 172–5.

Vlassopoulos, K. (2010) *Politics: Antiquity and Its Legacy*, London.

Watts, J. (2009) *The Making of Polities: Europe, 1300–1500*, Cambridge, UK.

Wolff, C. (2003) *Les Brigands en Orient sous le Haut-Empire romain*, Rome.

Wolpert, A. (2001) *Remembering Defeat: Civil War and Civic Memory in Ancient Athens*, Baltimore, MD.

Wrenhaven, K. L. (2012) *Reconstructing the Slave: The Image of the Slave in Ancient Greece*, London and New York.

2 Making law grip

Inequality, injustice, and legal remedy in Solonian Attica and ancient Israel*

David Lewis

'The most illuminating parallel for the *Seisachtheia* is still *Nehemiah* V 1–13, though I have yet to meet an Oxford ancient historian who uses it, and some have not heard of it'. Thus wrote G. E. M. de Ste. Croix in 1962 in a letter to his colleague A. Andrewes, part of a correspondence in which both scholars exchanged a number of ideas on Solon's reforms.[1] Several scholars have noted the comparative potential of Hebrew texts for studying archaic Greek history, and the many parallels between life in ancient Israel and archaic Greece.[2] Yet in many ways, the kind of comparison that de Ste. Croix envisaged is still a rarity. To be sure, classical scholars have not neglected the fact that Greek settlements of the archaic period were located in a much wider world, indeed one from which they were not hermetically sealed: literary scholars, as well as scholars of art, philosophy and religion, have for some time now studied the influences of Eastern thought and material culture on that of the Greeks.[3] This kind of study emphasises cultural connectivity and the transfer of ideas, persons, and objects. Much less common, however, is the sort of comparison that does not seek to chart cultural influence, but to examine similarity and difference in structural terms. In other words, how different was archaic Greece from its Eastern Mediterranean neighbours?[4]

In this essay, I aim to explore this question by analysing social problems and legal responses to these problems in two regions of the archaic Eastern Mediterranean: Attica and Israel. These two regions constitute a promising pair for the purposes of comparison: both were agrarian societies with comparable economic practices, and shared a similar climatic niche, systems of land tenure and inheritance practices.[5] Moreover, textual evidence from both regions deriving from or relating to the eighth through sixth centuries BCE enables us to address several questions in parallel. These questions can be formulated as follows. First, were the social ills that plagued Athenian society in the opening years of the sixth century unique to Attica, or even Greece broadly defined, or did they mirror similar, contemporary phenomena in non-Greek societies of the Eastern Mediterranean? Second, how did these problems relate to inequalities in wealth and power, and the inadequacy of formal legal institutions to curtail abuses? Third, were the legal solutions contrived by Solon to address these problems distinctive or unique (at least on a conceptual level), or were similar solutions devised elsewhere for ameliorating the plight of the poor and engendering peace and order? And finally, how unique were Solon's procedural reforms to the machinery of justice, the institutional innovations aimed at facilitating the effective application of the law in Athenian courts?

Issues of method

The materials selected for this study and the approaches employed to explore these problems attract no small measure of controversy. Let us first deal with Solon. Abundant information on the statesman can be found in Plutarch's *Life of Solon* and in chapters 5–12 of the Aristotelian *Athenaion Politeia*. Both of these texts provide valuable nuggets of sixth-century evidence, but these nuggets are embedded in a framework of fourth-century (and later) interpretation, speculation, and moralisation, some aspects of which may be correct, while other parts contain clear anachronisms. I should state at the outset that this essay will depend predominantly on the sixth-century material, and less upon the later accretions that built up in the classical period and thereafter to give a context and meaning to those poems of Solon that had been passed down to posterity and his (probably rather tersely-worded) laws that could still be consulted in classical Athens.

In this, I aim to steer a course that avoids two problematic approaches. The first is one that accords the same evidential value to the fourth-century (and later) writers as it does to the laws and poems. This is too risky, for at times it can be positively demonstrated that later writers have misunderstood Solon's laws and poems and invented anachronistic explanations to account for their form and wording.[6] It is better to leave aside the later material altogether and try to construct a coherent picture from the early evidence, an approach that has enjoyed notable successes in areas such as Spartan history.[7] The second problematic method is more objectionable: this approach aims to solve the problems created by the scanty and skeletal nature of our evidence for Solon by fattening up these bare bones on a diet of speculation and adventurous hypotheses about *inter alia* imaginary systems of land tenure and population pressure; these theories depend upon so many conjectural variables that they cannot possibly be correct.[8] They may exercise the imagination and ingenuity of scholars, but any approach of this kind is epistemologically flawed, as it invariably deals not so much with the evidence we have, but with speculation about what might be missing. The approach to Solon employed here is a drastic but methodologically necessary one: that is, to take Ockham's Razor to these speculative theories and cut away the large number of unverifiable elements. This leaves us only with the bare bones of sixth-century evidence contained in the laws and poems, but this can be interpreted cautiously in the context of what we know about early Greek law and social structure to provide as robust an interpretation of Solonian Attica as possible.[9]

Perhaps more difficult is using the Hebrew Bible to study social history (here, though, we will focus mainly on the prophetic texts); a little background may therefore help. The prophets of the Hebrew Bible were active in two Levantine states, the wealthier northern kingdom of Israel, and the smaller but longer-lived kingdom of Judah in the south. Both territories had perhaps belonged to a larger polity governed by Saul, David, and Solomon, but this allegedly split in two due to internal squabbles during the tenth century.[10] From the northern capital of Samaria and the southern capital of Jerusalem, the monarchs of these states imposed administrative structures that regulated local governance. Both states were, however, small principalities in a world of tectonic shifts between much larger empires; Assyria swallowed up the northern state of Israel in 722 BCE, and its southern neighbour survived only until 586 BCE, when it was conquered by the Babylonian king Nebuchadnezzar II. It was only after the return of the exiled elite of Judah under the Persians that the writings of the defunct monarchical age were (re)crafted (with numerous additions) into what we know today as the Hebrew Bible.[11]

This complex anthology of Israelite literature is replete with methodological controversies, most pressingly the processes of compilation and redaction, as well as the dating of its constituent texts. However, much of the material we shall be utilising here does not suffer so acutely from these complications. I refer primarily to the Hebrew prophets. Not only can most of these individuals be assigned a *floruit* and their oracles a temporal context, but their words, recorded by scribal groups and passed down as sacred text, preserve extremely valuable observations on the fabric of society around the time they were composed.[12] More problematic is the use of legal texts in the Torah, for there still exists disagreement about how and when these texts were compiled, the chronological sequence in which they were written, the influence of one section of text upon others, the degree of redaction and the question of how far they were followed in daily life, or were rather academic scribal compositions (to name a few). These issues rule out certain types of analysis, and we shall be forced to tailor our approach to one that lets us use the legal texts meaningfully despite these many uncertainties.

Inequality and injustice in Attica, archaic Greece, and Iron II Israel

The admonitions of the Hebrew prophets provide remarkably familiar reading for the student of archaic Greece. Gift-devouring judges rendering crooked verdicts, rich landowners increasing their holdings at the expense of impoverished neighbours (often by violent means), poor individuals borrowing money from the wealthy and becoming their slaves in the event of default; these and other problems plagued Greek and Israelite society during our period.[13] We will examine the textual evidence for these problems shortly, but it is necessary first to ground our analysis in an appreciation of the material inequalities that existed in Attica and Israel. The problem essentially boils down to this: both the prophetic texts and Solon's poetry portray dysfunctional societies in which various abuses of the lower classes occurred. How do we characterise either of these situations? The texts themselves could describe societies that merely exhibited unjust and dysfunctional (and occasionally violent) elements, but they could equally describe societies characterised by complete social breakdown and mayhem. It is important to acknowledge the basic ambiguity of the evidence on this point at the outset.

One element, however, that may afford us some purchase on this problem is the degree of economic inequality in either society, since not only is this factor related to various social ills, but it also can enable us to gauge the power of the elite compared to the rest of society.[14]

Our evidence for Israel is decidedly better than that for Attica. Few regions of the world have been as thoroughly surveyed and excavated as modern Israel, and the results have recently been synthesised in a groundbreaking study by Avraham Faust.[15] Drawing on a large data set of household remains, Faust has shown that rural settlements were rather egalitarian, with extended families dwelling together in relatively large houses, with little differentiation between house sizes; furthermore, on the village level there is ample evidence for cooperation between households in the processing of foodstuffs.[16] In the cities, however, inequality is highly visible: small numbers of large, well-built houses exist amid a mass of much smaller houses of the poor, the latter apparently inhabited by nuclear families.[17] This somewhat militates against old-fashioned views that misused the prophetic texts (or, to be more specific, Is. 5:8) to posit a wholesale 'latifundization' of Israel by the elite and the widespread displacement of a peasant proletariat.[18] Faust's work does not contradict the prophetic texts; rather, it contextualises them, showing that the abuses of the poor largely belong to an urban context, and that the countryside was not for the most part 'latifundized' by the elite, even if they did own extensive estates.

We unfortunately lack such datasets for Solonian Attica, and reconstructions of inequality cannot be based on more reliable 'bottom-up' approaches such as these. Instead, 'top-down' methodologies based on calculations regarding the Solonian census groups, combined with estimates of crop yields per hectare, constitute the chief variables on which historians have focused in attempting to understand inequality in sixth-century Athens. Studies such as these have produced a picture of more acute inequality, with a narrow elite controlling much of the land, and vastly richer than a broad stratum of poor Athenians. This picture is certainly plausible, but the margins for error inherent in this sort of approach are extremely large, and the proposed models should be seen as tentative, and possibly very far off the mark.[19] These points must be kept in mind as a check on the confidence of any proposed reconstruction of the Solonian 'crisis'. We might know of specific aspects of that crisis, but our present state of knowledge does not enable us to measure its intensity in any meaningful way. If we cannot measure its intensity, then we can at least describe some of its specific aspects; let us now turn to these in earnest.

Debt, exploitative lending and the enslavement of debtors

Debt and enslavement for debt was a notable problem in Solon's Attica. In fr. 4, Solon mentions some of the poor sold into slavery and living in foreign lands, a detail that is supplemented in fr. 36 by the claim that he brought back to Attica Athenians who had been sold abroad, legally or illegally,[20] as well as others who had fled on account of their debts; others, trembling at the feet of their masters, he claims, he set free. We also find the problem of the sale of free persons into slavery in the fragmentary laws. Plutarch (*Sol.* 13) believed that many Athenians sold their children to their creditors, and although the sale of children is not specifically mentioned in the poems, it surely occurred: Solon passed a law banning the sale of one's daughters and sisters, unless they had lost their virginity (R&L F31a = Plut. *Sol.* 23.2), and this implies that the Athenian *kyrios* before Solon's reforms had extraordinary powers over his dependants. One of the most famous of Solon's innovations was his ban on loans contracted on security of the person, which prevented enslavement for debt (R&L F69a-c = [Arist.] *Ath. Pol.* 2.2, 4.4, 6.1, 9.1; Plut. *Sol.* 13.4, 15.2, *Mor.* 828f).[21] This could potentially apply to contracting loans on the security of one's children and dependants, as well as on oneself. The dangers of debt and exploitative lending by the wealthy were not restricted to Attica, but were a structural feature of early Greek society more generally.[22]

As in archaic Attica, individuals in Israel and Judah faced the problem of debt and the threat of enslavement due to debt and poverty. One proverb claimed that the borrower was the creditor's slave, a figurative expression, but all the same, one that speaks volumes of the peril associated with borrowing money during this period (Prov. 22:7). The head of a household exercised complete authority over his dependants, and this extended to the right to pledge or sell children. During times of economic distress, children could be sold or pledged in order to meet financial obligations such as the payment of debts or taxes, and this practice was deplored from an early period. The eighth-century prophet Amos criticises the wealthy on two separate occasions for selling the poor into slavery (Amos 2:6; 8:4–6). A story concerning the prophet Elisha, who was apparently active during the ninth century, reflects the difficulties faced by the destitute (whether this is a strictly historical story or not is irrelevant for our purposes); it relates how Elisha visited a widow and helped alleviate her poverty when she faced creditors who were about to seize her children as slaves (II Kings 4:1). Similarly, Deutero-Isaiah (50:1) uses the sale of a son to pay off creditors as a metaphor for YHWH abandoning Israel. As we shall see, laws were created that aimed at limiting the rights of creditors, or those who 'acquired' poor Israelites as slaves; but two historical incidents illustrate how these laws, even if they were not utopian or academic, might be ignored if central authorities lacked the power to enforce them. The first incident dates to shortly before the sack of Jerusalem by Nebuchadnezzar II, and describes abuses perpetrated in Judah during the reign of Zedekiah, who sat on the throne of Judah at the same time as Solon was enacting his reforms in Attica hundreds of miles to the northwest (Jer. 34:8–22):

> The word which came to Jeremiah from YHWH after King Zedekiah had made a covenant with all the people in Jerusalem to proclaim a release (*deror*) among them – that everyone should set free his Hebrew slaves, both male and female, and that no one should keep his fellow Judahite enslaved. Everyone, officials and people, who had entered into the covenant agreed to set their male and female slaves free and not to keep them enslaved any longer; they complied and let them go. But afterwards they turned about and brought back the men and women they had set free, and forced them into slavery again. Then it was that the word of YHWH came to Jeremiah from YHWH: thus

said YHWH, the god of Israel: I made a covenant with your forefathers when I brought them out of the land of Egypt, the house of bondage, saying: 'In the seventh year each of you must let go any fellow Hebrew who may be sold to you; when he has served you six years, you must set him free.' But your fathers would not obey me or give me ear. Lately you turned about and did what is proper in my sight, and each of you proclaimed a release to his countrymen; and you have made a covenant accordingly before me in the house which bears my name. But now you have turned back and profaned my name; each of you has brought back the men and women whom you had given their freedom, and forced them to be your slaves again.

This text refers to a law that limited the right of creditors to retain fellow countrymen whom they had acquired as slaves for six years only. We can tease out several observations from this episode. First, Zedekiah (for whatever reason) proclaimed a general release (*deror*) for those of his Hebrew (i.e. Judahite) subjects who were being held as slaves. Second, it is clear that these subjects were not merely being retained as temporary servants as the 'law' (see infra) stipulated, but as permanent slaves, hence the complaint in Jeremiah's oracle. Third, this release was unenforceable; having initially agreed to it, the people holding these individuals turned around and re-enslaved them. More than a century later, the same abuse was still going on: the following passage, Nehemiah 5:1–13, concerns events which took place in the mid-fifth century BC, after the return of the exiles to what was now the Persian province of Yehud (Judah).

There was a great outcry by the common folk and their wives against their brother Jews. Some said, 'our sons and daughters are numerous; we must get grain to eat in order that we may live!' Others said, 'we must pawn our fields, our vineyards, and our homes to stave off hunger.' Yet others said, 'we have borrowed silver against our fields and vineyards to pay the king's tax.[23] Now we are as good as our brothers, and our children as good as theirs; yet here we are subjecting our sons and daughters to slavery – some of our daughters are already subjected – and we are powerless, while our fields and vineyards belong to others'. It angered me[24] very much to hear their outcry and these complaints. After pondering the matter carefully, I censured the nobles and the officials, saying, 'are you pressing claims on loans made to your brothers? Then I raised a large crowd against them and said to them, 'we have done our best to buy back our Jewish brothers who were sold to the nations; will you now sell your brothers so that they must be sold back to us?' They kept silent, for they found nothing to answer. So I continued, 'what you are doing is not right. You ought to act in a god-fearing way so as not to give our enemies, the nations, room to reproach us. I, my brothers, and my servants also have claims of money and grain against them; let us now abandon those claims! Give back at once their fields, their vineyards, their olive trees, and their homes, and abandon the claims for the hundred pieces of silver, the grain, the wine, and the oil that you have been pressing against them!'

de Ste. Croix was not far off the mark to claim that 'almost everything in the Solonian situation is there' in this passage. We should particularly note the sale of fellow countrymen to 'the nations' (*goyim, viz.* foreigners), and the attempt by Nehemiah to buy back those Jews sold to foreigners: this is precisely what Solon claims to have achieved in fr. 36. It is worth pointing out, however, that these passages are not 'anti-slavery' tracts: nothing is said about foreign slaves. The main complaint is that members of the same ethnic community are selling one other into slavery. Once 'commoditised', these fellow countrymen could be sold far from home; that is, to foreigners. Solon's image of poor Athenians serving far from their homeland is paralleled by the indignation expressed in Hebrew texts at the very same problem (Joel 4:3; Jer. 15:14, 17:4). Both show a keen appreciation of what Orlando Patterson calls the 'natal alienation' inherent in all systems of slavery: slaves cannot enforce the kinship ties they possess, and can be sold by their owners, in effect ripping them out of the social milieu to which they belong and casting them into commercial circulation. The Greek and Hebrew texts show that this experience was viewed as one that should not have been visited by members of the same community upon each other.

Judicial abuse

The passing of crooked legal judgements by elite judges, which is mentioned in fr. 4 and contrasted with Solon's own straight judgements enacted for good and bad alike mentioned in fr. 36, is a topic mentioned in other early Greek texts, especially Hesiod and Theognis, though hints of abuse go back to Homer.[25] As van Wees has shown, elite-controlled forms of adjudication provided ample scope for abuse: we should take seriously the accusations of judicial malpractice in early Greek texts.[26] The problem here was not that such arrangements were incapable of delivering justice to poor litigants: Hesiod (*Theogony* 81–90) and Homer (*Iliad* 18.497–508) both provide images of elite judges doing their job properly and rendering straight judgements. Rather, the problem was that there were no institutional checks and balances to inhibit crooked judges from passing corrupt and unfair verdicts had they been inclined to do so.

Likewise, judicial abuse is a recurrent theme in the complaints of the prophets. There were several kinds of judicial process in ancient Israel and Judah, ranging from judgements rendered by village elders to those of monarchs, but it would appear the most controversial was the lone judge, a royal official in the local town who enjoyed considerable power but also relative independence in his dealings. This group is often accused of selling justice for money, an apt parallel for the gift-devouring *basileis* of the *Works and Days*. Micah, a prophet active in the mid-eighth century, proclaims the following (Mic. 3:9–12):

> Hear this, you rulers of the house of Jacob, you chiefs of the house of Israel, who detest justice and make crooked all that is straight, who build Zion with crime, Jerusalem with iniquity! Her rulers judge for gifts, her priests give rulings for a fee, and her prophets divine for pay; yet they rely on YHWH,

saying, 'YHWH is in our midst; no calamity shall overtake us'. Assuredly, because of you Zion shall be ploughed as a field, and Jerusalem shall become heaps of ruins, and the Temple Mount a shrine in the woods.

A similar message is delivered at Mic. 7:2–4:

> The pious are vanished from the land, none upright are left among men; all lie in wait to commit crimes, one traps the other in his net. They are eager to do evil: the magistrate makes demands, and the judge judges for a fee; the rich man makes his crooked plea, and they grant it.

Amos, roughly contemporary, observed much the same thing (5:12):

> For I have noted how many are your crimes, and how countless your sins – you enemies of the righteous, you takers of bribes, you who subvert in the gate the cause of the needy![27]

Habakkuk, active during the period directly before the fall of Judah, asks God (Hab. 1:2–4):

> Why do you make me see iniquity, why do you look upon wrong? Raiding and violence are before me, strife continues and contention goes on. And so the law loses its grip and justice never emerges; for the villain hedges in the just man – therefore judgement emerges deformed.[28]

The same complaint is levelled in several proverbs.[29] Prov. 13:23 claims that the farms of the poor yield much produce, but that many perish for want of justice; Prov. 17:23 claims that 'the wicked man draws a bribe out of his bosom to pervert the course of justice' (cf. 18:16). The Hebrew Bible is littered with condemnations against those who fail to provide justice to the vulnerable, exhortations to provide fair and impartial rulings (Jer. 21:12; Zech. 7:9; 8:16; Prov. 18:5; 24:23–5; 29:14; 31:4–5), and to avoid vexatious litigation (Prov. 18:6; 20:3; 22:10). We can also turn to extra-biblical material. An ostracon from the late seventh century, found at Yavneh Yam, about 15 km south of Jaffa, bears a text that is either a letter, or a draft or copy of a letter, to a local governor (*śar*), requesting the return of a garment that has been unlawfully seized; the person making the request exhorts the governor not to dismiss his request.[30] Some judges clearly did just that: Jeremiah, active in the twilight years of the kingdom of Judah, criticised those who grew fat in their positions and dismissed the legal suits of the poor and needy (Jer. 5:26–8); Isaiah (1:23), active somewhat earlier, levelled the same criticism.

The acquisition of land and property at the expense of the poor

In one law (R&L F149/1 = Arist. *Pol.* 1266b14) Solon established a limit on the amount of land a single person could acquire.[31] This attests to inequality in landholding in Attica in the early sixth century; that land could change hands so that some individuals acquired large amounts of landed property and others were left destitute is clear evidence of its alienability. The same basic conditions pertained in Israel, and a similar drift towards inequality in landholding in at least some quarters can be seen from an early period. The admonitions of the prophets probably concern a mixture of arbitrary seizure, distraint upon pledged land when debts could not be repaid, and the opportunistic purchase of land from impoverished persons. The eighth-century prophet Isaiah (5:8) complains:

> Ah, those who add house to house and join field to field, till there is room for none but you to dwell in the land! In my hearing said YHWH of hosts: surely, great houses shall lie forlorn, spacious and splendid ones without occupants.

Micah (2:1–2) provides a similar indictment:

> Ah, those who plan iniquity in their beds; when morning dawns, they do it, for they have the power. They covet fields and seize them; houses, and take them away. They defraud men of their homes and people of their land.

This was not a problem that occurred in the eighth century alone: an oracle of Ezekiel forbids the prince to seize the land of others; instead, he must give grants of land from his own holdings only (Ez. 46:18; cf. I Kings 21:1–16). A related abuse was tampering with the boundary stones on the land of vulnerable people such as widows and orphans. By shifting these stones one could shrink their property and increase one's own holdings. Hosea (5:10) criticises the officials of Judah by likening them to those who shift boundary stones, and several proverbs roundly condemn this sort of behaviour (Prov. 22:28; 27:17; 23:10; cf. Job 24:2). Tampering with boundary stones is also a concern of several later Greek texts ([Dem] 7.39–40; Pl. *Leg.* 8.842e–843b; Theophr. *Char.* 10.9; IGT 62A).

Violence

In Solon's poems violence is deplored in fragments 4 and 13; his description of the opposing factions in fragments 4–7, 36 and 37 shows them at each other's throats. Violence is also prominent in the poems of Theognis.[32] A similar picture emerges from the Hebrew prophetic texts, which often use the language of violence and oppression to describe the conduct of the powerful towards weaker members of society (Hab. 1:2; Ezek. 18:10–13, 7:23; Hos. 4:2, 7:1; cf. Prov. 11:16). These references, however, are generic; as we noted above, it is not possible to establish the intensity of violent behaviour.

Levies on agricultural produce

The most contentious aspects of Solon's reforms are the nature of the cryptic reform known as the *seisachtheia* and the exact meaning of the word *hektemoros*.

There is no space here to enter this debate. Suffice it to say, there are strong reasons for rejecting the view of post-Solonian sources that the former was an abolition of debts;[33] the latter, some argue, were sharecroppers paying either one-sixth or five-sixths of their produce to landlords;[34] an alternative formulation is that the *hektemoroi* were peasant smallholders who paid one-sixth of their produce to their local lord in return for protection and the maintenance of justice.[35] Regardless of which picture is correct, it seems sufficiently clear that the elite were able to impose some form of compulsory levy on the agricultural produce of the poor. We find something comparable in Israel. Amos 8:4–6 addresses the wealthy thus:

> Assuredly, because you impose a tax on the poor and exact from him a levy of grain, you have built houses of hewn stone, but you shall not live in them; you have planted delightful vineyards, but you shall not drink their wine.

It is possible that this passage refers to royal taxes collected by local notables, who may have over-assessed the vulnerable and taken a cut of the levy.[36] Certainly, the list of impositions on the populace associated with monarchical government, which form Samuel's warning to the people of Israel when they demand a king, includes tithes, levies, and corvée labour (I Sam. 8:10–18). (This passage is better interpreted as a reflection of the abuses of kings informed by hindsight than an accurate report of the prophet's words.)

Dishonesty in transactions

Another abuse common in the prophetic texts is the use of false weights and scales. By tampering with weights and measures wealthy merchants could defraud their clients (Amos 8:4–6; Ezekiel 45:9; Hosea 12:8–9; Micah 6:9; cf. Prov. 11:1, 16:11, 20:23). Some of these false weights have been excavated.[37] It is difficult to be certain, but Solon's reform of weights and measures may have been aimed at redressing similar problems in Athenian society.[38]

Let us set out a few conclusions so far. Leaving aside the highly problematic task of assessing the prevalence and intensity of social abuses in either region, we can at least set out a basic taxonomy of what sort of abuses took place. It is striking that in both regions the list of principal abuses matches up quite closely. Does this make Greece and Israel a special, stand-alone pair for comparison? Probably not: the same kind of abuses can be found in many pre-industrial societies that lack strong judicial institutions.[39] Whilst that does not make these societies unique, it does provide a common baseline for further investigation, and advances us past standard assumptions of the putative difference between Greek and Near Eastern societies.[40]

Legal solutions

Let us now turn from material and social parallels to intellectual similarities. The abuses studied in the previous section merited legal solutions, and those can be grouped as substantive and procedural/structural in nature. In substantive terms, laws could be crafted to shape the behaviour of individuals by commanding them to act in a certain way in a given situation, as well as forbidding specific types of behaviour. In terms of procedure and structure, some Greek and Hebrew texts display an acute awareness of the weakness of existing forms of adjudication and the scope for the perversion of justice by unscrupulous individuals in positions of authority. Steps could therefore be taken to reform the courts and to undercut or circumvent the ability of corrupt judges to render crooked verdicts. We shall consider the notion of procedural reform in section IV; for now, let us deal with the issue of substantive law, that is, rules on conduct.

Laws appear in several distinct groups in the Torah: the earliest collection is the so-called 'Covenant Code' of *Exodus*, dating in all likelihood to the tenth and ninth centuries BCE.[41] The laws of *Deuteronomy* represent a re-working of the Covenant Code's rules in the context of seventh-century reforms, most probably those of Josiah.[42] The legal material in *Leviticus* and *Numbers* contains a large number of sacrificial laws, plus some other laws that represent the latest phase of Israelite legal thinking, probably compiled in the exilic period and essentially utopian in thrust, at least in term of the social justice legislation.[43] It is vital to note that there is no sure way of determining whether or not any of these laws were ever applied in the courts of ancient Israel. Indeed, it is quite possible that these texts merely represent a scribal tradition based on Mesopotamian legal-theoretical antecedents, in other words, the intellectual dimension of Israelite law. All the same, they are excellent evidence for *conceptual* solutions to real-life problems, and therefore tell us a great deal about how some individuals believed laws could and should counteract the injustices present in Israelite society.

Leaving aside those aspects of Hebrew law that relate to sacred issues, the substantive solutions in Hebrew texts to many of the problems we have examined above show remarkable similarities with early Greek, and specifically Solonian, law. Solon and other Greek lawgivers produced laws regulating the conduct of individuals regarding neighbouring farms: comparable laws exist in the Torah (R&L F60a-64b; IGT 127; 133; 137; 145; 146; 155; cf. Ex. 22:4–5, 9–14; Deut. 19:14, 23:25–6). Hebrew laws aim to hinder the centrifugal forces whereby property drifts towards the hands of the wealthy with the concomitant impoverishment of the poor, not by setting a ceiling on the amount of land one person could acquire, as did Solon (R&L F149/1 = Arist. *Pol.* 1266b14), but by enabling the redemption of land by kinsmen of the impoverished (Lev. 25:13–34; cf. Jer. 32:8–12); different means, but the same fundamental end.[44] Hebrew laws ring-fence certain items as impermissible as security for loans (Deut. 24:6, 12–13, 17). Hekataios of Abdera (*FGrHist* 264 F25, fourth century BCE) mentions that many early Greek lawgivers forbade pledging items such as weapons or ploughs as security for loans, and a law from Gortyn provides a concrete example of this (IGT 147; like Deut. 24:6, mentioning millstones). But perhaps the most detailed parallels between Hebrew and early Greek law lie in the rules protecting impoverished or indebted members of the community from becoming slaves. We have already seen that the ability to sell or pledge free persons in times of distress led to such individuals being cast into commercial circulation and scattered quite widely.[45] Solon enacted a ban on pledging the body as security for loans, but a recent study by Harris has shown that he permitted the existence of debt bondage, an institution whereby creditors could recover their loans by imposing compulsory labour services on the debtor or one of his dependants. The rights of the creditor over his bondsman fell short of the property rights of a slaveholder over his slave. Harris describes Solon's law as follows:

> Debt-bondage provided the Athenians with a crude way of reconciling the rights of creditors and debtors. The law granted creditors the right to seize borrowers who failed to repay their loans and to hold them until they were able to work off their debts. Yet at the same time, the law protected the freedom of debtors by denying creditors the ability to sell them into slavery as a way of recovering their loans.[46]

We possess no actual regulations on this practice in Attica, although they surely existed. However, extensive regulations of this sort survive from Gortyn (IGT 128; cf. 138) and suggest that a similar step was taken there, protecting indebted citizens from enslavement and providing them with a legally regulated method of repaying their obligations through indentured labour.[47] The Hebrew Bible contains three sets of rules that aim to achieve a very similar end. The oldest is *Exodus* 21:2–11,[48] which states that 'when you buy/acquire a Hebrew slave, he shall serve six years; in the seventh he shall go free, without payment.'[49] Despite the language of slavery, the law is in fact limiting the right of the buyer, radically changing the Hebrew's position from property of the buyer, i.e. a slave *sensu stricto* into an indentured servant. The text goes on to consider the circumstance of the bondsman being given a wife by his master (Ex. 21:3–4), and describes a procedure whereby the bondsman can become the master's permanent slave (Ex. 21:5–6); further rules follow regulating the position of concubines (Ex. 21:7–11). *Deuteronomy* 15:12–18 reworks this law, making it briefer and more streamlined: it retains the six-year term and the procedure for becoming a permanent slave, but changes the location of this procedure from a shrine to a household (in line with the Deuteronomic programme of cultic centralisation); it subsumes women into the same condition as men, not providing separate rules (as in Ex. 21:7–11); and it changes the language of the rules to emphasise the dignity of the indentured Hebrew.[50]

The later laws of Leviticus 25:39–55 are something of a departure: they also aim to protect Israelites from the full horrors of slavery, making the most explicit distinction in any Hebrew text between the legal position of the indentured Israelite (which ought to be akin to a hired worker) and non-Israelite slaves, who may be bought, sold and inherited (Lev. 25:40–1, 44–6). Unlike the laws in *Exodus* and *Deuteronomy*, there is no six-year limit to the bondsman's service; instead, the institution of indenture is subsumed into the institution of the Jubilee, a utopian project that scholars agree was never put into practice (Lev. 25:40; cf. 25:8–12). In this system, the indentured servant is released in the Jubilee year (once every fifty years), but can be redeemed by a kinsman at any point, if his master is a non-Israelite (Lev. 25:47–55).

These laws differ in their details, but what they aim to achieve is very close to Solon's ban on enslavement for debt and the aforementioned laws of Gortyn: a way of regulating the repayment of debts by indentured labour that prevents the master from treating the bondsman as a slave. The main differences in substantive terms are the exclusivity of the Hebrew laws for Israelites, whereas Solon's law appears to have protected all free residents of Attica; and the use of fixed term limits in the former case.

It is impossible to do full justice to the complexity of this issue in this brief review. However, the evidence cited should be adequate to demonstrate that in both Greece and Israel specific legal solutions were devised in order to counteract many of the social abuses analysed earlier in this essay, solutions that are often strikingly close to one another in detail. Thus we can track similarities between both regions not only in terms of material and social variables, but also in terms of conceptual solutions to specific problems. Not only were the societies of these two Eastern Mediterranean regions experiencing similar social ills: they were attempting to solve them in similar ways.

Reforms to the courts and legal procedure

One of the striking features of the history of Greek law and adjudication is its progress from corruptible, elite-dominated trials of the early archaic period to the popular courts of the classical period, which (at least in Athens) were elaborately organised to prevent bribery. Solon's contribution to this change in Attica was substantial, for he enacted two particular innovations that greatly improved the chances of the non-elite litigant receiving a fair trial: first, he made it possible for any litigant to appeal to a *dikasterion*, and second, for volunteer prosecutors to bring public charges, meaning that third parties could sue offenders even if victims would not ([Arist] *Ath. Pol.* 9.1).[51] More broadly, the growth of *polis* institutions during the same period across the Greek world is marked by the division of power among various magistrates and an attempt to limit the influence of individuals: this process includes features such as term limits on offices, penalties for magistrates who misuse their authority, and the growth of the concept of the rule of law.[52]

Given the similar structural weaknesses of Israelite and early Greek forms of adjudication, as well as the similar social problems in both regions, we must ask the following question: were the Israelites blind to the need for reform? Clearly, the answer is a resounding 'No.' Hebrew texts show that from an early period the problem of corrupt judges was viewed as a major issue of which people were perfectly aware.[53] Reform was indeed planned in Judah. In a seminal article, Bernard Levinson has drawn attention to the highly innovative programme of reform in *Deuteronomy*, which in several major respects diverges from Near Eastern constitutional and legal tradition. During the late eighth and seventh centuries BCE, under threat from Assyria (which had not long before dissolved the northern kingdom of Israel), Judah was whittled down to a rump state. Two Judahite kings,

Hezekiah and Josiah, attempted centralising reforms. The book of *Deuteronomy* is associated with the reforms in 622 BCE of the latter king, who centralised the cult of YHWH on Jerusalem and abolished local centres of worship in the countryside. The 'draft constitution', as Levinson terms it, probably represents a utopian restructuring of power and law in Judah compiled in the closing years of the Judahite state, or perhaps in the early years of the exile.[54]

It is a radical programme. First, it aims to replace the old local system of village courts presided over by local elders with a system of centrally appointed judges in the local settlements (Deut. 16:18–20). The capacity of these judges to pass crooked verdicts is hampered by laws on witnesses that allow only for decisions in cut-and-dry cases (Deut. 17:6, 17:8–9, 19:15–21). Difficult cases for which witnesses cannot be found, or possible cases of malicious litigation, are referred to a priestly court in Jerusalem, and the decisions passed by this court are final and binding (Deut. 17:11; cf. Ezek. 44:24). These judgements must be carried out exactly; if they are not, death is set as the penalty for whomever subverts them (Deut. 17:12). Second, the judicial role of the king is nullified and transferred to the temple priests: remarkably for a Near Eastern king, the king of Judah is made subordinate to the law (Deut. 17:14–20). Furthermore, state offices of Levitical priest and prophet are delimited, penalties are set for false prophets (Deut. 18:1–22), and the laws are entrenched so that future generations might not alter them (Deut. 4:2, 13:1).

A few remarks are necessary regarding these reforms. They do not go quite as far as those occurring in contemporary Greek societies: for instance, they do not set term limits for magistrates, and the optimistic assumption is that the Levitical priests in Jerusalem are cut from a different cloth than the corruptible officials and elders they are supposed to replace. The 'draft constitution' also stems from religious scribal circles, and thus has a strong religious thrust, albeit one concerned with constructing a socially just and cohesive society. We cannot, therefore, claim that the reforms here are identical in every respect to those of archaic Greek communities. Furthermore, the Greek examples that we possess exist for the most part as a mass of individual enactments of one sort or another spread over a lengthy period of time and deriving from a multitude of regions: *Deuteronomy*, by contrast, articulates a comprehensive and unified package of reforms. But these differences aside, we can see that the need for procedural and constitutional reform was perceived in both regions. Laws were not enough on their own, but required new and improved institutional mechanisms to enable their enforcement.

Conclusions

As Levinson notes

> [i]t remains unclear whether the political, social, and religious transformations called for by Deuteronomy's authors were ever actually implemented . . . the orientation of the unit thus seems far closer to utopian political science, a revisioning of the possibilities of political, religious and social life, than to any immediate description of the status quo.[55]

Whether or not these projected reforms would ever have been carried through is a moot point: a little more than two decades after Josiah's death the Babylonian king Nebuchadnezzar II sacked Jerusalem, deported thousands of its inhabitants and subsumed Judah into his empire, spelling its end as an independent kingdom. The Greek *poleis* were more fortunate: lying further afield, their independence was not menaced by a Near Eastern superpower until the end of the archaic age, and they were able to drive off this behemoth in the battles of 480 and 479 BCE. The reforms of Solon survived the autocratic Peisistratid regime of the mid- to late sixth century intact, and his programme of centralisation and promulgation of the rule of law was given firmer footing by the reforms of Cleisthenes in 508/7 BCE.

Faced with similar social ills, individuals in Greece and Israel conceived some strikingly similar legal solutions, including structural innovations to the machinery of justice that were designed to improve the chances of these laws gaining grip in real-life cases. The transformation of Athenian society and legal procedures into the classical *politeia* of the fifth and fourth centuries certainly owed much to Solon's ability to compromise between antagonistic elite and popular factions, although he had no inkling of where his reforms (with their short-term objectives) would eventually lead. Yet this all needs to be seen in a larger context: the conceptual solutions followed in many Greek societies did not spring from a 'Greek Genius' which somehow failed to obtain in a more tradition-bound and submissive East.[56] Much is due to historical circumstance and the capricious variable of external threat: this factor rendered reform and innovation a pipe dream in Israel, but a practical proposition across the Greek world.

Notes

*   References to archaic poetry follow West 1989–92; references to Solon's laws follow Rhodes and Leão 2015, which I have abbreviated to R&L. References to archaic Greek legal inscriptions are abbreviated as IGT = Körner 1993. Translations of Hebrew texts have been taken from the *Jewish Publication Society Tanakh* (*JPS Hebrew-English Tanakh: The Traditional Hebrew Text and the New JPS Translation,* Philadelphia, 1999), but I have modified some of these (and indicated the modifications where relevant). I would like to thank Edward Harris, Keith Rutter, Mirko Canevaro, and the anonymous reader at Ashgate for reading drafts of this essay and offering advice on style and content.

1   See de Ste. Croix 2004: 118. He follows this by writing 'almost everything in the Solonian situation is there'. Cf. de Ste. Croix 2004: 123, a copy of a later letter of 1968, where Ste. Croix again uses material from the Hebrew Bible in reference to Solonian Attica.

2   See e.g. Bremmer 1993; Snell 2001: 63–74; Naiden 2006. Yamauchi 1980 compares Solon to Nehemiah, whilst Seybold and von Ungern-Sternberg 2007 compare Solon to Josiah; whereas these scholars focus on individuals, this essay will focus on broader structural issues. Raaflaub 2007 provides a somewhat pessimistic response to Seybold and von Ungern-Sternberg's study. Hagedorn 2004 treats several aspects of Greek and Hebrew law in parallel. Nielsen 2014 argues that knowledge of Solonian Attica influenced the writers of the Hebrew Bible, an unusual view that stems from the 'minimalist' school, on which see Halpern 1995. Eagerly awaited are the published proceedings of the Tel Aviv conference 'Ancient Greece and Ancient Israel: Interactions and Parallels' (October 28-30, 2012).

3   For an excellent recent overview, see Vlassopoulos 2013.

4 See Vlassopoulos 2007 for the intellectual trends behind traditional assumptions on the uniqueness of Greece.

5 Foxhall 1997: 64 writes: 'when we look at the comparanda most often used for the agrarian economy of archaic Attica, the methodology appears alarmingly shaky. Most of the ethnographic case studies drawn on by Rihll, Manville, Gallant, Finley and others have come from tropical environments, usually Africa, South-East Asia, and the South Pacific.' Israel, as I hope to show, presents a much better starting point for comparison.

6 One of the most telling clues that later writers often misunderstood Solon's laws is the mention in [Arist.] *Ath. Pol.* 9.2 (cf. Plut. *Sol.* 18) of a tradition which held that Solon deliberately made his laws obscure in wording to increase the power of the popular courts. Whilst this explanation of the wording of Solon's laws seems fairly unlikely, anyone familiar with early Greek legal inscriptions can sympathise with the accusation of terse or obscure wording. These inscriptions are normally brief texts that (as we have them) are amputated from the social context within which they were designed to be read. Having lost the context, it is up to the interpreter to guess it; and some guesses are more educated than others (cf. Rhodes 1981: 162). The author of the *Athenaion Politeia* may have been mistaken, but the example shows how classical Greek readers of archaic laws faced some of the same challenges of interpretation we face today (cf. the explanation of Solonian legal language at Lys. 10.15–20). These later writers, however, were too often satisfied to read the terse archaic inscriptions in terms of current concerns, often introducing anachronisms. For demonstrations of these anachronistic interpretations, see Rhodes 1981: 164–9 and Kroll 1998 on coinage; Harris 1997 on the abolition of debts. Another clue is the too-often dismissed debate between Androtion (Plut. *Sol.* 15) and the writer of (or source behind) the *Athenaion Politeia* on the nature of the *seisachtheia*. The very existence of this debate, to my mind, speaks volumes on how little was known about the exact content of this reform by the fourth century.

7 See Hodkinson 2000 *passim*.

8 To note several examples: Rihll 1991 interprets Solon's reforms by recourse to the unverifiable notion of large tracts of public land in early Attica, and is in general highly speculative. Sancisi-Weerdenburg 1993 contains much careful analysis, but again depends on a hypothetical connection between marginal land and the *hektemoroi* (it seems to me that this 'marginal land', if it was indeed where *hektemoroi* farmed, can only have created a marginal problem, not the widespread problem suggested by the sources). A number of scholars have viewed the Solonian problem in relation to an 'agricultural crisis' – again, not attested in the sixth-century sources (e.g. French 1956; Gallant 1982). This now seems to be out of vogue: the evidence of archaeological surveys suggests that such a crisis is extremely improbable (Foxhall 1997; Bintliff 2006). Cf. Stanley 1999: 203 for a very speculative and elaborate theory on *hektemorage*, and Ober 2006, who argues that the *horoi* mentioned in Solon fr. 36 marked the segregation of different social groups (*hektemoroi*, *eupatridae*, etc.) into different regions of Attica, like the 'peace walls' separating Israelis from Palestinians.

9 Examples of this method: Rosivach 1992; Foxhall 1997; Harris 1997; Mitchell 1997; van Wees 1999, though these scholars often disagree on points of detail, and clearly even a slimmed-down approach contains much scope for debate. On the authenticity of Solon's laws, see Rhodes and Leão 2015: 1–9.

10 The 'united monarchy' is a controversial topic. See Carr 2010: 356–75 for a sensible view.

11 For the scribal culture in which this composition and redaction occurred, see van der Toorn 2007. For the historical method of Hebrew scribes, see Halpern 1988. Carr 2010 offers a compelling view of the evolution of the Hebrew Bible and discussion of methodology.

12 Van der Toorn 2007: 173–204 is essential reading on the process whereby prophetic speech came to be frozen in written texts. To summarise briefly his conclusions: many if not most of the prophetic oracles in the Hebrew Bible were written by scribes drawing their information from groups of followers of the prophet; often the scribe was a member of the group itself. The scribe was not therefore an amanuensis writing up a word-perfect transcript of the prophet's words. On the other hand, the contents of the prophetic books are for the most part immediate artefacts of the prophet and his followers, and for our purposes can be used as sociological observations on contemporary life. There was a certain degree of editing and addition made over time to the prophetic collections, but this had little to do with the observations on social abuses with which we are dealing, but more with religious and political themes (van der Toorn 2007: 199–204; see also Carr 2010: 248–9, 318–31). One should note that the use made in this essay of the observations of the prophets is strengthened by the recurrent mention of the same abuses by multiple voices; what follows is for the most part a typology of abuses corroborated by multiple texts, not generalisations based on single utterances.

13 Cf. Millett 1984: 103, though rightly dismissive of reducing Hesiod to an anti-aristocratic prophet of doom and judgement.

14 The topic of social inequality is generating a rapidly growing literature, too large, indeed, to be engaged with here in detail. For an introduction to the problems caused by various kinds of inequality, see Wilkinson and Pickett 2009.

15 Faust 2012.

16 Faust 2012: 128–77.

17 Faust 2012: 39–127.

18 Lods 1932: 397–8; cf. Faust 2012: 14–27.

19 See Foxhall 1997; van Wees 2006. These studies suffer from two problems: first, they depend on assumptions regarding crop yields and cultivation strategies that are open to question. Second (and more significantly), the produce totals attached to the Solonian census classes in [Arist.] *Ath. Pol.* 7.4 are very likely later figures that had nothing to do with Solon at all, which, if correct, undermines any calculation of this sort whatsoever. For this argument see Rosivach 2002; de Ste. Croix 2004: 48–9. It seems likely to me that these kinds of quantitative approaches to archaic Attic inequality are wholly unreliable.

20 This refers, I think, to two different scenarios: first, the enslavement of defaulting debtors: this was a legal means of enslaving an Athenian before Solon's ban on the practice was put in place. Second, arbitrary seizure and sale: such events are already envisaged in Homer (*Od.* 17. 249–50; 20.374–83).

21 See Harris 2006: 249–69.

22 Van Wees 1999: 25–9.

23 The King of Persia here imposed a tax in silver, not in kind; this posed various difficulties for peasant farmers, who had to borrow money from wealthy individuals against their property in order to pay the tax. For the kind of solutions to this quandary pursued in contemporary Babylonia, see Stolper 1985.

24 Nehemiah, who was sent as governor to the province by Artaxerxes I in 445 BCE. On the date of the Nehemiah memoir, Carr 2010: 208.

25 Van Wees 1999 *passim*.

26 Van Wees 1999. Hawke 2011: 105–7 brushes aside accusations of bribery, and believes that Hesiod (*Op.* 263–4) is the only source describing this. But he overlooks several texts discussed by van Wees that show it was a wider problem. Moreover, the structural weaknesses of these early courts show that whatever the frequency of such abuse, it potentially *could* happen: the checks and balances that inhibited the practice of bribery in classical courts were a later development.

27 Courts were often held at the gates of walled settlements. For an unconventional view of the 'needy at the gate', see Faust 2012: 103–9.

28 The translation of מוֹט as 'loses its grip' follows the New Jerusalem rendering. cf. *Psalm* 77:3, *Lamentations* 2:18, where the word signifies numbing or slackening.

29 On the date of *Proverbs*, see Carr 2010: 403–31.

30 For the text, see Dobbs-Allsopp et al. 2005: 359. Cf. the seventh- or sixth-century BCE ostracon from the Moussaieff collection, a request from a widow to an official: 'May YHWH bless you in peace. And now, let my lord, the official, hear your maidservant: my husband has died without children. May it happen that your hand be with me and that you give into the hand of your maidservant the inheritance about which you spoke to Amasiah. As for the wheat field which is in Naamah, you gave (it) to his brother': Dobbs-Allsopp et al. 2005: 570–3.

31 Rhodes and Leão 2015: 195 treat this law as spurious, but there are no strong reasons to do so, and I am inclined (as is van Wees 1999: 14–17) to take it seriously.

32 Van Wees 2000.

33 See Harris 1997. Van Wees 1999: 17–18 is equally sceptical as Harris of the idea that 'horos' in Solon's poems means 'security marker', but nonetheless insists that the abolition of debts is historical, even though the whole notion of debt cancellation stems from this interpretation of Solon's poem.

34 See van Wees 1999: 21–4. Edward Harris points out to me the basic flaw in any model in which a *hektemoros* is interpreted as a sharecropper: the abolition of *hektemorage* would leave the putative sharecropper worse off than before, since he had no title to the land on which he worked. The only way around this is to postulate that liberated sharecroppers were given the land on which they worked, which was therefore confiscated from the landlord, but this requires explaining *ignotum per ignotius*.

35 Harris 1997.

36 De Vaux 1961: 140.

37 Dever 2001: 221–30.

38 See Rhodes 1981: 164–8. I am not convinced by the argument of Davis 2012 that the mention of drachmas in Solon's laws is a later interpolation. He demonstrates convincingly that the Athenian economy of Solon's day was overwhelmingly agrarian and that few Athenians had personal stores of silver bullion. However, it does not follow from this that fines in Solon's laws would not have been set in silver drachmas (a weight, not a coin: Kroll 1998). In Achaemenid Babylonia, hardly anyone had personal stores of silver to pay the royal taxes, but they were imposed in silver nonetheless, meaning that entrepreneurs such as the Murašu family could make a good deal of money from providing a 'tax-paying' service (Stolper 1985; cf. Nehemiah 5:4, quoted previously). I do not wish to imply that identical businesses existed in Athens, but Davis does admit that merchants often utilised silver. If there were facilities for obtaining silver in Solonian Attica, then fines could have been set in silver.

39 Lenski and Lenski 1974: 228.

40 For example, Finley 1981: 162 characterises class struggle and resultant historical change in the Greco-Roman world as generated by an active, revolutionary proletariat, whereas in the Ancient Near East, change came from above, and the rather bovine lower orders never proceeded beyond 'grumbling' and 'dissatisfaction'. This essay shows, I hope, that we cannot fairly posit such a drastic fault line in terms of behaviour between the peoples of these regions.

41 Carr 2010: 470–2.

42 See Levinson 2008 for a splendid introduction to Deuteronomy and the methods of inner-biblical exegesis.

43 For the date, see Faust 2008 and Carr 2010: 297–303.

44 The promulgation of inheritance and property laws aimed at keeping land within the family is also clear in Gortyn: see Davies 2005: 319–22.

45   Ezekiel 27:13, around the turn of the sixth century BCE, mentions Greek and Anatolian slaves being imported into Tyre. Certain social practices in Greece may have led to this (see n. 20 previously). The same Phoenician middlemen, according to Joel (4:6) sold Judahite slaves to Greek merchants. It is entirely possible, if not distinctly likely, that some of the Greek slaves sold eastwards were Athenian and ended up labouring for Judahite owners, and conversely that some of the Judahite slaves sold to Greek merchants ended up in Attica. For the entangled nature of the slave trade in the eastern Mediterranean, see Lewis 2011: 108–10. On the importance of slavery to archaic elites, see Harris 2012.

46   Harris 2006: 269.

47   See Kristensen 2004.

48   One should note that these are not fully original solutions, but stem from an older tradition in cuneiform law; cf. *Laws of Hammurabi* § 117–8. The most convincing argument on the chronology and intertextual relationship of these laws is Levinson 2006a.

49   The use of the term *eved* is proleptic: Lemche 1975. On the term 'Hebrew slave' see Levinson 2006c. There has been much debate over the term 'Hebrew slave', some contending that the term 'Hebrew' should be linked to itinerant bands called *hapiru* known from Late Bronze Age texts. Na'aman 1986 shows that whatever the origins of the term 'Hebrew', its usage in the laws of Exodus has nothing to do with the *hapiru*, but is a simple gentilic.

50   Levinson 2006a: 303–4.

51   Rhodes 1981: 159–60.

52   Harris 2006: 3–28.

53   For example, Ex. 18:17–22 with Levinson 2006b: 1858–71.

54   Levinson 2006b: 1885. See also Berman 2006.

55   Levinson 2006b: 1885.

56   On the reductive contrast between 'The Greek Mind' and 'The Hebrew Mind' see the sensible comments of Hagedorn 2004: 14–37.

Bibliography

Berman, J. (2006) 'Constitution, class, and the Book of Deuteronomy', *Hebraic Political Studies* 1.5, 523–48.

Bintliff, J. (2006) 'Solon's reforms: an archaeological perspective' in J. Blok and A. P. M. H. Lardinois (eds.), *Solon of Athens: New Historical and Philological Approaches*, Leiden, Netherlands, 321–33.

Blok, J. and Lardinois, A. P. M. H. (eds.) (2006) *Solon of Athens: New Historical and Philological Approaches*, Leiden, Netherlands.

Bremmer, J. (1993) 'Prophets, seers, and politics in Greece, Israel, and early modern Europe', *Numen* 40.2, 150–83.

Burckhardt, L., Seybold, K. and von Ungern-Sternberg, J. (eds.) (2007) *Gesetzgebung in antiken Gesellschaften: Israel, Griechenland, Rom*, Berlin.

Carr, D. (2010) *The Formation of the Hebrew Bible: A New Reconstruction*, Oxford and New York.

Davies, J. K. (2005) 'The Gortyn laws' in M. Gagarin and D. Cohen (eds.), *The Cambridge Companion to Ancient Greek Law*, Cambridge, UK, 305–27.

Davis, G. (2012) 'Dating the drachmas in Solon's laws', *Historia* 61.2, 127–58.

De Vaux, R. (1961) *Ancient Israel: Its Life and Institutions*, London.

Dever, W. G. (2001) *What Did the Biblical Writers Know and When Did They Know It? What Archaeology Can Tell Us about the Reality of Ancient Israel*, Cambridge, MA.

Dobbs-Allsopp, F. W., Roberts, J. J. M., Seow, C. L. and Whitaker, W. E. (2005) *Hebrew Inscriptions: Texts from the Biblical Period of the Monarchy with Concordance*, New Haven, CT and London.

Faust, A. (2008) 'Cities, villages and farmsteads: the landscape of Leviticus 25:29–31' in J. D. Schloen (ed.), *Exploring the Longue Durée: Essays in Honor of Prof. Lawrence E. Stager*, Winona Lake, IN, 103–12.

Faust, A. (2012) *The Archaeology of Israelite Society in Iron Age II*, Winona Lake, IN.

Finley, M. I. (1981) *Economy and Society in Ancient Greece*, London.

Foxhall, L. (1997) 'A view from the top: evaluating the Solonian property classes' in Mitchell and Rhodes (1997), 61–74.

French, A. (1956) 'The economic background to Solon's reforms', *CQ* 6, 11–25.

Gallant, T. (1982) 'Agricultural systems, land tenure, and the reforms of Solon', *BSA* 77, 111–24.

Hagedorn, A. (2004) *Between Moses and Plato: Individual and Society in Deuteronomy and Ancient Greek Law*, Göttingen, Germany.

Halpern, B. (1988) *The First Historians: The Hebrew Bible and History*, San Francisco.

Halpern, B. (1995) 'Erasing history: the minimalist assault on ancient Israel', *Bible Review* 11.6, 26–47.

Harris, E. M. (1997) 'A new solution to the riddle of the seisachtheia' in Mitchell and Rhodes (1997), 103–12.

Harris, E. M. (2006) *Democracy and the Rule of Law in Classical Athens*, Cambridge, UK.

Harris, E. M. (2012) 'Homer, Hesiod and the "origins" of Greek slavery', *Revue des Études Anciennes* 114, 345-66.

Hawke, J. (2011) *Writing Authority: Elite Competition and Written Law in Early Greece*, Dekalb, IL.

Hodkinson, S. (2000) *Property and Wealth in Classical Sparta*, London.

Körner, R. (1993) *Inschriftliche Gesetzestexte der frühen griechischen Polis*, Cologne; Weimar, Germany and Vienna.

Kristensen, K. R. (2004) 'Gortynian debt bondage: some new considerations on *IC* IV 41 IV-VII, 47 and 72 I.56-II.2, X.25–32', *ZPE* 149, 73–9.

Kroll, J. H. (1998) 'Silver in Solon's laws' in R. Ashton and S. Hurter (eds.), *Studies in Greek Numismatics in Memory of Martin Jessop Price*, London, 225–32.

Lemche, N. P. (1975) 'The "Hebrew slave": comments on the slave law Ex. XXI 2–11', *Vetus Testamentum* 25.2, 129–44.

Lenski, G. and Lenski, J. (1974) *Human Societies: An Introduction to Macrosociology*, New York.

Levinson, B. (2006a) 'The manumission of hermeneutics: the slave laws of the Pentateuch as a challenge to contemporary Pentateuchal theory' in A. Lemaire (ed.), *Congress Volume 2004: Vetus Testamentum Supplements 109*, Leiden, Netherlands, 281–324.

Levinson, B. (2006b) 'The first constitution: rethinking the origins of the rule of law and separation of powers in light of Deuteronomy', *Cardozo Law Review* 27.4, 1853–88.

Levinson, B. (2006c) 'The "effected object" in contractual legal language: the semantics of "If you purchase a Hebrew slave" (Exod. xxi 2)', *Vetus Testamentum* 56, 485–504.

Levinson, B. (2008) *Legal Revision and Religious Renewal in Ancient Israel*, Cambridge, UK.

Lewis, D. M. (2011) 'Near Eastern slaves in classical Attica and the slave trade with Persian territories', *CQ* 61, 91–113.

Lods, A. (1932) *Israel, From Its Beginnings to the Middle of the Eighth Century*, London.

Millett, P. (1984) 'Hesiod and his world', *PCPS* 30, 84–115.

Mitchell, L. (1997) 'New wine in old wineskins: Solon, *arete* and the *agathos*' in Mitchell and Rhodes (1997), 75–81.

Mitchell, L. and Rhodes, P. J. (eds.) (1997) *The Development of the Polis in Archaic Greece*, London and New York.

Na'aman, N. (1986) 'Ḥapiru and Hebrews: the transfer of a social term to the literary sphere', *Journal of Near Eastern Studies* 45, 278–85.

Naiden, F. (2006) 'Rejected sacrifice in Greek and Hebrew religion', *Journal of Ancient Near Eastern Religions* 61, 189–223.

Nielsen, F. A. J. (2014) 'Israel the antithesis of Hellas: enslavement, exile and return in the Greek Solon tradition and the Hebrew Bible' in T. L. Thompson and P. Wadjenbaum (eds.), *The Bible and Hellenism: Greek Influence on Jewish and Early Christian Literature*, London and New York, 175–86.

Ober, J. (2006) 'Solon and the horoi: facts on the ground in archaic Athens' in J. Blok and A. P. M. H. Lardinois (eds.), *Solon of Athens: New Historical and Philological Approaches*, Leiden, Netherlands, 441–56.

Raaflaub, K. (2007) 'Josias und Solons Reformen: Der Vergleich in der Gegenprobe' in L. Burckhardt, K. Seybold and J. von Ungern-Sternberg (eds.), *Gesetzgebung in antiken Gesellschaften: Israel, Griechenland, Rom*, Berlin, 163–91.

Rhodes, P. J. (1981) *A Commentary on the Aristotelian Athenaion Politeia*, Oxford, UK.

Rhodes, P. J. and Leão, D. (2015) *The Laws of Solon: A New Edition with Introduction, Translation and Commentary*, London and New York.

Rihll, T. E. (1991) 'EKTHMOPOI: partners in crime?', *JHS* 111, 101–27.

Rosivach, V. J. (1992) 'Redistribution of land in Solon, fragment 34 West', *JHS* 112, 153–7.

Rosivach, V. J. (2002) 'The requirements for the Solonic classes in Aristotle, AP 7.4', *Hermes* 130, 36–47.

Sancisi-Weerdenberg, H. (1993) 'Solon's hektemoroi and Pisistratid dekatemoroi' in H. Sancisi-Weerdenberg, R. J. van der Spek, W. C. Teitler and H. T. Wallinga (eds.), *De Agricultura: in memoriam Pieter Willem de Neeve (1945–1990)*, Amsterdam, 13–30.

Seybold, K. and von Ungern-Sternberg, J. (2007) 'Josia und Solon: Zwei Reformer' in L. Burckhardt, K. Seybold and J. von Ungern-Sternberg (eds.), *Gesetzgebung in antiken Gesellschaften: Israel, Griechenland, Rom*, Berlin, 107–61.

Snell, D. C. (2001) *Flight and Freedom in the Ancient Near East*, Leiden, Netherlands.

Stanley, P. V. (1999) *The Economic Reforms of Solon*, St. Katharinen, Germany.

Ste. Croix, G. E. M. de (2004) *Athenian Democratic Origins and Other Essays*, Oxford, UK.

Stolper, M. (1985) *Entrepreneurs and Empire: The Murašu Archive, the Murašu Firm and Persian Rule in Babylonia*, Leiden, Netherlands.

van der Toorn, K. (2007) *Scribal Culture and the Making of the Hebrew Bible*, Cambridge, MA.

van Wees, H. (1999) ' "The mafia of early Greece": violent exploitation in the seventh and sixth centuries BC' in K. Hopwood (ed.), *Organized Crime in Antiquity*, London: 1–51.

van Wees, H. (2000) 'Megara's mafiosi: timocracy and violence in Theognis' in R. Brock and S. Hodkinson (eds.), *Alternatives to Athens: Varieties of Political Organisation and Community in Ancient Greece*, Oxford, UK, 52–67.

van Wees, H. (2006) 'Mass and elite in Solon's Athens: the property classes revisited' in J. Blok and A. P. M. H. Lardinois (eds.), *Solon of Athens: New Historical and Philological Approaches*, Leiden, Netherlands, 351–89.

Vlassopoulos, K. (2007) *Unthinking the Greek Polis: Ancient Greek History beyond Eurocentrism*, Cambridge, UK.

Vlassopoulos, K. (2013) *Greeks and Barbarians*, Cambridge, UK.

West, M. L. (1989–92) *Iambi et Elegi Graeci*, 2nd ed., Oxford, UK.

Wilkinson, R. and Pickett, K. (2009) *The Spirit Level: Why More Equal Societies Almost Always Do Better*, London.

Yamauchi, E. (1980) 'Two reformers compared: Solon of Athens and Nehemiah of Jerusalem' in G. Rendsburg, R. Adler, M. Arfa and N. H. Winter (eds.), *The Bible World: Essays in Honour of Cyrus S. Gordon*, New York, 269–92.

3 How to cast a criminal out of Athens

Law and territory in archaic Attica[*]

Mirko Canevaro

Athens in classical times was an untypical *polis*. If ancient historians have for a long time assumed that the level of urbanisation in the Greek city-states, although remarkable, still saw a vast majority of the population living in the countryside,[1] recent research by the Copenhagen Polis Centre has shown that this was not in fact the case.[2] I will not spend too much time summarising the results of this enterprise, which are well known to ancient historians and historians of city-state cultures alike. It will suffice to point out that in Boeotia, a region of around the same size as Attica, which contained about twenty-five city-states, out of a population which has been reckoned between 150,000 and 200,000 inhabitants, 120,000 Boeotians lived in the cities, a percentage between 60% and 80%.[3] However precise one is willing to consider these results, they certainly indicate a trend. In general, it seems that the majority (around 60%) of Greek *poleis* had a territory between 25 and 100 square kilometers, and 80% had a territory of less than 200 square kilometers.[4] Most of their population lived within the territory of the city itself. A considerable number of the inhabitants of these *poleis* were *Ackerbürger*, as Weber called them, city farmers who lived in the city and every morning left for the fields, to come back in the evening.[5]

Athens controlled a territory of 2,500 square kilometers, spreading all over the Attic peninsula and enclosed on the north and northwest by the mountain ranges of the Parnes and Cithaeron. Estimates of the total population of this territory have been calculated in the region of 250,000–300,000 people, 50,000 of whom, the free Athenian-born males, had at the beginning of the Peloponnesian War full political rights.[6] Some areas of Attica lay at one or two days walking distance from the city, and we have direct evidence from Thucydides that more than half of the population in 431 lived in the countryside (Thuc. 2.16.1; cf. also Arist. *Pol.* 1319a35–7). Modern studies have argued that in the fourth century between two-thirds and four-fifths of the population lived in the countryside.[7] In such a context one would expect hegemonic city dwellers dominating an extensive countryside subject population, with different rights based on the actual access to the city institutions, something similar to the division between city and *contado* in Italian mediaeval *communi*.[8] Yet, in fourth-century Athens all free Athenian-born inhabitants of Attica shared the same political rights, had access to all of the polis' institutions, and considered themselves Athenian. The logistic difficulties of a population spread over such a vast territory were overcome through the impressive territorial organisation of Attica, which was divided in demes, *trittyes* and tribes which were at the same time constituent parts of the *polis* and enjoyed some level of self-government. Every deme, and therefore tribe, had representatives in the council, which prepared the agenda for the assembly, and moreover demes had considerable powers of their own. This organisation, which has been explored in the work of scholars such as Whitehead and Osborne, made Attica into a fully integrated political reality in which everyone, wherever he came from, considered himself an Athenian and had a real chance not only to enjoy the security provided by the institutions of the *polis*, but also to contribute to its running.[9]

The Athenians were aware that this organisation had a date and an author: Cleisthenes had reorganised demes and tribes at the end of the sixth century, after the Peisistratid tyranny was eventually overthrown (Hdt. 5.66–72, [Arist.] *Ath. Pol.* 20.1). Cleisthenes is often considered by modern historians the founder of democracy, but this idea was not shared by the Athenians, who, at least from the fourth century, saw democracy as the product of Solon's legislation more than 80 years earlier.[10] Cleisthenes was at the most considered to have restored the Solonian order. Likewise, as I mentioned, Cleisthenes was thought to have reorganised the territorial arrangement of Attica; yet, that Attica was already an integrated political unit with arrangements that needed reforming is never questioned by later Athenian (and non-Athenian) writers. Attica had been unified in mythical times by king Theseus, with his famous *synoikismos*, and had since always been politically unified.[11] Theseus or not, ancient historians have traditionally accepted that Attica through the archaic age developed into a city-state, a *polis*, as a whole, and when we hear of Athens we should understand Attica, whether we are talking about the fourth century or the late seventh.[12]

In recent years, however, these assumptions have been questioned from different angles: Manville has pointed out that there is no trace during the seventh century of 'state' institutions developed, complex and strong enough to administer such a large region.[13] Frost has argued that it is impossible to account for the military shortcomings of archaic Athens, if we assume that the city was somehow strong enough to control the whole of Attica, with the manpower and resources that this would involve.[14] Finally, in a groundbreaking monograph Anderson has argued that there is in fact evidence that Attica was not unified until Cleisthenes' reforms, and this is reflected in funerary practices such as the use of *kouroi*, which are used consistently all the way through the sixth century in southern Attica, but disappear in Athens from around 580 to 530 BCE, probably following Solon's sumptuary legislation. Anderson has also convincingly argued that during the Peisistratid tyranny aristocratic families such as the Alcmaeonids, when forced into exile, did not relocate outside Attica: there is evidence that the Alcmaeonids relocated on the southern coast of Attica, at Anaphlystos and Sounion, that the Gephyraioi moved to Aphidna, and that Themistocles' branch of the Lykomidai relocated to Phrearrioi. Moreover, it can be argued that Peisistratus himself during his first period of exile relocated in the area of Brauron. These places were obviously considered suitable exile locations by the Athenians, yet they were part of what in classical times would have come to be considered the Athenian *polis*. A full political and territorial integration of Attica would have happened only with Cleisthenes' political action, and his 'reorganisation' would be in fact the first proper organisation, which Cleisthenes himself linked with a mythical *synoikismos* by Theseus to grant the authority of tradition to his arrangement.[15]

This view of a late unification of Attica has many advantages: first, it fits in my opinion more convincingly the source material and the archaeological evidence for the development of the Athenian 'state'. Second, it goes some way into making the necessary distinctions recommended by Davies between town formation, state formation and *polis* formation.[16] Based on Anderson's analysis, one seems to be able to make an educated guess about the area that Athens actually controlled around the time of Solon and the Peisistratids: the Attic plain enclosed between the sea, the Aigaleos, the Hymettos and the Pentelikos mountain ranges. This area is consistent with the size of most Greek *poleis*, and with a mostly urban population composed by a vast proportion of *Ackerbürger*, city farmers who reached their fields in the morning, but lived in the city. The town of Athens at the end of the seventh and the beginning of the sixth century was clearly already formed in Weberian terms, and its size, as in many Greek towns at this and different times, prompted the necessary development of political structures capable of regulating the life of growing numbers of inhabitants, while at the same time making progressive agricultural exploitation of the hinterland a necessity.[17] With previous reconstructions we had instead to postulate a dubious urban centre, still underdeveloped, behaving however as an actual *polis*, with a connected massive *chora* and political institutions capable of controlling it, and therefore typical of a fully formed state.

What is missing however from these reconstructions is the moment of the actual conceptualization of the hinterland, however extensive, as full part of the *polis*, and therefore of the limits of the *polis* as the borders of its *chora*, rather than of the nucleated urban settlement.[18] *Polis* in many archaic sources in fact indicates the urban centre, as synonym of *asty*, before state formation and the inclusion of the *chora* as constituent part of the *polis* developed the meaning of *polis* as a city-state composed of the town and its hinterland.[19] An inscription, *IG* I³ 1194 bis, is perhaps the only epigraphic evidence giving us a glimpse of the way an archaic Athenian saw the boundaries of his *polis*, and what we find is not encouraging. It is an epitaph inviting the passer-by to mourn a man called Tettichos; it identifies the passer-by either as an *astos*, an inhabitant of the city as urban settlement, or as a *xenos*, a foreigner. The epitaph was located on a road just outside Athens, between Sepolia and Levi, modern suburbs lying just north of Kolonos. This road did not lead out of Attica, but was rather of local use. This strongly suggests that the epitaph distinguishes between the inhabitants of the city and 'foreigners' including also the inhabitants of the hinterland.[20] No sign of integration between town and countryside here, nor of a conceptualization of a border of the *polis* which does not correspond with the end of the actual nucleated settlement. Despite this evidence, the borders of the territory of the Athenian *polis* are simply assumed to exist in scholarly reconstructions, without further reflection on how the inhabitants of the urban settlement first came to conceptualise them, and when. This is mostly due to the lack of relevant sources (Rousset has been collecting frontier-related inscriptions, and we have nothing from the archaic period),[21] but, I shall argue, the few surviving sources have been in this respect underexploited, and read too much at face value.

These sources are the homicide regulations that go collectively under the name of Draco's laws, and are preserved partially on a stele from the late fifth century (*IG* I[3] 104), in which Draco's law on unintentional homicide was republished,[22] and partially in a series of reliable quotations of archaic homicide statutes in Demosthenes' speech *Against Aristocrates*, which sometimes overlap with the stele, and which are partly Draconian and partly amendments to his laws. These texts are particularly important for our purposes because, first, they are nearly the only extant archaic textual evidence from Athens (Solon's poems are not very useful in this respect); and, second, because they actively attempt, probably for the first time, to define a public space.

These texts are concerned with exile for homicides, with places where they can or cannot return, or which they can or cannot access, and with the acceptable behaviour of the relatives of the victim, based on where and in what context the killer is found. Accordingly, they strive to define a space where their provisions are valid, the space from which the homicide is excluded as a consequence of his crime and pollution, and therefore they must reflect contemporary understandings of the limits of the city/*polis*/community.[23] A text attempting to mark a violence-free area is our first evidence for the Athenians' attempt to the define the limits of their community. Their formulation for the first time into written texts perhaps in some way even contributed to prompt Athenian reflections on these matters. The meaning of these texts in defining the physical limits of the *polis* community is however the object of a misplaced consensus: to give a couple of examples, Manville claims that Draco's law is evidence that by the end of the seventh century the Athenians had formed a community with legally enforceable territorial boundaries, and that this community extended to all of Attica.[24] The use of the term *Athenaios* in the law, according to Frost, evokes an Athenian identity which already extended to a vast territory.[25] Even Anderson accepts that Draco's law unmistakably refers to clear territorial limits, although he insists that they didn't extend to all of Attica.[26]

The origin of this consensus is a statement in Demosthenes' speech *Against Aristocrates* (Dem. 23.39), the orator's explanation of a mysterious expression in Draco's law, and the connected modern interpretation of another provision a few lines later. I will first quickly summarise the contents of Draco's law, and then discuss the relevant parts and Demosthenes' interpretation. The law of Draco preserved in *IG* I[3] 104 starts defining its range of application, unintentional homicide,[27] and the penalty; the latter has been restored as *pheugen*, which in classical Attic Greek indicates the penalty of exile, and which in the context of a very archaic law must in any case be interpreted as 'escape', 'flee Athens'.[28] The restoration is based on an *epsilon* read in the inscription by Stroud.[29] So 'if one unintentionally kills someone, he shall escape' or 'go into exile'. Provisions about the trial follow, with the mention of authorities and magistrates concerned with judging the killer himself, or whoever has been 'cause of the homicide'. The next provisions, heavily restored on the basis of the *Against Macartatus*, define the conditions for pardon, which can be granted only by the father or the brothers, or by the agnatic relatives of the victim, if they all agree. If the victim has no family, the phratry is to decide.

The next provision states that the law must be valid retroactively. Next, the statute goes back in time and prescribes that a proclamation that one is a killer must be made in the *agora*, and defines who is responsible for this proclamation. This is supposedly the first step, which starts the whole procedure against a killer. The next few lines in the inscription are very fragmentary, and it is impossible to work out their contents. Gagarin has argued for a logical sequence of provisions moving from the proclamation in the *agora* to provisions for the safeguard of the exiled homicide while he stays in exile, which are restored at ll. 26–9. These would be a provision for the protection of the killer before the trial, and another about the treatment of the convicted killer and his safe passage into exile (this is mentioned at Dem. 23.72).[30] This interpretation is very dubious: first it relies on understanding *androphonos* (l. 27) as 'convicted killer', trusting a very tendentious interpretation of the term at Dem. 23.29, which contradicts plenty of evidence in the orators and elsewhere that *androphonos* was used much more loosely, and could refer to a killer in general.[31] Second, there is little trace of logical and temporal sequence in the law, and we should not therefore postulate it here. The statute starts with provisions about the penalty, moves back to the procedure and officials responsible for the trial, then forward again to the rules about pardon, and then all the way back to the original proclamation in the *agora*. We should just admit that we have no idea of what the provisions at ll. 23–6 were about.

At ll. 26–9 we find the first of the provisions relevant for our purpose. The law (restored on the basis of Dem. 23.37) states that 'If then someone kills the murderer or is the cause of his death, as far as the murderer steers clear of the *agora ephoria*, of the athletic contests and of the Amphictyonic rites, he is to be liable to the same punishment as if he kills an Athenian, and is to be judged by the Ephetai' (Ἐὰν δέ τις τὸν ἀνδροφόνον κτείνῃ ἢ αἴτιος ᾖ φόνου, ἀπεχόμενον ἀγορᾶς ἐφορίας καὶ ἄθλων καὶ ἱερῶν Ἀμφικτυονικῶν, ὥσπερ τὸν Ἀθηναῖον κτείναντα, ἐν τοῖς αὐτοῖς ἐνέχεσθαι, διαγιγνώσκειν δὲ τοὺς ἐφέτας). Demosthenes (Dem. 23.39) argues that this provision was intended to protect convicted killers in exile as long as they stayed abroad. He claims that this was the purpose of the mention of the *agora ephoria*, an expression and institution, he admits, which needs explanation, since it is no longer existent: this indicates the frontiers of the territory (τῶν ὁρίων τῆς χώρας). Thus the mention of the *agora ephoria* would be a metonymic allusion to the borders of the Attic *chora*. Demosthenes' explanation has been universally accepted in modern scholarship, and has been consistently translated as 'frontier markets', with an interpretation of *agora* which fits the fifth century, but is more problematic for the seventh.[32] But does Demosthenes deserve such trust? He seems not to be so sure himself: he introduces his explanation with the words ὥς γ᾽ ἐμοὶ δοκεῖ, which could be translated as 'I suppose', and carries on supposing that 'in ancient times' (τἀρχαῖα) the inhabitants of the Attic borders went to gather with those of neighbouring lands. He is clearly guessing, but has no idea of the meaning of the expression.[33] Nevertheless, scholars have unconditionally trusted his words, and interpreted this expression as evidence of a fully institutionalised border of the *chora* in the late seventh century.

This interpretation, needless to say, is very problematic. First of all, although Demosthenes does not specify what happened in this *agora ephoria*, modern scholars have usually interpreted this as a market place.[34] Yet this meaning of the word *agora*, obvious for classical times, is anachronistic for the seventh century.[35] This is not to say that in archaic times the *agora* could not have the function of a market; in fact, there is evidence that it did, but this meaning and this function are derivative on the establishment of the *agora* as a physical public space of a city or community.[36] In archaic sources the *agora* can indicate the assembly of a *polis* or community, and this seems to be the meaning found in Hesiod's *WD* ll. 29–30 (Hesiod even uses the plural *agorai*), or in the 'resounding *agorai* and councils' of Alcaeus (fr. 130 Lobel-Page), an individual meeting of such an assembly, as in the *Hymn to Demeter* (296), as well as the venue in which such assembly meetings took place, like the *agora* of Scheria in Hom. *Od*. 6.262–72, *Il*. 18.127, and the *agora* of Megara found at l. 826 of the *corpus Theognideum*.[37] The *agora* seems to be strictly linked with the reality of a *ptolis/polis* in Homer, and in all instances represents a public space connected with a specific community, where decisions are taken and the public running of the community takes place.[38] This is in fact the meaning of *agora* which can be extrapolated from Draco's law itself, when at l. 20 *agora* is designed as the appropriate place for proclamations against homicides in Athens. The word is never used in archaic sources with the unequivocal and exclusive meaning of market place. Demosthenes in fact does not explicitly state that the *agora ephoria* is a 'market' on the borders; he simply states that this is where the borderers gather, without specifying for what purpose. The reason for which modern scholars have consistently read this expression as referring to 'markets' is that if this *agora ephoria* is only a market, then it is easy to paint a picture of the inhabitants of border areas, coming from different communities, meeting in the *ge methoria* for the purpose of trading and commerce. However, as the sources make necessary to postulate, an *agora* in the late seventh century must have been more than a market; it was the meeting and assembly (place) of a community, where communal business was dealt with and decisions were taken. *Agorai* in archaic sources are always found in connection with a *polis/ptolis* or some kind of political community, as an institution of such a community, and not as a random, casual meeting (place) for people from various, different communities.[39] If we recognise this, the interpretation of *agora ephoria* as an *agora* on or beyond the borders of Attica, or of the Athenian territory (with Anderson), becomes hard to accept. If we accept that *ephoria* means 'on' or 'beyond the borders', we must also accept that this *agora* was not the meeting place of a community, but a casual meeting place for random people, belonging to separate and often hostile political and territorial realities, doing business around the borders. Such an institution is nowhere attested, nor is such a use of the word *agora*.

But the problems with this interpretation are even greater: in accepting the met-onymic reading of the expression as 'the borders of the *chora*', scholars assume that the law here refers to 'frontier markets' in the plural. A series of markets presumably dispersed along the western and northern border of Attica. Yet the law has the singular *agora ephoria* without article, exactly as before when referring to the *agora* where the proclamation of the homicide must be made.[40] This use of the singular strongly suggests that the law is referring to one specific *agora*, and not to a series of *agorai* along the border (if this were the case, then why did the lawgiver not use a plural?). This makes even harder to believe that the expression must be a metonymic reference to the frontiers of the Athenian ter-ritory, and strongly suggests that the law is banning a homicide from specific locations, rituals and events, rather than specifying the territorial dimension of his exile. Moreover, if *ephoria* means 'on' or 'beyond the border', this implies a fully formed border of the Athenian territory. But if such a border existed, what was the need for the legislator to use a metonymic expression to allude to it? Why did he mention an *agora* if he did not mean to refer to an *agora*?

Beyond this point, due to the lack of parallel evidence and to the fragmentary state of Draco's law, any attempt to understand precisely what *agora ephoria* means cannot be anything more than an educated guess. One should notice how-ever that we have no epigraphical evidence of border *horoi* for Attica, nor of border *horoi* anywhere from the archaic age, neither actual *horoi* nor instructions to set them in place. A recent investigation has shown that in fact even in clas-sical and Hellenistic times marking a border with an *horos* was the exception rather than the rule.[41] Of course, uninscribed *horoi* would be difficult to iden-tify, and therefore border *horoi* might in fact have existed from very early times. Nevertheless, we have literary evidence for the use of *horoi* as boundary stones for cornfields in the *Iliad* (12.421–3; 21.404–5), (field) *horoi* are mentioned by Solon ([Arist.] *Ath. Pol.* 12.4–5), and we have considerable epigraphical evidence for archaic *horoi* from around the Greek world marking the boundaries of fields, sanctuaries and *agorai*.[42] In particular we have three *horoi* from the late sixth century which mark the limit of the area of the Athenian *agora* (*IG* I³ 1087–9). This evidence strongly suggests that the use of *horoi* as frontier markers, as well as the use of the word *horos* as border in general, rather than the physical marker of a border, must be derivative, and have developed from the original meaning of *horos* as a boundary stone. If this is the case, then any interpretation of *agora ephoria* as related to the borders of a *polis*, whatever the extent of the territory and its level of conceptualization, runs the risk of being anachronistic and is unwar-ranted by the source material.[43]

This *agora* 'by the *horoi*' or 'within the *horoi*' could refer to any sort of *horoi*. These may be the *horoi* of a sanctuary, if we want to read the whole range of prohibitions as referring to the Amphictyonic games, rites and, perhaps, an *agora* by the sanctuary at Thermopylai, as suggested by Sánchez.[44] More likely, these *horoi* could be those of the *agora* of Athens itself, which is mentioned at l.21 of Draco's law. The three inscribed *horoi* from the Athenian *agora* are clear evidence that archaic *agorai* were marked by *horoi*, and we should not consider the later date of these *horoi* a problem: archaeological research has shown that the classical Athenian *agora* was developed and in use only from the late sixth century, and earlier, as reported by Apollodorus (*FGrHist* 244 F113), the Athenians used a different *agora* (*archaia agora*), whose exact location is debated.[45] This is the *agora* mentioned in Draco's law, and in all likelihood it was also marked by *horoi*. The practice of marking an *agora* with stones is attested already in Homer (*Od.* 6.266 ff., 7.43 ff., 8.5 ff. and 16; *Il.* 18.497 and 504 ff.).[46] Of course, this is only an educated guess, but it seems plausible and probable that the expression *agora ephoria* would refer to the *agora* of Athens as a physical space, and therefore as delimited by *horoi*, to define clearly where a homicide is not to be admitted. This interpretation is in any case more likely than postulating an *agora* which is not attached to any particular political community (which would hardly be an *agora*), where members of different political communities met, set on the border between separate and potentially hostile territories, and assume that the mention of such an assembly place is a metonymic reference to a fully conceptualised border of the *polis* as the union of city and *chora*.

It seems therefore likely that the provision prohibited killing a homicide that kept clear of the *agora* (whatever the *agora* here concerned), the athletic games (possibly the Amphictyonic ones) and the Amphictyonic rites. We do not know what the previous lines of the law contained, but this obviously implies a soft form of *atimia*. *Atimia* in the archaic period has been explained as a condition of full outlawry, which made the *atimos* completely bereft of any rights.[47] He could be killed at any point, by anybody and without consequences, and therefore this *atimia* equated to a death sentence, unless the *atimos* chose to escape into exile. That this was the case is shown by Dem. 9.44, who, in explaining the meaning of a decree attributed to the first half of the fifth century (but probably a fourth-century reconstruction) making Arthmeios of Zeleia an *atimos*, refers back to an archaic statute (Draconian?) about murder, presumably concerned with intentional homicide, which states καὶ ἄτιμος τεθνάτω, 'and the *atimos* be dead'.[48] The same status of *atimia* is implied e.g. in a law about tyranny probably also Draconian ([Arist.] *Ath. Pol.* 16.10) and in the entrenchment clause of Draco's homicide laws quoted at Dem. 23.62. Full *atimia*, which involved the loss of any right and allowed anyone to kill the *atimos* without restrictions, was apparently the penalty for intentional homicide and treason. That the penalty for unintentional homicide was instead a softer version of *atimia* is shown by another homicide provision, probably an amendment to Draco's law adding further protection to unintentional killers in exile (see below): this law refers to such killers as *androphonoi* ὧν τὰ χρήματα ἐπίτιμα, 'whose goods are not *atima*'. In normal cases of *atimia*, as Dem. 23.62 shows, the goods were also *atima*, and could be pillaged without consequences. The goods of unintentional killers could not.[49]

Accordingly, one could conclude, the condition of a man who had committed unintentional homicide was different from that of a full *atimos*: he still was supposed to go into exile until pardoned, and he could no longer take part in the public and religious life of the community, but he could not be freely killed without consequences, unless he was found in certain specific places, which were forbidden to him. The lawgiver here clearly attempted to define the terms of the exile by marking a legal space that was to remain unpolluted and which the killer could not access. It is remarkable that he did this by marking certain specific areas, closely connected with the key moments of political and social life, and not by simply excluding the killer from the 'territory' and sending him beyond the 'borders'.

To go back to our expression, *agora ephoria*, this analysis has shown that there is no need to postulate any reference to a 'territory' of the *polis* with precise borders, and in fact all the evidence militates against such an interpretation. This provision of Draco's law bars unintentional killers from some specific places, which shows an attempt to define a legal space, but does not imply a notion of *polis* as a legal and political space composed by the city and its *chora*, with definite borders marking its limits. A few lines later in the inscription (ll. 30–31) a very fragmentary passage has been plausibly restored as [ἐξ]εῖ[ναι δὲ τοὺς ἀνδροφόνους ἀποκτείνειν ἢ ἀπάγειν, ἐὰν ἐν] τῇ ἡμεδ[απῇ[50] on the basis of a law quoted at Dem. 23.28. This law refers back to Draco's law, of which this provision clearly constituted an amendment, and states that it is allowed to kill, or use *apagoge* against, an *androphonos*, but not to maltreat him or demand ransom. Whatever the reliability of the restoration, the inscription clearly preserves the word τῇ ἡμεδ[απῇ, which has been usually understood and translated as 'our territory'.[51] This would be acceptable if one could show from other passages that the law does define the penalty of the unintentional killer as exclusion from the 'territory' of the *polis*, marked by its borders. Yet since this is very unclear, and the previous lines of the law lack, as we have seen, such a definition precisely when one would expect it, *hemedape* should not be read in this sense. The adjective simply means 'our own', 'from our own fatherland', as opposed to ἀλλοδαπός, 'belonging to another people', or 'city' or 'land'. It does not carry the precise meaning of 'territory' marked by borders, it simply refers to belonging to a community or political reality, however this is defined.

To sum up, there is nothing in Draco's law which implies an understanding of the political community as marked by borders, the limits of a territory which is part of the *polis* as much as the nucleated urban settlement. In fact, when we would expect the law to exploit such an understanding to define the conditions of the exile of the unintentional killer, the concept is instead conspicuous by its absence, and the law tries to define a legal space for the community by marking some specific significant places, connected to important social and political activities, as beyond the reach of the killer. In such a context, interpreting the term *athenaios* at l. 28 as referring to a status of Athenian citizenship which transcends the urban centre and encompasses all inhabitants of the Attic (or Athenian) territory is unwarranted by the evidence.[52] The term *athenaios* need not refer to any more than the inhabitant of Athens in full possession of his rights, and therefore not barred from any *agora*, athletic game or ritual. Its use in Draco's law does suggest that being *athenaios* involved not only dwelling in a certain place, but, perhaps for the first time, also having certain rights (and that violence, against the laws, could lead to the loss of those rights). It does not however grant that this newly-found status extended any further than the nucleated urban settlement called Athens.

There is however a passage in Thucydides that seems to imply that the Athenians, even before Draco, were both those living in the city and those living in the countryside, and that therefore a status of *athenaios* existed which encompassed people in a distinctly Athenian 'territory', whether this included the whole of Attica or not. Thucydides (1.126) narrates the story of Cylon, an aristocrat, Olympic victor in 640 BCE and son in law of Theagenes, the tyrant of Megara, who seized the Acropolis in 632 BCE[53] and tried to install a tyranny. Thucydides reports that the Athenians came in from the fields en masse, besieged Cylon and forced him and his men to surrender (οἱ δὲ Ἀθηναῖοι αἰσθόμενοι ἐβοήθησάν τε πανδημεὶ ἐκ τῶν ἀγρῶν ἐπ᾽ αὐτοὺς καὶ προσκαθεζόμενοι ἐπολιόρκουν). Even if reliable (which is far from clear, since this account dates from more than 200 years after the facts),[54] this account does not need to refer to any kind of integration between the inhabitants of the city and the countryside. As has been convincingly shown, one of the most widespread forms of land exploitation in *poleis* of small and medium size was through *Ackerbürger*, farmers who lived in the city and reached the fields every morning to go back to the city every evening.[55] These would farm fields at moderate distance from the city, and would be in every sense Athenians, since they inhabited the urban settlement and were members of the community of the city. If we assume that many Athenians were at the time *Ackerbürger*, then it is easy to understand how the events developed so fast and who were the Athenians who *pandemei* came to the city from the fields: they were the Athenian *Ackerbürger*. Of course, there is no way to prove conclusively that this interpretation is correct, but it has the advantage of not postulating out of no evidence a level of city/countryside integration which is completely unattested at this point in time.

The law of Draco does not seem to show any clear legal notion of territory as legally defined beyond the city, with its own clear limits, and no other evidence from late seventh-century Attica shows any sign of such a notion. Yet the need to keep the killer out of the community, and to define a violence-free civic area, clearly forced the lawgiver to define some kind of legal space, through the definition of particular places, events and therefore functions from which the killer is barred. About a century later, as we have seen, Cleisthenes was to devise a complex territorial organisation of the whole of Attica which made all free-born male inhabitants of the region into full Athenians. In order to account for such an organisation we need to assume that an understanding of a growing countryside as part of the *polis*, including other communities and villages, had by then developed to such an extent that this reorganisation seemed feasible and desirable.

Evidence of attempts to integrate the countryside (whatever its extent, which probably grew in time) into the Athenian 'state' are clearly attested at the time of the tyrants. Peisistratus and his sons are credited with the institution of deme judges, who would adjudicate quarrels in villages outside Athens, and there is evidence that Peisistratus himself used to visit the countryside to be seen and affirm his power.[56] Hippias even set herms on the roads of Attica which marked the distance of each place from the newly-built Altar of the Twelve Gods in the new *agora*.[57] The tyrants have also been credited with cultic policies aimed at spreading a sense of common belonging in the whole of the Athenian territory, although Anderson has (not fully convincingly) contested these reconstructions.[58] At the time of the tyrants we can therefore see a growing territory under direct or indirect control of the Athenian *polis*, encompassing also villages and separate communities. The problem of the status of such pre-existing communities was probably already of concern to Solon: the *Digest* (47.22.4) preserves a Solonian law on associations which, while declaring valid the decisions of various groups (*demoi*, phratries, dining groups, *orgeones*, *homotaphoi*, *thiasotai*, or people engaged in common enterprises for the purpose of trade or plunder), creates a hierarchy between their decisions and the 'public' decisions of the *polis*.[59] If, as seems likely, many of these associations had a territorial basis, this law must be a very early attempt to integrate external communities into the workings of the *polis*.[60] If, as argued by Ismard, the process of *polis* formation already involved the progressive integration of 'associations' within the wider organisation formed by the *polis*, it is easy to see how communities far from Athens could progressively also be integrated into the *polis*, as the territory it controlled grew.[61]

Progressive attempts to integrate a growing countryside into the *polis* must have forced the Athenians to imagine a political space beyond the urban settlement, which eventually came to encompass other settlements, and therefore to conceptualise its limits, however unstable these were. Such a development of a notion of borders of the territorial and political space of the *polis*, unsurprisingly, is exploited, and perhaps was in part fostered, by parallel attempts to define a legal space. We have seen how Draco's law, where we would expect it to define the legal space of the *polis* through the borders of its territory, struggled instead to create such a legal space by marking particular places, rites and events as barred to the killer. Conversely Dem. 23.44 reports a homicide provision stating that 'if someone, beyond the border, pursues or despoils some murderer in exile, whose goods are not confiscated, he is to incur the same penalty as if he did it in the *hemedape*' (Ἐάν τίς τινα τῶν ἀνδροφόνων τῶν ἐξεληλυθότων, ὧν τὰ χρήματα ἐπίτιμα, πέρα ὅρου ἐλαύνῃ ἢ φέρῃ ἢ ἄγῃ, τὰ ἴσα ὀφείλειν ὅσα περ ἂν ἐν τῇ ἡμεδαπῇ δράσῃ). This law clearly implies a formed notion of borders of the Athenian territory. When should we date it? This is an archaic statute, as is clear from the reference to an archaic notion of *atimia*, as well as from the similarities in wording with Draco's law. It has in fact often been considered a Draconian statute,[62] but should rather be interpreted as an amendment to Draco's law: first, it cannot be restored anywhere in the inscription reporting Draco's law about unintentional homicide, although the mention of the χρήματα ἐπίτιμα makes it certain that it is a law about unintentional homicide. Second, the law presupposes and refers to a provision declaring the goods of an unintentional killer not disfranchised, and to the penalties for those that despoil someone of his goods. It extends these penalties also to those who despoil the goods of an unintentional homicide abroad. A provision allowing the killing in retaliation of those who forcibly despoil someone of his goods is found at Dem. 23.60 and convincingly restored at ll. 36–8 of Draco's law (towards the end of the 'axon'). This law is therefore an amendment to other provisions about homicide (in the same way as Dem. 23.28 was), which were in all likelihood part of Draco's law, and which specified the conditions of the soft *atimia* of unintentional killers.[63] The amendment covered the case of an unintentional killer despoiled of his goods while abroad, and made the perpetrator liable to the same penalties as if he did it in Athens. It is impossible to date this amendment precisely, but this is clearly an archaic statute to be dated some time after Draco's law. It must have been approved at some point in the sixth century, and therefore in the same context in which Solon's and Peisistratus' attempts to bring about some level of integration between city and countryside were taking place. It is evidence that in the context of these attempts, the Athenians were in fact starting to understand their *polis* as a city with a territory, and the limits of this territory as the limits of Athens. These could therefore be used as the limits of the legal space were their laws were valid. In Draco's law the *hemedape* stays undefined, and nothing suggests that it was supposed to include any more than the city of Athens. Instead, at some point in the sixth century, the Athenians, when they had to define what is outside the *hemedape* as a legal space, naturally expressed this concept with the words πέρα ὅρου, 'beyond the border'.

One last piece of evidence can help us to form an idea of how this conceptualisation of the *horoi* (boundaries or boundary stones) of the territory as the limits of the *polis* came about. This is a version of the Oath of the Ephebes preserved in an inscription from Acharnae from the middle of the fourth century (*R&O* 88 ll. 5–20), and in slightly modernising (and stylistically improved) versions in Pollux (8.105–6a) and Stobaeus (43.48). There has been much debate about the authenticity of this text, and whether it was a fourth-century invention or reconstruction or a transcription (however much edited and modified through the centuries) of a very ancient oath.[64] Lycurgus has it read out (but no document is found in the speech) and discusses it in the *Against Leocrates*, and his words are consistent with the contents of the inscription (Lyc. 1.76–8). Close analyses have shown that references to the wording of the oath can in fact be found in fifth-century Athenian literature, which makes it virtually certain that it was at the time well known; moreover several features of the oath (the use of *thesmos* instead of *nomos*, the choice of deities, many not worshipped in classical Athens, the word κραινόντων) show that its origin is archaic. Siewert has argued that it should be considered pre-Peisistratid, and perhaps even pre-Solonian.[65] Exact dating is difficult, but it is safe to consider it another product of the sixth century, however much it has been edited in the following centuries.

The Ephebes swear that they 'shall not hand on the fatherland [*patris*] lessened, but greater and better [in size and strength]'. The oath, like the law at Dem. 23.44, seems to imply a definite concept of the territory of the *patris*, that can be extended, and therefore a *patris* which does not equate to the city alone, but to the city and its territory. At the end of the oath the Ephebes swear by 'the Gods Aglauros, Hestia, Enyo, Enyalios, Ares and Athena Areia, Zeus, Thallo, Auxo, Hegemone, Heracles, and the boundaries of my fatherland, wheat, barley, vines, olives, figs'. The word *theoi* is followed by a list of deities, and after the list is complete we have the expression *horoi patridos*, 'the borders of the fatherland'. This expression specifies that the fatherland, as the territory of the *polis*, has *horoi*, proper boundaries (or boundary stones, by which the Ephebes swear). These borders are the limit of the *patris* that the Ephebes swear to expand. After the mention of the *horoi patridos* we have a list of agricultural products: 'wheat, barley, vines, olives, figs'. These should be read as specifications of the *horoi patridos*, as the parallelism *theoi/horoi* suggests, which would imply that these agricultural products are particular instances of *horoi patridos*.[66] This is the reading used by Alcibiades to argue for the Sicilian expedition: the Athenians have sworn to extend the borders of the *patris* as far as these agricultural products are grown (Plut. *Alc.* 15.4). But even if we prefer a paratactic reading of this last part of the list,[67] there is little denying that the *horoi patridos* are tightly connected with agricultural products. Ober has suggested that the *horoi patridos* linked to agricultural products should be read as a metaphoric allusion to the boundary stones of the fields (concrete objects by which the Ephebes could swear) where these products were grown.[68] The Ephebes, and therefore the Athenians, visualised the limits of their territory at this time as the outer boundary stones of the arable land that belonged to them. Whether we accept this interpretation of physical field *horoi* on the border marking the border itself, or we believe that the use of *horoi* is here simply figurative,[69] it is clear that in the oath the concept of *horoi patridos* was tightly connected with agricultural products, and therefore the limits of the fatherland were understood as the limits of the land farmed by the Athenians. The Ephebes in archaic times swore to leave a *patris*, conceived as the city plus the arable land farmed by its members, bigger than they found it.

It is easy to see how such a concept could develop into a fully formed understanding of the *polis/patris* composed of both the city and its countryside, with precise political borders. It probably originated as the conceptualization of the territory of the *polis* by city dwellers who farmed its immediate hinterland, the *Ackerbürger*. But as the size of the farmed territory grew, together with the size and importance of Athens itself, the territory, the *horoi patridos*, came to encompass previous settlements, villages, autonomous and semi-autonomous political realities. At the same time, the cultural and political influence of this considerable urban centre grew even wider in Attica, a region which showed already significant similarities in cultural, material, linguistic and religious terms, developed over centuries and perhaps partially stemming back to previous phases of political unification in Mycenaean times.[70] Solon's law on associations seems to be one of the first attempts to integrate the various realities by then encompassed in the *horoi patridos* within a system based on the centrality of Athens. Peisistratus and his sons, through their trips to the *chora*, their deme judges and their markers of the distance from the Altar of the Twelve Gods, were attempting to integrate an even vaster territory. This integration would not be complete until Cleisthenes' reorganisation of Attica, yet all these successive attempts relied on the understanding by the Athenians that the *polis* was not simply the nucleated urban settlement, but also the fields that the *Ackerbürger* farmed. Gradually all that was included in the farmed territory of Athens, including pre-existing villages and semi-autonomous political realities became part of what Athens was, so that the *polis*, in the minds of its members, started having borders, marking the end of its political authority. The conceptualization of an Athenian legal space, and the attempt to control violence and create institutional means to prevent it and punish it, through the first written laws of Draco and Solon, developed hand in hand with this process, so that different stages of this conceptualization survive as cultural trace fossils in the texts of these laws. These laws in turn help us to see what Athens exactly was, and where it ended, as the people who wrote them saw it.

Notes

* I would like to thank the editors for organising the original panel, and for their work and advice during the production of the volume. Versions of this chapter have been delivered in Prague, Chicago and at the Universidade de São Paulo, and I have benefited from the feedback of the audiences. David Lewis, Edward Harris, John Bintliff, Sylvian Fachard, Josiah Ober and Lisa Eberle have read drafts of this essay, offering much invaluable feedback.

1 Cf. e.g. Finley 1987–89: 304–5; Brun 1999: 19; Horden and Purcell 2000: 105; Cartledge 2002: 20.

2 Cf. Hansen 2006b: 69–72; Hansen and Nielsen 2004: 70–9.

3 Cf. Hansen and Nielsen 2004: 437–59; Bintliff 1997; Hansen 1997: 62–3, 2006a: 13, 2006b: 84–7.

4 Hansen and Nielsen 2004: 70–2.

5 Weber 1999: 67–8. Scholars such as Finley 1963: 45 and Osborne 1987: 194 have argued against his belief that *Ackerbürger* were typical of the ancient city, but see Isager and Skydsgaard 1992: 149–55; Hanson 1995; Bintliff 2006: 27; Hansen 2006a: 93–4.

6 Garnsey 1998: 89–90; Hansen 1988: 12. Osborne 1987: 47 gives the more conservative estimate of 150,000.

7 Bintliff 2006: 13 n. 4 and Hansen and Nielsen 2004: 636. The only extensive archaeological study of a rural deme (Lohmann 1993; cf. also Lohmann 1995) shows extensive agricultural exploitation and intensive occupation of the *chora*. Many of these people must have lived in isolated farmsteads (Langdon 1991; cf. Steinhauer 2001; Hoepfner 1999: 247, 253, 259–60; Jones 2000; Hansen and Nielsen 2004: 625–6), but the existence of several town-like centres in Attica, given the overwhelming literary evidence for them, cannot be denied (Hansen and Nielsen 2004: 626). Bintliff 1994 shows that by the classical period a regular network of villages had developed in the rural areas of Attica.

8 Cf. Jones 1997: 359 ff.; Scott 2012: 217–21.

9 Osborne 1985; Whitehead 1986.

10 Cf. Anderson 2003: 206–11. On Solon and the later debates about the *patrios politeia*, see Fuks 1953; Ruschenbusch 1958: 399–408; Mossé 1979; Hansen 1990. For various views on the 'foundation' of democracy by Cleisthenes, Solon or Ephialtes, see e.g. Raaflaub et al. 2007.

11 Cf. e.g. Thuc. 2.25 with Ruschenbusch 1958: 408–18; Walker 1995: 35–82, 143–94; Parker 1996: 11–17. Moggi 1976: 44–81 collects all the evidence.

12 Cf. e.g. Hignett 1952: 34–8; Jeffery 1976: 84; Snodgrass 1977; Andrewes 1982: 360–3; Diamant 1982; Morris 1987: 195; Hansen and Nielsen 2004: 624–6. Osborne 1994 dates this process to the seventh century BCE.

13 Manville 1990: 76.

14 Frost 1984, 1994.

15   Anderson 2003, especially pp. 1–42, with a discussion of this evidence.

16   Davies 1997: 15–6.

17   Weber 1999. For recent discussions of town definition in the ancient world according to Weberian paradigms see Davies 1997: 15–6 and Hansen 2006a: 85–97.

18   The stage, that is, of the invention of the *polis* as it was understood in classical times, and of the conceptualization of this *polis*. Hölkeskamp *BMCR* 2004.04.03 laments that even Hansen in his work with the 'Polis Centre' neglects the 'the early, unfinished or "primitive" polis', and highlight the dangers of applying generalisations based on classical sources to the archaic *polis*.

19   Hansen 1998: 17–34, 2000: 178–9, 2006a: 56–61.

20   Cf. Frost 1994: 51; Anderson 2003: 24.

21   Rousset 1994: 99–100.

22   Cf. the republication of this inscription in Stroud 1968, with abundant exegetic material. I believe that the law preserved in this stele was concerned only with unintentional homicide, *pace* Gagarin's attempt to interpret the beginning of the law as 'even if', which would make these provisions valid also for intentional homicide (Gagarin 1981: 65–110).

23   On the role of pollution in Athenian homicide legislation cf. Salvo 2011 and Harris 2015, who argues that pollution played a key role in homicide laws and procedures at all stages (*pace* Parker 1983: *passim* and especially 125–6; MacDowell 1963: 141–51).

24   Manville 1990: 80–2.

25   Frost 1994: 48–9.

26   Anderson 2003: 21.

27   Gagarin 1981 argues that the expression 'καὶ ἐὰμ μὲ ʼκ {ἐκ} [π]ρονοί[α]ς [κ]τ[ένει τίς τινα' must refer not only to unintentional homicide, but also to intentional, and that nothing is missing at the beginning of the law: it should be read as 'even if someone does not kill someone intentionally', therefore *a fortiori* also if someone kills someone intentionally. His reconstruction has been mostly met with scepticism (cf. e.g. Sealey 1983: 292; Wallace 1989: 16–18; Rhodes 1991: 91 n. 24; Westbrook 2009), and it is assumed here that the sentence refers only to unintentional homicide. But even if Gagarin were right, this would make little difference for the arguments laid down here.

28   In classical Attic Greek the term has often the meaning of 'being the defendant', 'stand trial' (cf. Lys. 12.4; Pl. *Rep.* 405b; Ar. *Eq.* 442; Dem. 49.1; Aeschin. 3.201). Some scholars have argued that this must be the meaning also in Draco's law: 'even if someone does not kill someone intentionally, he is to stand trial' (Treston 1923: 195; Tsantsanoglou 1972: 170–9; Mirhady 2008: 15 ff.; Phillips 2008: 51, n. 74). The problem with this interpretation is that the verb *pheugein* with this meaning is not attested in the seventh or sixth century BCE (or in the first half of the fifth). Moreover Dem. 23.51 reports a law, in all likelihood a sixth-century BCE amendment to Draco's law on homicide (cf. Canevaro 2013: 62–4 about the authenticity of the document and the contents of the law), which uses the term unequivocally in the sense of 'escaping', 'going into exile': Φόνου δὲ δίκας μὴ εἶναι μηδαμοῦ κατὰ τῶν τοὺς φεύγοντας ἐνδεικνύντων, ἐάν τις κατίη ὅποι μὴ ἔξεστιν. The clause ἐάν τις κατίη ὅποι μὴ ἔξεστιν makes clear the meaning of the verb, which is not 'to stand trial'. Given therefore that the only Athenian archaic evidence for this verb in a legal context has the meaning 'to escape', 'to go into exile', it is safer to assume that *pheugein* means 'to go into exile' also in Draco's law (e.g. Ruschenbusch 1960: 147; Stroud 1968: 6; Gagarin 1981: 30; Carawan 1998: 33).

29   Stroud 1968: 41–2.

30   Gagarin 1981: 58–61.

31   Stroud 1968: 53 discusses the evidence and rejects Demosthenes' explanation of the term.

32   E.g. Stroud 1968: 53; Gagarin 1981: 59, 1986: 87, 2008: 98; Daverio Rocchi 1988: 30, 225; Manville 1990: 80; van Effenterre and van Effenterre 1990: 257–8;

Lambert 1993: 50; Ampolo 1999: 453–9; Schmitz 2001: 18; Stanton 2005: 18; Lape 2010: 10; Erdas 2012: 59; Fachard 2013: 104 (who, however, tells me *per litteras* that he now agrees that this *agora ephoria* must be the *agora* of Athens); Bresson 2016: 237, 491 n. 65.

33 This is recognised also in Ampolo 1999: 54–5 and Cerri 2013.

34 Ampolo 1999, in an article titled 'La frontiera dei Greci come luogo del rapporto e dello scambio: I mercati di frontiera fino al V secolo A.C.', discusses the nature, cultural implications and modalities of the exchanges across borders in archaic Greece. Yet, despite the title of his contribution, the only evidence for 'frontier markets' he provides is once again ll. 26–9 of Draco's law together with Dem. 23.39, while all the other evidence he discusses is for different kinds of exchanges that do not involve frontier markets. Ampolo (1999: 54–5) recognises that Demosthenes' interpretation must be no more than a guess, yet after pointing this out he strangely proceeds to use this interpretation as a building block in his analysis without substantiating it with further evidence that *agora ephoria* must mean 'frontier market'.

35 The dangers of applying classical concepts of *agora* to the archaic age are rightly stressed by Hölkeskamp, *BMCR* 2004.04.03.

36 See Hölkeskamp 1997, 1999: 270–85; Longo 2009: 202–4.

37 This passage, which should probably be dated to the second half of the sixth century BCE, also clearly alludes to the boundary of the (cultivated) land, γῆς δ' οὖρος, in a fashion which is very consistent with the Athenian Ephebic oath, and reminds of an amendment to Draco's law which should probably also be dated in the late sixth century BCE (Dem. 23.44). See below.

38 For the meaning of *agora* in the archaic period see Martin 1951; Kolb 1981: 1 ff.; ; Höllkeskamp 1997, 1999: 270–85; Ruzé 1997: 14–106; Kenzler 1999: 31 ff., 53 ff., 62 ff., 304 ff.

39 Cf. also Edwards 2004: 66: 'This explicit identification of the *polis*, the city, as the locale for the *agore* [. . .] This survey of references to the kings in the *Works and Days* evidences a consistent association of these figures with the *agore* and the *polis*'.

40 *Pace* the references at n. 33. ἀπέχω in the middle takes the genitive – ἀγορᾶς ἐφορίας is a genitive singular, and ἄθλων καὶ ἱερῶν genitive plurals (the ??[α]ὶ [ἄθλον καὶ ἱερ??ν restored in *IG* I³ 104 l. 28 translates the wording of Dem. 23.37 into Attic script). It is unclear whether the adjective 'Amphictyonic' is supposed to define only the rites, or also the games (cf. Stroud 1968: 54). Regardless, the law is banning a homicide from certain places, events and rituals.

41 Rousset 1994: 109–12. See also Freitag 2007. *Pace* Daverio Rocchi 1988: 53–4.

42 See Lalonde 1991: 1–52 for all the epigraphical evidence of *horoi* in Attica, which provides a very good sample of the range of their uses.

43 The first attestation of the term *ephorios* is in Strabo (12.3.22), too late to be relevant, and a passage in Harpocration (*s.v.* Ἐφορία) shows that the term was explained on the basis of Demosthenes' interpretation at Dem. 23.39, which might have conditioned later uses (cf. also Poll. 9.8–9; Suda 2.489 Adler; Phot. s.v. Ἐφορία; see Ampolo 1999: 455–6). Cerri's (2013) very speculatve interpretation of *agora ephoria* as a covert reference to Salamina (apart from the lack of corroborating evidence, which Cerri acknowledges) runs into the same problem: it assumes that the word *ephoria* can be read as an unequivocal reference to the frontier of the *polis*, yet *horos* is never used with this meaning in archaic texts.

44 Sànchez 2001: 53.

45 For different theories about the location of this *agora*, see Schnurr 1995; Robertson 1998; Greco 2000, 2001; Hitzl 2003; Schmalz 2006.

46 Cf. Hölkeskamp 2002: 320.

47 Cf. Hansen 1976: 75–82 with previous references; MacDowell 1978: 73–5. The meaning of *atimia* is different in classical times, when the *atimos* is disfranchised and

therefore deprived of certain rights, like that of entering the *agora*, the temples, taking part in the political running of the *polis* and even appearing in court, but is not an outlaw and still possesses certain rights and protections.

48 The decree was probably a fourth-century BCE reconstruction (see Habicht 1961), but the meaning of *atimia* there implied must date back to the early fifth century BCE and to the archaic period.

49 See below on Dem. 23.44.

50 Stroud 1968: 54–6, n. 102. His integration is suggested *exempli gratia*, and Gagarin 1981: 61 n. 85 is right in pointing out that, according to the general usage of the stele, we would expect here the verb κτείνειν rather than ἀποκτείνειν. But, even with a slight rewording (Gagarin's καὶ κτείνειν κἀπάγειν), Stroud's guess is still valid.

51 *LSJ* s.v. goes as far as to mention Draco's law with the words 'ἡ ἡμεδαπή (sc. γῆ)'.

52 *Pace* Manville 1990: 76, 80–2; Frost 1994: 48–9.

53 His exact dating is discussed in Moulinier 1946: 636, 628, 624 BCE are also possible dates for the attempt of coup.

54 On the reliability and distortions of oral traditions with reference to Thucydides see Thomas 1989: 272–81.

55 Isager and Skydsgaard 1992: 149–55; Hanson 1995; Hansen 2006a: 93–4; Bintliff 2006: 27.

56 Cf. [Arist.] *Ath. Pol.* 16.5.

57 [Pl.] *Hipparch.* 228b-229d; Hesych. s.v. *Hipparcheios Hermes*; Harp. s.v. *Hermai*. On the Altar of the Twelve Gods cf. Thuc. 6.54.5–7 with Thompson and Wycherley 1972: 129–36. One of these herms has been found near Koropi (cf. Kirchner and Dow 1937: 1–3).

58 Kolb 1977; Stahl 1987; Eder 1988, 1992: 28–31. *Contra* Anderson 2003: 121–211 *passim*.

59 Cf. Jones 1999: 311 ff. *Pace* Arnaoutoglou 2003: 44–50 (who believes that the law must be dated to the time of Adrian), the law is probably archaic, although it is possible that some expressions were modified in the last decade of the fifth century. Cf. Ismard 2010: 44–57 and van Wees 2013: 59–60.

60 Cf. Manville 1990: 55–69, esp. 63–66 on the territorial basis of such associations, and Osborne 1985: 127–50 on the negotiation of local and kinship ties in classical Athens. Cf. Schmitz 2004 for the importance of the neighbourhood in the development of archaic society and archaic law, and p. 258 about this law of Solon.

61 Ismard 2010, who stresses that the *polis* came into existence as the combination of these separate communities. Cf. Seelentag 2015 for the case of Crete. For an introduction to recent studies of communities and associations within and beyond the *polis*, see Taylor and Vlassopoulos 2015: 1–31.

62 *Cf.* e.g. Carawan 1998: 77; Drerup 1898: 271.

63 Cf. Canevaro 2013: 58–61.

64 Cf. Siewert 1972, 1977; Rhodes and Osborne 2003: 440–9; Sommerstein and Bayliss 2013: 13–22.

65 Siewert 1977; cf. Sommerstein and Bayliss 2013: 13–14.

66 Cf. e.g. Siewert 1977: 109.

67 This is assumed in Vidal-Naquet 1986: 122.

68 Ober 1995: 105–14. Cf. Mikalson 2005: 143, who also sees these as physical objects.

69 Cf. Burkert 1985: 251, who suggests that they are 'epitomizing the fruitful, ancestral earth'. Sommerstein and Bayliss 2013: 21 link them to the gods of the underworld.

70 But the unity of Attica in Mycenean times is very dubious, see e.g. Diamant 1982: 43, Parker 1996: 11, Hansen and Nielsen 2004: 625.

Bibliography

Ampolo, C. (1999) 'La frontiera dei Greci come luogo del rapporto e dello scambio: I mercati di frontiera fino al V secolo A.C.' in *Confini e frontier nella grecità d'Occidente: atti the trentasettesimo Convegno di studi sulla Magna Grecia, Taranto, 3–6 ottobre 1997*, Taranto, 451–64.

Anderson, G. (2003) *The Athenian Experiment: Building an Imagined Political Community in Ancient Attica, 508–490 B.C.*, Ann Arbor, MI.

Andrewes, A. (1982) 'The growth of the Athenian state' in J. Boardman and N. G. L. Hammond (eds.), *The Cambridge Ancient History: The Expansion of the Greek World, Eighth to Sixth Centuries B.C.*, Cambridge, UK, 377–89.

Arnaoutouglou, I. N. (2003) *Thusias heneka kai sunousias: Private Religious Associations in Hellenistic Athens*, Athens.

Bintliff, J. (1994) 'Territorial behaviour and the natural history of the Greek polis' in E. Olshausen and H. Sonnabend (eds.), *Stuttgarter Kolloquium zur Historischen Geographie des Altertums 4*, Amsterdam, 207–49.

Bintliff, J. (1997) 'Further considerations on the population of Ancient Boeotia' in J. Bintliff (ed.), *Recent Developments in the History and Archaeology of Central Greece*, Oxford, UK, 231–52.

Bintliff, J. (2006) 'City-country relationship in the "normal polis"' in R. M. Rosen and I. Sluiter (eds.), *City, Countryside and the Spatial Organization of Value in Classical Antiquity*, Leiden, Netherlands, 13–32.

Bresson, A. (2016) *The Making of the Ancient Greek Economy*, Princeton, NJ.

Brun, P. (1999) 'Les nouvelles perspectives de l'étude démographique des cités grecques' in M. Bellancourt-Valdher and J.-N. Corvisier (eds.), *La démographie historique antique*, Arras, France, 13–25.

Burkert, W. (1985) *Greek Religion: Archaic and Classical* (trans. J. Raffan), Oxford, UK.

Canevaro, M. (2013) *The Documents in the Attic Orators: Laws and Decrees in the Public Speeches of the Demosthenic Corpus*, Oxford, UK.

Carawan, E. (1998) *Rhetoric and the Law of Draco*, Oxford, UK and New York.

Cartledge, P. (2002) 'The economy (economies) of ancient Greece' in W. Scheidel and S. von Reden (eds.), *The Ancient Economy*, Edinburgh, 11–32.

Cerri, G. (2013) 'L'agora ephoria di Dracone e l'elegia Salamina di Solone: tra legge orale e legge scritta', *QUCC* 105.3, 45–52.

Daverio Rocchi, G. (1988) *Frontiere e confini nella Grecia antica*, Rome.

Davies, J. K. (1997) 'The "origins of the Greek polis": Where should we be looking?' in L. G. Mitchell and P. J. Rhodes (eds.), *The Development of the Polis in Archaic Greece*, London and New York, 24–38.

Diamant, S. (1982) 'Theseus and the unification of Attica' in *Studies in Attic Epigraphy, History and Topography Presented to Eugene Vanderpool*, Princeton, NJ, 38–47. *Hesperia* Supp. 19.

Drerup, E. (1898) 'Über die bei den attischen Rednern eingelegten Urkunden', *Jahrbücher für classische Philologie* 24.Suppl. 2, 221–366.

Eder, W. (1988) 'Political self-confidence and resistance: the role of the Demos and Plebs after the expulsion of the tyrant in Athens and the king in Rome' in T. Yuge and M. Doi (eds.), *Forms of Control and Subordination in Antiquity*, Leiden, Netherlands, 465–75.

Eder, W. (1992) 'Polis und Politai: Die Auflösung des Adelsstaates und die Entwicklung des Polisbürgers' in I. Wehgartner (ed.), *Euphronios und seine Zeit*, Berlin, 24–38.

Edwards, A. T. (2004) *Hesiod's Ascra*, Berkeley, CA.

Erdas, D. (2012) 'Aspetti giuridici dell'*agora* greca' in C. Ampolo (ed.), *Agora greca e agorai di Sicilia*, Pisa, Italy, 57–70.

Fachard, S. (2013) 'Eleutherai as the Gates to Boeotia' in C. Brélaz and S. Fachard (eds.), *Pratiques militaires et art de la guerre dans le monde grec antique: Études offertes à Pierre Ducrey*, Paris, 81–106.

Finley, M. I. (1963) *The Ancient Greeks*, London.

Finley, M. I. (1987–89) 'The city', *Opus* 6–8, 303–13.

Freitag, K. (2007) 'Überlegungen zur Konstruktion von Grenzen im antiken Griechen-land' in R. Albertz, A. Blöbaum and P. Funke (eds.), *Räume und Grenzen: Topologische Konzepte in den antiken Kulturen des östlichen Mittelmeerraums*, Munich, 49–70.

Frost, F. J. (1984) 'The Athenian military before Cleisthenes', *Historia* 33, 283–94.

Frost, F. J. (1990) 'Peisistratus, the cults and the unification of Attica', *Ancient World* 21, 3–9.

Frost, F. J. (1994) 'Aspects of early Athenian citizenship' in A. L. Boegehold and A. C. Scafuro (eds.), *Athenian Identity and Civic Ideology*, Baltimore, MD, 46–56.

Fuks, A. (1953) *The Ancestral Constitution*, London.

Gagarin, M. (1981) *Drakon and Early Athenian Homicide Law*, New Haven, CT.

Gagarin, M. (1986) *Early Greek Law*, Berkeley, CA and London.

Gagarin, M. (2008) *Writing Greek Law*, Oxford, UK.

Garnsey, P. (1998) *Cities, Peasants and Food in Classical Antiquity*, Cambridge, UK.

Greco, E. (2000) 'Note di topografia e di urbanistica IV', *AION* 7, 223–33.

Greco, E. (2001) 'Tripodes. Appunti sullo sviluppo urbano di Atene', *AION* 8, 25–38.

Habicht, C. (1961) 'Falsche Urkunden zur Geschichte Athens im Zeitalter der Perser-kriege', *Hermes* 89, 1–35.

Hansen, M. H. (1976) *Apagoge, Endeixis and Ephegesis against Kakourgoi, Atimoi and Pheugontes: A Study in the Athenian Administration of Justice in the Fourth Century B.C.*, Odense, Denmark.

Hansen, M. H. (1988) *Three Studies in Athenian Demography*, Copenhagen.

Hansen, M. H. (1990) 'Solonian democracy in fourth-century Athens', *Classica & Medi-evalia* 40, 71–99.

Hansen, M. H. (1997) 'The polis as an urban centre: The literary and epigraphical evi-dence' in M. H. Hansen (ed.), *The Polis as an Urban Centre and as a Political Com-munity*, Copenhagen, 9–86.

Hansen, M. H. (1998) *Polis and City-State: An Ancient Concept and Its Modern Equiva-lent*, Copenhagen.

Hansen, M. H. (2000) 'A survey of the use of the word polis in archaic and classical sources' in P. Flensted-Jensen (ed.), *Further Studies in the Ancient Greek Polis*: *Papers from the Copenhagen Polis Centre* 5, Stuttgart, 173–215.

Hansen, M. H. (2006a) *Polis: An Introduction to the Ancient Greek City-State*, Oxford, UK.

Hansen, M. H. (2006b) *The Shotgun Method: The Demography of the Ancient Greek City-State Culture*, Columbia, MO.

Hansen, M. H. and Nielsen, T. H. (eds.) (2004) *An Inventory of Archaic and Classical Poleis*, Oxford, UK.

Hanson, V. D. (1995) *The Other Greeks: The Family Farm and the Agrarian Roots of Western Civilization*, New York and London.

Harris, E. M. (2015) 'The family, the community and murder: the role of pollution in Athenian homicide law' in C. Ando and J. Rüpke (eds.), *Public and Private in Ancient Mediterranean Law and Religion*, Berlin, 11–35.

Hignett, C. (1952) *A History of the Athenian Constitution to the End of the Fifth Century B.C.*, Oxford, UK.

Hitzl, K. (2003) 'Pausanias und das Problem der alten Agora Athens', *Mouseio Benaki* 2, 101–12.

Hoepfner, W. (ed.) (1999) *Geschichte des Wohnens 5000 v.Chr. – 500 n.Chr. Vorgeschichte – Frühgeschichte – Antike*, Ludwigsburg, Germany.

Hölkeskamp, K.-J. (1997) 'Agorai bei Homer' in W. Eder and K.-J. Hölkeskamp (eds.), *Volk und Verfassung im vorhellenistischen Griechenland*, Stuttgart, 1–19.

Hölkeskamp, K.-J. (1999) *Schiedsrichter, Gesetzgeber und Gesetzgebung im archaischen Griechenland*, Stuttgart.

Hölkeskamp, K.-J. (2002) '*Ptolis* and *agore*: Homer and the archaeology of the city-state' in F. Montanari (ed.), *Omero tremila anni dopo*, Rome, 297–342.

Horden, P. and Purcell, N. (2000) *The Corrupting Sea: A Study in Mediterranean History*, Oxford, UK.

Isager, S. and Skydsgaard, J. E. (1992) *Ancient Greek Agriculture*, London.

Ismard, P. (2010) *La cité des réseaux. Athènes et ses associations, vie-ier siècle av. J.-C.*, Paris.

Jeffery, L. H. (1976) *Archaic Greece: the City States c. 700–500 B.C.*, London.

Jones, N. F. (1999) *The Associations of Classical Athens: A Response to Democracy*, Oxford, UK and New York.

Jones, N. F. (2000) 'Epigraphic evidence for farmstead residence in Attica', *ZPE* 133, 75–90.

Jones, P. (1997) *The Italian City-State: From Commune to Signoria*, Oxford.

Kenzler, U. (1999) *Studien zur Entwicklung und Struktur der griechischen Agora in archaischer und klassischer Zeit*, Frankfurt am Main.

Kirchner, J. and Dow, S. (1937) 'Inschriften vom attischen Lande', *MDAI* 62, 1–3.

Kolb, F. (1977) 'Die Bau-, Religions- und Kulturpolitik der Pisistratiden', *Jahrbuch des Deutschen Archäologischen Instituts* 92, 99–138.

Kolb, F. (1981) *Agora und Theater: Volks- und Festversammlung*, Berlin.

Lalonde, G. V., Langdon, M. K. and Walbank, M. B.. (1991) *Inscriptions: Horoi, Poletai Records, Leases of Public Lands*, Princeton, NJ.

Lambert, S. D. (1993) *The Phratries of Attica*, Ann Arbor, MI.

Langdon, M. M. (1991) 'On the farm in classical Attica', *CJ* 86, 209–13.

Lape, S. (2010) *Race and Citizen Identity in the Classical Athenian Democracy*, Cambridge, UK.

Lohmann, H. (1993) *Atene: Forschungen zu Siedlungs- und Wirtschaftsstruktur des klassischen Attika*, Cologne.

Lohmann, H. (1995) 'Die Chora Athens im 4. Jahrhundert v. Chr.: Festungswesen, Bergbau und Siedlungen' in W. Eder (ed.), *Die athenische Demokratie im 4. Jahrhundert v. Chr.*, Stuttgart, 515–48.

Longo, F. (2009) 'L'agore di Omero: Rappresentazione poetica e documentazione archeologica', *AION* 31, 199–224.

MacDowell, D. M. (1963) *Athenian Homicide Law in the Age of the Orators*, Manchester, UK.

MacDowell, D. M. (1978) *The Law in Classical Athens*, London.

Manville, P. B. (1990) *The Origins of Citizenship in Ancient Athens*, Princeton, NJ.

Martin, R. (1951) *Recherches sur l'agora grecque*, Paris.

Mikalson, J. D. (2005) *Ancient Greek Religion*, Oxford, UK.

Mirhady, D. C. (2008) 'Drakonian procedure' in C. G. Cooper (ed.), *Epigraphy and the Greek Historian*, Toronto, 15–30.

Moggi, M. (1976) *I sinecismi interstatali greci. I: Dalle origini al 338 a.C.*, Pisa.

Morris, I. (1987) *Burial and Ancient Society: The Rise of the Greek City-State*, Cambridge, UK.

Mossé, C. (1979) 'Comment s'élabore un mythe politique: Solon', *Annales ESC* 34, 425–37.

Moulinier, L. (1946) 'La nature et la date du crime des Alcméonides', *Revue des Études Anciennes* 48.3, 182-202.

Ober, J. (1995) 'Greek horoi: artifactual texts and the contingency of meaning' in D. B. Small (ed.), *Methods in the Mediterranean: Historical and Archaeological Views on Texts and Archaeology*, Leiden, Netherlands, 91–123.

Osborne, R. (1985) *Demos: The Discovery of Classical Attika*, Cambridge, UK.

Osborne, R. (1987) *Classical Landscape with Figures: The Ancient Greek City and Its Countryside*, London.

Osborne, R. (1994) 'Archaeology, the Salaminioi and the politics of sacred space in archaic Attica' in R. Osborne and S. E. Alcock (eds.), *Placing the Gods: Sanctuaries and the Sacred Landscape of Ancient Greece*, Oxford, UK, 143–60.

Parker, R. (1983) *Miasma: Pollution and purification in early Greek religion*, Oxford, UK.

Parker, R. (1996) *Athenian Religion: A History*, Oxford, UK.

Phillips, D. D. (2008) *Avengers of Blood: Homicide in Athenian Law and Custom from Draco to Demosthenes*, Stuttgart.

Raaflaub, K. A., Ober, J. and Wallace, R. W. (2007) *Origins of Democracy in Ancient Greece*, Berkeley, CA.

Rhodes, P. J. (1991) 'The Athenian code of laws, 410–399 BC', *JHS* 111, 87–100.

Rhodes, P. J. and Osborne, R. (2003) *Greek Historical Inscriptions, 404–323 BC*, Oxford, UK.

Robertson, N. (1998) 'The city center of archaic Athens', *Hesperia* 67, 283–302.

Rousset, D. (1994) 'Les frontières des cités grecques: Premières réflexions à partir du recueil des documents épigraphiques', *Cahiers du Centre Gustave Glotz* 5, 97–126.

Ruschenbusch, E. (1958) '*Patrios politeia*: Theseus, Drakon, Solon und Kleisthenes in Publizistik und Geschichtsschreibung des 5. u. 4. Jh. v. Chr.', *Historia* 7, 398–424.

Ruschenbusch, E. (1960) '*Phonos*: Zum Recht Drakons und seiner Bedeutung für das Werden des athenischen Staates', *Historia* 9, 129–54.

Ruzé, F. (1997) *Délibération et pouvoir dans la cité grecque de Nestor à Socrate*, Paris.

Salvo, I. (2011) *Mani impure: Contaminazione dell'omicidio e rituali civici di purificazione nel mondo greco antico*, Disseration, Pisa, Italy.

Sànchez, P. (2001) *L'Amphictionie des Pyles et de Delphes*, Stuttgart.

Schmalz, C. R. (2006) 'The Athenian Prytaneion discovered?', *Hesperia* 75, 33–81.

Schmitz, W. (2001) '"Drakonische Strafen": Die Revision der Gesetze Drakons durch Solon und die Blutrache in Athen', *Klio* 83, 7–38.

Schmitz, W. (2004) *Nachbarschaft und Dorfgemeinschaft im archaischen und klassischen Griechenland*, Berlin.

Schnurr, C. (1995) 'Die alte Agora Athens', *ZPE* 105, 131–8.

Scott, T. (2012) *The City-State in Europe, 1000–1600: Hinterland, Territory, Region*, Oxford, UK.

Sealey, R. (1983) 'The Athenian courts for homicide', *CP* 78, 275–96.

Seelentag, G. (2015) *Das archaische Kreta: Institutionalisierung im frühen Griechenland*, Berlin.

Siewert, P. (1972) *Der Eid von Plataia*, Munich.

Siewert, P. (1977) 'The ephebic oath in fifth-century Athens', *JHS* 97, 102–11.

Snodgrass, A. M. (1977) *Archaeology and the Rise of the Greek State*, Cambridge, UK.

Sommerstein, A. H. and Bayliss, A. J. (2013) *Oath and State in Ancient Greece*, Berlin.

Stahl, M. (1987) *Aristokraten und Tyrannen im archaischen Athen*, Stuttgart.

Stanton, G. R. (2005) *Athenian Politics, C. 800–500 B.C.: A Sourcebook*, London.

Steinhauer, G. (2001) 'The road-network and settlement pattern in the mesogaia in the area of the Spata Airport' in C. Doumas, K. Tsouni and G. N. Aikaterinidis (eds.), *Μεσογαία: ιστορία και πολιτισμός των Μεσογείων Αττικής*, Athens, 95–105.

Stroud, R. S. (1968) *Drakon's Law on Homicide*, Berkeley, CA.

Taylor, C. and Vlassopoulos, K. (eds.) (2015) *Communities and Networks in the Ancient Greek World*, Oxford, UK.

Thomas, R. (1989) *Oral Tradition and Written Record in Classical Athens*, Cambridge, UK.

Thompson, H. A. and Wycherley, R. E. (1972) *The Agora of Athens: The History, Shape and Uses of an Ancient City Center*, Princeton, NJ.

Treston, H. J. (1923) *Poine: A Study in Ancient Greek Blood-Vengeance*, London.

Tsantsanoglou, K. (1972) '*Phonou pheugein* (I.G. I² 115.11–13)' in G. Bakalakes and M. Andronikos (eds.), *Κέρνος: τιμητική προσφορά στον καθηγητή Γεώργιο Μπακαλάκη*, Thessalonike, Greece, 170–9.

van Effenterre, H. and van Effenterre, M. (1990) 'Le contrôle des étrangers dans la cité grecque' in G. Nenci and G. Thür (eds.), *Symposion 1988: Vorträge zur griechischen und hellenistischen Rechtsgeschichte*, Cologne, 1990, 257–8.

van Wees, H. (2013) *Ships and Silver, Taxes and Tribute: A Fiscal History of Archaic Athens*, London.

Vidal-Naquet, P. (1986) *The Black Hunter: Forms of Thought and Forms of Society in the Greek World*, Baltimore, MD.

Wallace, R. W. (1989) *The Areopagus Council to 307 B.C.*, Baltimore, MD and London.

Walker, H. J. (1995) *Theseus and Athens*, Oxford, UK.

Weber, M. (1999) 'Die Stadt: eine soziologische Untersuchung', *Archiv für Sozialwissenschaft und Sozialpolitik* 47, 1920–1, 621–772; repr. in W. Nippel (ed.), *Max Weber Gesamtausgabe*, I 22.5, Tübingen, Germany.

Westbrook, R. (2009) 'Drakon's homicide law' in E. M. Harris and G. Thür (eds.), *Symposion 2007: Vorträge zur griechischen und hellenistischen Rechtsgeschichte*, Vienna, 3–16.

Whitehead, D. (1986) *The Demes of Attica 508/7 – ca. 250 B.C.*, Princeton, NJ.

4 Macedonians in Bottiaea

'Warriors' and identities in late Iron Age and archaic Macedonia[1]

Ioannis K. Xydopoulos

The construction of an ethnic identity often presupposes a specific territory;[2] yet pre-modern societies display features that transcend our mental horizons, which have been shaped by modern national states and identities. Regarding the ancient Greek city-states, for instance, an individual's identity could be defined in multiple and not necessarily compatible ways; cultural, political and social boundaries were as alive in people's minds as were geographical ones. But what was the case in the complex entities called *ethne*, such as the Macedonians? Identity is equally a cultural product, subject to complex historical processes. While modern identities presuppose a specific imaginary feeling of participation in a national entity, pre-modern identities were more often constructed on the basis of allegiance to a certain centre of power.[3] Besides, they emerged as the result of a perceived differentiation between 'Us' and 'Others'. It is commonly through differentiation that members of a group conceive of themselves as a community adopting common traits which distinguish them from the others.

Identities and boundaries were closely connected during the early phase of the Macedonian expansion from their original nucleus towards Pieria and Bottiaea. It is useful to make some preliminary comments, focusing on the special difficulties arising from the specific topic. First of all, literary sources covering the period of expansion have not survived. All the information we possess derives from later traditions and, therefore, is subject to critique. Second, the use of archaeological evidence is not considered a reliable basis for drawing concrete conclusions regarding identities and ethnicity. And, third, the very character of the Macedonian kingdom after its first period of expansion, i.e. its multi-national form, is itself a problem. However, an effort will be made to enlighten this obscure – but not dark – period. We think that the case of the Bottiaeans is a fine example of 'successful violence', exercised in the Early Iron Age Macedonia by warriors who were alien to the *polis* culture. Through this violence emerged new notions of community, both for the defeated and the victors. In this chapter, we will be dealing mainly with the former, i.e. with the defeated.

The Bottiaeans: the literary evidence

According to Thucydides, Bottia (a variation used by Thucydides for Bottiaea) was the second successive area to be spear-won (μάχῃ) by the Macedonians, the first one being Pieria (Thuc. 2.99.3).[4] Regarding the chronology of the Macedonian expansion in general, various theories have been suggested.[5] As for its first stage, which primarily interests us in this chapter, Hammond placed it in the period 650–550 BCE.[6] The inhabitants of Botti(ae)a, the so-called Bottiaeans were expelled from their ancestral region and, by Thucydides' times, were dwelling next to the Chalcidians (in the Chalcidice peninsula). They moved to Chalcidice and settled in the area north of Poteidaia in the seventh century BCE. This area was called Bottike (*Βοττική* – Thuc. 1.65.2), and was located to the southeast of Krousis. The name was derived from the ethnic name *Βοττιαῖος* (Hdt. 8.127). The new place took the name Bottike in order to be distinguished from Bottiaea and also to imply that it was the region inhabited by the Bottiaeans (see below).

Herodotus is the first to give the exact location of Bottiaea: it was located between Mygdonia to the east and the *Makedonis ge* to the south, where the rivers Loudias and Haliakmon join before ending at the Thermaic Gulf.[7] Bottiaea thus covered the middle part of Macedonia, north of Pieria (and Elimeia), east of Eordaia, south of Almopia and west of Amphaxitis and Mygdonia. The term used by Thucydides in his passage (*Bottia*) is slightly different from the one used when describing the area around the central Macedonian plain (*Bottiaea* – see e.g. 2.100.4).[8] However, one can safely link the specific area with the Bottiaeans who originally lived in the plain of Central Macedonia surrounded by the rivers Loudias, Axios and Aliakmon. The very term *Βοττιαῒς γῆ* used by the historian (and taken from Hecataeus)[9] may imply that this region was the original nucleus of this people, since Herodotus uses (only once) an analogous term for the original core of the Macedonians (7.127.5). This could be related to the 'ancestry' of the Bottiaeans and the 'antiquity' of their presence in the area around Pella.

Scholars seem to agree that the expulsion of the Bottiaeans was made at the earliest stage of the Macedonian expansion. According to the archaeological data found in Olynthos, the major Bottiaean city in the Chalcidice, the earliest finds are to be dated in the second half of the seventh centuryor around 600 BCE.[10] Thucydides informs us that in his time Spartolos was the main Bottiaean polis.[11] There were approximately between six and twelve other Bottiaean poleis[12] which have not been positively identified, although various archaeological sites of the area have been suggested. It is also interesting that Herodotus (8.127) includes Olynthos, the biggest and most important, among the originally Bottiaian communities.[13] Olynthos was originally a Bottiaean city, but became the centre of the Chalcidic Federation from 432 BCE onwards. The city was built on two hills, the southern, where the archaic city of the Bottiaians is located, and the northern, where the city of the Chalcidians was built in 432 BCE. Both cities have been systematically investigated. The archaic city was organised with two parallel avenues running north-south and roads running off between them: simple houses, shops, store pits, and public buildings have been investigated there. The Chalcidian city on the northern hill was organised quite differently, built according to the rectangular Hippodamian system.[14]

The issue of the Bottiaean ethnic identity has a long scholarly history. Some think that they were a non-Greek native population, and that they were hellenized sometime after they reached Chalcidice.[15] Others regard them as Greeks, and in particular of Minoan origin; the literary sources provide arguments in support of this theory. Strabo writes that the Bottiaeans originated from Crete and left their island together with Minos, when the latter was pursuing Daedalus. After reaching Iapygia in Italy first, a part of them crossed the Ionian Sea and via the northern Pindus range came eventually to the central Macedonian plain. They took their name from their leader, a certain Botton.[16] Some scholars have tried to trace this Minoan origin in the archaeological data of Macedonia.[17] For example, there have been found three double axes (*pelekeis*) at the Tomb cemetery at Vergina. They were found as tomb offerings in female burials and were acknowledged as status symbols of the dead. Still, despite the fact that the then excavator connected them with Minoan Crete, he hesitated to link these offerings with the nearby Bottiaeans.[18] This was done by Hammond (see n. 17) and is also accepted by others.[19] Furthermore, back in 1986 Anna Michailidou and Iris Tzachili published a stone cast from Vergina, probably dating to the archaic period.[20] Among its forms was one for a double axe, something that led the two archaeologists to speak of 'Minoan inspiration'.[21] Recently, it has been argued that the presence of a nymph and a bull (Zeus and Europe?) on Bottiaean coins of the early fifth century attest the Bottiaean perception of their Greek identity. This perception was widely accepted by the fourth century, as we can conclude from Aristotle, who included the Bottiaeans among his *Politeiai*.[22]

However, we think that a distinction is needed at this point. By this, we mean that the myth regarding the Minoan origins may be true for the Bottiaeans who were living in the Chalcidice. Constructing a myth of being Greek in the late fourth century was a common phenomenon, often found in the Greek world, particularly in the Hellenistic period.[23] But this also implies that one should accept that the Minoans were of Greek descent – something not proven. However, Christos Gatzolis and Selene Psoma seem to accept this, when they write that 'Bottiaeans claimed Cretan origin, meaning Greek origin in the fourth century BCE'.[24] As we said previously, it is unclear how we should interpret this form of 'Greekness' related to the Minoans.

Minos' case, as well as others – e.g. the Egyptian Danaus in Aeschylus' *Suppliant Women* – clearly show that shared kinship still mattered much to the Greeks who had already developed a model of polarity between the Greek and the Barbarian.[25] Minos was a foreigner who became Hellenized. Greek myth, mainly focused on both Greek and foreign heroes, was used either to differentiate the Greeks from the Barbarians or to link the Greeks at a local level.[26] As Kostas Vlassopoulos put it, 'the fact that Greek myth reserved an important role for foreign heroes, even if these heroes existed only in the Greek mythic tradition, is a factor of crucial importance that created a wide range of opportunities'.[27] Still, I think that it had nothing to do with ethnic identification: it was just convenient enough for the pre-Macedonian residents of the area to identify themselves with the original inhabitants of the Greek peninsula, in terms of ancestry and of being indigenous, in contrast to the 'newcomers', i.e. the Macedonians.[28] Even if the Bottiaeans were of Greek origin, then one would expect that their burial customs would be different from the ones the Macedonians had. Unfortunately, to date, no mortuary evidence can be securely associated with the Bottiaeans (see below).

Identities

Modern scholars, considering ancient population groups and trying to define ethnicity, tend to apply anachronistic and problematic criteria, such as a shared language. Furthermore, it is inappropriate to apply the term *ethnicity*, invented in the mid-twentieth century, to an ancient phenomenon.[29] It has been argued that in the archaic period of the Greek mainland, the culturally authoritative criteria of ethnicity were descent and homeland, not language. Jonathan Hall has denied that Macedonia was a 'melting pot' for ethnic groups. He based his objection on three arguments: i) it is not language, religion, and culture that ultimately define ethnic identity, but shared kinship; ii) Macedonia was not on the periphery of a consolidated Greek world, since other non-Greek populations resided in the Greek peninsula and the Aegean islands; and iii) the fifth century constitutes a transitional phase 'during which the form (aggregative>oppositional) and the content (ethnic>cultural) of Greek identity underwent a profound development'.[30] Hall might be right in assuming that Macedonia was not peripheral to the Greek world; but the fact that the sources themselves, such as Herodotus, Thucydides, or Strabo,[31] refer to various pre-Hellenic peoples or *ethne* actually living in the northern region of the Greek peninsula, some of whom were later incorporated into the Macedonian kingdom, disproves his rejection of the 'melting pot' theory.[32] Absolute boundaries are difficult to draw for the historian, and as Edith Hall has stated, 'ethnic groups shade off into one another and interaction and interdependence have led to a high degree of acculturation'.[33]

Definitions of community are extremely problematic and have been the subject of debate in the social sciences. Certain criteria were used for all these definitions, such as common interests, the role of ecology or social structure, and an essential commonality. Nevertheless, notions of community have changed, based on the various functionalist and structuralist approaches. Fredrik Barth and Anthony Cohen have argued that communities should be seen not only as symbolic and contrastive constructs, but also as products of the perception of situational boundaries dividing social groups from each another. For them, the very existence and consciousness of boundaries play a crucial role in the awareness of community.[34]

However, it is only recently that the landscape has been taken into account regarding the formation of boundaries (physical or subjective) and communities. Since community is a term which both sustains diversity and expresses commonality, its members are related by their perception of these commonalities, and equally, they are differentiated from other communities and their members by these relations and the patterns of association to which they give rise.[35] Does landscape play a role in the formation of these commonalities? This seems highly plausible, as the relationship between people's actions and the landscape is close. An ethnic landscape represents a collective perception of identity and can be reconstructed through the study of literary sources, archaeological evidence, and other evidence that belongs also to the field of environmental archaeology. According to Cifani, there are two approaches regarding the definition of ethnicity. The first one is linked to be the elements of landscape archaeology. This means that the effects of geographical distribution and the climate on behaviour and culture are of equal importance for the understanding of an ethnic group as the elements that belonged to the second approach such as the customs, language and culture.[36]

Additionally, according to cultural anthropologists, we can trace four characteristics that contribute to an overall definition of an ethnic group: 1) the *epos*: the feeling of identity within a community and its cultural memory; 2) the *ethos*: the sharing of moral values; 3) the *logos*: the common language or languages inside a group; 4) the *oikos* or *topos*: the territory where a community is based. The methodology used for such a study leads us to follow a multidisciplinary approach which can be traced in five kinds of data: 1) literary sources, 2) epigraphic evidence, 3) burial customs, 4) material culture and 5) the spatial organisation of territories.[37] Thus, the initial inspiration for the articulation of time and change of a past landscape was based on Braudel's theory, based on which we can observe three different domains (landscape, social structure and events). However, many landscape archaeologists take a step beyond Braudelian or processualist approaches.[38]

Already in the Bronze Age, one can see complex societies in the Greek world, societies which could maintain 'coexisting forms of identity, some linked to a larger, "foreign" political world and some linked to a more ethnic and ritual world of "national" identity'.[39] Similar forms of identity are met in archaic Greece. As far as the northern Aegean is concerned, the arrival of Greek colonists must have caused major changes. The Euboeans settled in Chalcidice around 900 BCE and we must assume that their numbers were significant.[40] However, we do not know whether conflicts arose between them and the locals. Already by the mid-sixth century, the Greek presence in the northern shores of the Aegean had a serious impact, not only in terms of the burial customs, but also in pottery and architecture. It seems that the city-states of southern Greece engaged in economic and political activities in these areas, and the indigenous populations had to find ways to respond. Burials in Sindos and Trebenishte indicate that these interactions date back as early as the sixth century.[41] It is therefore no coincidence that on the island of Samothrace there have been discovered inscriptions in Greek script recording a non-Greek language, which has been interpreted as being Thracian.[42] Not only do these dedications clearly show that both Greeks and non-Greeks used the Samothracian sanctuary of Kabeiroi from the second half of the sixth century, but they are an early and interesting example of mixed settlements, which may be compared to those on Akte, mentioned by Thucydides.[43]

While it is generally admitted that 'the 'Hellenisation' of the north was accompanied by major social changes,[44] the sense of continuity from the Early Iron Age into archaic times comes mainly – if not exclusively – from the rich burials (primarily the so-called warrior graves), while large grave mounds can be found in many places. In Macedonia, despite some problems concerning chronology, 'the Iron Age warrior burial tradition may have been in decline by 650 or 600 BCE'.[45] Regarding burials, the evidence for the areas in the northern Aegean available up to 1998 gave Ian Morris the impression of a slow evolution. Although Snodgrass argued that the eighth century was a century of dramatic transformations all over

Greece,[46] there are some objections as to whether such radical changes took place in the northern Aegean on the basis of evidence found in burial sites.[47] However, the systematic excavations in northern Greece since then have revealed a large number of burial sites, some of them dating from the archaic period.

Warrior graves?

Until fairly recently, the archaeological exploration regarding the early stages of the Macedonian expansion had no impressive results, but the situation has changed dramatically after the excavations conducted in the last two decades.[48] Our data is confined mainly to the mortuary rituals, as these were conducted in the cemeteries of the period in Macedonia, something that brings us to the next problem, that of the so-called 'warrior graves'.

In one of his many papers regarding the Greeks and their armour, Hans van Wees argued that during the Dark Ages quite a few graves contained arms, including swords, spears and daggers. The term used by scholars when referring to such burials is 'warrior graves', meaning that the weapons placed in the tomb were the 'full combat gear' of the deceased.[49] These weapons were 'laid out as if the dead were carrying them'. Van Wees is quick to point out that not 'all men were buried with arms or armour', thus suggesting that 'burial with arms was the prerogative of the wealthy'. His assumption is based on relevant finds from the Dark Age graves from Athens and Argos. He finally suggests that 'when we occasionally encounter burial groups in which *most* of the dead are accompanied by arms, (. . .) we may safely conclude that these represent cemeteries used exclusively by members of the elite'.[50]

'Warrior graves' are a well-known phenomenon in Aegean archaeology.[51] It is a practice already encountered during the Late Bronze Age, with the most famous examples being the graves at Mycenae.[52] Similar finds of the same period were known from other parts of the Argolid, Athens and Lefkandi, and also from Knossos in Crete.[53] However, as it has been pointed out, not all of these graves belong necessarily to warriors.[54] In the Early Iron Age it seems that the identity implied by the grave goods begins to be associated with the concept of the 'hero' as described in the *Iliad*. New social identities seem to be in vogue in Early Iron Age Greece and this is depicted in such material assemblages.[55]

Post-Mycenaean finds deposited at Bronze Age tombs and unrelated with skeletal remains seem to be related with the emergence of 'hero cults' in Geometric Greece. The relationship between early states and hero cults has its roots in the late eighth and early seventh centuries, although this practice was geographically restricted to southern Greece, mainly Attica, Messenia and the Argolid.[56] It has been suggested that the phenomenon should be associated with the spread of the epic tradition and that its absence from regions like Crete or Thessaly was due to the absence of heroic monuments in these places to remind the local populations of the Age of heroes, and the fact that the burial customs in Geometric times in these places were similar with those of the Mycenaeans.[57] However, the suggestion that has prevailed is that this phenomenon should be taken as 'an integral,

ideological component in the process of state formation'[58] and that it is encountered in areas where a rise of the population is (archaeologically) attested for the
period under examination.[59] In particular, it has been argued that the practice is
met in communities that were trying to emphasise their ties with the land, thus
implying autochthony; it is further argued that the authors of this practice were
the local elites.[60]

As far as Macedonia is concerned, the tumuli cemetery at Vergina is one case of
tombs with weapons, while these are also found at other sites, such as Agrosykia
Pellas and Pateli (Agios Panteleemon Amyntaiou Florinas).[61] It seems that being
buried with weapons was commonplace in this part of the Greek world, and was
not depicting the actual status of the dead during his lifetime. Rather, it was a
depiction of how the dead would like to be seen in their tombs, or would like to
have been when alive.

Regarding our case study, i.e. the Bottiaia region in Central Macedonia, the
main archaeological data come from the ancient settlement of Archontiko, near
modern Pella. The settlement is situated very close to the innermost point where
the Thermaic Gulf penetrated in ancient times and approximately 14 km west of
the Axios River; thus Arhontiko controlled the east-west and north-south roads
of the region. According to its excavators, the town was continuously inhabited
until the Byzantine era. It seems that Archontiko was one of the most (or, perhaps,
the most) significant settlement in northern Bottiaea, until replaced by the new
capital of the Macedonian realm, namely Pella. Although the *trapeza* (plateau) of
the settlement had been excavated from 1992 to 1998 under the direction of the
archaeologists Pavlos and Anastasia Chrysostomou, it was the rescue excavation
that began in 2000 in the western cemetery, located 1 km west of the settlement,
that brought to light extremely important finds. As reported so far by the two colleagues, 'a total of 1,001 burials were excavated from 2000–2010 in six adjacent
fields over an area of approximately 1.1 hectares (2.7 acres)'. From this total, 260
belong to the Late Iron Age (dating from the second half of the seventh century
until *c.* 580 BCE)[62] and 474 to the archaic period (580–480 BCE). Among the rest,
261 belong to the classical and early Hellenistic periods (480–279 BCE), while
six cannot be safely dated.[63]

The excavators have classified what they call 'warrior graves' into four categories, based on the different types of armour found in the graves.[64] According
to their classification, the more fully geared with weapons a deceased was, the
higher his status. Furthermore, it has been recently pointed out that the sympotic
vessels found in these graves represent the status of the deceased in the localsoci-
ety: a great number and a large variety of these vessels are indicative of the high
status of the dead.[65] If one adds the presence of weaponry in the male burials[66] and
the existence of such differentiations in wealth also among female burials,[67] then
the issue regarding these 'warriors' becomes very interesting.[68] These forms of
social differentiation are strengthened by the very existence of another burial site,
smaller and poorer in grave goods, at the eastern cemetery of Archontiko, which
was used simultaneously.[69] The same forms of social differentiation are encountered also in many family burial plots at the western cemetery of Archontiko.

Funerals were occasions either of projecting personal and cultural identities or of creating new ones. These identities were 'outcomes or reflections of contemporary ideas, beliefs or social structures', closely connected with claims (or, perhaps, an ideology) about the status of the deceased.[70] It was a symbolic ritual, closely connected with 'a certain kind of masculine ideal'. Apart from the important social status it was implying for the dead, burial with weapons meant that the deceased were linked with a nexus combining masculinity, bravery in battle and political authority, a kind of a 'big man' in these societies.[71] But these identities were not uniform. Since regionalism seems to be the most striking feature of the Dark Ages, one should not make general assumptions regarding the whole of the Macedonian mainland. Material diversity goes along with social diversity, and there were many Dark Age societies instead of one, i.e. societies developed along 'different lines'. In other words, one cannot speak of a 'uniform Homeric society'.[72]

This lack of uniformity is depicted in 'the regional patterns in pottery, the different burial customs, and settlement structure'.[73] All these differences made some researchers suggest that the Bronze Age societies were considerably fragile as far as their political structures were concerned, since they depended on the 'big man' and his abilities as a leader; for example, a case in point is to be found in the *Odyssey* (assuming that the world of the *Odyssey* is the world of Bronze Age societies).[74] One of the main features of such societies is the 'investment in display' and, it seems that the *symposion* was such a place where the 'big man' would (or could) advertise his prowess.[75] So, cemeteries are a usually flattering, indirect representation of society, which 'tells us much about the collective habits and (material) values of particular societies'.[76] In stable settlements, the grave plots – i.e. a group of graves that probably represent the burial area of a particular burying group – may suggest a notion of continuity that was not dependent on the notion of a 'big man'.[77]

Archontiko seems to cover many – if not all – of these elements. Given Thucydides' mention of the Macedonian conquest of Bottiaea, it is worth exploring the links between Archontiko and Macedonia. The burial customs there are similar to those of Aigai. Those buried at the tombs of Archontiko seem to share the same material culture as those at other sites of Central Macedonia (we say 'seem' because, notwithstanding these similarities, they are different from many other burial sites in Central Macedonia, possibly a reflection of the multi-national character of the kingdom already in its early stages). And, although it has been suggested that at Vergina, in particular, the evidence of wealth – as well as the number of graves – seems to decline after 700–650 BCE,[78] recent excavations have altered the picture dramatically. In the male burials of the Iron Age tumuli cemetery at Vergina we find daggers and swords (but no remains of shields).[79] Also, sympotic vessels were found in the Macedonian cemeteries from Vergina (Aigai)[80] and Archontiko.[81] Similar drinking vessels with the ones at Archontiko have been found at Vergina and Sindos. At Vergina, although none of the burials from the archaic cemetery has been fully published,[82] one can see similarities with the east cemetery of Archontiko, since drinking equipment has a strong presence among the grave goods. Although it mainly consists of clay vessels (either imported or local), with the more wealthy finds to be limited in 'a few bronze phialai, oinochoai and lekanides', one cannot exclude the possibility that other, more precious artefacts could have existed simultaneously, given the fact the these graves were ruthlessly looted.[83] However, large metal sympotic sets have also been found.[84]

Regardless of the possible connection of these wealthy graves with the Macedonian royal family (with the so-called 'Lady of Aigai' being the most spectacular example),[85] these archaic burials suggest a stratification in society analogous to the societies of other Macedonian settlements. At Sindos, 24 of the 25 unlooted graves of the archaic period have yielded sympotic vases, differing in number per grave.[86] Seven of these 25 graves, belong to men, women and children, and are strikingly different from the rest, regarding the quantity and quality not only of the metal drinking vessels, but also of the other offerings.[87] Sympotic equipment almost identical to those found at Vergina and Archontiko is also attested at some archaic burial sites to the east of the Axios River, reaching up to the Anthemous valley, with that at ancient Sindos being the best known.[88] Particularly remarkable is that the mortuary practices at Sindos are the same with those attested at Vergina and Archontiko.

The excavation of the cemeteries in the Chalcidice peninsula provides evidence on the social structure and everyday life in the cities. On the other hand, these cemeteries provide evidence concerning religious ideology and burial customs. The similarities to the burial procedure of the cemeteries of southern Greece reveal the close contacts of the colonies with the south. Inhumation of adults in pit graves, cist graves, clay or stone sarcophagi, inhumation of children in hydriae and amphorae and of adults in pithoi prevailed in the archaic period, e.g. in Mende.[89] One could suggest that these burials contain many artefacts according to the social and economic status of the deceased and his family, his profession and social role (but this suggestion cannot be generally and diachronically applied): local and imported vases as well as other objects imported from the Eastern Mediterranean, Corinth and Attica, terracotta figurines, amulets, metal and glass vases and jewellery. Burials of children yielded many terracotta animal figurines and dolls.

The excavations of the cemetery of Akanthos brought to light more than 13,000 burials dating from the seventh century BCE to the Roman period. The graves are found in the sandy coast parallel to the sea with the head of the deceased to the east. The children were buried in the same area with the adults. The investigation yielded a few inscribed *stelai*, used for burial monuments.[90] The organisation of the cemetery of Mende was different. Approximately 250 burials were excavated, inhumations of infants in pots produced locally, dating from the eighth to the fourth centuries. The grave goods were placed inside the pot, mainly smaller vases, aryballoi, cylices etc. A small part of the cemetery of Aphytis, located to the west of the ancient city, has been excavated; the graves and the burial customs are similar to the ones found in southern Greece. Its excavation yielded a great number of artefacts that reveal the prosperity of the city. Among them there are many pieces of jewellery recalling the so-called 'Macedonian bronzes'.[91]

Still, the main difference comes from the excavation of the cemetery at Agia Paraskevi, in the area of Anthemous, which has yielded different finds: the 435 graves that were investigated were covered with low mounds and were organised in parallel lines. The graves contained rich grave goods, gold lozenge-shaped sheets which covered the mouth of the deceased, silver and bronze jewellery of the so-called 'Macedonian bronzes', bronze and iron arms and weapons made locally, clay figurines and local and imported pottery.[92] The finds present similarities to those of the Macedonian kingdom, such as the neighbouring cemetery of Thermi, Nea Philadelphia or Sindos, and imply a flourishing community with contacts with various areas of the Aegean (Ionia, Corinth, Attica, Chios, etc.) and close relations to Macedonia.[93] How, then, should one interpret these similarities? In an effort to answer that question, the reconstruction of the history of Macedonia in the sixth century and of the possible Macedonian expansion in the areas east of the Axios River is decisive.

Macedonians east of the Axios River

The suggestion that the Macedonians advanced deep into these areas already during Amyntas I's reign is fascinating; Eugene Borza, for example, takes it for granted that Anthemous was part of Amyntas' realm,[94] a recent acquisition together with the regions of Mygdonia and Krestonia.[95] We have argued elsewhere that we can be sure that Anthemous was part of the Macedonian kingdom when offered to Hippias, with Persian approval, since the area east of the Axios up to Anthemous must have been annexed to Macedonia before 480 BCE.[96] By this, we mean that the Macedonians, having reached the western bank of the Axios river already in an early period, i.e. the middle of the sixth century, had expanded their political territory also in the immediate regions east of the river (Amphaxitis, part of Mygdonia, and Anthemous).[97]

The first question that comes to mind is to what extent 'can the literary sources define or even guide our handling of the archaeological data?' This seems to have been the problem in many cases.[98] Thucydides was clear enough, but archaeology seems to provide strong evidence for the progress of acculturation among the various peoples on the shores and in the hinterland of the northern Aegean. The political expansion of the Macedonians east of the Axios cannot be confirmed by archaeology, despite the fact that, as mentioned above, the already excavated tombs in the Archontiko cemetery (in Bottiaea) are strikingly similar to those that have been discovered in Vergina (in modern Emathia, but in ancient Bottiaea),[99] in Sindos, in Agios Athanasios and in Agia Paraskevi.[100] These similarities, then, perhaps indicate a common cultural environment, regardless of the inhabitants' ethnic identity in these regions (Thracians, Macedonians, non-Greeks, or Greek colonists),[101] but nothing more. The interpretation of these similarities between the various sites mentioned earlier and the Macedonian cemeteries is not firmly agreed to date. Some scholars believe that the first expansion of the kingdom to the east of Axios took place sometime around 510–05 BCE, shortly after the region was conquered by the Persians;[102] others place this event not long before the arrival of the Persians, or even soon after their departure.[103] Yet, the similar mortuary practices attested here are hard to ignore.[104]

A first suggestion could be that these similarities were due to the existence of a Mycenaean substratum, or the 'memories of the Mycenaean burial customs'.[105] Snodgrass thought of Macedonia as a 'special category' regarding the 'Dark Ages'.[106] Its indigenous culture was affected by a shallow Mycenaean element, but the remoteness of the country and 'a major wave of non-Greek settlers which arrived at the end of the Bronze Age' were the key factors for the particular character Macedonia had. Still, the pottery has local imitations of Mycenaean patterns and Protogeometric pottery found at Vergina marks the new beginning of contacts with southern Greeks.[107]

A second – and stronger – suggestion would be that since, as Catherine Morgan has put it, 'ethnic expression requires a political framework',[108] one could suggest that this framework was the Macedonian state itself, having already expanded up to the Anthemous area by the end of the sixth century.[109] Territoriality and the definition of regional boundaries at *ethne*-states had close ties with natural boundaries, such as rivers or mountains, but also with 'the overall patterns of material culture'.[110] The importance of watercourses as such natural boundaries is not a parameter preventing a territorial change of frontiers. The Macedonians proved that in action, when advancing to the north and northeast, in their attempt to subjugate the neighbouring *ethne*, an attempt also connected with their effort to control the main passes from the north to the Thermaic Gulf. Land routes, which connected the western part of the kingdom with the Axios and Echedoros waterways, as well as with the Thermaic Gulf, would be extremely vital for the linking of all coastal settlements with those in the hinterland, thus providing 'access to markets for mountain economies'.[111] We do not know whether Amyntas' successor, Alexander I, could exercise his control in a similar way at the areas east of Anthemous; therefore, it is not possible to speak of a Macedonian expansion there prior to 480 BCE.[112] We believe that, in spite of the Anthemous case, territorial expansion is unlikely to have happened; archaeological evidence does not indicate a strong Macedonian presence in these regions, as well as in Bisaltia, before 480 BCE.[113]

But, what about Bottiaea? Or, to put it another way: is it possible to trace the identities of those buried at the western cemetery of Archontiko? Were they Macedonians, Bottiaeans or others? Very recently it has been suggested that 'the possibility that the dead were simply Macedonian aristocrats is excluded', on the basis that 'this burial custom does not appear in the Macedonian royal cemetery of Aigai'. To perceive them as 'the rulers of the Bottiaeans', whose constitution was studied by Aristotle, is merely a guess,[114] since there are some objections to this suggestion. The main one is that it is not safe to speak of Greeks from southern Greece, Macedonians, Bottiaeans, or Thracians in these regions based exclusively on archaeological material. It has been 'generally accepted that a typological approach to reading ethnic expression in material data does not work'.[115] Furthermore, the displacement of the Bottiaeans and the foundation of their new city of Olynthus are placed at the seventh century, as the data from Olynthus seem to confirm. Thucydides and his narrative of the Macedonian expansion are ignored in such an interpretation, while Aristotle must have known the constitution of the Bottiaeans living in their city-states at Bottike, thus being neighbours to his home-town of Stageira. One cannot overlook the way 'the various different territories of action add up to the political territory of a community, defined as an *ethnos* in our case, *i.e.* the Macedonians.[116] And, last but not least, as already known from the seminal work of Fredrik Barth, ethnic groups are defined by 'categories of ascrip-tion and identification by the actors themselves' and self-ascription.[117] Therefore, the existence of variations in the burials at Archontiko and Vergina may be consid-ered as variations within the group, i.e. the Macedonian aristocrats.[118]

Conclusion

It is well known that in antiquity abandonment of the original homeland was a common phenomenon, not only among individuals but also among whole popula-tions. Mobility around the Mediterranean was heavily affected by the distribution of resources and ancient Greece is a typical example of such a kind of forced movement.[119] The original locus of the Macedonians was a mountainous region,[120] thus providing its inhabitants with a number of options regarding the resources on which their life depended. As transhumant pastoralists and peasants, the Macedo-nians had no distinctive or well-defined boundaries within a certain microregion; on the contrary, their horizon was wide, related to the pastoralist's or peasant's own needs for the environment wanted to be used.[121] The topographical diversity one finds in central Macedonia and the subsequent Macedonian expansion toward the rich in waters and fertile land of Bottiaea seem to confirm this hypothesis.

However, as we saw in Thucydides, the challenge Macedonians faced was to impose (rather, to enforce) their authority upon all other tribes located in the region. They achieved this by expelling all of them from the area. And, since 'an ethnic group is more than just a social unit with distinctive traits and ori-gins',[122] we can suppose that the Macedonians who had conquered Bottiaea and belonged to the elite were 'compelled' in a way to demonstrate their status in the 'new lands' and to ensure their prominence in them, after the violent expul-sions they had conducted. The use of metal is perhaps indicative of the status of the dead. Morris argued, based on the Vergina finds, that 'the main difference between Athenian and Macedonian metal use would be that Macedonians thought along the lines iron/bronze=male/female, while Athenians thought along the lines iron/bronze=elite/commoner'.[123] This is not the case at Archontiko, where iron is abundant in women's burials.[124] The organisation of the space at the western Archontiko cemetery, as well as the grave goods, indicate in my opinion the elite/commoner distinction, thus implying a 'hierarchical community with an internal value system'.[125] If this had something to do with the epic poems, is not known, as well as if the burials at Archontiko and other places in Macedonia imply that the deceased were equal members of an inter-regional aristocracy, nourished by the competitive values of the epics. One could suppose that the presence of Greeks from the south on the shores of Macedonia was accompanied with the epic tradi-tion or, at least, with a spread of those who were versed in it.[126] What seems to be certain, though, is that there is a definite link between war for expansion the Macedonians had practised and violence among the burial finds at Archontiko: passing from the private enmities found in the *Iliad* to full-scale war for the exist-ence of the tribe was a violent reality, which apparently ended up in favour of the attackers. But, it is also connected with honour and valour. These sentiments were depicted in the graves of those who had fought.

Regarding identity, labelling material traits as 'ethnic' is tempting, but it is also dangerous.[127] It must be noted here that one cannot be certain about the eth-nic identity of the indigenous inhabitants in the areas of Bottiaea, Amphaxitis and Mygdonia during the sixth century. However, there have been suggestions of identifying some sites with settlements of Greek colonists,[128] or with other ethnic entities existing in the area. For example, one could suppose on a quite solid basis that the adult male buried in the late archaic grave at a site near the later Amphi-polis was apparently a prominent Thracian, as the grave goods indicate.[129] It will be sufficient to note at this point that the issue is extremely complicated, as the area called in the ancient sources *Thrace* was inhabited by various tribes, whose identification through the surviving archaeological data is in most cases no more than a guess. The case of the *ethnos* of the Bottiaeans, residing in the Chalcidice peninsula, is one example that justifies Edith Hall's remark (see previous section in this chapter on 'Identities') and proves that central Macedonia to the east of the Axios River (*i.e.* the new lands) *was* a melting pot in the archaic period.[130] What matters here is that it cannot be determined whether they were of Greek origin or not. While, as we saw, some scholars take their Greek origin for granted, others have suggested, on the basis of archaeological finds, that the Bottiaeans were not Greeks, but instead a Hellenized *ethnos*.[131] Thucydides, who always referred to them in close connection to the Chalcidians in Thrace, does not make any com-ments about their origin, probably because he also thought of them as Greeks.

The expelled Bottiaeans in Chalcidice developed a new, different identity: except for the name of their new dwellings (Bottike), they seem to have adopted the *polis* culture. Could this have been a result of being neighbours to the Greek colonists coming from the south? Perhaps, the ethnic BOTTIAIΩN on their coins[132] meant a new civic and/or ethnic Bottiaean identity constructed in a new political environment (or, a normal political evolution to another stage of politi-cal existence), linked with the myth of their Cretan origins and influenced by the interaction with the Greek settlers and the polis culture they were bringing with them. It can thus explain the reference Aristotle made to their constitution.[133] So, one could suggest that the violence exercised by the Macedonians upon the Bot-tiaeans led to a series of events, which illustrate the efforts made by the defeated to cope with the new circumstances: war, defeat, expulsion, resettlement, crea-tion and projection of a new identity, a new political culture, construction of a memory and origins from Minos. On the other hand, one could assume that also the victorious Macedonians had to deal with the costs of exercising their power, costs associated with the impact of their violent expansion.[134] But, in this case, the evidence is missing. Still, they had created during this stage of their expan-sion a political framework visible in the fifth century by Thucydides, who named the tribes of Upper Macedonia as 'allied to and subjugated by' the Macedonians (2.99.2), thus depicting the surviving variations of political status inside the Macedonian kingdom.

Notes

1 This paper has been benefited by the precious remarks made by the friends and colleagues Anastasia and Pavlos Chrysostomou, Anna Panayotou, Kostas Vlassopoulos and Vivi Saripanidi. Giorgos Kalogeras made the English text much better with his expertise. Any remaining mistakes are, of course, my own.
2 See generally Smith 1986.
3 Anderson 1983; Smith 1986.
4 Thuc. 2.99.3: τὴν δὲ παρὰ θάλασσαν νῦν Μακεδονίαν Ἀλέξανδρος ὁ Περδίκκου πατὴρ καὶ οἱ πρόγονοι αὐτοῦ, Τημενίδαι τὸ ἀρχαῖον ὄντες ἐξ Ἄργους, πρῶτοι ἐκτήσαντο καὶ ἐβασίλευσαν ἀναστήσαντες μάχῃ ἐκ μὲν Πιερίας Πίερας, οἳ ὕστερον ὑπὸ τὸ Πάγγαιον πέραν Στρυμόνος ᾤκησαν Φάγρητα καὶ ἄλλα χωρία (καὶ ἔτι καὶ νῦν Πιερικὸς κόλπος καλεῖται ἡ ὑπὸ τῷ Παγγαίῳ πρὸς θάλασσαν γῆ), ἐκ δὲ τῆς Βοττίας καλουμένης Βοττιαίους, οἳ νῦν ὅμοροι Χαλκιδέων οἰκοῦσιν· τῆς δὲ Παιονίας παρὰ τὸν Ἀξιὸν ποταμὸν στενήν τινα καθήκουσαν ἄνωθεν μέχρι Πέλλης καὶ θαλάσσης ἐκτήσαντο, καὶ πέραν Ἀξιοῦ μέχρι Στρυμόνος τὴν Μυγδονίαν καλουμένην Ἠδῶνας ἐξελάσαντες νέμονται. The first one was Pieria, whose inhabitants (the Pieres) were expelled by the victors and they finally inhabited Phagres and some other settlements, beyond the river Strymon, *i.e.* to the east. See also Hdt. 8.127; *cf.* Pikoulas 2001: 22 and 39; Vasilev 2011: 94–6 for details on the Pieres.
5 See nn. 112, 113, 123.
6 Hampl 1935: 120 (seventh-sixth century, BCE); Hammond 1972: 433–41, 1996: 69; Zahrnt 1984: 357 (mid-seventh century BCE); Flensted-Jensen 2004: 81 (seventh-sixth century BCE). See also Vasilev 2011: 95 (mid-seventh century BCE); in the beginning, P. Chrysostomou 1990: 218 (based on Hammond's arguments and before the excavations in the western cemetery of Archontiko), thought that the Bottiaeans were expelled in the late sixth century from their places by the Macedonians. However, after the systematic excavations there, he is convinced that the Macedonians, after having expelled the Bottiaeans, were living at Archontiko in the second half of the seventh century BCE. See, e.g., Chrysostomou and Chrysostomou 2010: 90; 2012: 126ff.; 2013: 204. Rosen 1978: 24 believes that there had been no radical expulsion of the other tribes from the area, but a rather peaceful integration of the original populations to the Macedonian kingdom. Flensted-Jensen (2004: 81) leaves the issue open, when writing that the Bottiaeans were expelled from their original place of habitation either in the seventh or the sixth century BCE. *Cf.* Mallios 2011: 167 (mid- to late seventh century). For the Bottiaeans and their early expulsion by the Macedonians, see also the following indicative articles or papers by I. Vokotopoulou: 1985: 133 and 150, 1993b: 12ff., 1994: 79–98, 1996: 319–28.
7 This comes from two passages in Herodotus, 7.123.19 (Ἀπὸ δὲ Αἰνείης, ἐς τὴν ἐτελεύτων καταλέγων τὰς πόλις, ἀπὸ ταύτης ἤδη ἐς αὐτόν τε τὸν Θερμαῖον κόλπον ἐγίνετο τῷ ναυτικῷ στρατῷ <ὁ> πλόος καὶ γῆν τὴν Μυγδονίην, πλέων δὲ ἀπίκετο ἔς τε τὴν προειρημένην Θέρμην καὶ Σίνδον τε πόλιν καὶ Χαλέστρην ἐπὶ τὸν Ἀξιον ποταμόν, ὃς οὐρίζει χώρην τὴν Μυγδονίην τε καὶ Βοττιαιίδα, τῆς ἔχουσι τὸ παρὰ θάλασσαν, στεινὸν χωρίον, πόλιες Ἴχναι τε καὶ Πέλλα) and 7.127.5 (Ἐπέσχε δὲ ὁ στρατὸς αὐτοῦ στρατοπεδευόμενος τὴν παρὰ θάλασσαν χώρην τοσήνδε, ἀρξάμενος ἀπὸ Θέρμης πόλιος καὶ τῆς Μυγδονίης μέχρι Λυδίεώ τε ποταμοῦ καὶ Ἀλιάκμονος, οἳ οὐρίζουσι γῆν τὴν Βοττιαιίδα τε καὶ Μακεδονίδα, ἐς τὠυτὸ ῥέεθρον τὸ ὕδωρ συμμίσγοντες). See also Hatzopoulos 1995: 164–5, 1996: 232ff. (esp. 239–45). For Bottiaea, see also Oberhummer 1897: 794–5; Hammond 1972: 142ff.; Girtzy 2001: 108ff. Cf. Zahrnt

1984: 334ff. and Gschnitzer 2003: 30. The place name is rather of Greek origin: see Chrysostomou 1990: 204; Gschnitzer 2001: 34. For the topography, see Chrysostomou 1990: 205; Flensted-Jensen 1995: 105–6 (Bottiaea-Bottike); Chrysostomou 1999: 260, and n. 8;

8   Thuc. 2.100.4: ἔσω δὲ τούτων ἐς τὴν Βοττιαίαν καὶ Πιερίαν οὐκ ἀφίκοντο, ἀλλὰ τήν τε Μυγδονίαν καὶ Γρηστωνίαν καὶ Ἀνθεμοῦντα ἐδῄουν. See also the term Βοττιηὶς in Diodorus 7, fr. 16. Hatzopoulos and Paschidis (2004: 794) place it between Mt. Bermion and the Axios.

9   Hammond 1972: 154; Zahrnt 1984: 353. How and Wells (1912: 173) place Βοττιαΐδα 'between the lower courses of the Axios and the Haliakmon'.

10 Robinson (1939: 326) assumes that the Bottiaeans reached Olynthos *c.* 650 BCE. See also Hammond 1972: 358–9 (675–25 BCE).

11 Thucydides 2.79; see also the Athenian tribute lists (*e.g. IG* I³ 277, 15). Flensted-Jensen 2004: 843–4, no. 612.

12 Aioleion (Flensted-Jensen 2004: 822–3, no. 558); Milkoros (Flensted-Jensen 2004: 833, no. 585); Pleume (Flensted-Jensen 2004: 837, no. 595); Prasilos (Flensted-Jensen 2004: 839, no. 599); Sinos (Flensted-Jensen 2004: 841, no. 606); and Strepsa (Flensted-Jensen 2004: 845–6, no. 615).

13 Flensted-Jensen 2004: 834–6, no. 588.

14 For a full account of the Bottiaeans in Chalcidice, see also Psoma 1999: 41–55 (esp. for the silver and bronze coinage of the Bottiaeans in the fourth century BCE).

15 E.g. Hatzopoulos 1989: 61. Regarding the origins of the Bottiaeans and the various opinions expressed, see Flensted-Jensen 1995: 108–11, esp. 109; *cf.* Mari 2002: 26; Mallios 2011: 167. Hornblower 1991: 101 says that the Bottiaeans in Thuc. 1.57.5 (i.e. those who were the inhabitants of Bottike) 'are not to be confused with the Bottiaeans who inhabited Bottiaea'.

16 See Strabo 6.3.2: τούτους δ' εἶναί φασι τοὺς μετὰ Μίνω πλεύσαντας εἰς Σικελίαν, καὶ μετὰ τὴν ἐκείνου τελευτὴν τὴν ἐν Καμικοῖς παρὰ Κωκάλῳ συμβᾶσαν ἀπάραντας ἐκ Σικελίας κατὰ δὲ τὸν ἀνάπλουν δεῦρο παρωσθέντας, ὧν τινὰς ὕστερον πεζῇ περιελθόντας τὸν Ἀδρίαν μέχρι Μακεδονίας Βοττιαίους προσαγορευθῆναι; 6.3.6: Βρεντέσιον δ' ἐποικῆσαι μὲν λέγονται Κρῆτες οἱ μετὰ Θησέως ἐπελθόντες ἐκ Κνωσσοῦ, εἴθ' οἱ ἐκ τῆς Σικελίας ἀπηρκότες μετὰ τοῦ Ἰάπυγος (λέγεται γὰρ ἀμφοτέρως)· οὐ συμμεῖναι δέ φασιν αὐτούς, ἀλλ' ἀπελθεῖν εἰς τὴν Βοττιαίαν; 7a.1.11: κατεῖχον δὲ τὴν χώραν ταύτην Ἠπειρωτῶν τινες καὶ Ἰλλυριῶν, τὸ δὲ πλεῖστον Βοττιαῖοι καὶ Θρᾷκες· οἱ μὲν ἐκ Κρήτης, ὥς φασι, τὸ γένος ὄντες, ἡγεμόνα ἔχοντες Βόττωνα, Θρακῶν δὲ Πίερες μὲν ἐνέμοντο τὴν Πιερίαν καὶ τὰ περὶ τὸν Ὄλυμπον, Παίονες δὲ [τὰ] περὶ τὸν Ἀξιὸν ποταμὸν καὶ τὴν καλουμένην διὰ τοῦτο Ἀμφαξῖτιν, Ἠδωνοὶ δὲ καὶ Βισάλται τὴν λοιπὴν μέχρι Στρυμόνος· ὧν οἱ μὲν αὐτὸ τοῦτο προσηγορεύοντο Βισάλται, Ἠδωνῶν δ' οἱ μὲν Μυγδόνες οἱ δὲ Ἠδωνες οἱ δὲ Σίθωνες. See Mallios 2011: 162ff. for an exhaustive presentation.

17 Hammond 1972: 305, 335–6 and 359 (for the double axes found in Olynthos) places them among the descendants of a group of Minoans that reached Macedonia as early as the fourteenth century BCE. Chrysostomou 1990: 205–6.

18 Andronikos 1969: 251.

19 Mallios 2011: 167 for references.

20 Michailidou and Tzachili 1986: 365–76.

21 Michailidou and Tzachili 1986: 375. For recent finds of double axes as jewellery at Nea Philadelpheia, see Misailidou-Despotidou 2012: 471–80.

22 Gatzolis and Psoma 2009: 142 and n. 46; Mallios 2011: 166.

23 Scheer 1993, 2003; Curty 1995: 245–54; Jones 1999; Osborne 2012: 31.

24 Gatzolis and Psoma 2009: 141.

25 Vlassopoulos 2013: 195–6.

26 Vlassopoulos 2013: 164–8.

27 Vlassopoulos 2013: 167.

28 There is evidence of the importance of the criterion of descent also for the Macedonians, as at least two genealogies ascribe a Greek descent to their eponymous ancestor, Makedon (see e.g. Hesiod, *Catalogue of Women*, fr. 7). For an analysis, see Xydopoulos 2006: 47–8.

29 Malkin 2001b: 3; Todd 2001: 14.

30 Hall 2001: 165–7.

31 See e.g. the mention of various tribes in these northern areas in Hdt. 7.110–5; Thuc. 2.99.3; Strabo, 1.11.1.

32 See, e.g. Strabo 7.1.41.1ff. Hammond 1972: 405–41 undertakes a full-scale analysis of the sources and of the presence of various (non-Greek) tribes and *ethne* in Macedonia and Thrace.

33 Hall 1989: 170; Jones 1997: ch. 5.

34 Barth 1969; Cohen 1985.

35 Rapport and Overing 2000: 62–3.

36 Cifani 2012: 144.

37 Cifani 2012: 145–6.

38 Burgers 2012: 64.

39 Kristiansen 2011: 208–9.

40 Morris 1998: 51.

41 Hecataeus (*FGrHist* 1, F146). For mixed Greco-barbarian settlements see Hatzopoulos 1996: 106–8 (for Sindos, p. 108, n. 2; for Therme, 108, n. 3); Bouzek and Ondrejova 1988: 84–94.

42 For their language, see Bonfante 1955: 101–9; Lehmann 1960: 8–19.

43 Thuc. 4.109.1ff.

44 Morris 1998: 49–51. For objections regarding the 'Hellenization' process in the Balkan area during the Iron Age, see Vranić 2014: 33–47.

45 Morris 1998: 50 (700 BCE); Hammond 1996 (650 BCE). The latter had stressed the need for a full publication of the various excavations at the cemetery of tumuli at Vergina (1972: 326ff.), something recently done by Bräuning and Kilian-Dirlmeier 2013.

46 See in general Snodgrass 1980.

47 Morris 1998: 71.

48 For the annual results of the excavations in Macedonia and Thrace one can read the proceedings of the *AErgMak*.

49 Van Wees 1998: 339.

50 Van Wees 1998: 338. The same argument in Morris 1987: 151 is that the presence of weapons in the majority of the tombs in the Kerameikos cemetery for the period 1050–800 BCE is 'the result of exclusion in burial practices, rather than the consequence of a very egalitarian society'; see also Morris 1989: 506.

51 Whitley 2002: 218: 'one of the most tenacious legacies of Homeric archaeology is the so-called "warrior grave" . . . warrior graves have become an integral part of the conceptual furniture of Aegean archaeology'. See e.g. Kilian-Dirlmeier 1990: 158; Deger-Jalkotzy 1999; Papadopoulos 1999: 267–74.

52 Whitley 2002: 221 and 228 n. 3.

53 Whitley 1991: 357–9.

54 Whitley 2002: 219.

55 Whitley 2002: 226–7.

56 Coldstream 1976: 8–17.

57 Coldstream 1976: 9 and 14. For burial customs in the various regions of Greece during the so-called Dark Ages (1100–700 BCE), see Snodgrass 1971: 140–212 (esp. for Macedonia, 160–3). For the warrior graves in various places in Greece, other than those mentioned, see Bräuning 1995: 138–41 (Greece in general); Vlachopoulos 2012: 74ff. (Naxos). See also Vasic 2003: 111–34 for the 'princely tombs' of the late seventh to the fifth century BCE in the Central Balkans.

58 Whitley 1988: 175 with references.

59 Whitley 1988: 175. See also Morris 1987: 156–9 for tables regarding pottery and population, and updated data (but not from Macedonia).

60 Whitley 1988: 178; Lemos 2006: 89.

61 See lately Chrysostomou 2013: 59–60 with references. For the Iron Age finds at Agrosykia, see Chrysostomou in Chrysostomou et al. 2007: 209–79. It has become evident from the archaeological finds that 'burial with weapons was a common feature of aristocratic burials in general and "Royal tombs" in particular'. It has been argued that this must be true, *e.g.*, for tomb Beta at Derveni, where a man and a woman were cremated and were accompanied – among other vessels – with weapons (Whitley 2002: 220; for the Derveni tomb, see Musgrave 1990: 310–21; Themelis and Touratsoglou 1997: 60–92). The same goes for the tomb of Philip II at Vergina and other tombs in the wider area of Central Macedonia, while, as it has been pointed out, it is very interesting that weapons are not to be found in the contemporary tombs of the Greek colonies at Chalcidice, a striking difference from Central Macedonia (Chrysostomou 2013: 60 n. 123; however, see Bilouka and Graekos forthcoming about weapons next to the dead in Iron Age tombs at Nea Kallikrateia).

62 The term that has prevailed for the period 1000–700 BCE for Macedonia is 'Early Iron Age' (EIA), thus depicting the existence of the specific art in the region, an art that according to some scholars was implying a strong northern tradition (see e.g. Korti-Konti 2005: 12).

63 Chrysostomou and Chrysostomou 2012: 495.

64 Chrysostomou, A. and Chrysostomou, P. 2007: 113–29; Chrysostomou and Chrysostomou 2009: 482–7; Chrysostomou 2011: 305–6.

65 Saripanidi 2016, 83–103.

66 For these weapons, which often bear golden, silver and ivory decorations, see Chrysostomou and Chrysostomou 2009: 482–7, 2012: 497–9; Kottaridi 2009: 149 and 152, 2013: passim; Chrysostomou 2011: passim.

67 Chrysostomou, P. and Chrysostomou, A. 2007: 440, 442–3; Chrysostomou 2011: 306. For the golden masks in the female graves at Archontiko, see Chrysostomou 2011: passim; Chrysostomou and Chrysostomou 2012: 505. No golden masks were found at Vergina. However, this may be because the wealthiest burials found at this site, which could have yielded masks, were either cremations or plundered (Kottaridi 1997: 83 and 85, 2004, 2009: 143 and 151–2, 2013: 130–1), the exception being the so-called 'Lady of the Aigai', who is neither a cremation nor a plundered grave (Kottaridi 2012).

68 For these weapons, which often bear golden, silver and ivory decorations, see Chrysostomou and Chrysostomou 2009: 482–7, 2012: 497–9; Kottaridi 2009: 149 and 152, 2013: passim; Chrysostomou 2011: passim.

69 Chrysostomou and Zarogiannis 2005.

70 Morris 1998: 43–5; Whitley 2002: 220; Gallou and Georgiadis 2006: 126. For the 'big man', see Hall 2014: 126–53.

71 Whitley 2002: 227.

72 Whitley 1991: 342.

73 Whitley 1991: 343; Lemos 2006: 89. See Coldstream 1983: 17–25, in which the author argues that geographical determinism is not the reason for regionalism in pottery.

74 Finley 1979: 74–107; Qviller 1981: 109–55; Whitley 1991: 348.

75 Whitley 1991: 349 and n. 57.

76 Whitley 1991: 354–5.

77 For Athens, see Morris 1987: 72–4 and 92–3.

78 Morris 1998: 44–5.

79 Andronikos 1969: 119.

80 Kottaridi 1997, 2009 (with bibliography), 2013: 122–53; Saripanidi 2016: 83–103.

81 Chrysostomou, P. and Chrysostomou, A. 2005, 2007, 2008, 2009: 479–87 (with further bibliography), 2012; Saripanidi 2016. See also Chrysostomou 2011: mainly 302–13.

82 Kottaridi 1997: 79–83 and 85–91, 2009: 145–51; Drougou 2011: 183.

83 I owe this comment to Vivi Saripanidi.

84 Kottaridi 1997: 83 and 85, 2004, 2009: 143 and 151–2, 2013: 130–1.

85 See e.g. Kottaridi 2004, 2013.

86 Saripanidi 2012: 202–9, 264–7 (Appendix E), 268–73 (Appendix ΣΤ).

87 For these seven graves and some of their finds see Vokotopoulou et al. 1985: 52–65, 82–5 (grave 65), 104–19, 128–31 (grave 59), 120–27, 152–73 (grave 25), 132–41, 148–51 (grave 115), 182–205, 208–9 (grave 67), 214–7, 232–41 (grave 52), 242–5, 258–73 (grave 28).

88 Vokotopoulou et al. 1985; for comparisons between the various sites, see Saripanidi 2012.

89 Tsigarida 2011: 147.

90 Trakosopoulou-Sakakidou 1987: 295–304, 1996: 297–312, 2004: 157–64.

91 For references, see Tsigarida 2011: 137–58.

92 Sismanidis 1987: 787–803. See also Papacostas 2013: 167–72.

93 Saripanidi 2016: 92.

94 See Hammond 1972: 190–1 for the topography of Anthemous.

95 Borza 1990: 117–8, who quotes Thucydides (2.99.5–6). Also, Zahrnt (1984: 332–4 and 365) argued that by the term *Macedonia* (in the political sense) one meant also Mygdonia, Anthemous, Krestonia and Bisaltia, i.e. all these regions being to the east of the Axios river. See also Borza 1990: 87–8.

96 Xydopoulos 2012: 21–37.

97 Hammond and Griffith (1979: 28–31) seem convinced that the Macedonians had conquered Amphaxitis before the coming of the Persians. Tripodi (2007: 82) and Archibald (2010: 332) agree with Hammond and Griffith. Saripanidi (2016: 94) suggests that the Macedonians crossed Axios in the end of the first or the beginning of the second quarter of the sixth century. See also Chrysostomou forthcoming, who suggests that the Macedonians had advanced to the east of the Axios River by the end of the first or the beginning of the second quarter of the sixth century.

98 See, e.g. Snodgrass' comments on Carandini 2012: 5–23.

99 Papazoglou 1988: 131ff. (as well as others), places Aigai in Bottiaea.

100 Sismanidis 1987: 787–803, 1993: 170–95.

101 See e.g. Vokotopoulou 1996: 328. One cannot be sure about the ethnic identity of the indigenous inhabitants in these areas. Despini (2009: 20–65) argued that the deceased at Sindos were Greek colonists from southern Greece. It will be sufficient to note that the issue is extremely complicated, as the area was inhabited by various tribes.

102 See e.g. Hammond and Griffith 1979: 58–9, 64; Andronikos 1987–90: 32–3; Saatsoglou-Paliadeli 1999: 355 and n. 20.

103 Zahrnt 1984: 358–61 and Hatzopoulos and Loukopoulou 1992: 15–25, respectively.

104 Vokotopoulou et al. 1985: passim; Vokotopoulou 1998: 23–4; Despini 2011; Saripanidi 2012: passim.

105 See e.g. Despini 2009: 50. To give an example, similarities in burials (from Aiane, Vergina, Archontiko, and Sindos) and offerings (e.g. pottery) could perhaps imply that Macedonia was inhabited by Mycenaeans who had emigrated to the region after the collapse of the Mycenaean world in the Peloponnese and elsewhere and their contacts with the indigenous populations may have resulted in mixed cultural schemes. Still, that does not imply the rather discredited assumption that changes in material culture signify changes in population, an idea manifested in Hall 1997 and reiterated in Hall 2002; see also Reher and Fernández-Götz 2015: 401.

106 Snodgrass 1971: 73.

107 Snodgrass 1971: 74.

108 Morgan 2001: 75.

109 Panagiotou 1996: 134–6 and 147 n. 24; Xydopoulos 2012; Saripanidi 2016: 94. Tiverios (1991: 242–3) puts the crossing of the Axios by the Macedonians at a very early date, *c.* 700 BCE.

110   Morgan 1991: 142.
111   Morgan 2009: 28.
112   Otherwise the offer of Anthemous to Hippias cannot be explained: in 505 BCE Amyntas did not have the full jurisdiction of his realm, due to Macedonia's vassal status to Persia, particularly in those regions which were not included into Macedonia. See Hammond and Griffith 1979: 59; Zahrnt 1984: 360; Hammond 1989: 42–3; Borza 1990: 87–9; Xydopoulos 2012: 21–37. Macedonian expansion towards Anthemous seems to be confirmed by archaeological data: the cemetery in Archontiko is strikingly similar to the ones excavated in Sindos (Vokotopoulou et al. 1985; Despini 1993: 162–9), in Agios Athanasios and in Agia Paraskevi, in the region of Anthemous (Sismanidis 1987: 787–803, 1993: 170–95). See also Panti 2012: 475: based on tomb typology, the cemeteries of the interior of the Thermaic Gulf, e.g. those of Archontiko Pellas, Nea Philadelphia, Agios Athanasios and Lete, form a clearly identifiable group, defined by their great similarity to the archaic cemeteries of the Macedonian hinterland, such as those of Aigai, Trebenishte and Aiane.
113   Hatzopoulos and Loukopoulou 1992: 22–3. The dominant belief in research is that the occupation of the areas up to the Strymon occurred immediately after 479 BCE. See Touratsoglou 2010: 10–11 (with bibliography) and 36. Already Busolt (1895: 323, n. 4) accepted the end of the Persian Wars as a terminus post quem; cf. Edson 1947: 95, n. 56, 1970: 27, n. 54; Cole 1975: 42 and n. 1; Hammond and Griffith 1979: 102 ff. Zahrnt (1984: 363, n. 122) accepts Alexander's seizure of Ennea Odoi. See also Hatzopoulos 1996: 174; Zahrnt 1997: 546; Veligianni-Terzi 1999: 18–20; Psoma 2002: 42; Picard 2006: 270–1; Dahmen 2010: 41–62; Sprawski 2010: 140; Touratsoglou 2010: 10; Mari 2012: 84. Heinrichs and Müller (2008: 291) stressed that after 479 BCE the typology of the Macedonian coins changed as far as Alexander's representation was concerned: up to that moment, he was represented as a client-king of Persia, with oriental ornaments signifying his status and his proximity to the Achaemenid royal house. We think that this change simply meant the end of Persian influence in the coin typology, not a possible expansion to the east. According to those supporting this hypothesis, the Macedonian king clearly exploited the *vacuum potestatis* that had occurred after the departure of the Persians. For example, Hammond believes that Alexander conquered the Edonians and the Bisaltians immediately after the Persian withdrawal and before the two ethnic entities manage to organise themselves. Thus, Alexander had under his rule the rich mines near Kilkis, the gold of the Echedoros River, the mines at Theodoraki – which Hammond identifies with the Dysoron – while he places Alexander's attack at Ennea Odoi (the subsequent Amphipolis) 'probably' in 477 BCE (Hammond 1989: 45). Loukopoulou and Hatzopoulos (1992: 15–30) suggest an immediate occupation of Mygdonia and Lower Paeonia, and afterwords of Bisaltia, Anthemous and Krestonia. The coins struck by the Ichnaeans at the beginning of the fifth century belong to those dwelling at the Strymon area (see Zahrnt 1984: 358 and n. 104; Psoma and Zannis 2011: 38–40; Zannis 2014: 139, n. 491, 140, 212, 216, 388).
114   Kottaridi 2014: 212.
115   Morgan 2009: 20.
116   Morgan 2009: 21. See Morgan 2003: ch. 4 for discussion on the subject, with references.
117   Barth 1969: 10. See also Jones 1996: 66–7.
118   As far as Archontiko is concerned, there are no differences, either with the tomb type (pit graves) or the grave goods and rituals. The suggestion that cremation was the usual way of burial for the Temenid Macedonians at Aigai, while this was not the case at the western cemetery of Archontiko, is not supported. The archaic period cremations at Archontiko are rare indeed (as those at Aigai), however they are located at key points of the cemetery and their majority belongs to the sixth century. Almost

all of the 80 pit graves of Aigai investigated up to 2007 (about 90%) were looted (see Tsigarida 2007: 524; Kottaridi 2009: 143–53, 2011: 131–52. See also Graecos 2011: 75–92). Kottaridi suggests that by the end of the sixth century the Bottiaeans were incorporated into the Macedonian state, except for those belonging to the elite who were expelled to Chalcidice, a suggestion that is not based on any solid evidence.

119 Horden and Purcell 2000: 384.

120 Hdt. 7.127.5.

121 Horden and Purcell 2000: 385.

122 Morgan 1991: 133.

123 Morris 1989: 507. For a recent study on the funeral rites at Vergina, see Chemsseddoha 2014: 63–86.

124 Chrysostomou and Chrysostomou 2012: 494–519.

125 Babić 2007: 83–4; Chrysostomou and Chrysostomou 2012: 519.

126 Hammond (1972: 430–4, 1996: 67–71) argued that the Macedonian expansion was made after the foundation of Methone. If he is correct, then the Eretrians, who founded Methone on the Pierian coast in 733 BCE, must have met not only Thracians but also Macedonians in the area. See Tzifopoulos 2012: 16.

127 See e.g. the conclusions in Morgan 2001: 92–4; Reher and Fernández-Götz 2015: 400–16.

128 Despini 2009: 20–65.

129 For this grave, which was found at the site of Alepotrypa, see Malamidou 2006: 200 with pls. 30.3–5. For the finds from the hearth, which included large quantities of animal bones and cereal grains within ash layers, see Malamidou 2006: 200.

130 Contra Hall 1997.

131 Flensted-Jensen 1995: 109–10 for the references.

132 Psoma 1999: 41–55.

133 The same could be true for the expelled Ichnaeans and their fifth-century coins, belonging to the monetary zone of Thasos and Berge: they have also issued coins with their ethnic IXNAIΩN on the obverse (see n. 118). In their case, however, we regrettably do not know anything concerning their foundation myth.

134 Ulf 2009: 93.

Bibliography

Adam-Veleni, P. and Tzanavari, K. (eds.) (2009) *ΑΕΜΘ 20 χρόνια, επετειακός τόμος*, Thessaloniki, Greece.

Anderson, B. (1983) *Imagined Communities: Reflections on the Origin and Spread of Nationalism*, London.

Andronikos, M. (1969) *Βεργίνα I: Το νεκροταφείον των τύμβων*, Athens.

Andronikos, M. (1987–90) 'Πρώτες σκέψεις για τα τελευταία ευρήματα της Βεργίνας', *Θρακική Επετηρίδα* 7, 25–34.

Archibald, Z. H. (1998) *The Odrysian Kingdom of Thrace: Orpheus Unmasked*, Oxford, UK.

Archibald, Z. H. (2010) 'Macedonia and Thrace' in J. Roisman and I. Worthington (eds.), *A Companion to Ancient Macedonia*, London, 326–41.

Babić, S. (2007) 'Greeks, Barbarians and archaeologists: Mapping the contact', *AWE* 6, 73–89.

Barth, F. (1969) 'Introduction' in F. Barth (ed.), *Ethnic Groups and Boundaries: The Social Organization of Culture Difference*, Boston, 9–38.

Bilouka, A. and Graikos, I. (forthcoming) 'Small things next to the dead body', paper presented at the *The Gods of Small Things*, Ure Museum, University of Reading, 21–2 September 2009.

Bonfante, G. (1955) 'A note on the Samothracian language', *Hesperia* 24, 101–9.

Borza, E. N. (1990) *In the Shadow of Olympus: The Emergence of Macedon*, Princeton, NJ.

Bouzek, J. and Ondrejova, I. (1988) 'Sindos – Trebenishte – Duvanli: interrelations between Thrace, Macedonia, and Greece in the 6th and 5th centuries B.C.', *Mediterranean Archaeology* 1, 84–94.

Bräuning, A. (1995) 'Untersuchungen zur Darstellung and Ausstattung des Krieges im Grabbrauch Griechenlands zwischen dem 10. und 8. Jahrhundert v. Chr.', *Internationale Archaeologie* 15, 138–41.

Bräuning, A. and Kilian-Dirlmeier, I. (2013) *Die eisenzeitlichen Grabhügel von Vergina: Die Ausgrabungen von Photis Petsas 1960–1961*, Mainz, Germany.

Burgers, G.-J. (2012) 'Landscape and identity of Greek colonists and indigenous communities in southeast Italy' in G. Cifani and S. Stoddart (eds.), *Landscape, Ethnicity and Identity in the Archaic Mediterranean Area*, Oxford, UK, 64–76.

Busolt, G. (1895 [repr. 1967]) *Griechische Geschichte bis zur Schlacht bei Chaironeia*. Band II, 2nd ed., Hildesheim, Germany.

Carandini, A. (2012) 'Urban landscapes and ethnic identity of early Rome' in G. Cifani and S. Stoddart (eds.), *Landscape, Ethnicity and Identity in the Archaic Mediterranean Area*, Oxford, UK, 5–23.

Chemseddoha, A.-Z. (2014) 'Quelques observations sur les thématiques funéraires en Macédoine à l'âge du Fer: le cas de la nécropole de Vergina', *Pallas* 94, 63–86.

Chrysostomou, A. (1999) 'Οι περιοχές της βόρειας Βοττιαίας και της Αλμωπίας την Εποχή του Σιδήρου' in *Αρχαία Μακεδονία VI*, 259–80.

Chrysostomou, A. (2000) 'Οι περιοχές της βόρειας Βοττιαίας και της Αλμωπίας στην Εποχή του Σιδήρου και τα αρχαϊκά χρόνια. Παραδείγματα ταφικών τύπων' in P. Adam-Veleni (ed.), *Μύρτος: Μελέτες στη μνήμη της Ιουλίας Βοκοτοπούλου*, Thessaloniki, Greece, 229–42.

Chrysostomou, A. (2013) *Νέοι θησαυροί της Εδεσσαϊκής γης*, Edessa, Greece.

Chrysostomou, A. and Chrysostomou, P. (2007) 'Τάφοι πολεμιστών των αρχαϊκών χρόνων από τη δυτική νεκρόπολη του Αρχοντικού Πέλλας' in *Αρχαία Μακεδονία VII*, 113–29.

Chrysostomou, P. (1990) 'Η τοπογραφία της βόρειας Βοττιαίας. Η Πέλλα, η αποικία της Πέλλας και οι χώρες τους' in *Μνήμη Δ. Λαζαρίδη. Πόλις και χώρα στην αρχαία Μακεδονία και Θράκη*, Thessaloniki, Greece, 205–31.

Chrysostomou, P. (2011) 'The ancient settlement of Archontiko' in M. Lilibaki-Akamati, I. M. Akamatis, A. Chrysostomou and P. Chrysostomou (2011) *The Archaeological Museum of Pella*, Athens, 299–389.

Chrysostomou, P. (forthcoming) *Χρυσά και αργυρά επίχρυσα ελάσματα προσώπου των αρχαϊκών χρόνων από το δυτικό νεκροταφείο του Αρχοντικού Πέλλας – Συμβολή στη μακεδονική χρυσοχοΐα*.

Chrysostomou, P., Aslanis, I. and Chrysostomou, A. (2007) *Αγροσυκιά: Ένας οικισμός των προϊστορικών και ιστορικών χρόνων*, Veria, Greece.

Chrysostomou, P. and Chrysostomou, A. (2005) 'Δυτική νεκρόπολη του Αρχοντικού Πέλλας: συστάδα τάφων αριστοκρατικής οικογένειας των αρχαϊκών χρόνων', *AErgMak* 17, 505–16.

Chrysostomou, P. and Chrysostomou, A. (2007) 'Ανασκαφή στη δυτική νεκρόπολη του Αρχοντικού Πέλλας κατά το 2005', *AErgMak* 19, 435–47.

Chrysostomou, P. and Chrysostomou, A. (2008) 'Σωστική ανασκαφή στο δυτικό νεκροταφείο του Αρχοντικού Πέλλας κατά το 2006', *AErgMak* 20, 703–12.

Chrysostomou, P. and Chrysostomou, A. (2009) 'Τα νεκροταφεία του αρχαίου οικισμού στο Αρχοντικό Πέλλας' in P. Adam-Veleni and K. Tzanavari (eds.), *ΑΕΜΘ 20 χρόνια, επετειακός τόμος*, Thessaloniki, Greece, 477–90.

Chrysostomou, P. and Chrysostomou, A. (2010) 'Ανασκαφή στο δυτικό νεκροταφείο του Αρχοντικού Πέλλας κατά το 2007: η ταφική συστάδα του πολεμιστή με τη χρυσή μάσκα και άλλες ταφικές συστάδες', *AErgMak* 21, 83–90.

Chrysostomou, P. and Chrysostomou, A. (2012) 'The "gold-wearing" archaic Macedonians from the western cemetery of Archontiko, Pella' in M. Tiverios, P. M. Nigdelis and P. Adam-Veleni (eds.), *Threpteria: Studies on Ancient Macedonia*, Thessaloniki, Greece, 490–517.

Chrysostomou, P. and Chrysostomou, A. (2013) 'Δυτικό νεκροταφείο του αρχαίου οικισμού στο Αρχοντικό Πέλλας: η σωστική ανασκαφική έρευνα του 2009', *AErgMak* 23, 195–204.

Chrysostomou, P. and Zarogiannis, A. (2005) 'Μεσιανό Γιαννιτσών: ένα νέο νεκροταφείο του αρχαίου οικισμού στο Αρχοντικό Πέλλας', *AErgMak* 19, 427–34.

Cifani, G. (2012) 'Approaching ethnicity and landscapes in pre-Roman Italy: the middle Tiber Valley' in G. Cifani and S. Stoddart, S. (eds.), *Landscape, Ethnicity and Identity in the Archaic Mediterranean Area*, Oxford, UK, 144–62.

Cifani, G. and Stoddart, S. (eds.) (2012) *Landscape, Ethnicity and Identity in the Archaic Mediterranean Area*, Oxford, UK.

Cohen, A. (1985) *The Symbolic Construction of Community*, London.

Coldstream, J. N. (1976) 'Hero-cults in the age of Homer', *JHS* 96, 8–17.

Coldstream, J. N. (1983) 'The meaning of the regional styles in the eighth century B.C.' in R. Hägg (ed.), The *Greek Renaissance of the Eighth Century B.C.*, Stockholm, 17–25.

Cole, J. W. (1975) 'Peisistratus on the Strymon', *G&R* 22, 42–4.

Curty, O. (1995) *Les parentés légendaires entre cités grecques*, Geneva.

Dahmen, K. (2010) 'The numismatic evidence' in J. Roisman and I. Worthington (eds.), *A Companion to Ancient Macedonia*, London, 41–62.

Deger-Jalkotzy, S. (1999) 'Military prowess and social status in Mycenaean Greece' in R. Laffineur (ed.), *Polemos: Le contexte guerrier en Égée à l'Âge du Bronze*, I–II, Liege, Belgium, 121–31.

Despini, A. (1993) 'Το αρχαίο νεκροταφείο της Σίνδου' in I. Vokotopoulou (ed.), *Ελληνικός Πολιτισμός. Μακεδονία. Το βασίλειο του Μεγάλου Αλεξάνδρου. Κατάλογος έκθεσης Marché Bonsecours, Μοντρεάλ 7 Μαΐου – 19 Σεπτεμβρίου 1993*, Athens, 162–9.

Despini, A. (2009) 'Gold funerary masks', *Antike Kunst* 52, 20–65.

Despini, A. (2011) 'Κτερίσματα και νεκρικές δοξασίες. Οι μαρτυρίες των τάφων της Σίνδου' in S. Pingiatoglou and T. Stefanidou-Tiveriou (eds.), *Νάματα: Τιμητικός τόμος για τον καθηγητή Δ. Παντερμαλή*, Thessaloniki, Greece, 335–43.

Drougou, S. (2011) 'Macedonian metallurgy: an expression of royalty' in *Heracles to Alexander*, 181–92.

Edson, C. F. (1947) 'Notes on the Thracian "phoros"', *CP* 42, 88–105.

Edson, C. F. (1970) 'Early Macedonia' in B. Laourdas and C. Makaronas (eds.), *Αρχαία Μακεδονία: Ανακοινώσεις κατά τὸ πρῶτον Διεθνὲς Συμπόσιο ἐν Θεσσαλονίκη, 26–9.8.1968*, Thessaloniki, Greece, 17–44.

Finley, M. I. (1979) *The World of Odysseus*, Harmondsworth.

Fisher, N. and van Wees, H. (eds.) (1998) *Archaic Greece: New Approaches and New Evidence*, Swansea, UK.

Flensted-Jensen, P. (1995) 'The Bottiaians and their poleis' in M. H. Hansen and K. Raaflaub (eds.), *Studies in the Ancient Greek Polis: Papers from the Copenhagen Polis Centre 2*, Stuttgart, 103–32.

Flensted-Jensen, P. (2004) 'Thrace from Axios to Strymon' in M. H. Hansen and T. H. Nielsen (eds.), *An Inventory of Archaic and Classical Poleis*, Oxford, UK, 810–53.

Gallou, C. and Georgiadis, M. (2006) 'Ancestor worship, tradition and regional variation in Mycenaean culture' in C. Gallou and M. Georgiadis (eds.), *The Archaeology of Cult and Death: Proceedings of the Session "The Archaeology of Cult and Death", 11th September 2003, St. Petersburg, Russia*, Budapest, 125–49.

Gatzolis C. and Psoma S. (2009) 'More on the Bottiaeans of Thrace' in Κερμάτια Φιλίας, τιμητικός τόμος για τον Ιωάννη Τουράτσογλου, vol. I: Νομισματική- Σφραγιστική, Athens, 135–43.

Girtzy, M. (2001) *Historical Topography of Ancient Macedonia*, Thessaloniki, Greece.

Graecos, I. (2011) 'War and hunting: the world of the Macedonian king and his companions' in *Heracles to Alexander*, 75–92.

Gschnitzer, F. (2001) *Kleine Schriften zum griechischen und römischen Altertum*, I, Stuttgart.

Gschnitzer, F. (2003) *Kleine Schriften zum griechischen und römischen Altertum*, II, Stuttgart.

Guimier-Sorbets, A. M., Hatzopoulos, M. B. and Morizot, Y. (eds.) (2006) *Rois, cités, nécropoles. Institutions, rites et monuments en Macédoine*, Athens and Paris.

Hall, E. (1989) *Inventing the Barbarian: Greek Self-Definition through Tragedy*, Oxford, UK.

Hall, J. M. (1997) *Ethnic Identity in Greek Antiquity*, Cambridge, UK.

Hall, J. M. (2001) 'Contested ethnicities: perceptions of Macedonia within evolving definitions of Greek identity' in I. Malkin (ed.), *Ancient Perceptions of Greek Ethnicity*, Cambridge, MA, 159–86.

Hall, J. M. (2002) *Hellenicity: Between Ethnicity and Culture*, Chicago.

Hall, J. M. (2014) *A History of the Archaic Greek World ca. 1200–479 B.C.E*, 2nd ed., Malden, MA.

Hammond, N. G. L. (1972) *A History of Macedonia*, I, Oxford, UK.

Hammond, N. G. L. (1989) *The Macedonian State: Its Origins, Institutions, and History*, Oxford, UK.

Hammond, N. G. L. (1996) 'The early history of Macedonia', *Ancient World* 27/1.1, 67–71.

Hammond, N. G. L. and Griffith, G. T. (1979) *A History of Macedonia*, II, Oxford, UK.

Hampl, F. (1935) 'ΟΙ ΒΟΤΤΙΑΙΟΙ', *RhM* 84, 120–4.

Hansen, M. H. and Nielsen, T. H. (eds.) (2004) *An Inventory of Archaic and Classical Poleis*, Oxford, UK.

Hatzopoulos, M. B. (1989) 'Grecs et barbares dans les cités de l'arrière-pays de la Chalcidique', *Klio* 71, 60–5.

Hatzopoulos, M. B. (1995) 'Τα ίρια της Μακεδονίας', *Πρακτικά της Ακαδημίας των Αθηνίν* 70, 164–77.

Hatzopoulos, M. B. (1996) *Macedonian Institutions under the Kings. I: A Historical and Epigraphic Study*, Athens.

Hatzopoulos, M. B. and Loukopoulou, L. D. (1992) *Recherches sur les marches orientales des Temenides*, Athens.

Hatzopoulos, M. B. and Paschidis, P. (2004) 'Makedonia' in Hansen and Nielsen (2004), 794–809.

Heinrichs, J. and Müller, S. (2008) 'Ein persisches Statussymbol auf Münzen Alexanders I. von Makedonien: Ikonographie und historischer Hintergrund des Tetrobols SNG ABC, Macedonia I,7 und 11', *ZPE* 167, 289–90.

Horden, P. and Purcell, N. (2000) *The Corrupting Sea: A Study of Mediterranean History*, Oxford, UK.

Hornblower, S. (1991) *A Commentary on Thucydides. I: Books I–III*, Oxford, UK.

How, W. W. and Wells, J. (1912) *A Commentary on Herodotus*, II, Oxford, UK.

Jones, C. P. (1999) *Kinship Diplomacy in the Ancient World*, Cambridge, MA.

Jones, S. (1996) 'Discourses of identity in the interpretation of the past' in P. Graves-Brown, S. Jones and C. Gamble (eds.), *Cultural Identity and Archaeology*, London and New York, 62–80.

Jones, S. (1997) *The Archaeology of Ethnicity*, London and New York.

Kilian-Dirlmeier, I. (1990) 'Remarks on the non-military functions of swords in the Mycenaean Argolid' in R. Hägg and G. C. Nordqvist (eds.), *Celebrations of Death and Divinity in the Bronze Age Argolid*, Stockholm, 157–61.

Korti-Konti, S. (2005) *Η ανατολίζουσα Μακεδονία*, Thesalloniki.

Kottaridi, A. (1997) 'Βεργίνα 1997', *AErgMak* 10, 79–92.

Kottaridi, A. (2004) 'The Lady of Aigai' in D. Pandermalis (ed.), *Alexander the Great: Treasures from an Epic Era of Hellenism*, New York, 139–47.

Kottaridi, A. (2009) 'Η νεκρόπολη των Αιγών στα αρχαϊκά χρόνια και οι βασιλικές ταφικές συστάδες' in P. Adam-Veleni and K. Tzanavari (eds.), *ΑΕΜΘ 20 χρόνια, επετειακός τόμος*, Thessaloniki, Greece, 143–53.

Kottaridi, A. (2011) 'Burial customs and beliefs in the royal necropolis of Aegae' in *Heracles to Alexander*, 131–52.

Kottaridi, A. (2012) 'The Lady of Aigai' in N. C. Stampolidis and M. Giannopoulou (eds.), *'Princesses' of the Mediterranean in the Dawn of History*, Athens, 412–33.

Kottaridi, A. (2013) *Aigai: The Royal Metropolis of the Macedonians*, Athens.

Kottaridi, A. (2014) 'The Macedonians and the Bottiaeans' and 'The discovery of the Bottiaean metropolis and the necropolis of Archontiko' in M. Andreadaki-Vlazaki and A. Balaska (eds.), *The Greek: Agamemnon to Alexander the Great*, Athens, 208–9 and 210–13.

Kristiansen, K. (2011) 'Constructing social and cultural identities in the Bronze Age' in B. W. Roberts and M. van der Linden (eds.), *Investigating Archaeological Cultures: Material Culture, Variability, and Transmission*, New York, 201–10.

Laffineur, R. (ed.) (1999) *Polemos: Le contexte guerrier en Égée à l'Âge du Bronze*, I–II, Liege, Belgium.

Lehmann, K. (ed.) (1960) *Samothrace, II.2*, New York.

Lemos, I. S. (2006) 'The "Dark Age" of Greece' in E. Bispham, T. Harrison and B. A. Sparkes (eds.), *The Edinburgh Companion to Ancient Greece and Rome*, Edinburgh, 87–91.

Lilibaki-Akamati, M., Akamatis, I. M., Chrysostomou, A. and Chrysostomou, P. (2011) *The Archaeological Museum of Pella*, Athens.

Malamidou, D. (2006) 'Les nécropoles d'Amphipolis: nouvelles données archéologiques et anthropologiques' in A. M. Guimier-Sorbets, M. B. Hatzopoulos and Y. Morizot (eds.), *Rois, cités, nécropoles. Institutions, rites et monuments en Macédoine*, Athens and Paris, 199–208.

Malkin, I. (ed.) (2001a) *Ancient Perceptions of Greek Ethnicity*, Cambridge, MA.

Malkin, I. (2001b) 'Introduction' in Malkin (2001a), 1–28.

Mallios, G. (2011) *Μύθος και ιστορία: Η περίπτωση της αρχαίας Μακεδονίας*, PhD dissertation, Aristotle University of Thessaloniki, Greece.

Mari, M. (2002) *Al di là dell' Olimpo: Macedoni e grandi santuari della Grecia dall'età arcaica al primo ellenismo*, Athens.

Mari, M. (2012) 'Archaic and early classical Macedonia' in R. L. Fox (ed.), *Brill's Companion to Ancient Macedon*, Leiden, Netherlands and Boston, 79–92.

Michailidou, A. and Tzachili, I. (1986) 'Λίθινη μήτρα για κοσμήματα από τη Βεργίνα' in *Αρχαία Μακεδονία IV*, 365–76.

Misailidou-Despotidou, V. (2012) 'Ο διπλός πέλεκυς στο νεκροταφείο της Νέας Φιλαδέλφειας' in P. Adam-Veleni and K. Tzanavari (eds.), *Δινήεσσα: Τιμητικός τόμος για την Κατερίνα Ρωμιοπούλου*, Thessaloniki Greece, 471–80.

Morgan, C. (1991) 'Ethnicity and early Greek states: historical and material perspectives', *PCPS* 37, 131–59.

Morgan, C. (2001) 'Ethne, ethnicity and early Greek states, ca. 1200–480 B.C.: an archaeological perspective' in I. Malkin (ed.), *Ancient Perceptions of Greek Ethnicity*, Cambridge, MA, 75–112.

Morgan, C. (2003) *Early Greek States beyind the Polis*, London.

Morgan, C. (2009) 'Ethnic expression on the Early Iron Age and early archaic Greek mainland: Where should we be looking?' in T. Derks and N. Roymans (eds.), *Ethnic Constructs in Antiquity: The Role of Power and Tradition*, Amsterdam, 11–36.

Morris, I. (1987) *Burial and Ancient Society: The Rise of the Greek City-State*, Cambridge, UK.

Morris, I. (1989) 'Circulation, deposition and the formation of the Greek Iron Age', *Man* 24, 502–19.

Morris, I. (1998) 'Archaeology and Archaic Greek history' in N. Fisher and H. van Wees (eds.), *Archaic Greece: New Approaches and New Evidence*, Swansea, UK, 1–91.

Musgrave, J. H. (1990) 'The cremated remains from tombs II and III at Nea Mihaniona and tomb Beta at Derveni', *BSA* 85, 310–25.

Oberhummer, E. (1897) 'Bottia – Bottike', *RE* 3.1, 794–5.

Osborne, R. (2012) 'Landscape, ethnicity and the *polis*' in G. Cifani and S. Stoddart (eds.), *Landscape, Ethnicity and Identity in the Archaic Mediterranean Area*, Oxford, UK, 24–31.

Panagiotou, A. (1996) 'Διαλεκτικές επιγραφές της Χαλκιδικής, της Μακεδονίας και της Αμφιπόλεως' in E. Voutiras (ed.), *Επιγραφές της Μακεδονίας: Γ' Διεθνές Συμπόσιο για τη Μακεδονία*, Thessaloniki 1996, 124–63.

Panti, A. (2012) 'Burial customs in the Thermaic Gulf and Chalcidice in the Archaic Period' in M. Tiverios, P. M. Nigdelis and P. Adam-Veleni (eds.), *Threpteria: Studies on Ancient Macedonia*, Thessaloniki, Greece, 470–93.

Papacostas, T. (2013) 'Τοπική κεραμική από το αρχαϊκό νεκροταφείο της Αγίας Παρασκευής Θεσσαλονίκης' in P. Adam-Veleni, E. Kefalidou and D. Tsiafakis (eds.), *Κεραμικά εργαστήρια στο Βορειοανατολικό Αιγαίο (8ος – αρχές 5ου αι. π.Χ.)*, Thessaloniki, 167–72.

Papadopoulos, T. J. (1999) 'Warrior graves in Achaean Mycenaean cemeteries' in R. Laffineur (ed.), *Polemos: Le contexte guerrier en Égée à l'Âge du Bronze*, I–II, Liege, Belgium, 267–74.

Papazoglou, F. (1988) *Les villes de Macédoine à l'époque romaine*, Paris.

Picard, O. (2006) 'Mines, monnaies et impérialisme: conflits autour du Pangée (478–413 av. J.-C.)' in Guimier-Sorbets, Hatzopoulos and Morizot (2006), 269–83.

Pikoulas, I. (2001) *Η χώρα των Πιέρων: Συμβολή στην τοπογραφία της*, Athens.

Psoma, S. (1999) 'Les Bottiéens de Thrace aux Ve et IVe siècles', *Revue Numismatique* 154, 41–55.

Psoma, S. (2002) 'Το βασίλειο των Μακεδόνων πριν από τον Φίλιππο Β': νομισματική και ιστορική προσέγγιση' in *Η Ιστορική Διαδρομή της Νομισματικής Μονάδας στην Ελλάδα*, Athens, 25–45.

Psoma, S. H. and Zannis, A. G. (2011) 'Ichnai et le monnayage des Ichnéens', *Tekmeria* 10, 23–46.

Qviller, B. (1981) 'The dynamics of Homeric society', *Symbolae Osloenses* 56, 109–55.

Rapport, N. and Overing, J. (2000) *Social and Cultural Anthropology: The Key Concepts*, London.

Reher, G.-S. and Fernández-Götz, M. (2015) 'Archaeological narratives in ethnicity studies', *Archeologické Rozhledy* LXVII.3, 400–16.

Robinson, D. M. (1939) 'Olynthos', *RE* 35.1, 325–42.

Roisman, J. and Worthington, I. (eds.) (2010) *A Companion to Ancient Macedonia*, London.

Rosen, K. (1978) 'Die Gründung der makedonischen Herrschaft', *Chiron* 8, 1–27.

Saatsoglou-Paliadeli, C. (1999) 'In the shadow of history: the emergence of archaeology', *BSA* 94, 353–67.

Saripanidi, V. (2012) *Εισαγμένη και εγχώρια κεραμική στο βορειοελλαδικό χώρο: η περίπτωση της Σίνδου*, PhD dissertation, Aristotle University of Thessaloniki.

Saripanidi, V. (2016) 'Too young to fight (or drink): a warrior krater in a child burial at ancient Sindos' in T. Carpenter, E. Langride-Noti and M. Stansbury-O'Donnell (eds.), *The Consumers' Choice: Uses of Greek Figure-Decorated Pottery*, Boston, 83–103.

Scheer, T. S. (1993) *Mythische Vorväter. Zur Bedeutung griechischer Heroenmythen im Selbstverständnis kleinasiatischer Städte*, Munich.

Scheer, T. S. (2003) 'The past in a Hellenistic present: myth and local tradition' in A. Erskine (ed.), *A Companion to the Hellenistic World*, Oxford, UK, 216–31.

Sismanidis, K. (1987) 'Το αρχαϊκό νεκροταφείο της Αγίας Παρασκευής Θεσσαλονίκης' in *Αμητός: Τιμητικός τόμος για τον καθηγητή Μ. Ανδρόνικο*, Thessaloniki, Greece, 787–803.

Sismanidis, K. (1993) 'Το αρχαϊκό νεκροταφείο της Αγίας Παρασκευής' in I. Vokotopoulou (ed.), *Ελληνικός Πολιτισμός. Μακεδονία. Το βασίλειο του Μεγάλου Αλεξάνδρου. Κατάλογος έκθεσης Marché Bonsecours, Μοντρεάλ 7 Μαΐου – 19 Σεπτεμβρίου 1993*, Athens, 170–95.

Smith, A. D. (1986) *The Ethnic Origins of Nations*, Oxford, UK.

Snodgrass, A. M. (1971) *The Dark Age of Greece: An Archaeological Survey of the Eleventh to the Eighth Centuries B.C.*, Edinburgh.

Snodgrass, A. M. (1980) *Archaic Greece: The Age of Experiment*, London.

Sprawski, S. (2010) 'The early Temenid kings to Alexander I' in J. Roisman and I. Worthington (eds.), *A Companion to Ancient Macedonia*, London, 127–44.

Themelis, P. G. and Touratsoglou, Y. P. (1997) *Οι τάφοι του Δερβενίου*, Athens.

Tiverios, M. (1991) 'Αρχαιολογικές έρευνες στη Διπλή Τράπεζα της Αγχιάλου (Σίνδος) κατά το 1991', *AErgMak* 5, 235–46.

Tiverios, M., Nigdelis, P. M. and Adam-Veleni, P. (eds.) (2012) *Threpteria: Studies on Ancient Macedonia*, Thessaloniki, Greece.

Todd, M. (2001) *Migrants and Invaders*, Charleston, SC.

Touratsoglou, I. P. (2010) *Συμβολή στην οικονομική ιστορία του βασιλείου της Μακεδονίας (6ος–3ος αι. π.Χ.)*, Athens.

Trakosopoulou-Sakakidou, H. (1987) 'Αρχαία Άκανθος: πόλη και νεκροταφείο', *AErgMak* 1, 295–304.

Trakosopoulou-Sakakidou, H. (1996) 'Αρχαία Άκανθος: 1986–1996', *AErgMak* 10A, 297–312.

Trakosopoulou-Sakakidou, H. (2004) 'Άκανθος. Το ανασκαφικό έργο της χρονιάς του 2004', *AErgMak* 18, 157–64.

Tripodi, B. (2007) 'Aminta I, Alessandro I e gli hyparchoi in Erodoto' in *Αρχαία Μακεδονία VII*, 67–85.

Tsigarida, E.-B. (2007) 'Χρυσά και αργυρά κοσμήματα από το αρχαϊκό νεκροταφείο της Βεργίνας' in *Αρχαία Μακεδονία VII*, 515–29.

Tsigarida, E.-B. (2011) 'Chalcidice' in R. L. Fox (ed.), *Brill's Companion to Ancient Macedon*, Leiden, Netherlands and Boston, 137–58.

Tzifopoulos, G. Z. (ed.) (2012) *Μεθώνη Πιερίας Ι: Επιγραφές, χαράγματα και εμπορικά σύμβολα στη γεωμετρική και αρχαϊκή κεραμική από το "Υπόγειο"*, Thessaloniki, Greece.

Ulf, C. (2009) 'Rethinking Cultural Contacts', *AWE* 8, 81–132.

van Wees, H. (1998) 'Greeks bearing arms. The state, the leisure class, and the display of weapons in archaic Greece' in Fisher and van Wees (1998), 333–78.

Vasic, R. (2003) 'To the north of Trebenishte' in C. M. Stibbe (ed.), *Trebenishte: The Fortunes of an Unusual Excavation*, Rome, 111–34.

Vasilev, M. (2011) 'Thucydides II,99 and the early expansion of the Argeadae', *Eirene* 47, 93–105.

Veligianni-Terzi, C. (1999) 'Το ανατολικό πολιτικό όριο της Μακεδονίας κατά την αρχαιότητα' in *Πρακτικά ΙΘ΄ Πανελληνίου Ιστορικού Συνεδρίου, 29–31 Μαΐου 1998*, Thessaloniki, Greece, 15–34.

Vlachopoulos, A. G. (2012) *Η Υστεροελλαδική ΙΙΙΓ περίοδος στη Νάξο, Τα ταφικά σύνολα και η συσχετισμοί τους με το Αιγαίο. τ. ΙΙ: Η Νάξος και ο μυκηναϊκός κόσμος τη μετανακτορικής περιόδου*, Athens.

Vlassopoulos, K. (2013) *Greeks and Barbarians*, Cambridge, UK.

Vokotopoulou, I. (ed.) (1993a), *Ελληνικός Πολιτισμός. Μακεδονία. Το βασίλειο του Μεγάλου Αλεξάνδρου. Κατάλογος έκθεσης Marché Bonsecours, Μοντρεάλ 7 Μαΐου – 19 Σεπτεμβρίου 1993*, Athens.

Vokotopoulou, I. (1993b) 'Μακεδονία – γεωγραφικό και ιστορικό διάγραμμα' in I. Vokotopoulou (ed.), *Ελληνικός Πολιτισμός. Μακεδονία. Το βασίλειο του Μεγάλου Αλεξάνδρου. Κατάλογος έκθεσης Marché Bonsecours, Μοντρεάλ 7 Μαΐου – 19 Σεπτεμβρίου 1993*, Athens, 12–19.

Vokotopoulou, I. (1994) 'Anciennes nécropoles de la Chalcidique' in J. de la Genière (ed.), *Nécropoles et sociétés antiques*, Naples, 79–98.

Vokotopoulou, I. (1996) 'Cities and sanctuaries of the archaic period in Chalkidike', *BSA* 91, 319–28.

Vokotopoulou, I. (1998) 'Μακεδονικά συμπόσια' in *Αμπελοοινική ιστορία στο χώρο της Μακεδονίας και της Θράκης. Ε΄ τριήμερο εργασίας, Νάουσα 17–19 Σεπτεμβρίου 1993*, Athens, 21–30.

Vokotopoulou, I., Despoini, A., Misailidou, V. and Tiverios, M. (1985) *Σίνδος*, Athens.

Vranić, I. (2014) 'The "Hellenization" process and the Balkan Iron Age archaeology' in M. A. Janković, V. D. Mihajlović and S. Babić (eds.), *The Edges of the Roman World*, Cambridge, UK, 33–47.

Whitley, J. (1988) 'Early states and hero cults: a re-appraisal', *JHS* 108, 173–82.

Whitley, J. (1991) 'Social diversity in Dark Age Greece', *BSA* 86, 341–65.

Whitley, J. (2002) 'Objects with attitude: biographical facts and fallacies in the study of Late Bronze Age and Early Iron Age warrior graves', *Cambridge Archaeological Journal* 12.2, 217–32.

Xydopoulos, I. K. (2006) *Κοινωνικές και πολιτικές σχέσεις των Μακεδόνων και των νοτίων Ελλήνων*, 2nd ed., Thessaloniki, Greece.

Xydopoulos, I. K. (2012) 'Anthemous and Hippias: the policy of Amyntas I', *Illinois Classical Studies* 37, 21–37.

Zahrnt, M. (1984) 'Die Entwicklung des makedonishen Reiches bis zu den Perserkriegen', *Chiron* 14, 325–68.

Zahrnt, M. (1997) 'ΠΟΛΙΣ ΜΑΚΕΔΟΝΙΑΣ – ΠΟΛΙΣ ΘΡΑΚΗΣ' in *Αφιέρωμα στον Ν. G. L. Hammond*, Thessaloniki, 543–50.

Zannis, A. G. (2014) *Le pays entre le Strymon et le Nestos. Géographie et histoire (VIIe – IVe siècle avant J.-C.)*, Athens.

5 Socialisation, identity and violence in classical Greek cities

Nick Fisher

Introduction

σὺ δ᾽ ἐν τόποισι τοῖς ἐμοῖσι μὴ βάλῃς
μήθ᾽ αἱματηρὰς θηγάνας, σπλάγχνων βλάβας
νέων, ἀοίνοις ἐμμανεῖς θυμώμασιν,
μήτ᾽, ἐκζέουσ᾽ ὡς καρδίαν ἀλεκτόρων,
ἐν τοῖς ἐμοῖς ἀστοῖσιν ἱδρύσῃς Ἄρη
ἐμφύλιόν τε καὶ πρὸς ἀλλήλους θρασύν.
θυραῖος ἔστω πόλεμος, οὐ μόλις παρών,
ἐν ᾧ τις ἔσται δεινὸς εὐκλείας ἔρως·
ἐνοικίου δ᾽ ὄρνιθος οὐ λέγω μάχην.
τοιαῦθ᾽ ἑλέσθαι σοι πάρεστιν ἐξ ἐμοῦ,
εὖ δρῶσαν, εὖ πάσχουσαν, εὖ τιμωμένην
χώρας μετασχεῖν τῆσδε θεοφιλεστάτης.
In my territories please do not hurl
Blood-stained whetstones, damaging to the passions
Of the young, making them mad with rage not fuelled by wine,
Neither should you, making their hearts seethe like fighting cocks,
Establish the god of War among my citizens
Internal and savage against each other.
Let war be beyond the gates, present in abundance,
For the man in whom there will be a dread love for glory.
I do not value the fight of a bird inside its home.
These are the things which are there for you to choose from me,
Doing good, receiving good, being well honoured,
To have your share in this land most loved by gods.

Aeschylus, Eumenides 858–69.

This speech, part of Athena's persuasive appeal to the Furies, sets out a problem of violence, civil war and the young which would have been felt by all Greek states.[1] 'Athena' suggests that solutions lie in terms both of institutions and of civic and religious values. For the new democratic Athens represented as emerging in Aeschylus' trilogy, the plan recommended by the goddess is to avoid civil war and violent and feuding criminality by a system of laws, approved and passed by the popular assemblies and enforced by trials before juries which represent the people. By these means the aggressive emotions of competitiveness and anger to which the young are especially prone, whether or not aided by wine, will be restrained, while on the other hand their longing for honour and fame will be channelled into wars against the foreign enemies (which will not be lacking). The successful embedding into this judicial system of these Furies, now called the *Semnai Theai* and located under the Areopagos, an institutionalisation which is powerfully backed by Zeus and his Olympians, is seen as reflecting a growing social cohesion in the community and its acceptance of the fundamental idea that internal conflicts and crimes such as homicide should be settled by legal process involving citizen juries.[2]

While levels of violence inside and between Greek cities in the archaic and classical periods have been much discussed lately, they have also been the subject of broader debates across vast swathes of human history. For example, Steven Pinker's large-scale recent book *The Better Angels of our Nature* controversially argues that levels of violence – both between states and inside them – have undergone sustained and systematic reductions, especially from the early modern period (the 'Enlightenment') onwards. The analysis which deals with warfare, with its innumerable statistical tables, argues that the twentieth century has been marked by a 'Long Peace' and a decline, not an increase, in humans killed and destruction wreaked; this has been widely criticised, both for serious flaws in the statistics and for a tendency to be unduly apologetic towards Western, especially American, warmongering and neo-colonial imperialism. What is more relevant for this chapter is his identification of reductions in rates of homicide and other forms of violence, torture and cruelty inside nations and communities, particularly in Western societies, which have been less criticised. Many of Pinker's explanations for the steady bursts of decline in rates of homicide and violence from the Middle Ages to the twentieth century develop ideas found in Norbert Elias' pioneering *The Civilising Process*, originally written in German in the late 1930s.[3] Elias identified as key factors in the reduction of violent conflict the increasing acceptance of self-control in social contexts, and hence the adoption of social manners, politeness and the restraint of the impulses to honour, revenge and sexual licence; the development of a state's ability to monopolise violence; and forms of economic growth and greater prosperity through commerce involving sustained cooperation between organised groups. Pinker adopts these, and also places much weight on the gradual acceptance of libertarian or humanitarian ideals from the Enlightenment, on the concomitant decline in 'fundamentalist' ideals in religion, and on the widening acceptance of non-authoritarian, democratic or at least 'republican' forms of government.

Neither Pinker nor Elias pay much attention to the internal worlds of the classical Greek states, and Pinker does not suggest that classical Athens or other Greek states might have developed a good many of the features of the 'civilising process' and seen a corresponding reduction in levels of violence and homicide. Rather, he notes in passing that in 'ancient Greece' warfare and slavery were constant and fundamental, human sacrifice was not unknown (based, dubiously, on the *Iliad*), genocide occurred (e.g. Melos), female infanticide was common, and the 'moral circle' was limited to the members of the city-state.[4] But it might be profitable to consider whether in fact some of these constituents of the 'civilising process', which lead to diminishing levels of violence according to Elias and Pinker, did occur in some form in the political and social developments in Greek communities, and were incorporated in the ideals and values which its educational institutions sought to inculcate in their young.[5]

One justification for Pinker's neglect of ancient Greece may be that, as is universally agreed, no usable statistics for homicide or other violent crimes can be suggested for any Greek state at any time. Our limited evidence – from the archaic poets like Solon, Tyrtaeus and Theognis, and Herodotus and later fragmentary narratives – suggests that many archaic cities experienced high levels of political violence (murders, exiles, riots and so on), often leading to full-on civil wars; some cities evidently attempted to deal with this by passing laws, for example those against *hybris* (e.g. Solon in Athens), or against violence committed when drunk (Pittakos in Mytilene).[6] There is, on the other hand, a general agreement that in the fifth and fourth centuries, in democratic Athens at least, levels of homicide and violent crime became remarkably low (see pp.123–4). We lack evidence to uncover the ways in which other Greek cities developed their legal institutions and norms to achieve a comparable balance, and to assess their effectiveness. One can observe that many states continued to experience throughout the classical period much higher levels of internal strife and *stasis* than did Athens; but it is much harder to understand how effectively their laws and processes worked. Clearly in times of war and *stasis* legal processes might often be abused (e.g. at Corcyra: Thuc. 3.70).

The purpose of this chapter is to consider the role of education and military training in Greek cities in helping to contain violence in their societies, to channel legitimate violence against enemies, and to defend the boundaries of the community. All Greek cities must have developed a wide variety of mechanisms, practices and ideas to introduce their young males to their roles as citizens, trained to defend its territory and fight in its wars, to respect its laws and informal norms, and to understand its distinctive political ideologies and traditions. In relation to the avoidance of violence, Greeks recognised the particular need to focus on the upbringing of young males, given prevailing views about their characteristics (cf. Athena's plea previously quoted). Greeks generally held the young (e.g. between the ages of about 16–30) to be at their strongest, fittest and most effective in varied forms of organised combat, but also the least able to control their physical desires and anger, and the most likely to defend their sense of honour by engaging in unrestrained acts of insult and violence.[7]

Such standard views are set out most clearly and succinctly by Aristotle in his chapter on youth and age in the *Rhetoric* (2.12). The young are full of uncontrollable desires, especially those of sex; they are full of anger and hot-tempered, and, concomitantly, devoted to the pursuit of honour (*philotimoi*), victory and superiority, more than the desire for wealth. Being full of anger and hope, they are brave, tend to excess, and commit crimes from *hybris* rather than from wickedness. In conformity with this picture, Antiphon's *Tetralogy* 4 contains contrary arguments on whether the normally accepted assumption that the young are more prone to drunken violence can be relied on in a particular case; a comic fragment (Alexis 45/6K/A) suggests that aging in men operates as with wine, as the young froth in fermentation and work off their *hybris* and then settle down; a tragic fragment (Sophocles fr. 786R) states that *hybris* never reaches the sober stage of adulthood but blooms and withers among the young. More expansively, Theseus (and other characters) in Euripides' *Suppliants* agree that the decision to launch the campaign of the Seven against Thebes owed much to the powerful support of young men who:

> loved being honoured,
> and drove for wars regardless of justice,
> destroying the citizens, one seeking command in war,
> another to grab power in his hands and commit *hybris*,
> another to gain wealth, not considering
> the masses, whether they may be harmed by their suffering (232–7).[8]

Hence, when beginning to describe the supposedly excellent Spartan educational system, Xenophon claims that the early lawgiver Lycurgus realised that the most powerful pride grows in the young, *hybris* becomes prevalent, and the strongest desires for pleasures, so he prescribed as many labours as possible for them and no free time (Xen. *Lak. Pol.* 3.2).[9] Socialising systems, therefore, were needed to train and channel the energy and aggression of the young into socially and militarily useful directions, and seek to control their tendencies to *hybris*, drunken disorder and internal conflict.

Reconstructing the diachronic stages of development of socialising practices in different Greek cities in the archaic and classical periods is very difficult and has produced many controversies, as different theoretical approaches offer contrasting explanations of the lacunose source material. It is commonly held that one starting point, for many communities at least, was the existence in the Bronze Age or early Iron Age of secretive processes which may be considered as 'rites of passage' for males entering adulthood: systems of activities and rituals engaged in by boys and young men as part of their induction into kinship (or pseudo-kinship) cultic organisations, through which their civic identity, their membership of their communities, came to be mediated. If so, the argument goes, such practices were adapted and transformed over time in very different ways as the cities developed and introduced new forms of education and training appropriate to their ideals and values; aetiological myths containing elements of 'interpretative constructs' of originally initiatory practices, such as those of the cunning young hunter or warrior (the so-called 'Black Hunter'), may continue to inform the understanding of the processes of growing up.[10] These practices might involve elements such as military training, marginal or 'frontier'-based activities (e.g. hunting), organised pederastic pair-bonding, cross-dressing and collective rituals. No doubt during

the archaic period all cities developed their civic institutions and adapted requirements for citizenship in different ways; but for most of them they remain opaque
to us, as substantial evidence for their mechanisms tends to start only with the
Hellenistic epigraphic evidence for the institutions of the *gymnasia* and *ephebeiai*,
beyond the hints of myths and stories which possibly carry initiatory features. As
usual, the main exceptions where systematic explorations may be possible are
Sparta, the Cretan cities and Athens.

Sparta

Διαφέρομεν δὲ καὶ ταῖς τῶν πολεμικῶν μελέταις τῶν ἐναντίων τοῖσδε. τήν τε
γὰρ πόλιν κοινὴν παρέχομεν, καὶ οὐκ ἔστιν ὅτε ξενηλασίαις ἀπείργομέν τινα ἢ
μαθήματος ἢ θεάματος, ὃ μὴ κρυφθὲν ἄν τις τῶν πολεμίων ἰδὼν ὠφελη θείη,
πιστεύοντες οὐ ταῖς παρασκευαῖς τὸ πλέον καὶ ἀπάταις ἢ τῷ ἀφ᾽ ἡμῶν αὐτῶν ἐς
τὰ ἔργα εὐψύχῳ· καὶ ἐν ταῖς παιδείαις οἱ μὲν ἐπιπόνῳ ἀσκήσει εὐθὺς νέοι ὄντες
τὸ ἀνδρεῖον μετέρχονται, ἡμεῖς δὲ ἀνειμένως διαιτώμενοι οὐδὲν ἧσσον ἐπὶ τοὺς
ἰσοπαλεῖς κινδύνους χωροῦμεν.

We (*Athenians as opposed to the Spartans*) are different too from our opponents
in our policies in relation to warfare, in the following ways. We keep our polis
open, and we do not ever keep out anyone by foreigner-expulsions from learning
or viewing anything; we do not trust in anything which, if not kept secret, one of
our enemies might be able to see and benefit from, nor do we trust more in preparations and deceits than in the courage in action which stems from our own natures.
And in education they pursue manly virtue (*andreia*) right from early childhood
by a laborious training regime; we, however, while we spend our lives in a relaxed
fashion, we advance with no less determination to face the equivalent dangers.

—Perikles' funeral speech, Thuc. 2.39

In the late archaic and the classical periods Sparta developed a highly complex system of boys' education and socialisation, tightly organised by annual age-classes.
It seems to have been the most elaborate educational system of any Greek state (as
the succinct and pointed summary Thucydides attributes to Perikles suggests).[11]
Under its completed form (at the latest by the early fifth century) a complex pro-
gression took Spartan boys from c. 7–20, providing extensive training in physical
and military skills, endurance, and song and dance. It was all aimed at the inculca-
tion of political and social values designed to make them brave, loyal, cohesive
and effective citizens both in war and peace.[12] It was designed to foster the skills
appropriate to the defence of their polis against external attack and internal subver-
sion from their dependent labour force, the helots, involving intense military and
athletic training, the encouragement of controlled aggression and endurance, vol-
untary but pervasive homosexual pair-bonding, and ritual displays of endurance,
singing and dancing in festivals, which themselves reflected Spartan myths and
deities. All processes alike fostered appreciation of the state's laws and traditions.

There were three important stages in Spartan upbringing: boys (about 7–13),
youths (about 14–20) and young men (about 20–30). Boys up to about 13 (called

paides by Xen. *Lak. Pol.* 2) were organised in small sets, supervised by older youths (the *eirenes*), in a fairly unremitting life of gymnastics, fights and beatings; they were kept shoeless, on short rations and encouraged to steal. From c.14–21 the youths (called *paidiskoi* by Xen. *Lak. Pol.* 3) were organised in annual age-classes. Later sources record that each of these age-classes had its own peculiar name; most of these names appear in inscriptions of the Roman period, and all six of them are listed systematically in two late glosses on manuscripts of Herodotus and Strabo: this list seems to have been derived from Aristophanes of Byzantium's third-century treatise 'On the naming of Age-Groups' or *peri onomasias helikion* (see Table 5.2). Though these names do not appear in Xenophon's *Lakedaimonion Politeia* (see Table 5.1) or any other classical source, Aristophanes' date and his antiquarian interests in the language and literature of the classical past suggest that they were traditional names by his time, going back at least to the classical period, rather than very recent, archaising inventions of his own time, when the upbringing was radically reformed by Kleomenes III (235–22 BCE: Plut. *Kleom.* 11).[13] The precise meaning of many of the terms is unknown, but the general tenor is that they were reminded that they were not yet adults.[14]

A notable feature of this system is the insistence on accustoming the young at all stages of the process to mete out and accept violence and pain. Plato and Aristotle criticised Spartan education for being monolithically concerned with instilling courage and preparing for war (Pl. *Lg.* 688a; Arist. *Pol.* 1271a40–1271b7). Plato added that the system fostered an animal-like collective uniformity and did not repress tendencies to rage and savagery (*Lg.* 666e), while Aristotle argued that it deliberately encouraged an animal ferocity (*to theriodes*) through the labours

Table 5.1 Spartan age-groups according to Xenophon (*Lak. Pol.* 2–4)

Age	Name	Meaning
7–13	Paides	boy
14–20	paidiskoi	adolescents
20–21?	eirenes/irenes	near adults
20–30	hebontes	young adults

Table 5.2 Spartan age-groups (c. 14–21) according to Aristophanes of Byzantium

Age	Name	Meaning
14–15	Rhobidai	?
15–16	prokomizomenoi	?
16–17	mikizomenoi or mikichizomenoi	?
17–18	propaides	nearly boys?
18–19	paides	boys
19–20	melleirenes	about to be youths
20–21	eirenes	youths

imposed, which was not the same as proper courage and proved counterproductive (*Pol.* 1338b9–38).[15] According to Xenophon, whipping and tests of endurance were ubiquitous: the *paidonomos* in charge of all the boys was charged with administering severe punishments on any slackers, and he was assigned also a band of young men (*hebontes*) equipped with whips to punish boys where needed; where these controllers were absent, any citizen could instruct and punish the boys (*Lak. Pol.* 2.2, 2.10). Boys were encouraged to supplement their minimal rations by thefts, subjected to beatings if caught (Xen. *Lak. Pol.* 2.7–8; cf. Plut. *Lyc.* 17). Physical competitions at the festivals involved pain and struggle; at the ritual for Artemis Orthia boys and adolescents competing to steal the cheeses faced whippings (Xen. *Lak. Pol.* 2.7; Pl. *Lg.* 633b; Ducat 2006a: 253–6),[16] and the Gymnopaidia featured contests in naked dancing in intense summer heat (Hdt. 6.67; Xen. *Hell.* 6.4.16; Pl. *Lg.* 633; Plut. *Ages.* 29.3, *Lyc.* 21; Athenaeus 630d–631b). According to Pausanias, organised and savage fights and ball games between teams of 'ephebes' took place at the Platanistas (3.14.8–9); it is possible, but not certain, that precursors of organised fights occurred in the classical period.[17] According to Plutarch, ritualised fighting between the rival 'herds' (*agelai*) of youths was constant and encouraged (*Lyc.* 16–17); here hints in classical sources (e.g. Pl. *Lg.* 633b) and possible Cretan parallels (Strabo 10.4.20, see p. 111) may suggest these practices existed then.[18]

The emotional intensity and competition involved in growing up in this complex system of peer-groups and supervisors was, for most perhaps, enhanced by the practice of approved homosexual 'loves' between older and younger youths. While apparently not compulsory, this was seen as an important part of the upbringing. According to Xenophon (*Lak. Pol.* 2.12–13), such relationships, if based on admiration for the boy's character, were 'pure' and constituted the 'finest education', but for a youth's desire to be seen to focused on the boy's body was regarded as wholly disgraceful. A boy from about age 12 was invited to form a lasting relationship with an older 'lover' (*erastes*), who was to act as his role model, develop his character and encourage his performance in all aspects of the disciplined and competitive lifestyle. State approval is indicated by the rule that a lover might be fined by magistrates, if his boyfriend showed insufficient endurance (Plut. *Lyc.* 18).[19] While the youths up until c. 20 would normally eat their austere provisions collectively under supervision, their lovers might on occasion introduce their adolescent boyfriends into their adult common messes (*syssitia*), for them to get a taste of them as continuing 'schools of self-discipline', to hear political discussions and see entertainments appropriate for free men (Plut. *Lyc.* 12). The expectation was that in due course a boyfriend would be admitted to his lover's mess, when, at c. 20, they would also be admitted into the army, and very probably mess-members served in the same army units.

This programme of gymnastics, hunting and team-fighting clearly made young Spartans fit, tough, and inured to inflicting and receiving pain. They were probably also given more specific military preparations than in other states: Spartan hoplites were the only Greek soldiers trained to advance to the rhythm of the pipes (Thuc. 5.70), and could operate chains of command and perform complex manoeuvres on campaign more effectively (Thuc. 5.66; Xen. *Lak. Pol.* 12.5–10; cf. Polyb. 4.20.6). Until the fourth century, when other states paid more attention to military training, and their army began to suffer defeats, it was generally thought that Sparta's success rested on her much more extensive training, though Aristotle observed that later events showed no more than that other states had hitherto virtually ignored such practices (*Pol.* 1338b25–9).[20]

It is not clear to what extent those in the second and third stages of the upbringing (Xenophon's *paidiskoi* and *eirenes*) were charged with defending the frontiers and the countryside before and after c. 370 BCE. What sources there are concern the activities of select groups of near-adults and young adults, the so-called *kryptoi* and the *hippeis*, and, characteristically, their operations mostly concern internal security and operations against the helots, rather than defence against foreign raids or invasions. This may be thought to support Thucydides' famous statement 'most Spartan institutions have always been designed with a view to security against the helots' (4.80), and the remark attributed by Xenophon to the conspirator Kinadon that all classes in Spartan territory, except the ruling Spartiates, would happily eat their masters raw (*Hell.* 3.3.6).[21] Sparta was famously free from major land invasions from its sixth-century rise to hegemony in the Peloponnese to the Theban and Arcadian attacks following the defeat at Leuktra in 371 BCE. But from the start of the Peloponnesian War, Athenian seaborne raids and other threats to Spartan territory brought responses in the form of fortification systems along the eastern and western coasts, and many more frontier forts were built after 370 in response to the creation of Messene and the Arcadian federation centred on Megalopolis, both by Spartans and by their opponents.[22] Historical texts attest garrisons placed in or sent to frontier settlements to face wartime raids or invasion war (e.g. Thuc. 2.25, 2.56, 4.8, 4.55; Xen. *Hell.* 6.5.24–7), though specific evidence for the use of *paidiskoi* or *eirenes* as garrisoning troops is lacking.

The *hippeis*, 300 elite hoplites serving probably for one year, chosen mostly or entirely from the c. 20–30 age-groups, were selected in a public and competitive process, 100 each by the three *hippagretai*, who had themselves been chosen by the ephors. The selection process produced further possibilities for controlled inter-Spartiate violence. The process was intended, as Xenophon makes clear, to excite an intense and continuous competition to be seen to be among the very best of the young Spartiates; even following the selection those unsuccessful would scrutinise critically those chosen and often fight them, though any Spartiate passersby was obliged to part them, and any who obstructed a mediator might be fined by the ephors (Xen. *Lak. Pol.* 4).

The *hippeis* are recorded as acting as specialised troops operating in battle, as guards to the Kings, as scouts (here, perhaps, on horseback, as their name implies they originally formed the Spartan cavalry), and, often in smaller groups, as performing special missions especially in relation to internal security. The most significant example is the prominent role played by one of the *hippagretai* and six or seven of his men, presumably from his 100 of the *hippeis*, in arresting Kinadon and hence foiling his dangerous conspiracy (Xen. *Hell.* 3.3.8–11).[23] It was no doubt thought that the process of selection as those who excelled over decades of organised training and defended themselves effectively in constant personal fights with their rivals produced crack soldiers who would be alike cohesive, loyal, decisive and, where necessary, ruthlessly violent.

Secondly, but problematically, there was the 'Secret Service', the *krypteia*. Not mentioned in Xenophon, a force of this name is first discussed in Plato's *Laws* (c. 350), along with other examples of endurance tests for Spartans, whose members had to operate barefoot in winter, sleep without bedding, without slave attendants, roaming night and day across the whole territory (*Lg. 633b-c*). Plato's Spartan Megillos does not mention the elements of helot-control by killings which are central to the description in Plutarch (*Lyc. 28*);

ἡ δὲ καλουμένη κρυπτεία παρ' αὐτοῖς, εἴ γε δὴ τοῦτο τῶν Λυκούργου πολιτευμάτων ἕν ἐστιν, ὡς Ἀριστοτέλης ἱστόρηκε, ταύτην ἂν εἴη καὶ τῷ Πλάτωνι περὶ τῆς πολιτείας καὶ τοῦ ἀνδρὸς ἐνειργασμένη δόξαν. ἦν δὲ τοιαύτη· τῶν νέων οἱ ἄρχοντες διὰ χρόνου τοὺς μάλιστα νοῦν ἔχειν δοκοῦντας εἰς τὴν χώραν ἄλλως ἐξέπεμπον, ἔχοντας ἐγχειρίδια καὶ τροφὴν ἀναγκαίαν, ἄλλο δὲ οὐδέν· οἱ δὲ μεθ' ἡμέραν μὲν εἰς ἀσυνδήλους διασπειρόμενοι τόπους, ἀπέκρυπτον ἑαυτοὺς καὶ ἀνεπαύοντο, νύκτωρ δὲ κατιόντες εἰς τὰς ὁδοὺς τῶν εἱλώτων τὸν ἁλισκόμενον ἀπέσφαττον. πολλάκις δὲ καὶ τοῖς ἀγροῖς ἐπιπορευόμενοι τοὺς ῥωμαλεωτάτους καὶ κρατίστους αὐτῶν ἀνήρουν.

The so-called *krypteia* of theirs, if it really was one of Lycurgus' institutions, as Aristotle has recorded, may well be what led Plato as well to that opinion about the system and the man. It operated like this: the leaders from time to time would send out those of the young who seemed to have the most sense into the countryside in different directions, equipped with daggers and sufficient provisions, but nothing else. By day they would make their way in scattered groups to remote places and hide themselves and rest. At night they would come down into the roads and slaughter any of the helots they caught. Often too they journeyed into the fields and did away with the strongest and bravest of them. Aristotle makes the further notable point that immediately upon taking up office the ephors would declare war on the Helots, so that they could be killed without pollution.

It seems pretty certain that the whole of this section in Plutarch derives directly from Aristotle's *Constitution of the Spartans*; he cites Aristotle at the start and the end, and an Aristotelian fragment quoted by Herakleides (fr. 611R) confirms an Aristotelian origin for the crucial bit in the middle describing how the *kryptoi* hid by night and day and disposed of those helots they thought necessary. Plutarch later in the chapter takes the view that such harsh measures as the *krypteia* should not be attributed, as did Aristotle, to Lycurgus (or to the ancient system), but were introduced when the helots were thought to be a much greater threat after the earthquake and helot revolt in the mid-450s BCE. There is one further source, from the later commentaries on Plato's text (*Scholia on Laws* 633b) which expands on his, rather than Aristotle's, version, and may (or may not) be based on good earlier evidence: this adds the further details that this was another form of training for war and that it lasted one year.[24]

Unfortunately, the origins of this practice and the importance and frequency of helot-killing to it are greatly disputed. Three current views may be distinguished. First, more or less following Aristotle, many hold that the institution with its security function against the helots was introduced in the sixth or early fifth century, and was a heavily re-institutionalised adaptation, of the sixth or early fifth century, of old initiation practices.[25] Secondly, some follow Plutarch and see the helot-killing as a later response to a large crisis, for example after the earthquake and the major helot revolt c. 465 BCE, coupled with the growing awareness of the failure to reproduce the Spartiate population.[26] Most recently it has been proposed that it was only introduced after the bigger crises of the defeat at Leuktra in 371 BCE, the invasions of Laconia and the creation of the independent Messenia and a powerful federal Arcadian state in 370–69.[27]

This latest suggestion rests on the absence of any reference to the institution before Plato's in c. 350 BCE, most significantly its absence from Xenophon, and from some interesting observations by Azoulay 2006 on Isocrates' *Archidamos*, a pamphlet written c. 366 BCE as if it were a speech delivered by the young Spartan prince Archidamos to the Spartan assembly.[28] Azoulay argued that the speech's suggestion that the Spartans fight to the bitter end to recover Messenia, if necessary sending their wives, children and non-combatants away, abandon the city and live like an army on the move (wandering, *planasthai*), uses as its frames of reference both historical examples of desperate measures from the Spartan past (e.g. Heraklids), or of other Greeks (e.g. Athens at Salamis), mercenary armies like Xenophon's 10,000 in Asia, and also the current *krypteia*, where young Spartans roam across the countryside hunting helots. Azoulay contemplated two possibilities: first, that the *krypteia* existed as a helot-controlling measure before 371 BCE (and hence might have been originally modelled on initiatory practices), and was enhanced and refocused c. 370 to attack now in guerrilla fashion 'liberated' Messenians in a way comparable to the reformation of the Athenians *ephebeia* after 336; or second, that it was created as a new institution in 370, to attack and kill 'helots' across the territory. In either case, Azoulay argued, plausibly, that Isocrates was aware of the institution and is in effect suggesting its expansion to become the strategy of the whole army, who would operate like the *kryptoi* as a mobile, wandering force using the weapon of surprise. Christien then sought to build on Azoulay and to strengthen the case for his second alternative, a post-Leuktra creation of the *krypteia* itself.[29]

Against this, one can first explain Xenophon's silence by supposing that in a relatively brief and positive account of the upbringing he chose to omit any reference to a controversial element, part of the endurance tests imposed on the young. Second, Plato's emphasis on the endurance of the *kryptoi* might be odd if it was entirely a recent institution expressly directed at controlling the newly freed Messenians; and third, it seems to me unlikely that Aristotle, writing a detailed account of the Spartan system in the 330s and 320s BCE, would suppose it was part of the 'Lycurgan' system, i.e. ancient practice, if it had been created after the breakdown of much of that system which he analysed in the *Politics*. It seems more likely that at some time before the Peloponnesian War existing practices, whereby some of all of those approaching or at the end of the upbringing spent sustained spells in solitary hunting and roughing it in the mountains, following the patterns of adolescent initiation (the 'Black Hunter' model), were gradually transformed into groups focused onto an increasingly ruthless and violent form of purging of dissident helots.[30] Whether this occurred some time during the sixth century, or after the crisis of the mid-fifth, has to be left open.

These inadequate sources do not reveal the age of the *kryptoi*, and choice seems to rest between young men at the end of the second stage of the process (*melleirenes*, or ephebes as the later general Greek term would designate them)[31] or those at the start of the *eirenes* stage, perhaps some or all of the *hippeis*.[32] Nor is it clear what numbers participated, or for how long. If it was an institution with a long history, these details may well have been subject to change over time, probably in the direction of greater frequency and ruthlessness, in response to growing alarms.

The Spartan state, then, seems in principle to have asserted the monopoly of violence, but then, to an unusual degree, it encouraged fighting between young Spartiates under fixed conditions. Young Spartans, then, were inured to engage in violent action and endure pain in a wide variety of ways and contexts, most surprisingly in the form of socially encouraged fighting between competing subgroups of youngsters, or successful and less successful candidates to be *hippeis*. One aim, to produce tough men of action, ready to respond swiftly to threats or insults, seems to have been largely achieved. The training in controlled violence surely helped the authorities to sustain a ruthless approach to threats from dissidents or rebellious helots (e.g. Kinadon's uprising, the *krypteia*, or the alleged murder of c. 2000 helots during the Peloponnesian War: Thuc. 4.80). But the Spartans' confidence and ready recourse to violence upset many outside their frontiers, among both their enemies and their allies. Collectively, their treatment of captives and defeated enemies in the Peloponnesian War initiated chains of atrocities (e.g. Thuc. 2.67, 3.32, 3.68, 5.83; Ste. Croix 1972: 20–2, 157–9); and, as shown by the excellent article by Simon Hornblower, the arrogant and violent treatment of other Greeks, especially their supposed friends, by many Spartans in positions of authority, often wielding their official staffs or batons (*bakteriai*), damaged Spartan prestige and interests (e.g. Thuc. 1.95, 3.93, 8.84; Xen. *Anab.* 2.3.11; Plut. *Arist.* 11, *Lys.* 5.7; Hornblower 2000).[33]

Unfortunately, there is very little evidence enabling us to assess how far this fierce, constant, competitiveness and sustained customization to violence caused problems of disorder and violent crimes between Spartiates at home. Such evidence as we have for legal trials at Sparta concern kings, commanders or soldiers accused of treason, cowardice, bribery and the like; we do not even know what penalties were imposed for (e.g.) homicide or assault.[34] The aim presumably was that these tendencies would be kept under firm control by the pressures of social conformity, sociability and shaming procedures. The upbringing instilled a general emphasis on discipline and obedience;[35] the festivals with their contests in choral performances of traditional songs created a cohesive, competitive, spirit among the tribes and other sub-groups; for those older than twenty, comparable cohesion was, in theory, constantly reinforced above all by the messes (*syssitia*) with their shared meals, social enjoyments and peer pressures. Membership of such messes, each apparently small in number, remained the basis of citizens' political and social life.[36] As members were men of all ages, the atmosphere was supposedly set by the older and more experienced, restraining drunkenness or shameful behaviour and encouraging friendly cooperation and discussions of great deeds for the state (Xen. *Lak. Pol.* 5.5). Friendships emerging from the pederastic relationships and continuing in the messes were often of considerable political importance.[37] The centrality of courage and discipline as primary virtues (asserted at Hdt. 7.104) was reinforced by specific shaming procedures: a Spartan who showed cowardice in battle might be labelled a 'trembler' (*tresas*) and subjected to a number of dishonouring sanctions, designed to make life not worth living. In practice this penalty seems to have been applied rarely and decreasingly from the later fifth century, when Spartan citizen manpower was in sharp decline.[38]

In relation to violence, the expectation was that bystanders would prevent the regular group or individual fights from getting out of control (Xen. *Lak. Pol.* 4.6), and there were measures taken to restrain drunkenness at the meals of the *syssitia* (Xen. *Lak. Pol.* 5; Plut. *Lyc.* 10–12, 28).[39] We know of no certain internal cases of homicide or grievous injuries, and Hornblower is probably right to suspect that they were relatively rare.[40] One mythical anecdote and one dubiously historical case both emphasise how shocked Spartiates were expected to be at such violence: the mythical Alkandros, who poked out Lycurgus' eye with his *bakteria*, and Kleomenes I, who, when mad, went around poking Spartiates in the face (Hdt. 6.75). So another of the paradoxes fundamental to Spartan society may well have been the coexistence of a high degree of permitted, even expected, violence between aggressive, honour-sensitive and militarily well-trained citizens, and a relatively low level of serious fighting and killings. As with so many of its other paradoxes, one fundamental reason, as Thucydides saw, is the constant consciousness of the need for security against the unfree populations in Laconia and Messenia.

Crete

It makes sense to follow this treatment of Spartan institutions with a brief discussion of procedures in Cretan cities. Information about practices in the many Cretan cities in the archaic and classical periods rests in part on generalised accounts in fourth-century political theorisers such as Plato, Isocrates and Ephorus; these are fundamentally based on the common belief that there were close parallels and mutual influence between Spartan and Cretan institutions. Limited control can be imposed on this by use of archaic and classical inscriptions recording laws and procedures (most famously the Gortyn laws) and extrapolation back from the much more numerous Hellenistic inscriptions; considerable discrepancies emerge.[41] Historical texts suggest that small-scale wars, raiding and internal *stasis* in many of the Cretan cities were frequent in the classical period, and even more prevalent in the Hellenistic period.[42] It is hence appropriate that the general-ised account of rites of passage and preparations of the young for membership of their communities found in Strabo's account, explicitly based on Ephorus (Strabo 10.4.16–22; Ephorus *FGrHist* 70 F149), emphasises how Cretan cities demanded of their youths extensive collective training in athletics and warfare. The younger males were expected to learn their letters and songs derived from their customs and laws,[43] to attend the men's messes or dining clubs (*andreia*), wearing shabby and skimpy clothing all year round, and to engage in constant fights inside their messes and between different messes. Older youths trained, raced and hunted, living in groups called 'herds' (*agelai*) at public expense; the herds engaged in practice battles against each other.[44] Sexualised pair-bonding was evidently an important part of the system, at least for many. Lovers 'abducted' their socially approved beloveds and spent two months with them hunting and feasting in the countryside; the culmination of the relationship was when the pair returned to their *andreion* and the beloved received symbols of adulthood as presents (mili-tary equipment, an ox and a drinking cup). According to Strabo, it was an honour for boys to attract a reputable lover and a disgrace for an attractive or well-born boy to fail to attract one; it seems likely then that such pairings became not an initiatory requirement for all future citizens, but rather a commonly enacted and sanctioned affectionate relationship.[45] Such homoerotic practices would then seem to have been re-institutionalised to constitute entry requirements for the male *andreia*, through which community membership was negotiated.[46]

It is clear that the fourth-century intellectuals' supposition that all Cretan cities had very much the same constitution and institutions is at best a serious over-simplification, and we cannot know which city, if any, best exemplified the general patterns presented by Plato, Ephorus and Aristotle.[47] Nonetheless, some archaeological traces and many inscriptions lend support to the view that some social realities and institutions underlie these basic accounts.[48] For example, the eighth- or seventh-century bronzes of nude pairs of men and youths with hunting equipment found at Kato Simi provide plausible evidence for early homosexual pair-bondings.[49] Cretans in antiquity excelled at running, especially long-distance running in the mountains (cf. Pl. *Lg.* 625d).[50] Hellenistic inscriptions show the significance of running in the socialisation process and as an essential activity of citizens, and strengthen the impression of continuity of ancient initiation rites and practices featuring hunting, transvestism, military training, choral song and feast-ing. In inscriptions from many cities we find young men passing from the status of *apodromoi* (not-yet-runners)[51] to that of *dromeis* (runners) at rituals which typi-cally involved a transference from female to adult male dress (*Ekdysia*), as they swore their citizenship oath (elements of which may well be of archaic origin). As has been demonstrated by Tzifopoulos,[52] these runners' (*dromeis*) are those of immediate post-'ephebic' age who have been admitted to adult status and with it gained access to the running events (*dromoi*) and training facilities (*gymnasia*), that is probably those aged c. 20–30.[53] Many Cretan festivals celebrated boys' coming of age; their titles, brief descriptions in some inscriptions and associated myths suggest rituals involving exchanges of clothing or the temporary adoption of nudity.[54] For the *Ekdysia* ('Taking off') at Phaistos we have the description of its related myth, which featured Galateia, Lampros and their daughter, who was raised as a boy and in accordance with her mother's wishes was transformed at maturity into the youth Leukippos (Antonius Liberalis *Met.* 17); youths at Mallia, Lyttos, Dreros and Axos are said to strip (*egduomenoi*) when swearing their citizenship oaths.[55] Hence it seems that in many places at the culmination of the rite new citizens shed ('*ekdyesthai*') their perhaps feminised clothing, were seen naked, and then received adult male clothes or armour.[56]

It seems evident that such training and socialisation, which persisted over centuries, produced warrior citizens who fought in the constant warfare between the cities, in piratical raiding, or served as mercenaries across the eastern Mediterranean.[57] There is very little evidence to enable an assessment of how far this emphasis in socialisation on collective rigour and discipline, coupled with the acquisition of respect for the detailed laws of the Cretan cities, achieved social cohesion and restrained too easy a recourse to violence to resolve disputes, or express self-assertion and drunken aggression. Aristotle thought that the Cretan constitutions did not work well, community spirit was weakened, and anarchy, *stasis* and internal wars were prevalent in the Cretan cities; but not all of his reasoning is supported by the inscriptions. He claimed that the *kosmoi*, the chief magistrates, were selected from a restricted set of families (*gene*) and that the *gerontes* (councillors), who were ex-*kosmoi*, were not accountable and tended to make decisions on their own initiative, and not according to written laws (*Pol.* 1272a27-b16), but the inscriptional record from Gortyn and other cities does not support these positions on the constitutions.[58] But even so the apparent prevalence of *stasis* as well as wars on the island, at least from the fourth century BCE onwards, encourages one to doubt how effectively violence between citizens was in practice controlled.

Athens

"We, however, while we spend our lives in a relaxed fashion, we advance with no less determination to face the equivalent dangers" (Thuc. 2.39). As Thucydides' Perikles implies, fifth-century Athenian education and military training, largely kept separate, were both rudimentary and uncoordinated compared to the picture at Sparta. His emphasis on the easygoing, but nonetheless effective nature of Athenian upbringing is part of his praise of Athens' democratic system and its ideal of the individual freedom of male citizens including the freedom of action ('living as one wishes') and freedom of speech (*parrhesia*). (Thuc. 2.37–45).[59] By the early fifth century, at the latest, schools and *gymnasia* and *palaistrai* were available at Athens, as across the Greek world, to teach boys the basic triad of literacy (*grammata*), music and singing (*mousike*), and athletics (*gymnastike*) (see e.g. Hdt. 6.27; Pausanias 6.9.6–8; Thuc. 7.29); and, increasingly from the mid-fifth century, the growing democratic system at Athens created a requirement of basic literacy for many citizens who participated in the system as councillors, jurors and other officials.[60] Attendance at Athens' schools and gymnasia was encouraged, but was not compulsory, and there was no state financial support

(Arist. *Pol.* 1337a5–25); as 'Protagoras' says in the speech given to him in Plato's dialogue, wealthy fathers were able to keep their sons at schools and *gymnasia* for longer than the poor (*Prot.* 323d-e).[61] The personified Laws in Plato's *Crito* (50d-e) claim – with exaggeration – that they 'required' Socrates' father to 'educate his sons in *mousike* and *gymnastike*'. In the later fourth century, Aeschines claimed that Solon passed laws regulating opening hours and teachers at schools and *gymnasia*, to protect the boys from abuse (1.9–10); the attribution to Solon is doubtful, but it is quite likely that these laws were established during the late sixth or early fifth century.[62]

These schools taught more than basic literacy and numeracy,[63] and it was held that they aimed also at the instilling of discipline, good order and the moral values suitable for 'good men'. There is little sign, however, that the schoolteachers did this by formal teaching of the institutions, laws or history of their city. But they taught 'letters' by making pupils learn and recite poetic texts, above all Homer and traditional choral songs (Pl. *Prot.* 325d-326e; Ar. *Nub.* 961–1062, *Ran.* 1054–5), in the belief that Homer would encourage preparedness to fight for their city and its political and moral principles, while choral songs would impart both discipline and awareness of their city's traditions, gods and religious rituals, and highlights of their mythical and historical past (cf. Pl. *Ion*; Xen. *Symp.* 3.4–6, *Mem.* 3.5.7–12; Lycurgus 1.102–4).[64] Discussions and memories inside the family no doubt reinforced some basic awareness of their political culture and the fundamental social values, above all those associated with honour, shame and reciprocity.[65]

Probably more important than schooling for young citizens in terms of the acquisition of understanding of the values of civilisation, cooperation and the traditions of the city and its gods was their membership of the sub-groups of the city and involvement in their activities. Boys were admitted, probably at c. 16 years, to an older pseudo-kinship group, the phratry, at the sacrifice and festival of the Apatouria, and at c. 18 to the institutions created in 508–7 by Cleisthenes, the local deme, and its linked wider groupings, the trittyes and the tribes (*phylai*).[66] In Plato's *Laws* book 2 all participants in the discussion agree that singing and dancing in a chorus throughout one's life was the right and proper way to learn and maintain the moral values of the community; an uneducated man was *achoreutos*, not a member of a chorus (654a). Further, performing and listening to the rhythms and tunes of music and song were thought to have the power to stir emotions and to instil moral character.[67] It is therefore significant that a good number – in my view, a very substantial number – of citizen boys and youths would participate in choral singing in the many contests involving competing teams from the ten tribes, the competitions in and cyclic contests (dithyrambs), tragedies and comedies, and in torch relay races, at state festivals such as the Dionysia, Lenaia, Panathenaia and Thargelia.[68]

The question of the development of measures designed to train future citizens for war, and use them in military contexts, has been as controversial as the issues of Spartan *krypteia*. But two recent major contributions encourage one to hope that many disagreements over the Athenian *ephebeia* can be put to rest. The unfortunately unpublished Oxford thesis by H. de Marcellus[69] and the first chapter of

A. Chankowski's book *L'Éphébie hellénistique*[70] are in essential agreement on many issues and present a largely compelling case.[71] It seems clear that it was not until Epicrates' reform of the mid-330s BCE – part of the widespread renewal of Athens' military, religious and moral order associated with the policies of Lycurgus and his colleagues – that the full two-year programme called the *ephebeia* was created, as described in Arist. *Ath. Pol.* 42 and reflected in a large number of inscriptions.[72] This imposed extensive training in different military skills and tours of duty garrisoning the frontiers, in tribal contingents under the control of ten 'Regulators' (*sophronistai*) and a single 'Director' (*kosmetes*); it became a model for similar institutions in many other states.[73]

Between the archaic period and 335–4 BCE we can see signs of organised ceremonies for those coming of age, and evidence for some training and garrison duties for future soldiers, rather unsystematic initially, but steadily increasing. The development may be divided into four chronological stages: (i) the archaic period before the reforms of Cleisthenes and his creation of the demes and tribes (508/7 BCE); (ii) from 507 BCE to the end of the Peloponnesian War; (iii) from the early fourth century to the beginning of the Lycurgan age, c. 400–340s; and (iv) the period of reform and the full programme established by Epicrates' law.

Stage 1: Pre-Cleisthenes

The essential piece of evidence for the pre-Cleisthenic period comes, ironically enough, from a text first put on stone and quoted in public speeches at around the time of the Lycurgan reform, namely the formal oath sworn collectively by new citizens, called by this time the 'oath of the *epheboi*'. It has been convincingly argued that the oath itself and much at least of the text we have must be archaic. The oath was quoted in the assembly by Aeschines in 348 BCE ('the oath of the ephebes in the sanctuary of Aglauros': Dem. 19.302); it was quoted again in the surviving speech by Lycurgus in the trial of Leokrates (1.76–7: 330 BCE).[74] A version of the text occurs in two later authors (Pollux 8.105–6; Stob. 43.48); another version which differs in subtle ways was inscribed, along with the oath sworn by Greeks before the battle of Plataea, on a dedication made by the priest of Ares and Athena Areia at Acharnai, accompanying a decision to build an altar at this sanctuary.[75] The style of the sculptural relief and the letter forms of the text suggest a date of this dedication c. 350–30 BCE; it could then have been set up either shortly before or after Epicrates' law of 335/4 BCE.[76] Here is the inscription:

θεοί.
ἱερεὺς Ἄρεως καὶ Ἀθηνᾶς
Ἀρείας Δίων Δίωνος Ἀχαρ-
νεὺς ἀνέθηκεν.

ὅρκος ἐφήβων πάτριος, ὃν ὀμνύναι δεῖ τ-
οὺς ἐφήβους. οὐκ αἰσχυνῶ τὰ ἱερὰ ὅπ-
λα οὐδὲ λείψω τὸν παραστάτην ὅπου ἂν σ-

τειχήσω· ἀμυνῶ δὲ καὶ ὑπὲρ ἱερῶν καὶ ὁσ-
ίων καὶ ὀκ ἐλάττω παραδώσω τὴν πατρίδ-
α, πλείω δὲ καὶ ἀρείω κατά τε ἐμαυτὸν κα-
ὶ μετὰ ἁπάντων, καὶ εὐηκοήσω τῶν ἀεὶ κραινόντων ἐμφρόνως καὶ τῶν θεσμῶν τῶν
ἱδρυμένων καὶ οὓς ἂν τὸ λοιπὸν ἱδρύσω-
νται ἐμφρόνως· ἐὰν δέ τις ἀναιρεῖ, οὐκ ἐ-
πιτρέψω κατά τε ἐμαυτὸν καὶ μετὰ πάντ-
ων, καὶ τιμήσω ἱερὰ τὰ πάτρια. Ἵστορες [[ο]]
θεοὶ Ἄγλαυρος, Ἑστία, Ἐνυώ, Ἐνυάλιος, Ἄρ-
ης καὶ Ἀθηνᾶ Ἀρεία, Ζεύς, Θαλλώ, Αὐξώ, Ἡγε-
μόνη, Ἡρακλῆς, ὅροι τῆς πατρίδος, πυροί,
κριθαί, ἄμπελοι, ἐλᾶαι, συκαῖ.

GODS

The priest of Ares and Athena
Areia, Dion, son of Dion, of Acharnai
set this up.

This oath was sworn in the shrine of Aglauros.   5
Ancestral Oath of the *epheboi* which is to be sworn by the
epheboi: . . . I will not shame the sacred
arms, nor will I abandon my comrade wherever
I am stationed. I will fight for the defence of things both sacred
and profane, and I shall not leave my country diminished,   10
but greater and more powerful, as far as I am able
and with the help of all. I will obey whoever may be at any time
holding offices in their wisdom, and the established
laws and any others which they may in their wisdom
establish in future. If any person seeks to overthrow them, I shall   15
not permit him, as far as I am able and with the help of all.
I will honour the ancestral sacred rites. Witnesses
to this shall be the gods Aglauros, Hestia, Enyo, Enyalios,
Ares and Athena Areia, Zeus, Thallo, Auxo,
Hegemone, Herakles, the boundaries of the country, wheat,   20
barley, vines, olive trees, fig trees.

The case for accepting the assertion of the priest and the orators that this is
in essence the ancient and traditional oath rests firstly on phrases which look
ancient: one might select 'I will fight for the defence of things both sacred and
profane (*hiera kai hosia*)';[77] 'those holding offices in their wisdom' – *krainontōn
phronimōs* – which also suggests a pre-democratic mode of making laws; or 'the
established ordinances' (*thesmoi*, not *nomoi*).[78] Secondly, it rests on echoes of the
language which can be found in fifth-century literary texts (Thuc. 1.144, 2.37;
Aesch. *Pers.* 955–62; Soph. *Ant.* 663–71);[79] and finally on the ancient-looking

collection of local deities, personifications and central elements of the community, which are adduced at the end as witnesses to the oath ('Aglauros, Hestia, Enyo, Enyalios, Ares and Athena Areia, Zeus, Thallo, Auxo, Hegemone, Herakles, the boundaries of the country, wheat, barley, vines, olive trees, fig trees').[80]

The occasions when the oath was sworn, however, must have changed with institutional developments. Before Cleisthenes, one might speculate that boys swore it at their incorporation (c. 16) into their phratry at its festival of the Apatouria, when on the third day, *Koureotis*, the phratry performed the larger ritual (*koureion*) of incorporation,[81] and cut and dedicated some of their hair, as a symbol of their change of status.[82] Some time after Cleisthenes, the oath must have been transferred to the occasion of their admission to their deme, and after 335/4 it became integrated into the formal ephebic process: according to Lycurgus, 'when they were inscribed on the deme list of citizens (*lexiarchikon grammateion*) and became ephebes' (Lyc. 1.76).[83] There is no evidence before the fifth century for specific collective activities – military, athletic, hunting or erotic – engaged in by specific groups of youths as they approached admission to membership of their phratries, or other local or pseudo-kinship groups.[84] Some training for Athens' wars by land and sea presumably occurred before an expedition set off or an enemy raid was resisted, but it was perhaps more likely to have been organised by the *naukraroi* through the 48 naucraries, than anything to do with the phratries or *gene*, if Lambert and van Wees are right to retain the connection of the naucraries with cavalry and ships (Pollux 8.108).[85] Aggressive raids, and defence against raids from outside, were apparently matters for the wealthy *naukraroi* and their supporters in the naucraries.[86] Athletic training, hunting and erotic pursuits of boys and youths by older young men were evidently all popular social pursuits from the sixth century on, particularly among the leisured classes, but they operated in optional settings such as the *gymnasia* and *symposia*.[87] It is possible that in earlier centuries there had been, as elsewhere, authorised homosexual bondings in connection to admission to pseudo-kinship groups such as the phratries; but no traces of them survive.

The argument for a pre-Cleisthenic association between phratry incorporation into manhood and citizenship and 'initiatory' ideas of hunting wild animals, defending the frontiers or cross-dressing, rests, as famously exemplified by Pierre Vidal-Naquet's 'Black Hunter' theory, on the myths connected with the Apatouria and with other festivals such as the Oschophoria, especially involving the exploits of the young Theseus. The Apatouria was a very ancient festival, celebrated by almost all the Ionian cities (Hdt. 1.147), and etymologically the name probably came from *homopatoria* ('from the same father'); this suggests that the Athenian phratry, in some form, was also an ancient, supposedly kinship, grouping.[88] The main myth associated with it featured a frontier war against the Boeotians, which was settled by a single combat between the Boeotian king Xanthios (Fair One) and Melanthos (Dark One), the champion of the Athenian King Thymoites, which the Athenian won by the well-known trick of pretending Xanthios had brought a companion (Hellanicus *FGrHist* 323aF23; Ephorus *FGrHist* 70F22).[89] Vidal-Naquet connected the elements of darkness, frontier fighting and trickery to suppose a mythical refashioning of the activities of bands of 'ephebic' youths pre-paring to defend the community and hunting: by the reversal of the norms com-mon in initiatory transitions during the 'liminal' period between childhood and adulthood, the youths roam on the frontiers and the uncultivated hills and practise trickery and light-armed warfare, in opposition to the forms of combat they would engage in as citizens (hoplite battle usually on the cultivated plains). Similarly, the festival and ritual of the Oschophoria seems to connect initiatory practices of youths and the myth of Theseus, travelling with seven youths and seven maidens to Crete to kill the Minotaur by the trick of Ariadne's thread: in the ritual, youths (by the fourth century at least the 'ephebes' in tribal teams) dress as girls and run races from the sanctuary of Dionysos in the city to the sanctuary of Athena Skiras at the old harbour at Phaleron, carrying vine branches bearing grapes (*oschoi*) (see e.g. Plut. *Thes.* 22–3; Athen. 495e; Photius *Library* 322a): the themes here are cross-dressing, nudity and the testing of young men by contests and activities at border countries.[90]

While it remains very attractive to see strong initiatory elements in these myths and their associations with festivals where young men have clear roles, many difficulties have been pointed out with the idea that these elements specifically reflect periods of time in pre-ephebic 'training', spent by those about to be admit-ted to membership of the archaic phratry, or the early classical deme.[91] Recent work has shown that full-scale hoplite warfare featuring the tight phalanx forma-tion and pitched battles on the plains did not become the norm until much later than supposed, perhaps not until the Persian Wars, and also that both before and after then hoplites commonly used trickery and deceits and engaged in different types of combat and on varied terrains.[92] Many mythical characters supposedly 'ephebic' may be rather slightly older youths (e.g. Melanion, Melanthios); the connection between frontiers and wild hilly country is not a clear-cut one,[93] and the notion of defending fixed frontiers seems unlikely to have been present before the time of Solon.[94] In general, Vidal-Naquet's original arguments were in danger of mixing the imaginary with the practical, or conflating historical with imaginary frontiers.[95] We remain quite in the dark concerning the (probably limited) forms of military preparations before the end of the sixth century; and the supposition that the 'proto-ephebe' was seen as an anti-hoplite lacks foundation.

Stage 2: c. 508–4 BCE

Cleisthenes' reforms centred on the new demes and tribes, which swiftly became the basis of military as well as political organisation; the infantry and cavalry fought in tribal contingents commanded by ten taxiarchs (infantry) and ten phy-larchs (cavalry), and the frontiers of the state were thereby fixed even more clearly.[96] Each of the tribes was also furnished with its own eponymous hero, with his associated myth as a benefactor of early Athens: Erechtheus, Aegeus, Pandion, Leon, Akamas, Oineus, Kekrops, Hippothon, Aias and Antiochos (Arist. *Ath. Pol.* 21.5; Dem. 60.27–31).[97] According to the *Ath. Pol.* (21.4), these ten were selected by Delphi from a 'long list' of 100 heroes submitted by Cleisthenes' reformers.

Evidence for use of young contingents as regular garrisons of the city walls and frontier forts and for patrols begins in the mid-fifth century and runs through the Peloponnesian War. At a crucial point in the so-called First Peloponnesian War, the Athenians chose not to disturb their troops besieging Aegina and sent 'the oldest and youngest troops' to face the Corinthians' incursion into Megara (Thuc. 1.105.3–5); at the start of the great war Perikles claimed that the numbers of hoplites engaged in defence in the garrisons and battlements were 13,000 of the oldest (probably those c. 40–59) and the youngest (2.13.6–7);[98] and some light-armed Plataean troops and some frontier guards (*peripoloi*) formed an ambush in Megara under Demosthenes (4.67.2; cf. 8.92.2).[99] There is also considerable evidence during the Peloponnesian war for the garrisons in frontier forts responding to raids, e.g. by Boeotians (Ar. *Ach*. 1020–87; Thuc. 2.32, 3.51, 4.67, 5.115ʹ, by raiding parties from the Spartan fort at Dekeleia (413–04; Thuc. 7.27–8, 8.98; *Hell. Oxy*. 17), or by brigands.[100] Such garrisons no doubt regularly included the young (Thucydides' *neotatoi*), but there is no certain evidence that these 'youngest' in the Athenian army in this period were specifically of the age (c. 18–19) as those later designated as ephebes, let alone that it was part of a two-year programme of training and patrolling; they may have been chosen more *ad hoc* from a wider age group of late teens and early twenties.[101] Presumably, however, even during this period young Athenians, as they began hoplite service, might be expected to have got themselves fit through gymnastic activities, and received some basic training in weapon use and hoplite and non-hoplite manoeuvres, before acquiring experience in varied forms of combat.[102] But at this time the Athenian casualness in regard to training was praised by 'Perikles' (Thuc. 2.37), and criticised as inadequate by Xenophon in the *Memorabilia*, where Socrates complains about the lack in Athens (compared to Sparta) of any systematic weapons training and frontier patrolling, as well as moral training in self-control, discipline and obedience (*sophronein, eutaktein, peitharchein*).[103]

Initiatory, Black Hunter-type, myths and stories of the violence and deceits of young hunters and warriors remained an important part of the Athenian 'imaginary' during the fifth century. As we have seen, myths retold at the Apatouria and Oschophoria, where the Athenian young went through admissions procedures or performed other roles, featured adolescents hunting, or acting as secretive, marginal and deceitful killers on frontiers. Myths associated with other festivals or pseudo-historical narratives known from Athens (such as Solon's attack on Salamis with beardless youths in female dress: Plut. *Sol*. 8), and from other communities, involve aggression and cross-dressing focused on wars against foreign enemies or tyrants.[104] A number of our surviving tragedies and comedies have been plausibly seen as playing with such themes of marginal young hunters or warriors, or sons in conflict with their fathers.[105] In these narratives, connections between the young and the frontiers, mountainous regions, or violence all seemed 'appropriate'; but there are very few signs that this 'imaginary' of the young had any influence on the detailed ways in which fifth-century Athenians were trained for warfare or the defence of the land boundaries.[106]

Stage 3: c. 400–340 BCE

For three or so decades after the end of the Peloponnesian War, the Athenians made many significant changes to their democratic and military systems, as they sought to learn the lessons of the war and to adjust to a changed political world.[107] In the unsettled period of new wars between 395 and 362 BCE, existing forts were developed and some more constructed across the Boeotian and Megarian frontiers; and between Eleusis and Athens the Dema wall, 4.3 km long, was built in the gap between mounts Aigealos and Parnes, perhaps in the early 370s. It is disputed whether there was a single policy, adopted soon after 404, to create a large-scale preclusive defensive system to protect the territory more effectively against major invasions, or whether there was rather a longer process of devising measures to deal with smaller-scale raiding parties, and provide places of refuge against invasions, especially once Thebes came to be seen as the major threat to Athens' security, and disputes continued over Oropos.[108]

It is during the 370s BCE that we find the first firm evidence that the term *ephebos* was being used for those aged c.18–20 engaged in a two-year stint of military preparation, which included garrisoning and patrolling the frontiers. Aeschines (2.167, of 343 BCE) says that he was a frontier guard (*peripolos*)[109] for two years on leaving boyhood, and calls his fellow-ephebes (*synepheboi*) and their officers (*archontes*) as witnesses. When Aeschines served depends on a passage from his earlier speech against Timarchos (1.49, of 346/5 BCE), where the preserved text states that he was a *synephebos* with Misgolas, and is now 45, whereas Timarchos, allegedly Misgolas' boyfriend, was of course younger. If the text is right, Aeschines was born c. 390 BCE and began as an ephebe c. 372 BCE. But at 1.109 Aeschines also claims that Timarchos was on the Council in the archon-year 361/60 BCE, and should therefore have been at least 30, and born c. 390 BCE, on the standard view that an age-limit of 30 was set for the Council and other magistracies.[110] Either the text at 1.49 has misstated Aeschines' age as 45, and he and Misgolas were born some years earlier,[111] or Aeschines attempted to mislead the jury, and all three were born c. 390 BCE and were ephebes c. 372–70 BCE.[112]

At about the same time that this two-year ephebate with frontier patrolling duties was introduced,[113] we find evidence for a change in conscription procedure and with that the earliest traces of a system of 42 age-classes for those between 18 and 59, each with their own eponymous heroes. In the same passage of Aeschines (2.167–9), as correctly interpreted by Christ (2001), he describes how, following his time as an *ephebos*, he served in the army (366 BCE) in 'what is called service in turns (*en tois meresin*)' with those in his age-group, and again later he served in 'expeditions in succession all those involving eponymous age-groups (*en tois eponymois*)'.[114] This last phrase is explained by the account of the arrangements both for ephebes and for arbitrators in the Aristotelian *Constitution of Athens*. This expounds, in the context of the creation of the Lycurgan ephebate of the late 330s BCE, that as well as the ten tribes with their tribal eponymous heroes, there were forty-two eponymous heroes who acted as the patrons of forty-two age-classes of adult Athenians: the set of new ephebes at c. 18 were assigned to the hero of those Athenians who, on reaching c. 60, ceased to be eligible for conscription, and became available for service as legal arbitrators (Arist. *Ath. Pol.* 53.4–7). Conscription of the hoplite army under the new system replaced the earlier system of selection by the ten generals and ten taxiarchs of individuals 'from the list'; this probably meant lists supplied by the demarchs, with the decision taken on each occasion which combination of age-sets to conscript, to rotate the requirements (hence called 'selection in turns' and 'with the eponymous groups') and presumably to achieve an appropriate mix of ages. Selection 'from the list' is attested at the time of the Corinthian War c. 395–87 BCE (Lys. 14.6, 15.5); hence conscription using the 42 age-groups came in between c. 386–66 BCE. The *Constitution of Athens* confirms that they were introduced some time before the Lycurgan reform of the *ephebeia*; it says, writing after the reform of 335/4 BCE, that lists of new 'ephebes', with the names of the current archon and the relevant age-hero, were posted on bronze *stelai*, but that previously they had been put on whitened boards, presumably since the first two-year *ephebeia* had been introduced some time before c. 372 BCE (*Ath. Pol.* 53.4–7).

It is conceivable that the division of adults into 42 age-sets, each named by an eponymous hero, might have begun earlier than the changes to conscription and the introduction of a two-year *ephebeia*: for example c. 399 BCE when the system of public arbitrators was introduced; or some time during the fifth century, for example during the period of other reforms c. 462–50 BCE; or even back in 508–0 BCE, as part of the Cleisthenic creation of demes and tribes and the new tribal army. We hear remarkably little about these eponymous heroes themselves. Only two or three can be named: Mounichos and Panops are securely attested, and most recently Kodros has been very plausibly added to the list.[115] Davidson and Steinbock have argued that their introduction should go back at least to the mid-fifth century, as a solidly democratic institution built on local traditions.[116] Sufficient local heroes were certainly available, as according to the Aristotelian *Ath. Pol.* (21.4) Cleisthenes' reformers submitted to Delphi a list of 100 heroes from which the ten tribal heroes emerged. It is not at all clear, however, what function they would have served before the introduction of conscription from age-classes and the two-year programme, and it would be surprising that we find no mention of age-class heroes in the relatively well-documented decades from c. 430–380 BCE (e.g. anywhere in Old Comedy). It is perhaps more likely that all three elements were created together as related attempts to enhance military effectiveness, by increasing the efficiency and fairness of conscription, improving the training and socialisation of the young and strengthening the civic cohesion and loyalty of new citizens by creating new, archaising bonds which linked coevals and fellow-soldiers to ancestral heroes, many of them perhaps early Attic kings, selected for their achievements in saving the city or making it greater.

Two of Xenophon's later works can be seen to pick up and comment on these developments in training. In his idealised description of Persian institutions in the *Cyropaedia* (probably composed in the 360s BCE), he described the initial forms of education among his (mythical) Persians (1.2.8–12); they attend school as *paides* up to c. 16 or 17, then they spend ten years designated as *epheboi*, sleeping at the central public buildings, both for the sake of security and for their own self-control *(sophrosyne)*, which was especially necessary for those of that age. They go hunting with the king (for fitness and endurance), receive weapons training and engage in contests, and were employed for guard duty and for seeking out criminals and brigands *(kakourgoi* and *leistai)*. It seems likely that Xenophon has chosen the name *epheboi* with an eye on the relatively recent designation in Athens, while his own prescriptions may combine elements from Sparta (e.g. central sleeping arrangements, strong emphasis on hunting, endurance and tests),[117] from Athens (guard duty, some weapons training, and perhaps helping to pursue criminals and brigands),[118] and others that may reflect more his own ideas: some of these may have been taken up by the Lycurgan reformers (particularly the moral emphasis on discipline and *sophrosyne*).[119]

A little later, in his *Poroi* (mid 350s BCE), the treatise which most explicitly offers practical advice to his native Athens, Xenophon addresses the issue of specific training of Athens' young directly and provides invaluable further evidence for the operations of these newish *epheboi*. At the end of Chapter 4, he sums up his argument and adds the comment that revenues saved would enable improvements in the training of the young (*Vect.* 4.51–2):

πραχθέντων γε μὴν ὧν εἴρηκα ξύμφημι ἐγὼ οὐ μόνον ἂν χρήμασιν εὐπορωτέραν τὴν πόλιν εἶναι, ἀλλὰ καὶ εὐπειθεστέραν καὶ εὐτακτοτέραν καὶ εὐπολεμωτέραν γενέσθαι. οἵ τε γὰρ ταχθέντες γυμνάζεσθαι πολὺ ἂν ἐπιμελέστερον τοῦτο πράττοιεν ἐν τοῖς γυμνασίοις τὴν τροφὴν ἀπολαμβάνοντες [πλείω] ἢ ἐν ταῖς λαμπάσι γυμνασιαρχούμενοι· οἵ τε φρουρεῖν ἐν τοῖς φρουρίοις οἵ τε πελτάζειν καὶ περιπολεῖν τὴν χώραν πάντα ταῦτα μᾶλλον ἂν πράττοιεν, ἐφ᾽ ἑκάστοις τῶν ἔργων τῆς τροφῆς ἀποδιδομένης.

If all I have mentioned were implemented, I agree that the city would be not only better provided with resources, but would also become more obedient, more disciplined and more effective in war. Now those assigned to perform exercises would train much more keenly in the *gymnasia* if they received a large allowance for maintenance than when they are receiving gymnastic training for the torch races, and those instructed to guard in the forts, to act as light-armed troops and to patrol the territory would perform all this much better if they were given maintenance for each of these tasks.

This seems to be suggesting a further intensification of youth training, to instil further the characteristic Xenophontic virtues of obedience and discipline (cf. *Cyr.* 1.2.8–12), by the addition of some public expenditure for maintenance *(trophe)*. He mentions two spheres of activity, gymnastic training focused on preparing tribal teams for the torch races and military training and activities in the garrisons and on patrols.[120] Xenophon's suggestion in part anticipates the later reform in the wish to see public money (which he would see deriving from his suggestions for revenue-building) put into their maintenance – presumably to increase both the numbers and the extent and efficiency of the training. One can conclude that between the 370s and the 330s the two-year ephebic service was not compulsory, perhaps not even for sons of hoplites, and the gymnastic training was essentially financed by the liturgy of the *lampadephoria*.[121]

Stage 4: The period of reforms and Epicrates' law

Debates on the inadequacy of military and moral training in Athens seem to have intensified over the next two decades, in parallel with the growing threat from Macedon, and reached their climax, with the decision for major reform, in response to the defeat at Chaeronea.[122] Epicrates' law, early in 334 BCE, established and funded, for most c. 18-year-old Athenians[123] a radically reformed and expanded system of military, political and cultural training, an essential part of the wide-ranging Lycurgan programme of renewal and preparation for future conflicts.[124] It imposed on the young two years of intensive and co-ordinated athletic, military, religious and civic training (Arist. *Ath. Pol.* 42). The nomenclature and qualifications of the new officials put in charge on the cadets, ten *sophronistai*, one from and for each tribe, and one *kosmetes*, from and for the whole citizen body, all of whom had to be older than 40, demonstrates the strongly moralising and Spartanising tone of the institution.[125] The *sophronistai* were chosen by the fathers of the new ephebes in each tribe, 'selecting those who were best and most suitable'; and the *kosmetes* was probably selected by the assembly and no doubt voters selected someone they believed to be even more suitable (Arist. *Ath. Pol.* 42.2, with Rhodes ad loc).

The primary responsibility of these officials was not the military training, for which there were specialist generals, athletic and combat trainers for both hoplite and light-armed combat (Arist. *Ath. Pol.* 42.3 with Rhodes ad loc); rather, they must have had general responsibilities for discipline and good order, moral instruction and protection.[126] The age requirement, as Aeschines said, implies the aim of ensuring that these officials had sufficient age and experience to exercise self-control over one's desires; that is that the aim was specifically to lessen the chances that they would be tempted to use their position to 'abuse' sexually the boys or youths in their charge.

Aristotle's description of the full programme of the new *ephebeia* starts with a description of how the elected *kosmetes* and *sophronistai* collected the ephebes together and 'they go around the shrines and then march to the Peiraeus and start guard duty, some at Mounichia, some at Akte' (Arist. *Ath. Pol.* 42.3): this constitutes an excellent example of learning what it is 'to share in and to defend the *hiera kai hosia*'.[127] This tour of the sanctuaries, which may or may not have occurred in the previous forms of training, is likely to have included visiting, and learning about, the major sanctuaries and buildings on the Acropolis and in the Agora, the sanctuaries of the ten tribal heroes, scattered across Attica (and not necessarily in the territory of the relevant tribe),[128] and probably the shrines of each age-class' particular eponymous hero, which are also likely to have been spread across the territory. These tours no doubt further embedded the multiple loyalties in the new ephebes and strengthened their links to their mythological role models, the heroes and kings who had notably protected the city, or set other standards by brave deeds of self-sacrifice.[129] As Kearns and Steinbock have shown, we find echoes of such appeals in speeches such as Lycurgus *Against Leokrates* and Demosthenes' funeral speech after Chaeronea.[130] In inscriptions of the Hellenistic and Roman periods ephebes are praised for their performances in a great many rituals (often lifting the sacrificial oxen) and for escorting images of the gods in a number of processions, for example to Eleusis or Phaleron.[131] Whether or not any of these functions had been performed by ephebes after they were created c. 386–66 BCE, or even by young men earlier, is uncertain; but it is very likely that a good number were assigned to the new ephebes immediately after Epicrates' reform, and soon became established parts of their programme. In that case these duties will have further increased their familiarity with the processes of identity-creation, confirmation of boundaries across the territory and reinforcement of good relations with the innumerable gods and heroes honoured by local groups and the city as a whole.

With increasing intensity and comprehensiveness, then, Athenians built a system of military training and cultural education on the basic idea of incorporation of new citizens into the constituent sub-groups (first the phratry, then after 507–2 BCE the deme), through an oath which insisted on fighting together in defence of the frontiers, land and gods and with the aim of increasing the city's power. Use of the new soldiers as reserve troops and frontier guards and patrols grew from the mid-fifth century and may have made limited play with cultural ideas and myths of initiatory heroes who hunt and deceive in border country; the reforms of c. 386–66 BCE and of 335/4 BCE greatly expanded the appeal of heroes and patriotic myths as role models specifically for the young.

In general, as stated at the start of this chapter (pp. 99–103; see also Vlassopoulos and Xydopoulos, this volume, pp. 4–19), it is agreed that in democratic Athens levels of homicide and seriously violent crime were kept remarkably low and the community was remarkably free from serious political *stasis*.[132] Some signs of this non-violent and civilised society may be given. While class-related violence and murders may have been common in the archaic period, between the establishment of democracy in 508/7 and the Macedon-imposed changes after 322 BCE, serious political violence or *stasis* was restricted to the assassination of Ephialtes, and serious tensions in the period of the democratic advances of 462–50 BCE (the period of Aeschylus' warnings in the *Eumenides* with which I started) and to the two brief periods of the rise and swift fall of oligarchic regimes in 411–10 and 404 BCE, resulting from the defeats of the Peloponnesian War and pressures from Sparta. Only a few cases of homicide between free persons can be cited from our law court speeches.[133] Serious weapons were not carried in the streets or in the Attic countryside,[134] and while quarrels and personal disputes (arising from inheritance disputes, erotic rivalries, drunken insults and arguments and the like) might often have produced fist, feet, stick or potsherd fights, or occasionally slave-like whippings, they were rarely settled by swords or daggers.[135]

Speakers in the law courts were alive to the forensic benefit of being seen to have responded with no more than appropriate retaliatory violence, and of preferring to choose legal remedies to escalation of violence (e.g. Lys. 3 and 4; Dem. 21 and 54). Litigants may express sympathy with others who did retaliate against an aggressor, even to the point of killing him, but they emphasise that the social and moral norms preferred citizens to seek recourse in the courts, rather than by direct action (e.g. Dem. 21.71–6). Athenians thus seem to have adopted the principles shown being established in the *Oresteia* and believed that trust in the effectiveness of the legal system served as an effective deterrent against homicide, extreme violence and retaliation outside the law.[136]

There is much disagreement about the reasons for these attainments of high levels of civilised sociability and restraint of violence. The issues have been addressed in a number of recent publications by Gabriel Herman, culminating in a substantial book. One central argument of that book is that democratic Athenians consistently believed, and mostly acted on that belief, that if attacked, wronged or insulted, a citizen should restrain his anger, avoid direct retaliation, and instead go to law, in order to protect the cohesion of a law-abiding and peaceful community; he goes considerably further than others in claiming that, in so acting, Athenians abandoned the legitimacy of revenge or of the defence of their honour (*time*) as ideals and redefined the idea of *timoria* from revenge to something closer to legally administered punishment.[137] This has proved controversial, and I agree with many reviewers that this is a fundamentally simplistic and one-sided presentation, and forms a central part of his strong idealisation of Athenian society as harmonious and free from tensions or contradictions. The evidence suggests rather that Athenians maintained a very powerful belief in personal honour and legitimate revenge, but mostly accepted that such revenge could be adequately achieved through the courts, which gave satisfaction for their wronged honour. They accepted this deal because it contributed to a more cohesive and less violent society, while retaining some sympathy with those who were unable to restrain their longing for revenge.[138]

One may then ask what other elements of Athenian society may have helped to acclimatise its citizens to accept this prioritisation of cohesive values, and whether the upbringing young Athenians received helped to instil these principles of restraint of aggression and preference for conflict resolution through legal means. One dominant model of cohesive commensality, the *symposion*, developed ritualised protocols of order and politeness designed to enhance the pleasures and harmony of the members of the group; emphasis was placed on self-control. It was well recognised that alcohol, witticisms, erotic pursuits and other forms of fun carried the serious danger of escalating from acceptable limits into intolerable insult and violence (*hybris*). Elements of these sympotic practices, originally perhaps exclusively practised by wealthy elites throughout Greece, seem to have spread, as far as resources permitted, further down the social scale in classical Athens, and were also adopted at the dinners and drinking parties organised by the many types of associations, some of them constituent parts of the citizen body like phratries and their *orgeones* and *thiasoi*, others more informal cult associations (often also called *orgeones* or *thiasoi*).[139] Young Athenians would perhaps become accustomed to observing and beginning to practise these protocols at festivals of their phratries, where they and their brothers were admitted, and at many other festivals of the demes, the polis and other associations; at least the better-off among them might learn the procedures by being taken to the fathers' private symposia.[140] Similarly, they would be inducted into the delicate processes of learning to cope with being objects of erotic pursuit at the gymnasia.

An equally important instigator of social cohesion and reciprocity throughout the Greek world was the pervasive performance of choral song and dance contests. At Athens, while women's choruses, curiously, seem largely absent, many festivals had choruses competing in tragedy, comedy and dithyramb (or cyclic choruses), which were often divided into boys and men, and organised through the ten tribes. A large proportion of young Athenians must have participated in such choruses, which formed important vectors for socialisation for future citizens. Their collective training and performances will have enabled them to acquire further knowledge of the city's myths, cults and traditions and enhanced awareness of political and moral issues, while they learnt to co-operate in disciplined ways in these intense but tightly controlled competitions.[141]

It is harder to assess how far the specific processes of military training and identity-creation for young Athenians – which as we saw, were developed slowly and unsystematically from the archaic period to the fully reformed Lycurgan *ephebeia* – may have contributed to their general adherence to the norms of military and civic life: how far did these processes help them to combine the application of controlled violence to enemies and outsiders, with disciplined restraint of their aggression to fellow Athenians and acceptance of the ideal of a measured response to assaults, ideally by seeking law-abiding remedies? We have seen that Xenophon thought that Athenians displayed much better habits of discipline when training in choruses, or as rowers on triremes, than in the land army or the cavalry (Xen. *Mem.* 3.3.12–13, 3.5.5–21, 3.4.4–5),[142] and he later recommended tightening the programmes of the proto-ephebes (*Vect.* 4.51–2). The little evidence we have of military discipline in the period from the end of the Peloponnesian War and the Lycurgan reform shows some hints of co-operative and friendly behaviour inside tribal regiments of the army, but rather more alarming signs of insubordination and disorder.[143] On the more positive side, Lysias' defence of the wealthy, young, long-haired cavalryman Mantitheus, facing his *dokimasia* and charges of undemocratic and licentious behaviour, and perhaps a dubious past under the Thirty, highlights the generous financial help (thirty *drachmai*) he gave himself and encouraged others to give to those hoplites from his deme who lacked resources for travel for a campaign in Boeotia in 395 BCE (Lys. 16.14).

The more alarming narratives also all come, naturally, from law court speeches. The generals (like other magistrates, presumably including other military officials like the taxiarchs) had, when operating the draft, the power to fine citizens refusing to serve. In another Lysias speech, a soldier who complained, abusively, that he was being unfairly drafted, was fined the usual sum of 50 *drachmai* by some of the generals, and was brought to court when he had still refused to pay it at the end of the year. His defence was first that the fine was illegitimately imposed, as the generals only had power to fine citizens where verbal abuse of officials took place in a public building (*synhedrion*) and he did it at a bank, which did not count as such, and second that the treasurers had agreed with him that the fine had not been properly imposed. It seems impossible to decide on the merits of the case, but as far as it goes, Lysias' defence speech, along with many references from Old Comedy,[144] suggests that the recruitment process 'from the list' often caused problems and grievances, and that resentful Athenian citizen-soldiers were not reluctant to criticise their elected officers, if they felt arbitrary or malicious injustice was being done, and might resort to abusive language. It seems further that the generals' powers were limited and were properly subject to democratic scrutiny and ultimately to the decision of a popular court.[145]

On campaign, *strategoi* in the fourth century had greater powers to discipline unruly soldiers, namely to imprison, to cashier and to fine (Arist. *Ath. Pol.*61.2). Their powers seem to have been diminished; *strategoi* seem to have lost the power summarily to execute deviant citizens at the end of the Peloponnesian War, and, according to Aristotle, in his time fines were not normally imposed.[146] One case we hear of, from the opponent in a case of assault arising from an erotic rivalry over a youth, presents what sounds a very serious case of unruly behaviour. Simon allegedly joined the Athenian army at Corinth late during the Corinthian War, c. 394 BCE, missed the battle (of the river Nemea) and the departure of some troops to Koroneia, and then got in a fight with Laches the taxiarch, the commander of his tribal regiment. Apparently this gross indiscipline produced no more serious penalty than a public dismissal or cashiering (*apokeryxis*) (Lys. 3.45).[147] The possibility however exists that a prosecution for non-performance of military service (*graphe astrateias*) back in Athens would be expected to follow a cashiering; but, if it did in this case, it presumably did not produce a conviction, which would have imposed loss of citizen rights (*atimia*) and made Simon unable to bring this prosecution.[148]

The impression that the laws regulating discipline were not very severe gains some support from the general, if vague, complaint made by Demosthenes in 348 BCE (3.11) about laws which allowed those guilty of lack of discipline (*tous ataktountas*) to get off. This discouraged those who were keen to serve and Demosthenes recommended that these laws be repealed; quite which laws he meant is not clear. But it is very difficult to know how frequent such cases were, nor are the full circumstances clear. The most alarming narrative, and most relevant because it involved young soldiers in the period not long before Epicrates' reform, is that of Konon's sons: when on garrison at the border fort of Panakton, they behaved allegedly in an appallingly rowdy, idle and drunken fashion, and pursued an enmity with the speaker Ariston and others camped nearby with violent and verbal abuse. They were restrained and rebuked by the general and taxiarchs, but no action is reported to have been taken (Dem. 54.3–6).[149] The military context is important, but unfortunately not certain. One possibility is that it occurred during a routine garrison duty of the *synepheboi* on the frontier; if so, the drunkenness, fighting and general indiscipline alleged is fairly shocking. Carey and Reid suggest that the wording 'when service at the garrison at Panakton was posted for us' does not suggest normal garrison duty for ephebes, but a specific campaign; this may not be decisive, given the less regularised and predictable garrison activities of the *ephebeia* between c. 386–366 and 334/3 BCE, as evidenced by Aeschines 1.49 and 2.167. Gernet ad loc and Ober, however, point out that the language of 'camp' and 'tents' and the presence of 'a general, taxiarchs and other soldiers' suggest that the garrison had been supplemented by citizen-hoplites for a specific purpose.[150] So if this episode was a military response to a particular threat from the Thebans (for example the hoplite expedition to Panakton of 343 BCE, mentioned at Dem. 19. 326), the indiscipline is even more disturbing. One must be alive to the possibility, however, that what occurred, and what instigated the lasting hostility between Konon and his sons and Ariston (and possibly his friends) was not so one-sided or grave, but rather repeated episodes of fighting between two gangs of high-spirited and hot-tempered youths.[151] This scenario still suggests inadequate levels of control by the military officers of young men of considerable wealth and influence, much given to casual abuse and violence.[152]

It is possible that the circulation of narratives such as this through the courts and outside created a more general alarm, and contributed to the sense that a much more rigorous and disciplined, and arguably more Spartan, system of training for military service and citizenship was needed. Hence this may be part of the background to the introduction of Epicrates' *ephebeia* law and ephebic training and new competitions in *eutaxia*, along with more important considerations, such as Athens' relatively unsuccessful military record since the Social War, culminating with the defeat at Chaeroneia. Some support for this suggestion may be given by the presence in speeches of Aeschines and Lykourgos of 343–30 BCE of arguments adopting Spartan moralising rhetoric and seeking Spartan solutions acceptable in the post-Chaeroneia climate, when Sparta herself was in decline and an ally.[153]

Conclusion

All cities considered here, and no doubt all other Greek cities, sought to instil in their new citizens patriotic feelings and respect for fellow members of their political and sacred communities, what it meant to 'share in the *hiera* and *hosia*'. All sought to teach these virtues and emotions through locally-based myths and rituals, shared religious practices and collective training, physical exercise and choral song and dance. All cities made use of the collective imaginaries, located in myth, of the stages of transition from childhood to adulthood, and all probably transformed earlier initiatory practices and beliefs, albeit in very different ways. There remained considerable differences between the approaches employed at Sparta and in the Cretan cities on the one hand, and those used at Athens on the other (and probably many other, less militarily-orientated societies). At Sparta and in Crete, socialisation involved more intensive levels of compulsory physical exercise and military discipline, aided by athletic and song-dance contests, common messes and institutionalised or strongly encouraged homosexual pair-bonding between age-unequals. At Athens formal schooling, and most participation in athletics, collective sociability and homosexual friendships, were mostly developed outside the formal structures associated with admission to the state and the sub-groups which regulated citizenship; but participation in all these activities, as in the choral performances and torch races which operated through the Kleisthenic tribes, was in all probability extended steadily across the social divisions of the citizens. Formal preparations for military service were also increased in stages between the archaic period and the end of the classical period; it seems likely, however, that while levels of disorder are hard to assess, strict discipline in the 'ephebic' training operations and on army campaigns may have frequently clashed with the democratic ideals of free speech. In conclusion, overall levels of violence in civic life seem to have been kept relatively low both in Sparta and in Athens (though possibly not in Crete or elsewhere), but by very different types of 'civilising processes' and as a result of radically different civic ideologies.

Notes

1 Cf. van Wees 2008b for a contextualisation of this plea in terms of the prevalence of violent *stasis* in Athens and elsewhere in the archaic period; also Vlassopoulos and Xydopoulos, Chapter 1 of this volume. Lines 858–66 are probably an addition to an existing speech, otherwise identical in length to Athena's other speeches in this epirrhematic section. If so, the likelihood is that they were added by Aeschylus himself, as a response to a moment of crisis at a late stage in the preparation of his performance text (see Sommerstein 1989, *ad loc.*), rather than by a later interpolator (as e.g. Taplin 1977, 407 n. 1).

2 Of course, homicide trials continued to be heard by Areopagites, constituted by ex-archons, not randomly selected ordinary citizens like most other offences. But the Areopagos as a court seems to have maintained general confidence through most of the period of the democracy. See e.g. Wallace 1985; de Bruyn 1995.

3 Elias 1978–82.

4 Pinker 2011: 4–7, 162, 184, 400, 505, 781–5. For assessments of the levels of the violence of warfare in the ancient Greek world, cf. e.g. van Wees 2004; Chaniotis 2005a; Richer 2005: 24–30.

5 Cf. also on use of Elias' idea of the civilising process, Herman 2006: 28–9, 266–7, 288–9; Richer 2005: 7–8.

6 Fisher 2000; van Wees 2000a, 2008b, 2011; Forsdyke 2005; Richer 2005: 16–24.

7 Cf. Roisman 2005: 12–25 with many more references.

8 The adjective *neanikos* (youthful) and verb *neanikeiuesthai* (behave in a youthful way) can have positive connotations, but more usually imply rash, headstrong or violent behaviour: see Dover 1974: 103–4.

9 In a more specialised way the author of the Xenophontic work on hunting argued that intense hunting helps to create the sort of successful young men who drive out the shameless and hubristic elements from their souls and bodies, and instil a growing desire for moral excellence; men who would not accept that their *polis* should be treated unjustly or their territory should suffer any harm (Xen. *Kyn.* 12.8–9). Cf. also Xen. *Cyr.* 1.2.9, see pp. 120–1; Plato *Laws* 884.

10 Powerfully explored initially by Vidal-Naquet 1986, and subject to much criticism, e.g. those in Padilla 1999 (especially Leitao 1999, on myths and rites as channelling the violent tendencies of the young); in Dodd and Faraone 2003; and Davidson 2007: 68–98. See the ingenious and thoughtful reviews of Ma 1994, 2008.

11 Perikles' use of 'manliness' (*andreia*) as the goal imposed on Spartan boys from an early age implies the denial of childhood (cf. Rusten ad loc.).

12 Our knowledge of the details is problematic, because our limited evidence comes from non-Spartan writers, many of them antiquarians from the Hellenistic and Roman

periods such as Plutarch. The best overall treatment is now Ducat 2006a. Cf. also Hodkinson 2006, arguing, like Ducat, that the military aspect of the training should not be over-emphasised to the repression of the civic and cohesive.

13 Ducat 2006a: 71–7, against the ultra-sceptical account of Kennell 1995. See also on the details of these names and textual problems, MacDowell 1986: 159–67; Chankowski 2010: 85–9, concluding that while changes took place, *ephebos/ephebeia* were never terms used by Spartans for their system of youth training.

14 Ducat 2006a: 74–6.

15 Cf. Ducat 2006a: 49–65.

16 By the Roman period, these whippings became much more intense, and were aimed in part at a tourist market delighting in antiquarian spectacle (Plut. *Lyc.* 30 and many other sources, set out in Kennell 1995: 149–61), but Xenophon's and Plato's testimony demonstrates that the classical upbringing included substantial endurance tests and multiple uses of the whip.

17 Cf. Kennell 1995: 45, 55–9, supposing these to be Hellenistic or Roman innovations, and Ducat 2006a: 208–10, who allows the possibility of earlier versions.

18 Cf. also e.g. Cartledge 1987: 25–6; Ducat 2006a: 209–10.

19 Cartledge 2001: 91–105; Ducat 2006a: 196–201; Davidson 2007: 315–43.

20 Cf. van Wees 2004: 89–90; also Hodkinson 2006: 129–33.

21 For defences of Thucydides' view that such concerns for internal security best explain many aspects of the Spartan political and social system, its uniform values and the upbringing designed to instil them, see e.g. Ste. Croix 1972: 89–94; Cartledge 2001: 127–52.

22 For fifth- and fourth-century forts, see Catling 2002: 224–56; Christien 2006.

23 On the *hippeis*, see above all Figueira 2006; also Ducat 2006a: 101–3, 168–75. The youngest hoplites (aged 20–30) might also be used as swift 'runners-out' (*ekdromoi*) in combat against loose formation: Thuc. 4.125, 4.127; Xen. *Hell.* 4.5.11–17; Rawlings 2000: 239.

24 It is unlikely that the *krypteia* described in *P. Lond.* 187, involving a two-year period of endurance in the mountains with rough clothes and a simple diet, is the Spartan institution; that 'Hagesilaos the Laconian' (=Agesilaus) is here said to have admired it suggests it was not. See Ducat 2006a: 309–11, against Cartledge 1987: 30. One might think perhaps of a Cretan city, but see also Ducat 2006a: 311–2.

25 Following above all the powerful articles of Vidal-Naquet 1986; Cartledge 2001: 87–8, 98–102, 129–30; also Ducat 2006a: 281–332.

26 Talbert 1989; Whitby 1994.

27 Christien 2006: 175–7.

28 Azoulay 2006.

29 Christien 2006.

30 Cf. also Leitao 1999: 269, suggesting that the practice as directing the aggression of the Spartan young against the helots, as in the Spartan myth recorded by Pausanias (4.4.2–3), young Spartans in female clothes attacked Messenians attempting to rape Spartan girls at a festival of Artemis.

31 Cartledge 1987: 30–2; Chankowski 2010: 87–8.

32 Figueira 2006.

33 Cf. also Hodkinson 2006: 130.

34 Cf. MacDowell 1986: 122–50.

35 On discipline in the Spartan army, see Pritchett 1974: 235–6; Hodkinson 2006: 145–7.

36 Cf. Fisher 1989; Hodkinson 2006: 142–3; Rabinowitz 2009.

37 Cf. Cartledge 2001: 103–5.

38 Ducat 2006b.

39 Fisher 1989; also Davidson 1997: 61–9.

40 Hornblower 2000.

41 Perlman 1992; Chaniotis 2005b.

42 Arist. *Pol.* 1269a29–1269b6, 1272b7–22; Polyb. 4.53–4, 24.3; Strabo 10.4.11. Fifth-century treaty between Knossos, Tylissos and Argos, much concerned with raiding: Meiggs and Lewis 1969: no. 42; fifth-century *stasis* at Knossos: Pind. *Ol.* 12; Paus. 6.4.11. See Chaniotis 1996: 13–56; 2005a: 9–17.

43 Ducat 2006a: 164 and n. 41, for the translation of *tas ek ton nomon odas*. As he observes, a number of states seem to have set their laws, or at least their underlying principles, to music, as Plato composed his statements of legal principles in prose (Pl. *Lg.* 721–3, 858–9).

44 On the clothes, diet, fights, etc. comparable to the Spartan ethos, see Ducat 2006a: 186–7, 203, 208–9.

45 Davidson 2007: 300–15; Link 2009. Arist. *Pol.* 1272a13–28 connects together regulations for the operations and funding of the *andreia* and the arrangements for male relationships, which he implausibly claims were designed, along with segregation of women, to control the birth rate.

46 See e.g. Scanlon 2002: 74–7. On Cretan *andreia*, see Lavrečić 1988; Chaniotis 1996: 21–2, 123–33, 2005b: 184–5; Erickson 2010: 309–45, 2011, who suggests also that more private *symposia* also occurred in archaic and classical Crete; Wallace 2010: 384–92; and Whitley 2015, who emphasises the indications in the material record for variable patterns of the institution and the buildings in which members may have sat and dined across the island.

47 Perlman 1992 demonstrates a gulf between the Ephoran and Aristotelian synthesis and actual political institutions, and suggests tentatively that the theorists assumed a strong connection between legislation at Sparta and at Sparta's colony Lyktos, which may have been the primary model for the rest of the island.

48 See especially Chaniotis 2005b; Link 2009: 92–3, esp. n. 6; Wallace 2010: 353–7.

49 Koehl 1986, who also argues for links further back to Minoan rituals at the site.

50 Tzifopoulos 1998.

51 They were said by a lexicographer to be those 'those not yet able to take part in the public *dromoi*' (Arist. Byz. *fr.* 48).

52 Tzifopoulos 1998.

53 Cf. also Chaniotis 2005b: 184–5.

54 A month *Dromeios* is attested at Priansos (*IC* III.3.4), which may suggest a festival there called the Dromeia; cult for Hermes Dromaios is attested at Polyrrhenia (*IC* II.23.10); according to Plutarch, Cretans, as well as Spartans, offered cult to Apollo Dromaios (*Mor.* 724b-c). Cf. Tzifopoulos 1998: 159–60.

55 Mallia and Lyttos, *IC* I.19.1, Dreros, *IC* I.9.1 11–12, 140–1; Axos, *IC* II.5.24.7–9. On the connections here between rites and myths, see Leitao 1995; Davidson 2007: 302–6; and also Chaniotis 1996: 123–33 and 2005b: 175–94.

56 Explicitly in Lato, *IC* I.16.5.21–5; at Lyttos at the festival of *Periblemaia* ('Putting on'), *IC* I.19.1.17–18.

57 See e.g. Chaniotis 2005a: 44–51, 78–82; Wallace 2010: 283–4, 358–60, 391–9.

58 Perlman 1992. The *kosmoi* in some cities did come from the same tribe and were its military leaders (Chaniotis 2005b: 177). More positively, Aristotle does note that, unlike the situation at Sparta, the Cretan cities, despite their constant mutual warfare, did not seek support from their enemies' slaves or serfs, for fear of reciprocal action (Arist. *Pol.* 1369a38-b7).

59 Cf. also Lys. 2.13; Arist. *Pol.* 1317a40–1318a3; see analyses of these Athenian claims of the advantages of freedom and education in rational courage in Liddel 2007: 17–30; Balot 2004, 2010; Ober 2010. Xenophon *(Lak. Pol.* 13.5, *Mem.* 3.12.5) thought the Spartan military training brought results, while Aristotle (*Pol.* 1338b), writing after the fourth-century Spartan defeats and Theban successes, held that Spartan dominance lasted only so long as they were the only ones to take training seriously.

60 See Missiou 2011. Some fifth-century archaeological evidence for schooling in Athens is provided by a small building, inside the hero shrine to Akademos, where a number of slate-like stones with letters scratched on them have been found, apparently schoolboys'

writing slates (Vanderpool 1959: 279–80); some Athenian vases show boys learning their letters together, or engaged in singing or gymnastics (Morgan 1998: 19).

61 Harris 1989; Pritchard 2003: 206–18.

62 Cf. Fisher 2001 ad loc.

63 Morgan 1998, 1999.

64 See e.g. Ford 1999; Steinbock 2011.

65 Cf. Steinbock 2013: 73–5.

66 On the phratries, see Lambert 1998; on Attic associations in general, see Ismard 2010.

67 See e.g. the discussions in Plato (*Rep.* 398–400) and Aristotle (*Pol.* book 8), with Ford 2003.

68 Fisher 2010, 2011, where I argue, against Pritchard (2003, 2004), that these tribal song-dance and racing contests required choruses and athletes drawn widely from middling citizen families as well as from elite, and that this active participation contributed greatly to Athens' stability, social cohesion and low levels of violence. Similar arguments on sport and democratisation, in much broader contexts, ancient and modern, can be found in Christesen 2012 (Ch. 9 on ancient Greece).

69 de Marcellus 1994.

70 Chankowski 2010.

71 Chankowski had not read de Marcellus' dissertation. It is available online from the Bodleian Library, University of Oxford.

72 For the law's author, see Harpokr. s.v. Epikrates = Lycurgus fr. V.3 Conomis, which records that a bronze statue of Epikrates was set up because of his 'law about the ephebes'. For the date of the law (335/4, not 336/5), see Knoepfler 2001: 381–2. The string of ephebic inscriptions praising ephebes and their officials, the *sophronistai* and the *kosmetes*, begins in 334/3 with Reinmuth 1971: no. 3; Reinmuth 1971: no. 2 = Rhodes and Osborne 2003: no. 89, a collection of decrees of Kekropis, states that ephebes being honoured were registered in the year of Ktesikles (334/3); so they were the first cohort. The law should have been passed in the spring of 335/4. Reinmuth's idea that the recovery of Oropos was one final determining cause in the decision to pass the law remains valid; and Knoepfler showed that to be 335, after the fall of Thebes to Alexander, not after Chaeronea (Knoepfler 2001: 367–89). Chankowski 2010: 128–9, also Lambert 2012: 224–35, 294–6, on the immediate institution of the *eutaxia* liturgy. For the connection between the reform and basic ideas which we can associate with Lykourgos, cf. Faraguna 2011: 69–70.

73 See now Chankowski 2010: passim.

74 A propos of this and other oaths sworn by citizens, Lykourgos claims that it is the element 'which holds the democracy together' (1.79). Cf. also Dem. 23.67–8; Herman 2006: 318–20.

75 Rhodes and Osborne 2003: no. 88.

76 Cf. Rhodes and Osborne 2003: 447–9 and Humphreys 2004: 190–1.

77 Blok 2011: 244 suggests that this phrase is likely also to have been present in the earliest version of the oath, as part of her general demonstration of the pervasiveness and importance of the language of 'sharing in *hiera* and *hosia*' as a mode of expressing membership of a community or citizenship.

78 Ostwald 1969 for the shift from *thesmos* to *nomos*.

79 Siewert 1977; de Marcellus 1994: 43–8; Finkelberg 2008 (adding Pl. *Apol.* 28d6–29a1 from the early fourth century to the list); Chankowski 2010: 127–8; Blok 2011: 244–5. The echoes in Pericles' Funeral Speech (Thuc. 2.37) are especially relevant here, suggesting that the orator on such a solemn occasion honouring the war dead would allude to the oath which all citizens had sworn.

80 Though Ares and Athena Areia were probably added by the loyal priest of this sanctuary; Siewert 1977: 109–10. On these 'earthy' gods, cf. also Lambert 2011: 186–7. See also Canevaro (this volume), pp. 61–3, suggesting that the reference to the 'boundaries of the country' would fit a date for the oath after the time of Draco's laws, which lacked the concept of definite frontiers of the state, and to some time during the sixth century, when this concept was solidifying.

81   'The third day they call *Koureotis*, because the boys (*kouroi*) and girls (*korai*) were enrolled in the phratries': *Scholia on* Ar. *Ach.* 142ff.

82   Hesych. s.v. *Koureotis*: 'a day in the month of Pyanepsion, on which they cut off the hair of the heads of the boys and sacrifice them to Artemis': see Cole 1984; Lambert 1998: 161–78. On haircutting in Greece generally, see Leitao 2003, who notes that Athenian boys offered cut hair on other occasions (112–3). On identity-creation in different types of phratries in the Greek world, see Parker 2008.

83   Though Pollux suggests it happened at the end of ephebic service.

84   Cf. de Marcellus 1994: 26–34.

85   Lambert 1998: 251–61; van Wees 2013: 44–61; Ismard 2010: 299–30 rejects the connection with the archaic Athenian navy.

86   Van Wees 2013: 53–61.

87   Cf. Sommerstein 1996. On hunting, cf. Xenophon's *Kynegetikos*, recommending it as a pursuit for young Athenians as opposed to the education offered by the sophists; see Schnapp 1997: ch. 4; Rawlings 2000: 243–5. On athletics and *symposia*, see e.g. Kyle 1987; Fisher 1998; Golden 1998; Scanlon 2002.

88   Cf. Parker 1996: 104–8, 2005: 458–61 on phratries and the *Apatoria*.

89   Cf. also Kearns 1989: 183–4; Lambert 1998: 144–52.

90   Vidal-Naquet 1986; see also Chankowski 2010: 99–103, and on the Oschophoria also Parker 2005: 211–17.

91   Cf. e.g. Lambert 1998: 148–52.

92   Leitao 1999: 254–6; Rawlings 2000, 2007: 63–78; Van Wees 2000a, 2004: 166–96.

93   Polinskaya 2003; see also Buxton 2013, 66–70, arguing that Melanthos fits the proposed 'ephebic' pattern, but Melanion does not.

94   See Canevaro, Chapter 3 in this volume, passim.

95   Leitao 1999; Poliskaya 2003: 98–9, This is in effect recognised by Vidal-Naquet 1989 in his revisionary 'Return to the black hunter'; cf. Ma 2008: 190.

96   See Canevaro, Chapter 3 in this volume, passim.

97   Kearns 1989: 80–92; de Polignac 2011; Steinbock 2013 72–3.

98   On the numbers and interpretation, see e.g. van Wees 2004: 241–3.

99   Vidal-Naquet 1986: 143 sees in the facts an ambush by light-armed troops which took place at night (Thuc. 4.67), indications that both the *peripoloi* (as young proto-ephebes) and the Plataeans (as new citizens) were selected as being on the margin of the city; cf. also Hornblower 2005 ad loc.

100   Thucydides and Lysias assert the presence of a good number of strongholds in Attica (Thuc. 2.13.6, 2.24.1; Lys. 12.40, 14.35), and Thucydides and Xenophon attest specific forts at Oenoe (Thuc. 2.18), Panakton (Thuc. 5.3.5 etc.), Oropos (Thuc. 8.60), Sounion (Thuc. 8.4) and Thorikos (Xen. *Hell.* 1.2.1); for Eleusis, cf. Ober 1985: 192–3; Hornblower 2005 on Thuc. 2.19.2. For the archaeological remains of forts, Ober 1985: 130–80; for their use in the Peloponnesian war, Ober 1985: 191–4. There was also much fighting between the oligarchs and democrats, and also brigandage, across the territory during the period of the Thirty and the democratic uprising at Phyle (see Lys. 7.6, 31.17–19): cf. Ober 1985: 49–50; Fisher 1999: 75–80.

101   Cf. Burckhardt 1996: 31–3; Sommerstein 1996; Chankowski 2010: 140–2.

102   Cf. van Wees 2004: 89–95.

103   *Mem.* 3.5.15–21, 25–7; cf. 3.12. Cf. Fisher 2007: 335; Plato (*Lg.* 831–2) blames excessive love of wealth as one cause for the fact that democratic states neglected military and gymnastic training and contests.

104   See especially Leitao 1999.

105   For example, Sophocles' *Philoctetes*; cf. contrasting interpretations in this respect in Vidal-Naquet 1988 and Dodd 2003; or Euripides' *Hippolytus* with Mitchell-Boyask 1999. See for comedies, Slater 1996 and the responses by Sommerstein 1996 and 2010. Cf. also Leitao 1999; Ma 2008, suggesting that 'marginality' through a lengthy process of integration into full adulthood is a more significant and useful analytical tool than is postulating a specific 'ephebic' phase.

106 See especially Sommerstein 1996, 2010; Polinskaya 2003.

107 For the political changes, see above all Hansen 1999: esp. 296–304.

108 Ober 1985 argued for the general policy; against, Harding 1988: 70; Munn 1993; de Marcellus 1994: 63–8; Rawlings 2007: 137–8. On Oropos, under Boeotian control between 402–386 BCE, independent until 374, when it chose to re-join Athens, lost again to Thebes in 367/6, cf. Hansen and Nielsen 2004: 448–9. On garrisons-deme in the fourth century, see also Whitehead 1985: 401–7.

109 The *peripoloi*, along with the cavalry, are mentioned by Xenophon in the 350s (*Vect.* 4.47–8) as providing an effective response to small-scale invasions by neighbours; commanders of the *peripoloi* are first attested in the inscription of 352/1 BCE setting out Athenian policy of the disputed sacred untilled land (*orgas*) near Eleusis and the Megarian frontier (*IG* II^2 204 = Rhodes and Osborne 2003: no. 58, 16–24). The *peripoloi* are listed along with the Areopagos, the general in charge of the security of the territory (*ton epi ten phylaken tes choras*), the demarchs, the council of 500, and any Athenian who wishes, as those deputed to look after the sacred *orgas*. The *peripolos* Smikythion of Kephale is honoured by the demesmen of Eleusis in *IG* II^2 1193, re-dated, along with *IG* II^2 1187 by Couvenhes (1998: 56–7) to c. 338 BCE, on the basis of the style of the relief and letter forms.

110 See e.g. Rhodes 1972: 1–2; Hansen 1999: 89–90. This rule is doubted by Develin 1985; Chankowski 2010: 115 n.266, in which case Aeschines' birth date c. 390 may be retained without accusing him of misleading the jury at this point. But I think the rule should be maintained.

111 So Lewis (1958) suggesting a change to 54.

112 So Harris (1988), accepted by Fisher (2001: 10–12).

113 The *peripoloi* were still probably a mixture of the young and other, especially light-armed, troops (some mercenary); but the new *ephebic* system probably considerably increased the numbers of the 18–20 year-olds.

114 Christ 2001: 412–4 shows, against Andrewes 1981, that both these designations refer to the same new system using the 42 age-groups, which replaced conscription from the list.

115 Mounichos: see Habicht 1961: 143 = Reinmuth 1971: no. 6, a dedication by ephebes of Aiantis to the hero Mounichos; Kearns 1989: 186–7. Panops: Photius s.v. Panops; Pl. *Lysis* 203a, see Vidal-Naquet 1968: 163n.9; Kearns 1989: 193. Kodros: see Steinbock 2011: 291–4, who plausibly adds him on the basis of the reference to him (Lyc. 1.88) as one of the ancient kings who were 'eponymous of the land' (*eponymoi tes choras*); Kearns 1989: 178.

116 Davidson 2006, 2007: 75–6; Steinbock 2011: 292–4.

117 See the nuanced account in Tuplin 1994: 150–61.

118 Hunter 1994: 153; Fisher 1999: 75–80.

119 De Marcellus 1994: 119–22; Chankowski 2010: 117.

120 The suggestion of Sekunda 1990 that the ephebes did gymnastic training in year one and frontier duties in year two is not justified; Chankowski 2010: 119. His assumption that at this period the tribal races were manned exclusively by the ephebes, rather than by a mixture of ephebes and slightly older youths, is not necessary; cf. Humphreys 2004: 114–5.

121 The liturgy is also illustrated by *IG* II^2 1250, where the tribe Aiantis honours its gymnasiarch and names the torch-racers, on which see Sekunda 1990; Whitehead 1991.

122 Humphreys 2004: 80–93, 110–20; also Fisher 2001: 53–67, on this as an important context for Aeschines' successful prosecution of Timarchos.

123 On the complex issues of who served as ephebes, cf. e.g. Rhodes and Osborne 2003: 452–4; Burckhardt 1996: 33–43; Humphreys 2004: 89. I agree with Humphreys that after 335/4 sons of hoplites would be expected to serve, and sons of the poor would not be excluded.

124 On the educational and cultural aspects of the programme cf. also Azoulay 2011: 211–17; Lambert 2011: 185–90.

125   Hansen 1999: 301; Fisher 2007: 336–8. As I mentioned there, two third-century inscriptions reveal Athenian special troops called *kryptoi,* evidently contingents of ephebes, one assigned covert duties in the countryside during the Chremonidean war of the 260s BCE, the other forming part of the garrison at Rhamnous c. 235–30. Plato had recommended in *Laws* (760–63) that squads of young men appointed to regulate the countryside of Magnesia might be called *agronomoi* or *kryptoi.* These Athenian *kryptoi* may have been created as part of the Lycurgan reorganisation of the *ephebeia,* or else a little later; hence the possibility exists that Lycurgus positively wished to give them these further Spartan and Platonic associations. Possibly the term *kosmetes* owed something also to the *kosmoi* of Cretan cities (a suggestion I owe to Roger Brock). These *kryptoi* seem to preserve elements of 'Black Hunter' thinking in their separate status and marginality: see Ma 2008: 194–5.

126   Cf. Steinbock 2011: 295. The institution of the *eutaxia* tribal contest, funded by liturgists, probably testing the ephebes in drill, will have greatly enhanced the emphasis on good discipline for the ephebes: *IG* II² 417; cf. Rhodes and Osborne 2003: no. 89, 40, 58. See de Marcellus 1994: 150–4; Humphreys 2004: 115–8; Liddel 2007: 202, 292; Lambert 2012: 224–35, 294–6.

127   Cf. Blok 2011.

128   Cf. Parker 1996: 118–20; see also de Polignac 2011 on Aiantis and Hippothontis, two tribes whose heroes and sanctuaries have strong associations with frontiers and marginal places.

129   See, in general, Kearns 1989: 44–63.

130   On Kodros' self-sacrifice, see Lyc. 1.83–9; Kearns 1989: 56; Herman 2006: 332–3; on the daughters of kings Erechtheus and Leos, cf. also Kearns 1989: 57–63; Leduc 2005.

131   On processions, see Kavoulaki 1999; Parker 2005: 162–73, 178–80; Sourvinou-Inwood 2011: 158–92.

132   The case for this in general is also made well by Herman 2006.

133   See e.g. Fisher 1998: 73–5; Herman 2006: 206–15.

134   Van Wees 1998; Herman 2006: 239–40.

135   E.g. Fisher 1998: 75–7.

136   Legal systems as the fundamental defence of freedom and justice for all: Eur. *Suppl.* 429–37; Dem. 21.209–11, 22.51–2, 24.24–6, 24.75–6; Ps.-Dem. 25.20–1; Aeschin. 1.4–6, 3.6–7.

137   See the full statement of his views in his large book (Herman 2006). He opposes in particular the view of Cohen 1995 that the courts, encouraging revenge, acted as stimuli to feuds.

138   See e.g. Fisher 1998: 80–6, 2000: 84–90; among reviews of Herman, see especially Christ 2007; Balot 2008; Kucharski 2008; van Wees 2008b; also Wohl 2010: 71–82, seeing some justification for both Cohen's and Herman's positions, in relation to the case of Konon (Dem. 54). See also now Alwine 2015.

139   See e.g. Murray 1990; Fisher 2000; Corner 2010; as D'Arms 1990: 317 noted, Elias' discussion of the development of sophisticated rules for collective commensality as a major part of his 'civilising process', identified as beginning in the Middle Ages (Elias 1978: 60–128), misses its significant elaboration in ancient Greece and Rome.

140   Cf. also Steinbock 2013, 75–80 on *symposia* as locations for acquiring social values and social memory.

141   For details see e.g. Osborne 1993; Wilson 2000, 2003, 2007; Fisher 2010, 2011.

142   Cf. Pritchett 1974: 235–6.

143   On the issue of the powers available to commanders to maintain discipline in the Greek world, see Pritchett 1974: 232–45; Couvenhes 2005. Couvenhes seeks to reduce somewhat the gulf between Spartan rigour and punishments and a greater laxity in Athens and other more democratic states seen by Pritchett and others; but arguably significant differences remain.

144   Ar. *Ach.* 1065, *Eq.* 1369–72, *Pax* 1180–90; cf. Christ 2001: 403–4.

145 On the details of this case, cf. MacDowell 1994; Dreyer 1994; Christ 2001: 400, 406–7; and Todd 2007: 581–93.
146 Harrison 1971: 31–2; Pritchett 1974: 238; Couvenhes 2005: 432–6; Todd 2007: 342, 608–9.
147 Van Wees 2004: 109 emphasises the leniency of the penalty, though the public shame of the proclamation, and its availability for being recalled by all his enemies (as in this speech) should not be missed.
148 Todd 2007: 341–2. If Simon had been acquitted (for whatever reason) on such a charge, there may have been another side to the story, and Lysias would not have admitted the fact.
149 Cf. van Wees 2004: 110.
150 Gernet 1959, 104; Carey and Reid 1985: 78; Ober 1985: 217–9.
151 So Carey and Reid 1985: 80–1, cf. 69–73; Wohl 2010: 78–82.
152 Ariston claims he came from a family of trierarchs (Dem. 54.44), and has some liturgy-performers among his friends and witnesses (Dem. 54.32); Konon also has similarly rich witnesses on his side (Dem. 54.7, 31, 34) and apparently his defence was to present himself and his sons as fine men (*kaloi kagathoi*), who belonged to the types of fun-loving clubs which encouraged whoring and getting into relatively harmless fights, as did their opponents (Dem. 54.14–17).
153 E.g. Aeschin. 1.180–2; Lyc. 1.105–7, 128–30; see Fisher 1994, 2007.

Bibliography

Alwine A.T. (2015) *Enmity and Feuding in Classical Athens*, Austin.
Andrewes, A. (1981) 'The hoplite *katalogos*' in D. S. Shrimpton and D. J. McCargar (eds.), *Classical Contributions: Studies in Honour of M. F. McGregor*, New York, 1–3.
Azoulay, V. (2006) 'L'*Archidamos* d'Isocrate: une politique de l'espace et du temps', *REG* 119, 504–31.
Azoulay, V. (2011) 'Les métamorphoses du *koinon* Athénien' in V. Azoulay and P. Ismard, P. (eds.), *Clisthène et Lycurgue d'Athènes*, Paris, 191–218.
Azoulay, V. and Ismard, P. (eds.) (2011) *Clisthène et Lycurgue d'Athènes*, Paris.
Balot, R. (2004) 'Courage in the democratic polis', *CQ* 54, 406–23.
Balot, R. (2008) 'Review of Herman 2006', *CP* 103, 320–5.
Balot, R. (2010) 'Democratizing courage in classical Athens' in D. M. Pritchard (ed.), *War, Democracy and Culture in Classical Athens*, Cambridge, UK, 65–108.
Bertrand, J.-M. (ed.) (2005) *La violence dans les mondes grec et romain*, Paris.
Blok, J. (2011) '*Hosie* and Athenian law from Solon to Lycourgos' in Azoulay and Ismard (2011), 233–54.
de Bruyn, O. (1995) *La compétence de l'Aréopage en matière de procès publics: des origines de la polis athénienne à la conquête romaine de la Grèce (vers 700-146 avant J.-C.)* Stuttgart.
Burckhardt, L. A. (1996) *Bürger und Soldaten: Aspekte der politischen und militärischen Rolle athenischer Bürger im Kriegswesen des 4. v. Chr.*, Stuttgart.
Buxton, R. (2013) *Myths and Tragedies in Their Ancient Greek Contexts*, Oxford, UK.
Carey, C. and Reid, R. A. (1985) *Demosthenes: Selected Private Speeches*, Cambridge, UK.
Cartledge, P. (1987) *Agesilaos and the Crisis of Sparta*, London.
Cartledge, P. (2001) *Spartan Reflections*, London.
Catling, R. W. V. (2002) 'The survey area from the Early Iron Age to the classical period' in W. G. Cavanagh, J. Crouwel, R. W. V. Catling and G. Shipley (eds.), *The Laconia Survey: Continuity and Change in a Greek Rural Landscape* II, London, 151–256.

Chaniotis, A. (1996) *Die Verträge zwischen kretischen Poleis in der hellenistichen Zeit*, Stuttgart.

Chaniotis, A. (2005a) *War in the Hellenistic World*, Oxford, UK.

Chaniotis, A. (2005b) 'The great inscription, its political and social institutions and the common institutions of the Cretans' in E. Greco and M. Lombardo (eds.), *La Grande Iscrizione di Gortyna: centoventi anni dopo la scoperta*, Athens, 175–94.

Chankowski, A. S. (2010) *L'Éphébie hellénistique: étude d'une institution civique dans les cités grecques des îles de la Mer Égée et de l'Asie mineure*, Paris and Brussels.

Christ, M. (2001) 'Conscriptions of hoplites in classical Athens', *CQ* 51, 398–422.

Christ, M. (2007) 'Review of Herman 2006', *BMCR* 2007.07.37, available at http://bmcr.brynmawr.edu/2007/2007-07-37.html.

Christesen, P. (2012) *Sport and Democracy in the Ancient and Modern Worlds*, Cambridge.

Christien, J. (2006) 'The Lacedaemonian state: fortifications, frontiers and historical problems' in S. Hodkinson and A. Powell (eds.), *Sparta and War*, Swansea, UK, 163–83.

Cohen, D. (1995) *Law, Violence and Community in Classical Athens*, Cambridge, UK.

Cole, S. G. (1984) 'The social function of rituals of maturation: the Koureion and the Arkteia', *ZPE* 55, 233–44.

Corner, S. (2010) 'Transcendent drinking: the symposium at sea reconsidered', *CQ* 60, 352–80.

Couvenhes, J.-C. (1998) 'Le Stratège Derkylos, fils d'Autoklès d'Hagnous et l'éducation des *paides* à Eleusis', *Cahiers du Centre Gustave Glotz* 9, 49–69.

Couvenhes, J.-C. (2005) '*De disciplina Graecorum*: les relations de violence entre les chefs militaires grecs et leur soldats' in J.-M. Bertrand (ed.), *La violence dans les mondes grec et romain*, Paris, 431–54.

D'Arms, J. H. (1990) 'The Roman *convivium* and the idea of equality' in O. Murray (ed.) *Sympotica: A Symposium on the Symposion,* Oxford, UK, 308–20.

Davidson, J. (1997) *Courtesans and Fishcakes: The Consuming Passions of Classical Athens*, London.

Davidson, J. (2006) 'Revolutions in human time' in S. Goldhill and R. Osborne (eds.), *Rethinking Revolutions through Ancient Greece*, Cambridge, UK, 29–67.

Davidson, J. (2007) *The Greeks and Greek Love: A Radical Reappraisal of Homosexuality in Ancient Greece*, London.

de Bruyn, O. (1995) *Le compétence de l'Aréopage en matière de procès public*, Stuttgart.

de Marcellus, H. V. (1994) *The Origins and Nature of the Attic Ephebeia to 200 BC*, PhD dissertation, University of Oxford.

de Polignac, F. (2011) 'D'Ajax à Hippothoon: héros marginaux et cohérence des tribus clisthéniennes' in V. Azoulay and P. Ismard (eds.), *Clisthène et Lycurgue d'Athènes*, Paris, 107–18.

Develin, R. (1985) 'Age qualifications for Athenian magistrates', *ZPE* 61, 140–59.

Dodd, D. B. (2003) 'Adolescent initiation in myth and tragedy: rethinking the Black Hunter' in D. B. Dodd and C. Faraone (eds.), *Initiation in Ancient Greek Rituals and Narratives: New Critical Perspectives*, London, 71–84.

Dodd, D. B. and Faraone, C. (eds.) (2003) *Initiation in Ancient Greek Rituals and Narratives: New Critical Perspectives*, London.

Dover, K. J. (1974) *Greek Popular Morality*, Oxford, UK.

Dreyer, M. (1994) 'Diskusionsbeitrag zum Referat von Douglas M. MacDowell' in Thür (1994), 165–8.

Ducat, J. (2006a) *Spartan Education*, Swansea, UK.

Ducat, J. (2006b) 'The Spartan "tremblers"' in S. Hodkinson and A. Powell (eds.), *Sparta and War*, Swansea, UK, 1–56.

Elias, N. (1978–82) *The Civilising Process*, I–II, Oxford, UK.

Erickson, B. L. (2010) *Crete in Transition: Pottery Styles and Island History in the Archaic and Classical Periods*, Princeton, NJ.

Erickson, B. L. (2011) 'Public feasts and private symposia in the Archaic and Classical periods' in K. T. Glowacki and N. Vogeikoff-Brogan (eds.), *ΣΤΕΓΑ: The Archaeology of Houses and Households in Ancient Crete*, Princeton, NJ, 381–91.

Faraguna, M. (2011) 'Lycurgan Athens' in V. Azoulay and P. Ismard (eds.), *Clisthène et Lycurgue d'Athènes*, Paris, 67–88.

Figueira, T. J. (2006) 'The Spartan *hippeis*' in S. Hodkinson and A. Powell (eds.), *Sparta and War*, Swansea, UK, 57–84.

Finkelberg, M. (2008) 'Plato Apology 28d6–29a1 and the Ephebic oath', *Scripta Classica Israelica* 27, 9–16.

Fisher, N. (1989) 'Drink, *hybris* and the promotion of harmony at Sparta' in A. Powell (ed.), *Classical Sparta: Techniques behind her Success*, London, 26–50.

Fisher, N. (1994) 'Sparta re(de)valued: some Athenian public attitudes to Sparta between Leuctra and the Lamian War' in S. Hodkinson and A. Powell (eds.), *Sparta and War*, Swansea, UK, 347–400.

Fisher, N. (1998) 'Gymnasia and the democratic values of leisure' in P. Cartledge, P. Millett and S. von Reden (eds.), *Kosmos: Essays in Order, Conflict and Community in Classical Athens*, Cambridge, UK, 84–104.

Fisher, N. (1999) '"Workshops of villains": was there much organised crime in classical Athens?' in K. Hopwood (ed.), *Organized Crime in Antiquity*, London and Swansea, UK, 53–96.

Fisher, N. (2000) 'Symposiasts, fish-eaters and flatterers: social mobility and moral concerns' in D. Harvey and J. Wilkins (eds.), *The Rivals of Aristophanes: Studies in Athenian Old Comedy*, London and Swansea, UK, 355–96.

Fisher, N. (2001) *Aeschines: Against Timarchos*, Oxford, UK.

Fisher, N. (2003) '"Let envy be absent": envy, liturgies and reciprocity in Athens' in D. Konstan and K. Rutter (eds.), *Envy in the Ancient World*, Edinburgh, 181–215.

Fisher, N. (2007) 'Lykourgos of Athens: Lakonian by name, Lakoniser by policy?' in N. Birgalias, K. Burasalis and P. Cartledge (eds.), *The Contribution of Ancient Sparta to Political Thought and Practice*, Athens, 327–41.

Fisher, N. (2008) 'The bad boyfriend, the flatterer and the sykophant: related forms of the *kakos* in democratic Athens' in I. Sluiter and R. Rosen (eds.), *KAKOS, Badness and Anti-Value in Classical Antiquity*, Leiden, Netherlands,185–231.

Fisher, N. (2010) '*Charis, Charites*, festivals and social peace in the classical Greek city' in I. Sluiter and R. Rosen (eds.), *Valuing Others in Classical Antiquity*, Leiden, Netherlands, 71–112.

Fisher, N. (2011) 'Competitive delights: the social effects of the expanded programme of contests in post-Kleisthenic Athens' in N. Fisher and H. van Wees (eds.), *Competition in the Ancient World*, Swansea, UK, 175–219.

Ford, A. (1999) 'Reading Homer from the rostrum: poems and laws in Aeschines' *Timarchus*' in S. Goldhill and R. Osborne (eds.), *Performance, Culture and Athenian Democracy*, Cambridge, UK, 231–56.

Forsdyke, S. L. (2005) *Exile, Ostracism and Democracy: The Politics of Expulsion in Ancient Greece*, Princeton, NJ.

Gernet, L. (1959) *Demosthène, Plaidoyers Civils III*, Paris.

Golden, M. (1998) *Sport and Society in Ancient Greece*, Cambridge, UK.

Goldhill, S. and Osborne, R. (eds.) (1999) *Performance, Culture and Athenian Democracy*, Cambridge, UK.

Habicht, C. (1961) 'Neue Inschriften aus dem Kerameikos', *MDAI* 76, 127–48.

Hansen, M. H. (1999) *The Athenian Democracy in the Age of Demosthenes*, 2nd ed., Oxford., UK

Hansen, M. H. and Nielsen, T. H. (eds.) (2004) *An Inventory of Archaic and Classical Poleis*, Oxford, UK.

Harding, P. (1988) 'Athenian defensive strategy in the fourth century', *Phoenix* 42, 61–71.

Harris, E. M. (1988) 'When was Aeschines born?', *CP* 83, 211–4.

Harris, W. V. (1989) *Ancient Literacy*, Cambridge, UK.

Harrison, A. R. W. (1968–71) *The Law of Athens*, I–II, Oxford, UK.

Herman, G. (2006) *Morality and Behaviour in Democratic Athens: A Social History*, Cambridge, UK.

Hodkinson, S. (2006) 'Was classical Sparta a military society?' in S. Hodkinson and Powell (eds.), *Sparta and War*, Swansea, UK, 111–62.

Hodkinson, S. (ed.) (2009) *Sparta: Comparative Perspectives*, Swansea, UK.

Hodkinson, S. and Powell, A. (eds.) (2006) *Sparta and War*, Swansea, UK.

Hopwood, K. (ed.) (1999) *Organized Crime in Antiquity*, London and Swansea, UK.

Hornblower, S. (2000) 'Sticks, stones and Spartans: the sociology of Spartan violence' in H. van Wees (ed.), *War and Violence in Ancient Greece*, London and Swansea, UK, 57–82.

Hornblower, S. (2005) *A Commentary on Thucydides, II: Books IV-V.24*, Oxford.

Humphreys, S. C. (2004) *The Strangeness of Gods: Historical Perspectives on the Interpretation of Athenian Religion*, Oxford, UK.

Hunter, V. (1994) *Policing Athens: Social Control in the Attic Lawsuits, 420–320 B.C.*, Princeton, NJ.

Ismard, P. (2010) *Le Cité des réseaux: Athènes et ses associations VIe–Ie siècle av. J.-C.*, Paris.

Kavoulaki, A. (1999) 'Processional performance and the democratic polis' in S. Goldhill and R. Osborne (eds.), *Performance, Culture and Athenian Democracy*, Cambridge, UK, 293–320.

Kearns, E. (1989) *The Heroes of Attica*, London.

Kennell, N. M. (1995) *The Gymnasium of Virtue: Education and Culture in Ancient Sparta*, Chapel Hill, NC.

Knoepfler, D. (1993) 'Les kryptoi du stratège Epichares de Rhamnonte et le début de la guerre de Chrémonidès', *BCH* 117, 327–41.

Knoepfler, D. (2001) *Décrets érétriennes de proxenie et de citoyenneté, Éretria* 11, Lausanne, Switzerland.

Koehl, R. B. (1986) 'The Chieftain cup and a Minoan rite of passage', *JHS* 106, 99–110.

Kucharski, J. (2008) 'Review of Herman 2006', *AHB* 22, 89–95.

Kyle, D. G. (1987) *Athletics in Ancient Athens*, Leiden, Netherlands.

Lambert, S. D. (1998) *The Phratries of Attica*, 2nd ed., Ann Arbor, MI.

Lambert, S. D. (2011) 'Some political shifts in Lycurgan Athens' in V. Azoulay and P. Ismard (eds.), *Clisthène et Lycurgue d'Athènes*, Paris, 175–90.

Lambert, S. D. (2012) *Inscribed Athenian Laws and Decrees, 352/1–322–1*, Leiden, Netherlands.

Lavrečić, M. (1988) 'Ἀνδρείον', *Tyche* 3, 147–61.

Leduc, C. (2005) 'La figure du père sacrificateur de sa fille dans les rituels athéniens' in J.-M. Bertrand (ed.), *La violence dans les mondes grec et romain*, Paris, 271–86.

Leitao, D. (1995) 'The perils of Leukippos: initiatory transvestism and male gender ideology in the Ekdusia at Phaistos', *CA* 24, 130–63.

Leitao, D. (1999) 'Solon on the Beach: some pragmatic functions of the limen in initiatory myth and ritual' in M. W. Padilla (ed.), *Rites of Passage in Ancient Greece: Literature, Religion, Society*, Lewisburg, PA, 247–77.

Leitao, D. (2003) 'Adolescent hair-growing and hair-cutting rituals in ancient Greece: a sociological approach' in D. B. Dodd and C. Faraone (eds.), *Initiation in Ancient Greek Rituals and Narratives: New Critical Perspectives*, London, 109–29.

Lewis, D. (1958) 'When was Aeschines born?', *Classical Review* 8, 108.

Liddel, P. (2007) *Civic Obligation and Individual Liberty in Ancient Athens*, Oxford, UK.

Link, S. (2009) 'Education and pederasty in Spartan and Cretan society' in S. Hodkinson, S. (ed.), *Sparta: Comparative Perspectives*, Swansea, UK, 89–112.

Ma, J. (1994) 'Black Hunter variations', *PCPS* 40, 49–80.

Ma, J. (2008) 'The return of the Black Hunter', *Cambridge Classical Journal* 54, 188–208.

MacDowell, D. M. (1986) *Spartan Law*, Edinburgh.

MacDowell, D. M. (1994) 'The case of the rude soldier (Lysias 9)' in G. Thür (ed.), *Symposion 1993: Vorträge zur griechischen und hellenistichen Rechtsgeschichte*, Cologne; Weimar, Germany and Vienna, 153–64.

Meiggs, R. and Lewis, D. (1969) *A Selection of Greek Historical Inscriptions to the End of the Fifth Century BC*, Oxford.

Missiou, A. (2011) *Literacy and Democracy in Fifth-Century Athens*, Cambridge, UK.

Mitchell-Boyask, R. (1999) 'Euripides' Hippolytus and the trials of manhood (the ephebia?)' in M. W. Padilla (ed.) *Rites of Passage in Ancient Greece: Literature, Religion, Society*, Lewisburg, PA, 42-66.

Morgan, T. J. (1998) *Literate Education in the Hellenistic and Roman Worlds*, Cambridge, UK.

Morgan, T. J. (1999) 'Literate education in classical Athens', *CQ* 49, 46–61.

Morrow, G. (1960) *Plato's Cretan City*, Princeton, NJ.

Munn, M. H. (1993) *The Defence of Attica: The Dema Wall and the Boeotian War of 378-375 B.C.*, Berkeley and Oxford.

Murray, O. (ed.) (1990) *Sympotica: A Symposium on the Symposion*, Oxford, UK.

Murray, P. and Wilson, P. (eds.) (2003) *Music and the Muses*, Oxford, UK.

Ober, J. (1985) *Fortress Attica: Defence of the Athenian Land Frontier, 404–322 BC*, Leiden, Netherlands.

Ober, J. (2010) 'Thucydides on Athens' democratic advantage' in D. M. Pritchard (ed.), *War, Democracy and Culture in Classical Athens*, Cambridge, UK, 65–87.

Osborne, R. (1993) 'Competitive festivals and the polis: a context for dramatic festivals at Athens' in A. H. Sommerstein, F. S. Halliwell, J. Henderson and B. Zimmermann (eds.), *Tragedy, Comedy and the Polis*, Bari, Italy, 21–37.

Oswald, M. (1969) *Nomos and the Beginnings of the Athenian Democracy*, Oxford, UK.

Padilla, M. W. (ed.) (1999) *Rites of Passage in Ancient Greece: Literature, Religion, Society*, Lewisburg, PA.

Parker, R. (1996) *Athenian Religion: A History*, Oxford, UK.

Parker, R. (2005) *Polytheism and Society at Athens*, Oxford, UK.

Parker, R. (2008) 'Πατρῷοι θεοί: the cults of sub-groups and identity in the Greek world' in A. H. Rasmussen and S. W. Rasmussen (eds.), *Religion and Society: Rituals, Resources and Identity in the Ancient Graeco-Roman World*, Rome, 201–14.

Perlman, P. (1992) 'One hundred-citied Crete and the "Cretan politeia"', *Classical Philology* 87, 193-205.

Piérart, M. (1974) *Platon et la cité grecque*, Brussels.

Pinker, S. (2011) *The Better Angels of our Nature*, London.

Polinskaya, I. (2003) 'Liminality as metaphor: initiation and the frontiers of ancient Athens' in D. B. Dodd and C. Faraone (eds.), *Initiation in Ancient Greek Rituals and Narratives: New Critical Perspectives*, London, 85–106.

Powell, A. and Hodkinson, S. (eds.) (1994) *The Shadow of Sparta*, London.

Pritchard, D. M. (2003) 'Athletics, education and participation in classical Athens' in D. Phillips and D. Pritchard (eds.), *Sport and Festival in the Ancient Greek World*, Swansea, UK, 293–350.

Pritchard, D. M. (2004) 'Kleisthenes, participation and the dithyrambic contests of late archaic and classical Athens', *Phoenix* 58, 208–28.

Pritchard, D. M. (ed.) (2010) *War, Democracy and Culture in Classical Athens*, Cambridge, UK.

Pritchett, W. K. (1974) *The Greek State at War: Part II*, Berkeley, CA and Los Angeles.

Rabinowitz, A. (2009) 'Drinking from the same cup: Sparta and late archaic commensality' in S. Hodkinson (ed.), *Sparta: Comparative Perspectives*, Swansea, UK, 113–92.

Rawlings, L. (2000) 'Alternative agonies: hoplite martial and combat experiences beyond the phalanx' in H. van Wees (ed.), *War and Violence in Ancient Greece*, London and Swansea, UK, 233–59.

Rawlings, L. (2007) *The Ancient Greeks at War*, Manchester, UK.

Reinmuth, O. W. (1971) *The Ephebic Inscriptions of the Fourth Century B.C.*, Leiden, Netherlands.

Rhodes, P. J. (1972) *The Athenian Boule*, Oxford, UK.

Rhodes, P. J. and Osborne, R. (2003) *Greek Historical Inscriptions, 404–323 BC*, Oxford, UK.

Richer, N. (2005) 'Introduction' in J.-M. Bertrand (ed.), *La violence dans les mondes grec et romain*, Paris, 7–35.

Roisman, J. (2005) *The Rhetoric of Manhood: Masculinity in the Attic Orators*, Berkeley, CA, Los Angeles and London.

Scanlon, T. F. (2002) *Eros and Greek Athletics*, Oxford, UK.

Schnapp, A. (1997) *Le chasseur et la cité: chasse et érotique dans la Grèce ancienne*, Paris.

Sekunda, N. V. (1990) '*IG* II² 1250: a decree concerning the *Lampadephoroi* of the tribe Aiantis', *ZPE* 83, 149–82.

Siewert, P. (1977) 'The ephebic oath in fifth-century Athens', *JHS* 97, 102–11.

Slater, N. W. (1996) 'Bringing up father: *paideia* and *ephebeia* in the *Wasps*' in A. H. Sommerstein and C. Atherton (eds.), *Education in Greek Fiction*, Bari, Italy, 27–52.

Sommerstein, A. H. (1989) *Aeschylus' Eumenides*, Cambridge, UK.

Sommerstein, A. H. (1996) 'Response to N.W. Slater' in A. H. Sommerstein and C. Atherton (eds.), *Education in Greek Fiction*, Bari, Italy, 53–64.

Sommerstein, A. H. (2010) 'Adolescence, ephebeia and Athenian drama' in A. H. Sommerstein, *The Tangled Ways of Zeus and Other Studies in and around Greek Tragedy*, Oxford, UK, 47–60.

Sommerstein, A. H. and Atherton, C. (eds.) (1996) *Education in Greek Fiction*, Bari, Italy.

Sourvinou-Inwood, C. (2011) *Athenian Myths and Festivals*, Oxford, UK.

Ste. Croix, G. E. M. (1972) *The Origins of the Peloponnesian War*, London.

Steinbock, B. (2011) 'A lesson in patriotism: Lycurgus' Against Leocrates, the ideology of the *ephebeia*, and Athenian social memory', *CA* 30, 279–317.

Steinbock, B. (2013) *Social Memory in Athenian Public Discourse: Uses and Meanings of the Past*, Ann Arbor, MI.

Talbert, R. J. A. (1989) 'The role of the helots in the class struggle at Sparta', *Historia* 38, 22–40.

Taplin, O. (1977) *The Stagecraft of Aeschylus*, Oxford, UK.

Thür, G. (ed.) (1994) *Symposion 1993: Vorträge zur griechischen und hellenistichen Rechtsgeschichte*, Cologne; Weimar, Germany and Vienna.

Todd, S. C. (2007) *A Commentary on Lysias Speeches 1–11*, Oxford, UK.

Tuplin, C. (1994) 'Xenophon, Sparta and the *Cyropaedia*' in Powell and Hodkinson (1994), 127–81.

Tzifopoulos, Y. Z. (1998) '"Hemerodromoi" and Cretan "Dromeis": athletes or military personnel? The case of the Cretan Philonides', *Nikephoros* 11, 137–70.

Vanderpool, E. (1959) 'News from Greece', *AJA* 63, 279–80.

van Wees, H. (1998) 'Greeks bearing arms: the state, the leisure class and the display of weapons in Archaic Greece' in H. van Wees and N. Fisher (eds.), *Archaic Greece: New Approaches and New Evidence*, London, 333–78.

van Wees, H. (2000a) 'The development of the hoplite phalanx: iconography and reality in the seventh century' in H. van Wees (ed.), *War and Violence in Ancient Greece*, London and Swansea, UK, 125–66.

van Wees, H. (ed.) (2000b) *War and Violence in Ancient Greece*, London and Swansea, UK.

van Wees, H. (2004) *Greek Warfare: Myths and Realities*, London.

van Wees, H. (2008a) 'Review article: violence', *JHS* 128, 172–5.

van Wees, H. (2008b) '*Stasis*, destroyer of men: mass, elite, political violence and security in archaic Greece' in C. Brélaz and P. Ducrey (eds.), *Sécurité collective et ordre public dans les sociétés anciennes*, Geneva, 1–39.

van Wees, H. (2011) 'The "law of hubris" and Solon's reform of justice' in S. D. Lambert (ed.) *Sociable Man: Essays on Ancient Greek Social Behaviour in Honour of Nick Fisher*, Swansea, UK, 117-44.

van Wees, H. (2013) *Ships and Silver, Taxes and Tribute: A Fiscal History of Archaic Athens*, London.

Vidal-Naquet, P. (1968) 'La tradition de l'hoplite athénien' in J.-P. Vernant (ed.), *Problèmes de la guerre en Grèce ancienne*, Paris, 161–82.

Vidal-Naquet, P. (1986) *The Black Hunter: Forms of Thought and Forms of Society in the Greek World*, Baltimore, MD.

Vidal-Naquet, P. (1988) 'Sophokles' *Philoctetes* and the *ephebeia*' in J.-P. Vernant and P. Vidal-Naquet, *Myth and Tragedy in Ancient Greece*, New York, 161–80.

Vidal-Naquet, P. (1989) 'Retour au chasseur noir' in M. M. Mactoux and E. Gény (eds.), *Mélanges Pierre Lévêque* II, Paris, 387–411.

Wallace, R. W. (1985) *The Areopagos Council, to 307 B.C.*, Baltimore, MD and London.

Wallace, S. (2010) *Ancient Crete: From Successful Collapse to Democracy's Alternatives, Twelfth to Fifth Centuries BC*, Cambridge, UK.

Whitby, M. (1994) 'Two shadows: images of Spartans and helots' in A. Powell and S. Hodkinson (eds.), *The Shadow of Sparta*, London, 87–126.

Whitehead, D. (1985) *The Demes of Attica*, Princeton, NJ.

Whitehead, D. (1991) 'The Lampadephoroi of Aiantis again', *ZPE* 87, 42–4.

Whitley, J. (2015) 'Agonistic aristocrats? The curious case of Archaic Crete' in N. Fisher and H. van Wees (eds.), *Aristocracy in the Ancient World*, Swansea, UK, 287–312.

Wilson, P. (2000) *The Athenian Institution of the Khoregia*, Cambridge, UK.

Wilson, P. (2003) 'The politics of dance: dithyrambic contest and social order in ancient Greece' in D. Phillips and D. Pritchard (eds.), *Sport and Festival in the Ancient Greek World*, Swansea, UK, 163–96.

Wilson, P. (2007) 'Performance in the *Pythion*: the Athenian Thargelia' in P. Wilson (ed.), *The Greek Theatre and Festivals: Documentary Studies*, Oxford, UK, 150–82.

Wohl, V. (2010) *Law's Cosmos: Juridical Discourse in Athenian Forensic Oratory*, Cambridge, UK.

6 Binding curses, agency and the Athenian democracy[*]

Zinon Papakonstantinou

In the ancient world, magical binding curses (*katadesmoi/defixiones*) were a popular way to influence, inhibit and harm an opponent. Although oral magical spells are attested since the archaic period, the earliest written specimens date to the late sixth/early fifth century. According to the extant record, the production of written binding curses, scratched on the surface of small lead tablets and other materials, increased exponentially since the fourth century, especially in Athens. In this essay I investigate Athenian written binding curses of the classical period in the light of perceptions and practices of individual and collective agency. Looking beyond the aspects of production and deposition of the tablets directly linked with magic, written binding curses can be considered as narratives on interpersonal relationships and public life. These narratives often stem from or implicate subaltern groups (women, slaves, urban labourers) not well represented in the extant Athenian literary corpus. Viewed from this vantage point, binding curses can provide insightful and, at times, unorthodox perspectives on social interaction and conflict management in the Athenian public sphere.

Binding curses in classical Athens

Binding curses are attested in Athens since the fifth century, although there should be no doubt that the practice is significantly older. They were performed orally or in conjunction with written magical texts scratched on various materials. According to the current orthodoxy, spells written on lead appear in small numbers for the first time in Athens around the mid-fifth century, and their numbers increase during the fourth. Even though the amount of Athenian curse tablets attributed to the fifth century remains low, extant specimens suggest a familiarity with the genre of written curses, at least among professional sorcerers, since the early/mid-fifth century. Hence *SGD* 1, a curse tablet of the mid-fifth century or slightly later, originally contained at least 70 lines of text and targeted numerous men and women. The tablet was then deposited in the right hand of a skeleton in a grave in Kerameikos. This is admittedly the most elaborate of the early written Athenian binding curses, and it presupposes a period of local acculturation of the practices of binding magic. Other Athenian curse tablets dated to the second half of the fifth century also suggest a fairly advanced level of sophistication in magical texts and rituals practised in Athens at least since the mid-fifth century.

The existence of binding curses is also explicitly alluded to in fifth-century Athenian literature. Aeschylus' *Eumenides* contains a 'binding song' uttered by the Erinyes against Orestes in the context of a murder trial.[1] The Erinyes assume a moral high ground, arguing for the righteousness of their intention to bind and punish a sacrilegious assassin. In language and content the song is reminiscent of a judicial binding curse, mixed with elements of a 'prayer for justice', i.e. a spell uttered against a target that had committed some form of crime and injustice.[2] Moreover, in *Prometheus Bound* (52–87) the binding of Prometheus' scene bears a strong resemblance to the language and rituals of binding magic. Prometheus is bound in shackles and is impaled with a wedge through his chest. The whole episode, which involves various agents (Kratos, Hephaistos, Zeus), corresponds to an on-stage re-enactment of a binding ritual.[3] These allusions to binding magic are near contemporary to the earliest written curse tablets from fifth-century Athens. It should be noted that in both the *Eumenides* and the *Prometheus Bound* binding practices are not explicitly acknowledged as magical, which points to magic as a rather underground practice that most people would have hesitated to admit any association with. By the same token, in both cases the playwright assumed that the audience would be conversant with the main features of binding magic.

The last point is also corroborated by another reference to a binding curse in fifth-century Athenian literature, this time concerning a well-known public figure. Thoukydides, the son of Melesias, was prominent on the Athenian political scene as the opponent of Perikles, primarily in the 450s and 440s. He was eventually ostracised in 443. At some point towards the end of his career, possibly soon after his return from exile in the late 430s, he was involved in a lawsuit. Aristophanes (*Vesp.* 946–8) records that during the trial the elderly Thoukydides was paralysed in the jaw and was thus unable to defend himself. The *scholia vetera*, which most likely drew from classical Athenian sources, further elaborate that Thoukydides was unable to plead his defence, as if his tongue had been tied from within. The language of these passages fits very well the language and actions envisaged in classical Athenian judicial curses.[4] In the *Acharnians* (703–18) Aristophanes presents a different explanation for this incident, i.e. that Thoukydides was completely outperformed by the prosecutor in court. This suggests that in the years following Thoukydides' trial there were at least two narratives in circulation regarding this incident. In the version recorded in the *Wasps* and the scholia, a version ostensibly sympathetic to Thoukydides, the politician's mishap was attributed to a binding curse. There are other known instances in the Greco-Roman world when orators and politicians attributed their sudden inability to speak in public to binding magic.[5]

In addition to corroborating the point that theatre-goers in fifth-century Athens were familiar with the language and rituals of binding magic, the passage from the *Wasps* that reproduces the rumour that Thucydides was the victim of a binding curse points to a rather neglected aspect of magic: the need for publicity. In the ancient world magical rites were furtively conducted, and scholars working on ancient magic are right to underscore secrecy as a vital component of the performance of binding curses.[6] Nonetheless, assuming that a magical rite works primarily by the power of suggestion, it is important, if not essential, that the intended victim becomes somehow aware that he or she is the target of a magical act. In other words, in the ancient world magical professionals and their clients had to carefully balance ritual secrecy with a certain degree of public awareness of the existence of the magical spell. In this sense, magical binding curses shared a feature with public imprecations, i.e. curses proclaimed against e.g. enemies of the state or potential desecrators of graves, which were publicly displayed in inscriptions.[7]

The case of Thoukydides demonstrates that instances of real or presumed magic against high-profile individuals could become part of popular lore in classical Athens. Other evidence suggests that targets of magical rites became aware of the existence of malicious magical spells in a number of ways. In the *Laws* (933 B) Plato decries men who are terrified at the sight of wax voodoo dolls on doors, public streets or tombs of their ancestors. Contrary to voodoo dolls, binding curses were not publicly displayed, as they were usually hidden in graves, wells or in the sites of sanctuaries. But knowledge of their existence could spread through gossip and hearsay, no doubt often initiated by the curser and his or her sorcerer. Plato once again alludes to that practice when he claims that sorceries, incantations and binding spells affect their intended victims, as they make them believe that they can inflict real harm (*Laws* 933A).

The existence of counter-curses also corroborates the argument that in order for a curse to be effective, the intended victim somehow had to be convinced that a potential harmful spell was in operation. An early fourth-century opisthographic curse tablet from Athens[8] illustrates this point. On side A the curser articulates a counter-curse:

> Whoever puts a binding spell on me, whether woman or man, or slave or free, or foreigner or citizen, or family member or stranger, whether for spite towards my work or my deeds, whoever puts a curse on me before Hermes *eriounios* or *katochos* or *dolios* or anywhere else, I put a counter spell on all my enemies.

The author of this curse has clearly come to believe that a binding spell against him was in operation or in the making. It is likely, although not necessary, that the counter-curse on side A was related to the binding curse against two *antidikoi* (trial opponents) on side B. If both sides of the tablet refer to the same legal dispute, then we can envisage the following situation of conflict: the author of *NGCT* 24 had a dispute with Dion and Granikos, which eventually ended up in court, and he binds them both on side B. But the *defigens* also had grounds to believe that he was the target of a curse commissioned by his adversaries or other individuals involved in the same dispute. He therefore commissions a reciprocal spell (side A) in addition to the aggressive curse on side B. To cover all bases the counter spell in *NGCT* 24, side A casts the net wide and targets anyone among the curser's opponents who could potentially employ binding magic against him.

NGCT 24 therefore demonstrates how practitioners of binding magic exploited the particularities of Athenian social life and polity, especially the continuous, partly unmediated social interaction between individuals of all genders, legal statuses and social backgrounds, and the relative open access of most aspects of the political and legal process to Athenian residents, in order to enhance the efficacy of binding curses. By spreading the word that a curse was in operation sorcerers and their clients aimed at psychologically manipulating their opponents by creating feelings of frustration and fear of imminent harm. For targets of binding curses, the possibility of pernicious consequences as a result of a curse was very real and the need for reprisals was urgent and mandatory. Many targets of magic responded by resorting to the supernatural themselves – as the author of *NGCT* 24 did with his counter-curse, or the petitioner in an oracular tablet in the sanctuary of Zeus in Dodona who, being aware that he was the target of a curse by an adversary, asks Zeus if it was still worth it going to court.[9] Despite their often esoteric language, furtive contexts of production and arcane rites of deposition, binding curses depended partially on their integration in daily social interaction to enhance their effectiveness.

These observations have wider implications for the way we interpret curse tablets and the role of magic in general in the ancient world. The need to publicise the existence, if not part of the contents, of a binding curse meant that besides being formulaic and secretive texts, written curse tablets were also narratives through which their authors articulated strategies of social interaction and advancement. In the case of classical Athens, several aspects of Athenian society and daily life facilitated this dual role of curse tablets. For instance, writing was widely used in classical Athens for official purposes, and there is evidence to suggest that many inhabitants of Attica possessed at least modest literacy skills.[10] But there should be no doubt that interpersonal communication was overwhelmingly conducted through oral discourse. That suited the nature of magical curse tablets, texts that were committed to writing but were not supposed to be read in public. Instead, their contents were communicated by word of mouth to interested parties. As we will see in the next section, aspects of the institutional setup of democratic Athens also made binding curses a suitable tool to employ in certain circumstances. And because binding spells were motivated by particular – most often personal – interests, they allow precious glimpses into how individuals responded to the challenges they faced in their interaction with the Athenian public sphere and its formal institutions.

Binding curses in the Athenian public sphere

A problem in any attempt to interpret the wider implications of binding curses is that in the overwhelming majority of cases we can only guess the identities and social backgrounds of the individuals who commissioned them. Agents of curses do not name themselves in the tablets, undoubtedly due to the fear that they might accidentally fall victims of their own curse. Moreover, in most cases we can deduce only part of the circumstances that led to the production of a binding curse. These features of binding curses has led scholars interested in curse tablets to move beyond the confines of magical rituals in a quest for overarching models of analysis, including a recent take on curse tablets as a means to pre-empt danger and manage risk.[11] The Athenian material is however equally amenable to more particularly Athenian socio-historical interpretations, both because there are hundreds of extant curse tablets from ancient Athens (including considerable amounts from the classical and early Hellenistic periods), but also because the Athenian social and cultural milieu can be adequately reconstructed to provide a context for the study of binding curses. Adopting such an approach, a recent study insightfully examines the role of curse tablets in the process of ritualizing and mediating violence in Athenian law courts and daily life.[12]

There is, to be sure, plenty of room for further study of Athenian curse tablets. The following analysis takes as its starting point some central features of Athenian democratic institutions and other well-known aspects of quotidian life in Athens during the classical period. Of particular interest is the principle that Athenian citizens were enjoying open access to various state institutions and governmental bodies. In theory, and contingent on some restrictions related primarily to rules of rotation and tribal proportional representation in decision-making bodies, all Athenian citizens could freely participate in the assembly, the courts of justice, the council of 500, religious festivals and other activities of the Athenian democracy. In practice, citizens who lived in or around the urban centre and were devoid of the need for daily labour in order to earn a livelihood had an advantage over citizens who lived in remote demes, small farmers and urban labourers. State authorities were aware of these disparities and, since the inception of the democracy and throughout the classical period, Athenians took various measures to mitigate them, including the use of allotment for the selection of representatives to the council of 500 and court juries and the introduction of the *misthos* (pay) for jury duty and attendance in assembly meetings. The purpose was to remedy social and geographical inequalities and ensure that, as much as possible, a wide cross-section of the Athenian population participated in the day-to-day operations of the Athenian democracy.

These initiatives had partial success; we are aware that many Athenian non-elites were able to share in some aspects of the running of the state. But surely, even after the various incentives introduced over time, for many the practical constraints of distance to the urban centre and the need to focus on day-to-day necessities were often difficult, if not impossible, to overcome. It should be noted however that even for Athenians who lived in remote areas of Attica there were some possibilities to participate in collective action, including deme politics, phratry activities, local festivals and theatrical performances. For citizens of inferior legal status and non-citizens – including women, metics and slaves – the opportunities for participation in civic activities were markedly reduced, and were regulated according to gender, age and status. But it should be noted that even members of these subaltern groups had opportunities, albeit marginal, to make their presence known in state organs from which they were formally excluded. One example concerns women in the Athenian courts of justice. In the overwhelming majority of cases women had an inferior standing in the courts, and could be represented only through a male *kyrios* (guardian), usually a male relative.[13] But there is evidence to suggest that women, as well as children and other groups, could at times attend the proceedings of trials, and that often they attempted to influence their outcomes through heckling and peer-pressure techniques directed at litigants and jurors.[14]

As the episode involving the alleged binding curse in the trial of Thukydides demonstrates, in classical Athens the content of high-profile legal and assembly proceedings were quickly shared in the Athenian public sphere, i.e. in all the discursive, communal spaces (e.g. the agora or civic festivals) where inhabitants of Attica could interact with each other. Narratives on aspects of public life were no doubt renegotiated and even distorted during this process; nevertheless, this process was fundamental in shaping communal perceptions on pressing political issues as well as on other matters that somehow had achieved notoriety among the wider public. All the above was feasible because in classical Athens individuals could interact to such an extent that often a blurring of identities occurred, especially between persons of differing legal statuses (e.g. citizens, metics and slaves).[15]

The interaction of individuals of all genders, legal statuses and social backgrounds also clearly emerges in Athenian binding curses from the classical period. In turn, this means that binding curses have the potential to contribute to our understanding of the functioning of the Athenian public sphere. Hence, in a legal curse tablet of the first half of the fourth century the curser targets 'those inscribed here, both men and women who are here inscribed' followed by an *adynaton* prescription, common in magical spells, that his opponents in court shall see an end to the trial when the dead make a journey home.[16] Following this preamble there is a list of names, all individuals bound by the curse. The list of targets includes a woman ('daughter of Euphranor', ll. 11–12), a 'saffron-seller' (l. 23), perhaps short for spice-seller, and several individuals identified with their demotics, including Aristophon of Azenia (1.29), known for his long public career and successful judicial record.[17] An Aristophanes Aristom[edous] targeted in the same curse (1.25) was very likely a nephew of Aristophon.

Equally revealing is a mid-fourth century Athenian curse tablet.[18] It targets at least 96 persons and provides the demotics of many of the targets. The list includes several Athenians prominent in politics and public life, including Xenokles of Sphettos,[19] Polyeuktos of Sphettos,[20] and the notorious sycophant Aristogeiton of Pithos. Moreover, among the targets we find a metic (1.50), a painter and individuals involved in the grain trade (chaff-sellers and a groats-seller), as well as four women and one man identified as prostitutes. How can we explain the impressive and diverse lineups of public figures and members of subaltern groups in *SGD* 42 and *SGD* 48? A plausible interpretation is that in both cases, in the mind of the agent of the curse, all the targets were somehow connected in a particular affair and were perceived as adversaries. Regardless of the exact circumstances of the disputes that led to the creation of these binding curses, the presence of representatives of a cross-section of Athenian society could only make sense in a context where virtually unhindered interaction, collaboration or interpersonal conflict by members of these groups was feasible.

Personal and collective agency

With this background in mind, we can return to some fundamental questions regarding binding curses and their role in the society that generates them: what did people in the ancient world believe they were achieving when they engaged in magic? Why did inhabitants of Attica, whether full citizens or otherwise, believe that magic was an appropriate and efficient strategy in coping with problematic situations? And finally, how did their actions affect the world around them, both in the short term and in the longer run? Binding curses were interventions in public life – be that the courtroom in the case of a showdown between prominent public figures, or a proactive response to a dispute confined to the microcosm of the neighbourhood. Moreover, curse tablets were personal responses to particular challenges faced by the individuals, and in some cases their friends and associates, who commissioned the curses. In other words, they reveal something of individual or group motivations, intentions and goals of people involved in interpersonal or intergroup disputes in the public sphere of classical Athens.

The concept of agency could be valuable in developing further this line of argument. Agency can be defined as a mode of social praxis, as the totality of choices made and acts executed by an individual or a group towards the realisation of a certain objective. In recent decades, agency, especially in its interplay with structure, has been a prominent theme in the social and cognitive sciences, and less explicitly in historical scholarship as well. It is widely recognised that in most cases the relationship between agency and structure is complex and uneasy; by the same token, it is acknowledged that some kind of dialectical relationship between agency and structure exists. Institutions and state-controlled entities have the capacity to confer power and impose constraints on individuals; yet at the same time individuals are capable through their agency to mediate, manipulate and partly control the operation of state and social structures.

Individuals act agentically when they act with intentionality and in a proactive manner. They construct plans and set goals that they set out to execute. From the scholar's point of view, several factors are taken into consideration when scrutinising the process of agency, including the social standing of the agent, his or her social environment, the availability of resources and the agent's ability to self-reflect and adjust strategies and objectives. Agency is exercised primarily in three modes: individual (or personal), collective and proxy. Individual agency can be manifested in various gradations. Low-level agents tend to focus on the mechanics and the immediate consequences of their actions, i.e. on how they act. Their actions are usually confined to everyday, routine acts, as low-level agents most often lack the skills and a sense of self-efficacy necessary to undertake successfully more complicated tasks. By contrast, high-level agents tend to set their plans and establish their objectives in an encompassing manner, taking into consideration their motives and the long-term social and self-evaluative implications of their actions, i.e. they identify why they act. High-level agents are more resourceful, are more adaptive to setbacks and have a more clear appreciation of themselves vis-à-vis other social agents and society at large. In practice, most people fall somewhere between the two extremes (high–low) of personal agency modes, and it is possible that the same person would exhibit traits of high or low agency in different situations, based on a number of variables (e.g. unfamiliarity with a situation or task involved). Nevertheless, individuals tend to incline towards one of the personal agency modes, i.e. high-level agents usually tend to think and act in high-level terms and vice versa. Finally, it should be noted that the environment, including the family and the wider social milieu, seems to be a significant factor in influencing the prevailing personal agency mode exhibited by an individual.[21]

How can these insights on human behaviour contribute to our understanding of Athenian binding curses? I argue that the institutional and social setup of democratic Athens encouraged individual and collective agency. People could organise and act in groups, often as part of a civic body (religious festivals, council of 500, assembly, jury), but they could also act individually or in unison with other collective configurations (family, friends and associates) and often, as we have already pointed out, in a manner that transcended strict age, gender and legal status divisions. Compared with modern, impersonal representative democracies, inhabitants of Attica had infinitely more opportunities to exercise their individual and collective agency on a daily basis and for a wider array of issues that affected the entire Athenian polity. Proxy agency, i.e. the state of seeking to influence one's environment and improve one's life conditions through the help and services of others, was not unknown in ancient Athens, but was less common in comparison to most modern and some ancient societies (e.g. Rome).

Furthermore, extant sources, including curse tablets, suggest that inhabitants of Attica often exercised high-level individual and collective agency. Individuals, especially residents in or near the urban area of Athens, intentionally engaged in a number of acts that had clearly defined long-term implications for the individuals in question and often for the city-state of Athens as a whole. Hence, Athenians participated in big numbers in the popular assembly which decided on issues that affected the entire community. Despite the questions surrounding their composition, Thucydides' narratives of debates in the Athenian assembly during the Peloponnesian War allow valuable insights on the dynamics of assembly meetings in late fifth-century Athens. For instance, in the Mytilene debate (Thuc. 3.37–49) speakers deliberated not only on the immediate fate of the rebels in the Aegean island, but also on the best way to serve Athenian interests, and in regards to the message that Athens, as an imperialist power, wanted to send to her allies and indeed the entire Greek world through this affair. Furthermore, in the debate before the Sicilian expedition (Thuc. 6.8–26) the discussion in the assembly of the long-term benefits that could accrue to Athens out of a military intervention in Sicily was pivotal in the demos' overwhelming vote in favour of the expedition.

Even if we allow that some of the arguments put in the mouths of assembly speakers by Thucydides and other ancient authors are rhetorical constructions, one would reasonably expect that long-term consequences and matters of civic expediency would have been considered and debated in a meeting that decided important issues of state, including war. That was especially so, since it was the assembly-goers who were going to bear the brunt of any decision they were going to vote for. Parallels are to be found in several defining moments in Athenian history during the classical period, for example the decision to award amnesty to oligarchs after the restoration of the democracy in 403. Even decisions on more humdrum issues, e.g. the awarding of honours or citizenship to individuals who benefitted Athens, had long-term implications: they encouraged the persons in question to continue their acts of munificence and invited other wealthy individuals to emulate them, all to the benefit of Athens and its people.

Speakers in the popular assembly no doubt hammered these points home to the assembly audience, who could not have failed to realise the import of their decisions. Assembly-goers were therefore able to think and act individually at a high-level agency mode and vote, in an instantiation of collective agency, according to what they thought were their best interests. The same pattern is detected in other spheres of life in classical Athens. For instance, inhabitants of Attica regularly engaged in religious festivals at the polis or regional level, *oikos* rituals and other acts of interaction with the divine with the firm belief that their acts propitiated the gods who were expected to reciprocate with well-being and prosperity for the individuals, their families and their city. Moreover, through communal worship, processions, athletic contests, theatrical performances and other features of these festivals, participants re-enacted and negotiated the meaning of what it meant to be a member of the Athenian community, as well as the image that Athens projected to the rest of the Greek world. Overall, although the means and motives for certain actions might appear irrational or counterproductive to modern audiences, the evidence overwhelmingly suggests that Athenians routinely acted in a high-level agency mode in multiple action domains, including politics, religion, law and family life.

It was the particular institutional and social framework of classical Athens, with the relative easy access to civic decision-making bodies by citizens and the open spaces in the Athenian public sphere where citizens and subaltern groups interacted, that largely accustomed inhabitants of Attica to think and act in a high-level agency mode. Forensic orations corroborate this inference. Most extant court speeches employ arguments based on the long-term consequences of the dispute for the litigants. The implication is that not only were the litigants high-level agents, but that the same applied to the jurors at large, since they were able to follow and decide on the basis of these arguments.

Curse tablets, interpersonal and group conflict

Binding curses can also elucidate Athenian patterns of interpersonal interaction as well as individual behaviours and modes of agency in the context of conflict. Curse tablets are especially valuable because they illustrate the immediate, cognized goals of the agent (in this case the person who commissioned a curse), and also allude to long-term aims. In the case of classical Athens, most curse tablets are very explicit about the adversaries and the objectives of the curse, which suggests that they were generated by specific situations of interpersonal conflict and not by generic grievances of the author of the curse against some people.

Moreover, even though some curse tablets indicate that at times animosities and conflict crossed social divides, on balance the evidence for dispute resolution in classical Athens (i.e. forensic oratory and curse tablets) cumulatively suggests that in most cases disputes and litigation involved social and economic peers.[22] In turn, this means that we can reasonably speculate about the social background of the curser by identifying the main target or targets of a binding curse.

The extant corpus of classical Athenian binding curses provides numerous examples of magical spells that touch upon the higher echelons of Athenian public life and politics. For instance, an early fourth-century curse tablet discovered at Kerameikos bears the shape of a ship and appears to be targeting a commercial boat, its crew and cargo. At the end of side B the curser targets [Ἀ]νδοκδης ἑρμοκο[πίδης].[23] This is undoubtedly a reference to the famous orator Andokides, whose name was involved in the scandals of the mutilation of the Hermaic stelae and the profanation of the Eleusinian mysteries in 415. Andokides felt the repercussions of his involvement with these religious scandals for the rest of his life. Among others, he was prosecuted for impiety in a trial that took place most likely in 400.[24] We know that besides his political activities, Andokides also actively engaged in commercial enterprises. Indeed he appears to have been a major entrepreneur, specialising in long-distance trade.[25]

Viewed in this light, it is reasonable to suggest that the curse tablet against Andokides was commissioned by a business rival, or even a former associate (e.g. crew member) in one of Andokides' commercial enterprises. Whatever his background, the agent of the curse in question possibly sought revenge against a perceived injustice. But it is equally likely that there were wider motives behind the curse tablet against Andokides, especially if the main context of the dispute that generated the curse is located in the world of business. Binding curses ostensibly motivated by business rivalries are discussed in more detail below. However, it is worth mentioning that very often one of the objectives of the agents of such curses appears to be the professional and financial ruin of business adversaries. Andokides profited greatly from his entrepreneurial undertakings, and there should be no doubt that he was at odds with other powerful commercial interests in the city of Athens. Andokides' potential business failures would have paved the way for great profit for other Athenian entrepreneurs.

Furthermore, although the bulk of the spell against Andokides is dedicated to specific commercial undertakings in which the orator was involved, the curse is noteworthy for the emphatic reference to Andokides' role in the mutilation of the herms in 415.[26] Once again, several possibilities present themselves. For example, the author of the curse might have genuinely resented the role of Andokides in the events of 415 and believed that a well-known act of sacrilege would motivate further the divine spirits to execute the curse against his target. Not incompatible with the previous possibility is an additional consideration, corroborated by the fact that the curse was most likely produced in the first years of the fourth century, i.e. around the time or soon after Andokides' impeachment for *asebeia* (impiety) in 400/399.[27] The trial of Andokides no doubt evoked memories of the mutilation of the herms and the profanation of the mysteries to a wider segment of the

Athenian population who treated with suspicion and ill will Andokides and his involvement in the public affairs of Athens. Although not all Athenians shared this view, as suggested by the fact that Andokides was acquitted of the *asebeia* charge, the agent of the curse against Andokides inserted the spell into the contemporary, public discourse on the role of Andokides in the infamous events of 415.

The spell against Andokides is therefore a great example of how an Athenian at the turn of the fourth century could concurrently engage in diverse action domains, i.e. business, politics, litigation. Experience and expertise in a wide range of activities are tokens of high-level social agents. In the case of the Andokides curse this high-level individual agency can be documented for the target and can be deduced for the author of the curse. Andokides, a well-known public figure, is targeted as a business rival, as a person who is disrespectful of the moral values and religious practices of the community and as an individual who might even be conceived as an opponent of the democracy itself. Interestingly, a detail of the *asebeia* trial reveals how such multi-domain agential behaviour was feasible in practice. In his defence speech Andokides points out that a certain Agyrrhios, one of the supporters of the chief prosecutor Kephisios, was also his business rival with whom he had a dispute at a tax auction.[28] The identity of the person who commissioned the binding spell against Andokides is of course unknown, but the context of Andokides' life in the early fourth century is sufficiently known to allow a reasonable reconstruction of the place of the curse in conflicts and disputes prominent in the Athenian public sphere during the same period. If, as argued above, authors of binding curses increased their potential effect on the intended victims by making their existence known through gossip-mongering, then the objective of the curse against Andokides was to sabotage his business dealings and undermine his public stature, especially in connection with the *asebeia* trial.

The use of binding magic as a conflict management strategy by high-level agents is also suggested by numerous other curse tablets. In most cases the context of the dispute and the personal history of the target are less known than in the case of the curse against Andokides. Nonetheless, even in the cases of obscure contexts a careful reading of certain curses provides valuable clues for various types of disputes and the role of binding magic in the process of dispute resolution. A good case study concerns local situations of conflict, i.e. disputes that did not obtain the publicity accorded to the religious scandals of 415.

DTA 24, a fourth-century curse tablet inscribed on two sides of a lead strip, is an example of a curse that refers to local factional strife. It targets nine individuals, with a certain Phokion topping the list of side A. Adolf Wilhelm first identified the Phokion in question as the famous Athenian public figure of the fourth century.[29] Once this identification is considered plausible, then several other features of the curse fall into place. For instance, l.2 of side A targets a certain Eupheros and an Aristokrates. We know that members of the family of Kallistratos of Aphidna, the prominent Athenian statesman of the first half of the fourth century, bore the same names.[30] Given the other circumstantial evidence linking Phokion and Kallistratos, it seems quite plausible that the Eupheros and Aristokrates targeted in *DTA* 24 were the two brothers of Kallistratos.[31] Moreover, side B of the same tablet targets five individuals, including a Euthemon and a Nikomenes. The individuals Euthemon Eupolidos Halieus[32] and Nikomenes Hieronos Halieus[33] are attested in decrees from the deme of Halai Aixonides.[34] Since *DTA* 24 was reportedly discovered in the territory of the same deme, and given that side A of the tablet ostensibly refers to prominent Athenian public figures, it is quite plausible that the Euthemon and Nikomenes targeted on side B should be identified with the two individuals prominent in the deme politics of Halai Aixonides in the 360s.

It has been reasonably suggested that *DTA* 24 is a judicial spell and that the individuals cursed on both sides of the tablet belonged, at least in the mind of the curser, to the same political group.[35] Wilhelm conjectured that the historical context of the curse was a series of administrative reforms in connection with the offices of treasurer and demarch.[36] The references to individuals prominent in state (side A) and local (side B) politics are not inconsistent with these interpretations.[37] But even if these particular interpretations are not accepted, it is evident that the author of *DTA* 24 clearly wants to impede and/or alter the course of action undertaken by the targets. Moreover, it is very likely that the dispute that generated *DTA* 24 was connected with issues that the aggregate of public men targeted in the curse would be involved with, i.e. issues of factional conflict that had wider implications on the local (deme) and civic-wide level. In other words, the author of *DTA* 24 was most likely another public figure involved in a multi-stage showdown with the targets. Furthermore, the tablet seems to allude to different stages of a dispute with local and civic repercussions. A multifaceted dispute that involved numerous individuals would inevitably generate variant meanings and invite the pursuit of far-flung objectives through the employment of different strategies, including magic.

Another example of a binding curse that elucidates agential behaviour in classical Athens, especially in instances of conflict management and resolution, is *SGD* 45. If in the case of *DTA* 24 the curser is pursuing a dispute related to demotic and civic factional strife, in *SGD* 45 the focus seems to be exclusively on the local level. *SGD* 45 binds eight individuals, six men and two women. Although none of the targets can be identified securely, the names of all but one are qualified by a demotic or kinship term. Most targets come from neighbouring demes of south-western Attica (Aigilia, Anaphlystos). Nausistratos from Aigilia, mentioned first, is presumably the main target; Nikonymos (l.2) and Kleostrate (l.6) are his offspring. An Aristaichmos from Anaphlystos, perhaps a descendant of the target bearing the same name (ll. 4–5) in our curse, is mentioned as a member of the *genos* of Kerykes in a late first-century inscription (*PAA* 163780). Smikythos from Aigilia, l.3 (*PAA* 826635) might be identical or related to a Smikythos, son of Deinostratos, from Aigilia, a *diaitetes* c. 330 (*IG* II² 1927, l. 178; *PAA* 826640). The curse concerns a dispute of local calibre, involving most likely locally prominent individuals. Family ties play a role, but the consequences of the dispute were clearly felt by other residents in the area as well. Perhaps we are dealing with a locally high-profile inheritance and property quarrel: considerable financial gain, as well as a person's and a family's social standing, were often at stake in such disputes.

Financial considerations and intra-group rivalries also seem to be at the core of curse tablets alluding to disputes that involved individuals identified by their profession. It is noteworthy that in some instances the agents of these curses envisage a formal legal stage in the dispute. An example is *DTA* 68, a two-sided, fragmentary fourth-century curse tablet from Athens. It binds at least twenty individuals, men and women, of various professions (a miller, several tavern-keepers, a pimp, a boxer, a prostitute). Some targets are clearly of non-Athenian origin (side B, l. 9, Lykios; l. 10, Lyde) and one (side B, l. 15) is identified as a slave. The text is repetitive, containing names of targets followed by a formula binding bodily parts and at times the speech, memory and workplace of the accursed. *DTA* 68 is suggestive of how individuals of different legal statuses could interact in democratic Athens, but the nature of the dispute is not very clear. The focus is clearly on taverns and the sex trade, and an isolated reference to 'witnesses' in a fragmentary part of the tablet (side A, l.10) suggests that legal proceedings were underway, or anticipated. The wide assortment of professions has perplexed some commentators, who suggested that the targets might belong to an association or society, or that *DTA* 68 might be a blanket curse, i.e. the author just listed all those who he or she wanted to harm.[38]

Another instance of a dispute seemingly involving several persons of a certain occupation is *DT* 49, a curse tablet of the late fourth century. Here many of the targets are identified as cooks/butchers (*mageiros*). Theagenes, mentioned first and twice more in the text of the tablet, is obviously the main target. He is represented as being in collusion with other individuals, ostensibly against the author of the curse. The tablet employs explicitly violent language (ll. 15–17: 'all these I bind, I hide, I bury, I nail down') and anticipates the prospect of litigation. In ll. 9–11 Pherekles' tongue and spirit are bound in connection with his potential testimony in support of Theagenes and the text of the tablet ends (ll. 17–21) with a curse against all future actions of the curser's adversaries in a court or arbitration.[39]

Both *DTA* 68 and *DT* 49 illuminate modes of interaction and conflict between labourers in the entertainment sector, in the sex trade, as well as other sectors of the Athenian economy. Many of the protagonists of these disputes were clearly of inferior legal status in the eyes of the Athenian state. The patterns of conflict management suggested by these curses is nonetheless comparable to dispute resolution practices involving elite Athenians as described in literary sources. In both cases disputes that originated as a rivalry between two individuals often escalated into group feuds in which kin, friends and associates of the main antagonists take an active part. Secondly, in literary narratives disputes frequently contain an element of physical violence which is also implied in the language of some of the tablets. Finally, in literary evidence interpersonal conflict is often depicted as escalating into litigation, an inference amply corroborated by binding curses.[40]

The adversaries of all the individuals targeted in *DTA* 68 and *DT* 49, i.e. the persons who commissioned the curses in question, most likely belonged to the same social milieu as most of their targets. This is a crucial point because, if accepted, it follows that some curse tablets can illuminate agential behaviour and conflict management practices of non-elite residents of Athens. Curse tablets suggest that non-elite Athenians actively exploited the institutional apparatus of Athenian democracy, as well as other options and strategies, including magic, in the course of a dispute. Moreover, individuals of metic and citizen status but of modest social backgrounds often anticipated that their disputes would reach formal arbitration or litigation.[41] Participants in a dispute often exhibited a self-reactive and self-reflective attitude, i.e. they not only constructed potential courses of action, but were willing to re-evaluate, adjust and eventually pursue additional or alternative modes of praxis towards a satisfactory resolution of a dispute. Such a conception and management of disputes as multi-stage affairs that encompass networks of supporters or adversaries are symptomatic of engaged, high-level individual and collective agents.

Conclusions

Curse tablets from classical Athens illustrate facets of interpersonal and intergroup interaction, conflict management and agential behaviour. They frequently present unorthodox narratives of social interaction deriving from non-privileged residents of Attica. Furthermore, the institutional setup and social conditions in classical Athens, primarily the principle of open access to key institutions of decision-making (assembly, council of 500) and adjudication (law courts), as well as the inter-mingling of individuals of all social backgrounds and legal statuses in numerous settings within the Athenian public sphere, encouraged high-level individual and collective agency. This is evident in the conflict management and dispute resolution strategies pursued through the curse tablets. Very often binding curses allude to long-term, multi-stage disputes and point to a self-reflective and adaptive atti-tude on the part of the authors of curses. Since individuals usually adopt the same agency mode in various aspects of their daily life (e.g. work, family life, disputes), it follows that the insights that the curse tablets provide on conflict managements and agential behaviour have wider, largely unexplored implications for the work-ing of the Athenian democracy and society during the fourth century.

Notes

  * Research for this chapter has been conducted at the University of Hamburg during the tenure of a Fellowship for Experienced Researchers awarded by the Alexander von Humboldt foundation. Special thanks go to Prof. Dr. Werner Riess for his hospitality, collegiality and feedback on various facets of my work on Athenian binding curses. I am solely responsible for any mistakes that this chapter contains. All ancient dates are BCE.
  1 *Eum.* 306–96, incorporated in the stasimon performed by the chorus of Erinyes. See Faraone 1985.
  2 For "prayers for justice" see Versnel 1991.
  3 See Marston 2007.
  4 See the discussion by Faraone 1989.
  5 See Faraone 1989: 152–5.
  6 E.g. Dickie 2001: 38–40; Eidinow 2007: 140–1.
  7 Teos, *Nomima* I, 104 and 105; Strubbe 1991.
  8 *NGCT* 24=Jordan 1999: no. 1.
  9 Lhôte 2006: no. 141 bis.
10 Pébarthe 2006; Missiou 2011.

11 Eidinow 2007.
12 Riess 2012, especially chapter 3.
13 Gagarin 1998.
14 Lanni 1997.
15 Cohen 2000; Vlassopoulos 2007. For oral communication, gossip and hearsay in classical Athens, see Hunter 1990.
16 *SGD* 42. See also Robert 1936: no. 11.
17 Oost 1977. Cf. Davies 1971: no. 2108.
18 *SGD* 48 = Jordan and Curbera 2008. See also Humphreys 2010.
19 Davies 1971: no. 11234.
20 Hansen 1983: 175.
21 For high and low levels of personal agency, see Vallacher and Wegner 1989 and 2012. For human agency and the related concept of self-efficiency, see Bandura 1989 and 1997. For the relationship between agency and structure, see Giddens 1984 and 1989.
22 Osborne 1985; Christ 1998: 79.
23 Costabile 2004–5: no. I.
24 MacDowell 1962: 204–5.
25 And. 1.62; [Lys.] 6.48; Davies 1971: no. 828, especially p. 31.
26 For the role of Andokides in the events of 415 see Furley 1996.
27 The arguments for the date of the curse tablet in the early years of the fourth century are expounded by Costabile 2004–5: 168–9.
28 And. 1.133–5.
29 Wilhelm 1904: 115–8. Regarding *DTA* 24, see Nisoli 2003.
30 See Davies 1971: 8157 IV; Hochschulz 2007: 16–17.
31 Nisoli 2003: 272ff.
32 *LGPN* II, p. 168, no. 2; Davies 1971: no. 5475.
33 *LGPN* II, p. 335, no. 2.
34 *IG* II² 1174; *IG* II² 1175; *IG* II² 2820.
35 Nisoli 2003.
36 Wilhelm 1904: 117–8.
37 *DTA* 24, side B, contain references to two women, Meideia and Syra, the latter almost certainly a slave. It is likely that the two women played only an auxiliary role in the dispute that instigated *DTA* 24, but their inclusion in the list of targets is a reminder of the involvement of individuals of inferior legal statuses in various facets of Athenian public life.
38 Eidinow 2007: 199.
39 For the possible identification of some of the targets of *DT* 49 see Ziebarth 1899: 110; Wünsch 1900: no. 10, pp. 63–4; Gager 1992: no. 44.
40 In addition to *DTA* 68 and *DT* 49, there are more than forty curse tablets from classical Athens that refer explicitly to litigation. Historians of Athenian law have by and large overlooked this evidence. An exception is Rubinstein 2000: 45 and 64–5, which contains a brief discussion on the networks of supporters (*syndikoi*, *synegoroi*) in legal curses. For the discourse and practice of violence in the context of disputes in classical Athens see Cohen 1995 and Riess 2012.
41 For a curse tablet referring to a dispute involving metics, see Costabile 1998 (with subsequent discussion by Costabile 2000, 2001 and Jordan 2004); and perhaps Jordan 2008.

Bibliography

Bandura, A. (1989) 'Human agency in social cognitive theory', *American Psychologist* 44.9, 1175–84.
Bandura, A. (1997) *Self-Efficacy: The Exercise of Control*, New York.

Christ, M. (1998) *The Litigious Athenian*, Baltimore, MD.

Cohen, D. (1995) *Law, Violence and Community in Classical Athens*, Cambridge, UK.

Cohen, E. E. (2000) *The Athenian Nation*, Princeton, NJ.

Costabile, F. (1998) 'La triplice *defixio* del Kerameikós di Atene. Il processo polemarchico ed un logographo attico del IV sec. a. C. Relazione prelimimare', *MEP* 1, 9–54.

Costabile, F. (2000) 'Defixiones dal Kerameikós di Atene – II. Maledizioni processuali', *MEP* 4, 37–122.

Costabile, F. (2001) 'La triplice defixio: nuova lettura. Processo e norma libraria attica nel V-IV sec. a.C. Defixiones dal Kerameikós di Atene – III', *MEP* 6, 143–208.

Costabile, F. (2004–5) 'Defixiones dal Kerameikós di Atene. IV', *MEP* 7–8, 137–92.

Davies, J. K. (1971) *Athenian Propertied Families 600–300 B.C.*, Oxford, UK.

Dickie, M. W. (2001) *Magic and Magicians in the Greco-Roman World*, London and New York.

Eidinow, E. (2007) *Oracles, Curses and Risk among the Ancient Greeks*, Oxford.

Faraone, C. A. (1985) 'Aeschylus' ὕμνος δέσμιος (*Eum.* 306) and Attic judicial curse tablets', *JHS* 105, 150–4.

Faraone, C. A. (1989) 'An accusation of magic in classical Athens (Ar. *Wasps* 946–48)', *TAPA* 119, 149–60.

Faraone, C. A. and Obbink, D. (eds.) (1991) *Magika Hiera: Ancient Greek Magic and Religion*, New York and Oxford, UK.

Furley, W. D. (1996) *Andocides and the Herms: A Study of Crisis in Fifth-Century Athenian Religion*, London.

Gagarin, M. (1998) 'Women in Athenian courts', *Dike* 1, 39–51.

Gager, J. (1992) *Curse Tablets and Binding Spells from the Ancient World*, Oxford, UK.

Giddens, A. (1984) *The Constitution of Society: Outline of the Theory of Structuration*, Berkeley, CA.

Giddens, A. (1989) 'A reply to my critics' in D. Held and J. B. Thompson (eds.), *Social Theory of Modern Societies: Anthony Giddens and His Critics*, Cambridge, 249–301.

Hansen, M. H. (1983) '*Rhetores* and *strategoi* in fourth-century Athens', *GRBS* 24.2, 151–80.

Hochschulz, B. (2007) *Kallistratos von Aphidnai: Untersuchungen zu seiner politischen Biographie*, Munich.

Humphreys, S. C. (2010) 'A paranoiac sycophant? The curse tablet NM 14470 (D. R. Jordan and J. Curbera, *ZPE* 166 2008, 135–150)', *ZPE* 172, 85–6.

Hunter, V. (1990) 'Gossip and the politics of reputation in classical Athens', *Phoenix* 44, 299–325.

Jordan, D. R. (1999) 'Three curse tablets' in D. R. Jordan, H. Montgomery and E. Thomassen (eds.), *The World of Ancient Magic: Papers from the first International Samson Eitrem Seminar at the Norwegian Institute at Athens, 4–8 May 1997*, Bergen, Norway, 115–24.

Jordan, D. R. (2004) 'Towards the text of a curse tablet from the Athenian Kerameikos' in A. Matthaiou (ed.), *Ἀττικαί Ἐπιγραφαί. Πρακτικά συμποσίου εις μνήμην Adolf Wilhelm (1864–1950)*, Athens, 291–311.

Jordan, D. R. (2008) 'An Athenian curse tablet invoking Palaimon' in A. Matthaiou and I. Polinskaya (eds.), *Μικρός Ιερομνήνων. Μελέτες εις μνήμην Michael H. Jameson*, Athens, 133–44.

Jordan, D. R. and Curbera, J. (2008) 'A lead curse tablet in the National Archaeological Museum, Athens', *ZPE* 166, 135–50.

Jordan, D. R., Montgomery, H. and Thomassen, E. (eds.) (1999) *The World of Ancient Magic: Papers from the first International Samson Eitrem Seminar at the Norwegian Institute at Athens, 4–8 May 1997*, Bergen, Norway.

Lanni, A. M. (1997) 'Spectator sport or serious politics? οἱ περιεστηκότες and the Athenian lawcourts', *JHS* 117, 183–9.

Lhôte, É. (2006) *Les lamelles oraculaires de Dodone*, Geneva.

MacDowell, D. (1962) *Andokides On the Mysteries*, Oxford, UK.

Marston, J. M. (2007) 'Language of ritual cursing in the binding of Prometheus', *GRBS* 47, 121–33.

Matthaiou, A. (ed.) (2004) *Αττικαί Επιγραφαί. Πρακτικά συμποσίου εις μνήμην Adolf Wilhelm (1864–1950)*, Athens.

Matthaiou, A. and Polinskaya, I. (eds.) (2008) *Μικρός Ιερομνήνων. Μελέτες εις μνήμην Michael H. Jameson*, Athens.

Missiou, A. (2011) *Literacy and Democracy in Fifth-Century Athens*, Cambridge, UK and New York.

Nisoli, A. G. (2003) 'Defixiones politiche e vittime illustri. Il caso della defixio di Focione', *Acme* 56, 271–87.

Oost, S. I. (1977) 'Two notes on Aristophon of Azenia', *CP* 72, 238–42.

Osborne, R. (1985) 'Law in action in classical Athens', *JHS* 105, 40–58.

Pébarthe, C. (2006) *Cité, démocratie et écriture. Histoire de l'alphabétisation d'Athènes à l'époque classique*, Paris.

Riess, W. (2012) *Performing Interpersonal Violence: Court, Curse and Comedy in Fourth-Century BCE Athens*, Berlin and Boston.

Robert, L. (1936) *Collection Froehner I. Inscriptions grecques*, Paris.

Rubinstein, L. (2000) *Litigation and Cooperation: Supporting Speakers in the Courts of Classical Athens*, Stuttgart.

Strubbe, J. H. M. (1991) 'Cursed be he that moves my bones' in C. A. Faraone and D. Obbink (eds.), *Magika Hiera: Ancient Greek Magic and Religion*, New York and Oxford, UK, 33–59.

Vallacher, R. R. and Wegner, D. M. (1989) 'Levels of personal agency: individual variation in action identification', *Journal of Personality and Social Psychology* 57.4, 660–71.

Vallacher, R. R. and Wegner, D. M. (2012) 'Action identification theory' in P. A. M. van Lange, A. W. Kruglanski and E. T. Higgins (eds.), *Handbook of Theories of Social Psychology: Volume One*, London, 327–48.

Versnel, H. S. (1991) 'Beyond cursing: the appeal to justice in judicial prayers' in C. A. Faraone and D. Obbink (eds.), *Magika Hiera: Ancient Greek Magic and Religion*, New York and Oxford, UK, 60–106.

Vlassopoulos, K. (2007) 'Free spaces: identity, experience and democracy in classical Athens', *CQ* 57, 33–52.

Wilhelm, A. (1904) 'Über die Zeit einiger attischer Fluchtafeln', *Jahreshefte des Österreichischen Archäologischen Instituts* 7, 105–26.

Wünsch, R. (1900) 'Neue Fluchtafeln I', *RhM* 55, 62–85.

Ziebarth, E. (1899) 'Neue attische Fluchtafeln' in *Nachrichten von der Gessellschaft der Wissenschaften zu Göttingen, Philologisch-historische Klasse*, 105–35.

7   Reintegrating the exiles

Violence, urban landscape and memory in early Hellenistic Tegea

Elias Koulakiotis

Introduction

The present study focuses on a crucial moment of a city's life; the reintegration of ex-citizens into the community of the polis. Such episodes are of major interest, because they pose questions regarding the identity of citizens and outcasts alike, the representation and management of violence within the city's members, and perceptions of property and urban landscape. This study takes into account the so-called spatial turn in the humanities and tries to investigate the role of urban landscape in the reintegration of exiles into the corps of citizens.[1]

As Hansen and Nielsen put it, in antiquity 'belonging' in a political context meant, principally, to belong to one's polis. Like the modern state, the polis provided its citizens with a feeling of common identity, based on traditions, culture, rituals, symbols and sometimes (presumed) common descent.[2] To these components one should add two more. First, a feeling of sharing a space that is controlled by this community (called often *patris*, fatherland).[3] This feature is important, especially if we think that the outcast member of a political community is in fact defined in spatial terms: this means that an exiled (*phygas*) is the member thrown out of the borders of the community in its legal dimension; that is out of its territory.[4] Second, that 'a polis was not a harmonious unit, but most *poleis* were split up into two opposed *poleis*'.[5] As a result of this opposition between the two factions within a polis there was a constant tension and discord;[6] this discord very often caused repeated outbursts of civil war. During such civil strife each faction was eager to collaborate with a congenial faction in another, neighbouring or distant polis, or, during the Hellenistic era, in a league of cities or in a kingdom. It seems that some cities were marked by such civil strife, which was accompanied by proverbial ferocity. The Hellenistic historian Polybius, when presenting the attitudes of his fellow Arcadians, insists on the violence provoked during such confrontations within the cities' populations.[7]

Macedonian kings and Greek cities: creating violence?

The fourth century BCE was a period of intense political and military confrontations in both mainland Greece and the Eastern Mediterranean. The mighty kings of Macedon Philip II and Alexander III, 'the Great', as well as their successors, proved to be decisive factors of huge geopolitical and cultural changes. Of equal importance were a great number of anonymous protagonists, i.e. soldiers and mercenaries, who originated from the Greek city-states, the *poleis* of the broader Greek world, and enrolled in the Greek and Persian armies.[8] These mercenaries were very often political allies or enemies of the new world rulers. By the end of the fourth century there existed a mass of political refugees and exiles, often of different generations, who searched for a solution so they could return to their home cities. Of course, not all virtual returnees were mercenaries, and not all mercenaries were exiles.

During the Olympic Games in August 324 BCE, Alexander communicated to the crowd of the exiled Greeks in Olympia his intention to let them return into their home cities.[9] The framework in which this 'decree' was ratified had to do with Alexander's own return from India to Babylon, and his intention to punish those of his satraps who were disloyal and ineffective in their administration. Some of them reacted by using mercenary forces against the threats of the king.[10] According to the historian Diodorus,[11] the scope of Alexander's 'Exiles' decree' was twofold: first, it would increase the number of Alexander's allies in these cities and the king's influence in them;[12] secondly, it would put under control those who recently challenged the status quo newly established by the Macedonians, such as most of the cities of the Arcadian League, like Tegea in the Peloponnese.[13] Tegea's general support of Alexander in the past[14] did not spare her from having to respect Alexander's rules. Tegea must have had to take back those responsible for leading her into an alliance with Sparta in 331 BCE, and thus into the war against Alexander's general, Antipater.[15]

By forcing[16] – against the 'international' commitment of the members of the Council of Corinth, which supervised the relations between Greek states in the 330s BCE – the return of a group of people who were long absent, it was almost certain that enmities would arise. Although the official intention of the decree (as propagated by the king's ambassador in Olympia, Nicanor) was to promote the unity of the corps of the citizens within every city, in fact the return of the exiles in their home cities could only undermine the concord of each city's population. In this way, the provoked tensions could be manipulated by the Macedonians so as to better control the divided cities.[17]

The novelty of this decision made by Alexander eventually underlined the king's intention to transform the citizens of an independent city-state into a sort of 'subjects' of his newly built empire. The decree was not a general law; it concerned only those who went to exile before Alexander's reign and those who were not accused of sacrilege and murder.[18] It was a kind of imposed 'international' framework (*diagramma*), which should be implemented in accordance with each city's legislation,[19] but in fact could only undermine the civic legislation of each city concerned.[20] As already remarked, there were two important exceptions: it did not concern those who committed a sacrilege and the murderers. Given the broad meaning of both categories (sacrilege and murder, which could be political murder), it was difficult to clearly define the group of people concerned (on murder, law and territory, see also the chapter by Canevaro in this volume).[21]

Articulating a response: royal *diagramma* vs. civic *nomos*

The case of Tegea is a good example of a city's reaction to Alexander's initiative, because we have the response of this city to the king's will. This response is preserved mainly on an inscription found about a century ago in Delphi.[22] The actuality of the text and the problems concerned with the persons referred in it could situate it into the 'international' constellation from 330–317 BCE.[23] I accept here the *communis opinio* of dating it in 324 BCE, and relating it to Alexander's "Exiles' Decree" (l. 4: τὸς φυγάδας τὸς κατενθόντας).[24]

It seems that there was more than one exchange of official correspondence between the city and the king's chancellery, and the text from Delphi preserves the final regulations made after agreement with the king.[25] Its contents represent a series of 'solutions' to particularly difficult problems, raised by the original *diagramma* and answered (partly) by a second *diagramma*.[26] Among the major issues raised by the text, it was the restitution of property, with provision for property that was burdened with debt; the establishment of arbitration procedures; the clarification of the property rights of wives and daughters of exiles; and, finally, the reassignment of liturgical obligations.[27]

In my view, the major idea that is subjacent in the whole text is to deal with a group of ex-citizens who were affected by a sort of *atimia*, since it is known that the exiles were probably fully or partially *atimoi*, that is without *timè*, without moral and economic honour.[28] The purpose of the text is to restore citizenship to these people; that is, to undo the state of *atimia* and to restore their own identity as citizens.[29] In fact it is an action of restitution, but also of redistribution,[30] since a series of real estate matters are regulated and rearranged. In the text a number of thematic units can be discerned, which address issues having to do with property and ancestry,[31] religion and public space,[32] law and adjudication,[33] public finances and private debts,[34] kinship,[35] and finally collective memory;[36] that is civic rights and crucial matters that define participation in a political community and constitute civic identity.

Arcadian landscape and Tegean territory: the importance of gardens for civic identity

I cannot discuss here all the regulations of the text; I will insist on those related to real estate, in particular houses and gardens, property that has to do with the right of *enktèsis gès kai oikias* (the civic right to possess land and house).[37] In the case of Tegea, we do not know which clauses of *atimia* were inflicted on the exiled and to what extent. As Plassart, the editor of the text, already remarked, the property of the exiled must have been confiscated, but the Tegeates did not tear down the houses of the exiled, a habit that was valid in the Greek world, especially in cases of treason.[38] This procedure symbolised the curse on the exiled families who suffered *atimia*. It was a kind of *damnatio memoriae* of the material existence of the citizen.[39] It seems that economic and eventually legal reasons led the Tegeates not to raze the houses; that was perhaps characteristic of the general financial situation in this period. The citizens of Tegea who stayed in the city very probably sold the properties of the exiles to new owners[40] and these latter had to handle them back to the prior owners. One can imagine that a series of problems would arise, and these problems should be settled down by three kinds of law courts (foreigners court, civic court and a court with judges from the neighbouring Mantineia) and within a limited time frame (within sixty days), so the abnormal and transitional situation could be over as quickly as possible.[41]

The original *diagramma* prescribed that if a house had been confiscated, then the new owner had to give it back unless the exiled had more than one house. Furthermore, according to the *diagramma*, the cultivated plots of land (l.15: χωρία) of the exiled were to be restored in half. It was a common phenomenon in antiquity that a family had more than one house, in both the city and in the fields; in this case, it is obvious that the old owner, i.e. the exiled, would prefer his urban residence, since generally its price was higher. In that case, the urban houses, that is the family houses, were to be restored in their entity. The gardens adjacent to these family houses or in near distance from them (within a distance of one *plethron* – about 30 m – that is within the urban district) were also to be restored in their entity; whereas the remote gardens, i.e. those not close to houses, were considered as simple cultivated land.[42] We should remember here that the territory of Tegea in southeast Arcadia was quite fertile and apt for agriculture, unlike the major part of Arcadia.[43] Therefore, it is understandable that disputes over fertile lands were unavoidable.[44]

Normally, gardens were outside the urban centre, near the city wall,[45] but it seems that in Tegea this was not entirely the case. As Osborne already remarked,[46] in Tegea we can find a really big city wall, enclosing a very extensive area.[47] As a result, the mixture of gardens and residences was very common and this was understandable for a city like Tegea, which had started as a confederation of villages and only at a late stage was fused into one centre by synoecism.[48]

It is then clear that a special value is attributed to the gardens close to the family houses.[49] Very probably house (*oikia*) and garden (*kèpos*) formed an entity, which guaranteed the existence of the *oikos*.[50] It seems that it was part of the citizens' identity, since real estate was a prerequisite of being a citizen.[51] Furthermore, perhaps this entity symbolised the continuity of a built and cultivated – that is, human – landscape. In this image it is very important to remember that the garden is an *enclosed* cultivated land, which helps to better conceptualise the borders not only between different properties, but between culture and nature as well.[52] This was eventually important in a land such as Arcadia, a region attributed with special 'qualities': here monstrosity (see the theriomorphic [animal-formed] Arcadian religion exemplified in its most representative deity, Pan)[53] and bestiality (see the ferocity of certain Arcadians commented by Polybius)[54] were pervasive. The Tegean community might perceive such qualities as a threat, both external and internal. For the citizen of Tegea house *and* garden might stand for a constant reminder of his condition as *zôon politikon* (political animal).[55]

The Aristotelian view on human communities described above should be supplemented by the philosopher's opinion on the formation and function of the city:

a *polis* not only consists of its parts, but the entire *polis* realised in a bigger scale the pattern embodied in the *oikos*,[56] which in Tegea consisted of house and garden. We should add here that the name of the city, Tegea, has to do with the Greek word *tegos*, which means sheltered, enclosed.[57] Therefore, would it be legitimate to argue that in the fourth century the entire city of Tegea with its huge wall[58] embodied a certain ideal of a garden city between secure dwelling and profitable farm?

As already said, sharing the territory and landscape of the city was the prerequisite of being a member of a political community, such as the ancient polis. This was important for an agrarian community, where labour and production had a strong ideological connotation echoed by the hoplitic ideal and thus mirrored citizen equality.[59] This was very important for an Arcadian city, where land meant also antiquity,[60] especially if we remember the Arcadians' self-representation as indigenous,[61] and where living in cities was almost homonymous to their identity.

It seems that not every soil, but the land as part of the *polis* mattered for the citizen identity and that is understandable even for 'pastoral' Arcadia. According to Arcadian self-presentation and myths reported by Pausanias,[62] their own mythical king Lykaon was the founder of the first city ever founded, Lykosoura, a pattern of urbanisation first invented in Arcadia and an institution imitated in the future by the rest of human beings.[63] Of course the notion and the content of the *polis* changed through the centuries, and especially in the fourth century we deal with a new concept as synoecisms (like that of Megalopolis) and leagues of cities (like the Arcadian one) created new realities; as a consequence, ethnic and civic identities were readjusted. Nevertheless, by the end of this century, and when the city of Tegea tries to reaffirm the profile of its citizens, the relation to the city landscape seems crucial for their identity.[64]

Forgetting violence: forging a new identity

If the above regulations on houses and gardens regarded the private space of the citizen, the next one has to do with the public one (ll. 21–3). Here we deal with restitution of the exiles' right to reintegrate themselves to the civic feasts (ll. 21–2: π|αναγορίαις), that is to reintegrate themselves into the collective life[65] through a re-appropriation of the public space, since it is known that public rituals connected with religious worship extended in the whole territory of the city, both urban and extra-urban.[66] In my view, it is relevant that this regulation is mentioned in the text of the inscription just after the prior ones regarding houses and gardens. In this way the city revokes the condition of the exiled by restoring their right of access to the totality of its territory.

The aforementioned evidence showed that the conceptualization and function of city space in Tegea could not avoid involving the management of violence, since this latter aspect was part of the civic life by the end of the fourth century. Furthermore, the citizens needed to share not only a physical, but also a mental landscape, like the one of collective memory. And that is the next step of the city's regulations as preserved in the text. After prescribing regulations on the female relatives of the exiles (ll. 57–66), the city intends to find out a way of transcending the traumatic situation of being divided by imposing an official oblivion of the misdeeds (ll. 57–66; l. 59: *ou mnasikakèsô*, "I shall not harbour grudges"). In the case of the Tegea decree this oath is the key to preserving the city's community in the future and it is forgetfulness of violence, amnesty that leads to a new, reassessed collective identity.[67]

Epilogue: transforming violence in antiquity and beyond

The case of Tegea represents a pertinent example of controlling inter- and intra-communal violence, with special reference to important economic and juridical matters which might ensue. The tensions caused by intracommunal violence because of the repatriation of the exiles could be overcome only by rendering the city to its ex-citizen,[68] that is by permitting them to reappropriate the private and public space, both built and cultivated, real and imagined. Sharing a common, rearranged fatherland as well as a 'purged' collective memory meant for the Arcadians of Tegea a reinvented common identity and a pacified future.

To conclude this study, it should be worth looking on what comes after the period examined until now. In the Hellenistic and Roman periods the Arcadian landscape was re-interpreted and Arcadia became a cultural symbol of utopia. In this period, external perceptions of land and people created an (invented) image,[69] in which the inhabitants of the land, the famous Arcadian mercenaries[70] – those who formed the biggest part of the exiled – became passionate lovers.[71] It was as if the violence of Pan was transformed into the violence of Eros (Amor).

This was a mostly Roman interpretation depending on Roman perceptions of both countryside and urban space. It is known that during the second and first centuries BCE Rome became gradually a garden city,[72] and the affinity with such a landscape as the Arcadian cities like Pallantion and perhaps Tegea virtually enforced the (presumed) Arcadian origin of Rome.[73] Centuries later, with the revival of the interest in antiquity after the Renaissance, gardens and garden architecture in particular became part of the movement of 'Arcadianism'[74] – which, in general, stood for absence of every kind of violence for the city dwellers of this period[75] – and as such perhaps a nice reminiscence of the Tegean landscape.[76]

Notes

1 On the 'spatial turn' in historiography, see Döring and Thielman 2008. See also Vlassopoulos 2007: ch. 7, on space and territory of the Greek *poleis*, and Bakke 2007: 1–19, on landscape and memory.
2 Hansen and Nielsen 2004: 124.
3 See Scheer 2011: 11; Velissaropoulos-Karakostas 2011a: 123.
4 See the contribution by M. Canevaro in this volume. On the content of the term *phygas* (exiled, banished), see Seibert 1979: 371–407. On the difference between *phygas* and *atimos* see Poddighe 1993 and Youni 1998: 49–58. On Tegea's borders (*horoi*) and defined territory see Hdt. 8.124.3: οὖροι οἱ Τεγεητικοί and further Nielsen 2002: 184 and 593.
5 Hansen and Nielsen 2004: 124.

6 Loraux 1980: 218: 'ce geste inaugural du politique qui est la reconnaissance du conflit dans la societé'. See also Lintott 1982: 252–63 and Gehrke 1985.

7 Polyb. 4.20–1. See also the bloody internal strives which took place in Tegea because of the city's participation in the Arcadian League in 370 BCE: Xen. *Hell.* 6.5.7 (see the map of the Peloponnese and Arcadia); see further Nielsen 2002: 596; Hansen and Nielsen 2004: 531; Loraux 2005: 62–5.

8 On the Peloponnesian origin of the biggest part of Alexander's mercenaries and furthermore on the economic aspects of their return after the Asian expedition see Rizakis and Touratsoglou 2008: 71 and 79.

9 The original text of the decree can only be partially reconstructed by later, mainly literary, evidence: Hyp. 5.18–9; Din. 1.82; Diod. 17.109.1, 18.8.2–7. For the discussion on the number of the exiled see McKechnie 1989: 26–8. See also Bencivenni 2003: 15–104.

10 Rizakis and Touratsoglou 2008: 79; Atkinson and Yardley 2009: 114–5.

11 Diod. 18.8.3–5.

12 Bosworth 1988: 220–8. See also Garland 2014: 192.

13 In 331/0 BCE Tegea took part in the war raised by the Spartan king Agis against the Macedonians: Curt. 6.1.20: *Tegeate veniam defectionis praeter auctores inpetrauerunt.* Megalopolis, another big Arcadian city, chose the opposite side.

14 Tegea did not take part in the battle of Chaironeia which opposed the allied Greeks against the Macedonian king Philipp, since in 336 BCE, when Philip died, Tegea had profited by Philip's policy in the Peloponnese. The Macedonian king took lands from the Lacedaemonians and gave them to Sparta's enemies, i.e. Messenians, Arcadians and Argives. For a brief survey of the events and the role of the Arcadian League see Lintott 1982: 231–3.

15 Atkinson and Yardley 2009: 117. For Heisserer 1980: 221–2, Alexander's decree had in scope more inter-Macedonian confrontations and was ratified in order to cause problems to Antipater; the decree wanted to restore those who opposed the Macedonian rule during the revolt of Agis and had been banished by Antipater.

16 Diod. 18.8.4: *if any of the cities are unwilling to receive you back he [sc. Alexander] will compel them to do so.* On the Council of Corinth see Poddighe 2011.

17 In 324 BCE Alexander had dissolved the Arcadian League: Hyp. 1.18; see Heisserer 1980: 228. Compare Philip's attitude towards the Aitolians, when he divided the *Koinon* in its *phylai*, or the dissolution (διοικισμός) of Mantineia by Sparta after 386 BCE. See also Dmitriev 2004: 375 and Faraguna 2004: 127 who insists on the fact that the exiles' return meant further political struggles in Greek cities, as Diod. 17.113.3 suggests: πέμπτοις δὲ τοῖς ἀντιλέγουσι περὶ τῆς καθόδου τῶν φυγάδων.

18 Diod. 18.56.4.

19 See the exemples of Chios and Mytilene: Velissaropoulos-Karakostas 1987: 80–1; Brun 1988; Worthington 1993; Malouchou 2000–3; Rhodes and Osborne 2003: nos. 84–5; Dimopoulou-Piliouni 2015: 250–67. For the Macedonian and Ptolemaic royal *diagrammata* see Hatzopoulos 1996: 398; Dmitriev 2004: 376–7; Velissaropoulos-Karakostas 2011a: 63–6; Poddighe 2013. See also Gawlinski 2011: 1–3 for the use of the term *diagramma* in some cities of the Peloponnese.

20 See Curt. 10.2.5: *quamquam solvendarum legum id principium esse censebant.* It is not clear whether this phrase was used in a political or legal sense; cf. Diod. 17.113.3, with ambassadors sent to Alexander. Compare also the reaction of Tegea, who proposed corrections to the decree (see following). Furthermore as Dmitriev 2004 argued, it is not clear if the protests against the regulations prescribed by the decree corroborate the impression that the Lamian War was the consequence of this decree.

21 See Arrian, *Anab.* 1.17.10–2 on the situation in Ephesos. Most of the exiles were banished not according to the legal procedure of their own cities (i.e. not by due process of law), but by political factions: Just. 13.5.5: *quia plurimi non legibus pulsi patria, sed*

per factionem principum fuerunt, verentibus isdem principibus, ne revocati potentiores in re publica fierent. For Dmitriev 2004: 375, 'the exiles' decree left open the possibility for negotiations and compromises [...] as well as the right of these cities to use their own laws and to organize a procedure for the restoration of exiles in the way it seemed best to each city'. See also O'Neil 2000, with a different point of view.

22 *IG* V, 2 p. xxxvi; *SIG*³ 306; Tod 202; Heisserer 1980: 205–25; Thür and Taeuber 1994: 51–70; Rhodes and Osborne 2003: no. 101. Here I follow the text and the traslation by Rhodes and Osborne 2003: 526–32 (see Appendix).

23 See the discussion in Thür and Taeuber 1994: 52–3 and Rhodes and Osborne 2003: 530.

24 Worthington 1993; Demandt 2009: 368.

25 Ll. 1–3: —– *With reference to the things about which the city sent the envoys and King Alexander sent back his judgment to us, the transcript (diagramma) shall be written according to the corrections made by the city of what was spoken against in the transcript.* See also Balogh 1943: 81: 'The settlement of 324 was an amnesty imposed from without in contrast to the Athenian measures in 403 and 401. It did not serve the interests of Tegea, but had its origins in the desire of Alexander to establish peace and order in the Greek motherland and to achieve a strong and close control of Greece', cited by Heisserer 1980: 228. See also Seibert 1979: 160–2.

26 Heisserer 1980: 222.

27 Atkinson and Yardley 2009: 117.

28 The economic aspect is important in Tegea's text; consider the terms *tima, timasia, timama* refered in ll. 16–19. See also Poddighe 1993 on a comparable case from Athens and with discussion on the *phygades/atimoi*; Velissaropoulou 1987: 94–5; Youni 1998: 81–6.

29 Dubois 1988: 75 suggests that the Tegeans endeavoured to satisfy the spirit of Alexander's decree, but accorded the returning exiles the minimum of civic dignity (cited by Atkinson and Yardley 2009: 117).

30 See the remarks by Lonis 1991: 103.

31 Ll. 4–21, with regulations concerning property from both paternal and maternal side that is evidence regarding the ancestry of the exiled: (4) *The exiles who are returning shall recover their paternal possessions from which they went into exile, or their maternal possessions, i.e. in cases when women were not remarried and held their property and did not possess brothers. And if it has happened to any remarried woman that her brother, both himself and his descendants, have perished, here too the man shall have the maternal possessions but no longer those from further back.(9) With reference to the houses, each (sc. returned exile) shall have one in accordance with the transcript. If a house has a garden adjacent to it, let him not take another; if there is not a garden adjacent to the house, but there is one nearby within a plethron, let him take the garden; if the garden is more than a plethron distant, let him take the half of this, as has been written also for the other plots of land. Let (sc. the men to whom property is returned) receive as the price (tima) of the houses two minas for each room, and the assessment (timasia) of the houses shall be as the city considers; but for the garden he shall receive double the valuation (timama) in the law. The city shall discharge the money (for the compensation), and shall not exempt from taxation either the exiles or those previously living at home as citizens.* See also Lonis 1991: 99–100.

32 Ll. 21–4 with regulations concerning taking part in public religious feasts: *With reference to the general festivals from which the exiles have been absent, the city shall deliberate, and whatever the city deliberates shall be valid.*

33 Ll. 24–37: *The foreign court shall give judgment for sixty days. As many as are not adjudicated in the sixty days, it shall not be possible for them to go to law in the foreign court with reference to property, but always in the city's court: if they find anything later, in sixty days from the day when the court is established; and, if it is*

not adjudicated in this period, it shall no longer be possible for him go to the law. If any return later, when the foreign court is no longer in existence, let him register the property with the strategoi in sixty days, and if there is any defense against him the court shall be Mantinea; and, if it is not adjudicated in these days, it shall no longer be possible for him go to law.

34 Ll. 37–48: *With reference to the sacred money in general together with the debts to the Goddess, in cases which the city has set right, let him who has the property give the half to the returned exile like the others. As many as themselves owned pledges to the Goddess or otherwise, if it appears that he who has the property has set the obligation right with the Goddess, let him give the half to him who has returned, like the others, leaving nothing aside; but if it does not appear that he has given back to the Goddess, let him give back to him who has returned the half of the property, and with the [sc. other] half let him himself settle the obligation. If he does not wish to settle, let him give back to him who has returned the whole property, and let him convey it and settle the whole obligation to the Goddess.* On these terms, see Velissaropoulos-Karakostas 2011b: 29–31.

35 Ll. 49–57: *As many wives of the exiles or daughters as have remained at home and married, or went into exile but subsequently married in Tegea, and bought their release by remaining at home, these shall not be subject to examination over their paternal or maternal possessions, nor their descendants; but as for those who did not go into forced exile after <their marriage> and who are now creeping back on the present occasion, themselves or their children, they shall be examined, both themselves and their descendants, in respect of their paternal and their maternal possessions in accordance with the transcript.* On these terms see Maffi 1994 and Velissaropoulos-Karakostas 2011a: 245–8 and 2011b: 48–50.

36 Ll. 57–66: *I swear by Zeus, Athena, Apollo, Poseidon, that I shall show good will to those who have returned whom the city resolved to receive back, and I shall not harbour grudges against any of them for what he may have plotted (?) from the day on which I have sworn the oath, nor shall I hinder the safety of those who have returned, neither in the – nor in the community of the city – transcript – towards those who have returned – the city – the things written in the transcript for – nor shall I give counsel against anybody.*

37 Velissaropoulos-Karakostas 1987: 98, 2011b: 94–101. On safety problems related to houses see the contribution by N. Giannakopoulos in this volume.

38 Plassart 1914: 136, n. 2, with bibliography. See also Connor 1985: 84 who notes the absence of evidence for the razing of the house (*kataskaphè*) in Arcadia. Furthermore it cannot be sure if *kataskaphè* should be considered as a penalty imposed through formal legal practices, or (as Forsdyke 2012: 159 suggests) as a means of popular justice.

39 Connor 1985: 86–8.

40 For the procedure and possible prices, see Carroll-Spiellecke 1989: 67–8.

41 Ll. 35–6: εἰ δ᾽ [ἂν μὴ] διαδικάσ|ητοι ἰν ταινὶν ταῖς ἀμέραις, μηκέτ[ι] ἦναι αὐτοῖ δι|κάσασθαι.

42 Ll. 14–6: ἐ|πὲς δὲ ταῖς οἰκίαις μίαν ἕκαστον ἔχεν κατὺ τὸ διά|γραμμα· εἰ δέ τις ἔχει οἰκία κᾶπον πὸς αὐτᾶι, ἄ<λλ>ον μ|ὴ λαμβανέτω· εἰ δὲ πλέον ἀπέχων ὁ κᾶπός ἐστι πλέθρω, τωνὶ τὸ ἤμι|σσον λαμβανέτω, ὥσπερ καὶ τῶν ἄλλων χωρίων γέγρα|πται.

43 See Hdt. 1.66.2: καλὸν πεδίον for the plain of Tegea; see also Voyatzis 1999: 142 and Roy 1999: 328.

44 Agriculture, even in a limited scale, was a major factor of wealth in ancient societies; on the nexus between wealth and passions, see the Introduction of this volume.

45 Carroll-Spillecke 1989: 40. This pattern of habitation was not the same all over Greece. In Delos for example the gardens were outside the urban district: Bruneau 1979.

46 Osborne 2002: 378.

47 See also Odegard 2005: 210, who stresses the affinity to the city wall of Mantineia, a neighbouring Arcadian city. As for the territory of Tegea in general, it seems that it

was clearly defined by borders (Nielsen 1996: 98; Pretzler 1999: 104). Furthermore, in Tegea, most important sanctuaries with a clear relation to Tegean community identity are located in the city itself whereas for the biggest part of the Greek cities' sanctuaries and monuments are scattered over the countryside. See Pretzler 1999: 103 and de Polignac 1995.

48 Nielsen 2002: 12 and 137–8; Odegard 2005: 216. According to Thür and Taeuber 1994: 60: 'Vermutlich geht es um kleine, standardisierte Gärten innerhalb des Siedlungsgebiets [. . .] Man kann sich also die Besiedlungsverhältnisse in Tegea in Gebäudekomplexen vorstellen, die im Eigentum einzelner, wohl politisch einflussreicher Bürger standen'. However, recent archaeological surveys by the Norwegian Archaeological School in Athens did not yet seem to verify this pattern of habitation in Tegea, since they have not yet examined the entire city.

49 Of course, there are different notions and uses of gardens: see Carroll-Spillecke 1989. Here I am primarily concerned in the 'Nützgarten'.

50 See Lonis 1991: 101, where he discusses the formula *enktèsis gès kai oikias* as a prerequisite of the civic identity, as well as p. 96, where he discusses the mobile furniture of the house.

51 As Plassart 1914: 137, n. 5 already noted, there are other examples connecting gardens to the right of citizenship like in a series of decrees from the late fourth-century BCE Zeleia (*GDI* 5533 = *Michel* 531, ll. 19, 27: δοῦναι . . . οἰκίην, κῆπον). Plassart mentions more inscriptions relevant to the connection between houses and gardens (Attica: *IG* II, 1132; Icaria: *IJG* I, no. VIII, 31; Amorgos: *Syll².*, 827–9), as does Carroll-Spillecke 1989 in her appendix with a list of literary and epigraphic sources. See also Osborne 2002: 378.

52 See Osborne 2002: 391, and in general Barbu et al. 2013. See also Giesecke 2007: 100–2 on the Roman perceptions of the polarity *nature/culture*.

53 See Jost 2005.

54 One could add here the tales of human sacrifice in Arcadian religion and mythology, as they are exemplified in Lykaon's (i.e. 'werewolf') myth.

55 On man as 'political animal' and 'polis-dwelling animal' as well, see Arist. *Pol.* 1253a2–4. On this passage see the discussion in Miller 2005: 329. Furthermore see the remarks by Osborne 2002: 374: 'consider the garden's place in the conceptual framework of man as a social animal'.

56 Arist. *Pol.* 1252b28–30, 1253a19–23. On the symbolic significance, which many cultures attach to human dwelling places and on the importance of the ancient Greek *oikos* that goes far beyond the needs for physical shelter and confort, see Connor 1985: 79. On the lost Aristotelian Τεγεατῶν πολιτεία (frr. 559–60 and 607–8 Gigon) see Nielsen 2002: 592.

57 See *LSJ* s.v. *tegos* and Stavridou 1996: 25.

58 However, we should not forget that strong city walls were quite common in the fourth century; see the parallel case of Mantineia in Xen. *Hell.* 6.5. On the construction of major public buildings during the Hellenistic period see Rizakis and Touratsoglou 2008: 78.

59 The Arcadian League was democratic in its institutions and political orientation: see Lintott 1982: 232. One should remember here the democratic associations to the Arcadian deity par excellence, Pan: Borgeaud 1979: 235–7. On *isomoiria* in relation to the distribution of gardens see Carroll-Spillecke 1989: 66–8.

60 On Arcadians as *proselenoi* (existing before the moon) see Arist. F549 Rose; see also Bergese-Burelli 1995: 78–83.

61 Consider also the altar of Gè (land) in the agora of Tegea mentioned by Pausanias, 8.48.8: πρὸς δὲ τῷ ἱερῷ τῆς Εἰλειθυίας ἐστὶ Γῆς βωμός.

62 Pausanias 8.38.1.

63 See Nielsen 1999: 32 and 42.

64 On the urbanisation of Tegea see also Strabo 8.3.2. On the impact of the landscape in the formation of the character of the citizens see Plato, *Laws* 707b-c: ἀλλὰ γὰρ ἀποβλέποντες νῦν πρὸς πολιτείας ἀρετήν, καὶ χώρας φύσιν σκοπούμεθα καὶ νόμων τάξιν.
65 Thür and Taeuber 1994: 64. On the importance of civic feasts for the self-representation of a community see Chaniotis 1995.
66 De Polignac 1995.
67 See Sommerstein and Bayliss 2013:143–4, who suggest that a second oath must have been sworn by the exiles themselves; consider also Loraux 1980, 1997: 141–3, and Carawan 2012: 580: 'the oath is not simply a pledge of forgiveness for wrongs that are not redressed, but a guarantee against any reprisal beyond the remedies that have been authorized'. On oaths in general see also Graf 2005. The above oath is also to be found in the database at http://www.nottingham.ac.uk/greatdatabase/brzoaths/public_html/database/index.php (oath ID 572)
68 Lonis 1991: 92.
69 See the remarks by Nielsen 1999: 21 on the fact that Arcadian identity was continually (re)created and (re)negotiated.
70 See Roy 1999: 346–9.
71 Started by Theocritus and Polybius, but really propagated by Vergil: see Jost 1989 and Irmscher 2006.
72 Grimal 1943; Giesecke 2007: xii–xiii.
73 Pallantion, an Arcadian city very close to Tegea, was considered the home city of Evandros, one of the mythical founders of Rome; see Mavrojannis 2003 and 2004. On the connection between the Tegeate Telephos (through Pergamon) and early Italian/Roman history based on the notion of συγγένεια (kinship) see Pretzler 1999: 114. On numismatic evidence of the actuality of this myth in the Hellenistic and Roman period, see also Pretzler 1999: 113–4.
74 Petropoulos 2012: 232.
75 See Panofsky 1955.
76 I would like to thank M. Youni for her help in this study.

Bibliography

Atkinson, J. and Yardley, J. (2009) *Curtius Rufus. Histories of Alexander the Great, Book 10: Introduction and Historical Commentary*, Oxford, UK.

Bakke, J. (2007) *Forty Rivers: Landscape and Memory in the District of Ancient Tegea*, Bergen, Norway.

Balogh, E. (1943) *Political Refugees in Ancient Greece*, Johannesburg.

Barbu, D., Borgeaud, P. and Volokhine, Y. (2013) *Mondes clos: Cultures et jardins*, Paris.

Bencivenni, A. (2003) *Progetti di riforme costituzionali nelle epigrafi greche dei secoli IV-II a.C.*, Bologna, Italy.

Bergese-Burelli, F. (1995) *Tra ethne e poleis: pagine di storia arcade*, Pisa, Italy.

Borgeaud, P. (1979) *Recherches sur le dieu Pan*, Geneva.

Bosworth, A. B. (1988) *Conquest and Empire: The Reign of Alexander the Great*, Cambridge, UK.

Brun, P. (1988) 'Les exilés politiques en Grèce: l'exemple de Lesbos', *Ktèma* 13, 253–61.

Bruneau, P. (1979) 'Deliaca 31. Les jardins urbains de Délos', *BCH* 103, 89–99.

Carawan, E. (2012) 'The meaning of *mê mnêsikakein*', *CQ* 62, 567–81.

Carroll-Spillecke, M. (1989) *ΚΗΠΟΣ: Der antike griechische Garten*, Munich.

Chaniotis, A. (1995) 'Sich selbst feiern? Städtische Feste des Hellenismus im Spannungsfeld von Religion und Politik' in M. Wörrle and P. Zanker (eds.), *Stadtbild und Bürgerbild im Hellenismus*, Munich, 147–72.

Connor, W. R. (1985) 'The razing of the house in Greek society', *TAPA* 115, 79–102.

Demandt, A. (2009) *Alexander der Grosse: Leben und Legende*, Munich.

de Polignac, F. (1995) *Cults, Territory and the Origins of the Greek City-State*, Chicago and London.

Dimopoulou-Piliouni, A. (2015) *ΛΕΣΒΙΩΝ ΠΟΛΙΤΕΙΑΙ. Πολίτευμα, Θεσμοί, Δίκαιο των πόλεων της Λέσβου*, Athens.

Dmitriev, S. (2004) 'Alexander's exiles decree', *Klio* 86, 348–81.

Döring, J. and Thielmann, T. (eds.) (2008) *Spatial Turn: Das Raumparadigma in den Kultur- und Sozialwissenschaften*, Bielefeld, Germany.

Dubois, L. (1988) *Recherches sur le dialecte Arcadien*, Part 2, Louvain-la-Neuve, Belgium.

Faraguna, M. (2004) 'Alexander and the Greeks' in J. Roisman (ed.), *Brill's Companion to Alexander the Great*, Leiden, Netherlands and New York, 99–132.

Forsdyke, S. (2012) *Slaves Tell Tales and Other Episodes in the Politics of Popular Culture in Ancient Greece*, Princeton, NJ.

Gaertner, J. F. (2007) *Writing Exile: The Discourse of Displacement in Greco-Roman Antiquity and Beyond*, Leiden, Netherlands and Boston.

Garland, R. (2014) *Wandering Greeks: The Ancient Greek Diaspora from the Age of Homer to the Death of Alexander the Great*, Princeton, NJ and Oxford, UK.

Gawlinski, L. (2011) *The Sacred Law of Andania*, Berlin and New York.

Gehrke, H.-J. (1985) *Stasis: Untersuchungen zu den inneren Kriegen in den griechischen Staaten des 5. und 4. Jahrhunderts v. Chr.*, Munich.

Giesecke, A. L. (ed.) (2007) *The Epic City: Urbanism, Utopia and the Garden in Ancient Greece and Rome*, Washington, DC, Cambridge, MA and London.

Graf, F. (2005) 'Oath' in *Thesaurus cultus et rituum antiquorum (ThesCRA). III, Divination, Prayer, Veneration, Hikesia, Asylia, Oath, Malediction, Profanation, Magic Rituals*, Los Angeles, 247–70.

Grimal, P. (1943) *Jardins romains à la fin de la république et aux deux premiers siècles de l'empire*, Paris.

Hansen, M. H. and Nielsen, T. H. (eds.) (2004) *An Inventory of Archaic and Classical Poleis*, Oxford, UK.

Hatzopoulos, M. (1996) *Macedonian Institutions under the Kings. I: A Historical and Epigraphic Study*, Athens.

Heisserer, A. (1980) *Alexander the Great and the Greeks: The Epigraphical Evidence*, Norman, OK.

Irmscher, J. (2006) 'Arcadianism' in *Brill's New Pauly: Classical Tradition*, vol. I, Leiden, Netherlands and Boston, 210–13.

Jost, M. (1985) *Sanctuaires et cultes d'Arcadie*, Paris.

Jost, M. (1989) 'Images de l'Arcadie au IIIe s. av. J.-C. (Lycophron, *Alexandra*, v. 479–483)' in M. Mactoux and E. Gény (eds.), *Mélanges Lévêque II*, Paris, 285–93.

Jost, M. (2005) 'Bêtes, hommes et dieux dans la religion arcadienne' in E. Østby (ed.), *Ancient Arcadia, Papers from the Third International Seminar on Ancient Arcadia, held at the Norwegian Institute at Athens, 7–10 May 2002*, Athens, 93–104.

Lintott, A. (1982) *Violence, Civil Strife and Revolution in the Classical City 750–330 BC*, London.

Lonis, R. (1991) 'La réintegration des exilés politiques en Grèce: le problème des biens' in P. Goukowsky and C. Brixhe (eds.), *Hellènika Symmikta*, Nancy, France, 91–109.

Loraux, N. (1980) 'L'oubli dans la cité', *Le Temps de la réflexion* 1, 213–42.

Loraux, N. (1997) *La cité divisée: l'oubli dans la mémoire d'Athènes*, Paris.

Loraux, N. (2005) *La tragédie d'Athènes*, Paris.

Maffi, A. (1994) 'Regole matrimoniale e successorie nell'inscrizione di Tegea sul rientro degli esuli' in H.-J. Gehrke (ed.), *Rechtskodifizierung und soziale Normen im interkulturellen Vergleich*, Tübingen, Germany, 113–33.

Malouchou, G. E. (2000–3) 'Χῖοι κατελθόντες', *Horos* 14–16, 275–87.

Mavrojannis, T. (2003) *Aeneas und Euander: Mythische Vergangenheit und Politik im Rom vom 6. Jh. v. Chr. bis zur Zeit des Augustus*, Perugia, Italy.

Mavrojannis, T. (2004) ' "Evandro sul Palatino". La canonizzazione delle tradizione arcade di Roma nel contesto politico della storia del II secolo a. C.', *Atene e Roma* 49, 6–20.

McKechnie, P. (1989) *Outsiders in the Greek Cities in the Fourth Century BC*, London.

Miller, F. D. Jr. (2005) 'Aristotle: naturalism' in C. Rowe and M. Schofield (eds.), *The Cambridge History of Greek and Roman Political Thought*, Cambridge, UK, 321–43.

Nielsen, T. H. (1996) 'A survey of dependent poleis in classical Arcadia' in M. H. Hansen and K. Raaflaub (eds.), *More Studies in the Ancient Greek Poleis*, Stuttgart, 63-105.

Nielsen, T. H. (1999) 'The concept of Arcadia – the people, their land and their organisation' in T. H. Nielsen and J. Roy (eds.), *Defining Ancient Arcadia*, Copenhagen, 16–79.

Nielsen, T. H. (2002) *Arkadia and Its Poleis in the Archaic and Classical Periods*, Göttingen, Germany.

Odegard, K. (2005) 'The topography of ancient Tegea: new discoveries and old problems' in E. Østby (ed.), *Ancient Arcadia: Papers from the Third International Seminar on Ancient Arcadia, held at the Norwegian Institute at Athens, 7–10 May 2002*, Athens, 209–21.

O'Neil, J. L. (2000) 'Royal authority and city law under Alexander and his Hellenistic successors', *CQ* 50, 424–31.

Osborne, R. (2002) 'Classical Greek gardens: between farm and paradise' in J. D. Hunt (ed.), *Garden History*, Cambridge, MA, 373–91.

Panofsky, E. (1955) '*Et in Arcadia ego*: Poussin and the Elegiac Tradition' in idem, *Meaning in the Visual Arts*, Garden City, NY, 295–320.

Petropoulos, M. (2012) 'Αρκαδία. Ιστορικό και αρχαιολογικό περίγραμμα' in A. Vlachopoulos (ed.), *Πελοπόννησος*, Athens, 230–41.

Pikoulas, Y. A. (ed.) (2012) *Ιστορίες για την Αρκαδία: Proceedings of the International Symposium in honour of James Roy*, Stemnitsa, Greece, 39–51.

Plassart, A. (1914) 'Règlement tégéate concernant le retour des bannis à Tégée en 324 av. J.-C.', *BCH* 38, 101–88.

Poddighe, E. (1993) 'La condition juridique des citoyens Athéniens frappés par le décret du 322 : ἄτιμοι ou φυγάδες?', *Métis* 8, 271–83.

Poddighe, E. (2011) 'Alexander and the Greeks: the Corinthian League' in W. Heckel and L. Trittle (eds.), *Alexander the Great. A New History*, Chichester, UK, 99–120.

Poddighe, E. (2013) 'Diagramma' in R. Bagnall, K. Brodersen, C. B. Champion, A. Erskine and S. R. Hubner (eds.), *The Encyclopedia of Ancient History*, Chichester, UK, 2067–8.

Pretzler, M. (1999) 'Myth and history at Tegea: local tradition and community identity' in T. H. Nielsen and J. Roy (eds.), *Defining Ancient Arcadia*, Copenhagen, 89–129.

Rhodes, P. J. and Osborne, R. (2003) *Greek Historical Inscriptions 404–323 BC*, Oxford, UK.

Rizakis, A. and Touratsoglou, I. (2008) 'L'économie du Péloponnèse hellénistique: un cas régional' in C. Grandjean (éd.), *Le Péloponnèse d'Épaminondas à Hadrien*, Paris, 69–82.

Roy, J. (1999) 'The economies of Arkadia' in T. H. Nielsen and J. Roy (eds.), *Defining Ancient Arkadia*, Copenhagen, 320–81.

Roy, J. (2007) 'The urban layout of Megalopolis in its civic and confederate context' in R. Westgate, N. Fisher and J. Whitley (eds.), *Building Communities: House, Settlement and Society in the Aegean and Beyond*, London, 289–95.

172   Koulakiotis

Roy, J. (2008) 'Perceptions of the Arkadian landscape' in P. Doukellis (ed.), *Histoires du paysage*, Athens, 49–65.

Roy, J. (2009) 'Living in the mountains: Arkadian identity in the classical period' in C. Gallou and M. Georgiadis (eds.), *The Past in the Past: The Significance of Memory and Tradition in the Transmission of Culture*, Oxford, UK, 57–65.

Roy, J. (2012) 'Fifty years in Arkadia. Πενήντα χρόνια στην Αρκαδία' in Pikoulas (2012), 39–51.

Scheer, T. (2011) 'Ways of becoming Arcadian' in E. Gruen (ed.), *Cultural Identity in the Ancient Mediterranean*, Los Angeles, 11–25.

Seibert, J. (1979) *Die politische Flüchtlinge und Verbannten in der griechischen Geschichte I*, Darmstadt, Germany.

Sommerstein, A. and Bayliss, A. (2013) *Oath and State in Ancient Greece*, Berlin and Boston.

Stavridou, A. (1996) *Τα γλυπτά του Μουσείου της Τεγέας*, Athens.

Thür, G. and Taeuber, H. (1994) *Prozessrechtliche Inschriften der griechischen Poleis: Arkadien (IPArk)*, Vienna.

Velissaropoulos-Karakostas, J. (1987) *Θεσμοί της Αρχαιότητας, I. Η πόλις*, Athens.

Velissaropoulos-Karakostas, J. (2011a) *Droit grec d'Alexandre à Auguste (323 av. J.-C. – 14 ap. J.-C.). Personnes – Biens – Justice*, I, Athens.

Velissaropoulos-Karakostas, J. (2011b) *Droit grec d'Alexandre à Auguste (323 av. J.-C. – 14 ap. J.-C.). Personnes – Biens – Justice*, II, Athens.

Vlassopoulos, K. (2007) *Unthinking the Greek Polis: Ancient Greek History beyond Eurocentrism*, Cambridge, UK.

Voyatzis, M. (1999) 'The role of temple building in consolidating Arkadian communities' in T. H. Nielsen and J. Roy (eds.), *Defining Ancient Arcadia*, Copenhagen, 130–68.

Worthington, I. (1993) 'The date of the Tegea Decree (Tod ii 202): a response to the Diagramma of Alexander III or of Polyperchon?', *AHB* 7, 59–64.

Youni, M. (1998) *Μορφές ποινών στο αττικό δίκαιο: Άτιμος έστω – Άτιμος τεθνάτω*, Thessaloniki.

Appendix: the Tegea decree
(Rhodes and Osborne, *GHI* nº101)

[– – 12 – – ἐπὲς δὲ τοῖς ἀ πόλις ἀπέστειλε τὸς π] |

1 [ρέσβεας, καὶ τὰν κρίσιν ἀπέπεμψε πὸ]ς ἡ[μέας ὁ βασι]|[λεὺς Ἀλέξ]ανδρος
τὸ διάγρ[α]μμα, γραφῆναι κατὺ τὰ ἐ|[πανωρ]θώσατυ ἀ πόλις τὰ ἰν τοῖ
διαγράμματι ἀντιλ|εγόμενα. τὸς φυγάδας τὸς κατενθόντας τὰ πατρῶια|
5 κομίζεσθαι, ἐς τοῖς ἔφευγον, καὶ τὰ ματρῶια, ὅσαι ἀ|νέσδοτοι τὰ πάματα
κατῆχον καὶ οὐκ ἐτύνχανον ἀδ||ελφεὸς πεπαμέναι· εἰ δέ τινι ἐσδοθένσαι
συνέπες|ε τὸν ἀδελφεὸν καὶ αὐτὸν καὶ τὰν γενεὰν ἀπολέσθα||ι, καὶ τανὶ
ματρῶια ἦναι, ἀνώτερον δὲ μηκέτι ἦναι. ἐ|
10 πὲς δὲ ταῖς οἰκίαις μίαν ἕκαστον ἔχεν κατὺ τὸ διά|γραμμα· εἰ δέ τις ἔχει οἰκία
κᾶπον πὸς αὐτᾶι, ἄ<λλ>ον μ|ὴ λαμβανέτω· εἰ δὲ πὸς τᾶι οἰκίαι μὴ πόεστι
κᾶπος, ἐ|ξαντίαι δ' ἔστι ἰσόθι πλέθρω, λαμβανέτω τὸν κᾶπον·| εἰ δὲ πλέον
ἀπέχων ὁ κᾶπός ἐστι πλέθρω, τωνὶ τὸ ἥμι|
15 σσον λαμβανέτω, ὥσπερ καὶ τῶν ἄλλων χωρίων γέγρα|πται· τᾶν δὲ οἰκιᾶν
τιμὰν κομιζέσθω τῶ οἴκω ἑκάστ|ω δύο μνᾶς, τὰν δὲ τιμασίαν ἦναι τᾶν οἰκιᾶν
κατάπε|ρ ἀ πόλις νομίζει· τῶν δὲ κάπων διπλάσιον τὸ τίμαμ|α κομίζεσθαι ἢ
ἐς τοῖ νόμοι. τὰ δὲ χρήματα ἀφεῶσθα|
20 ι τὰν πόλιν καὶ μὴ ἀπυλιῶναι μήτε τοῖς φυγάσι μήτ|ε τοῖς πρότερον οἴκοι
πολιτεύονσι. ἐπὲς δὲ ταῖς π|αναγορίαις, ταῖς ἐσλελοίπασι οἱ φυγάδες, τὰν
πόλ|ιν βωλεύσασθαι ὅ, τι δ' ἂν βωλεύσητοι ἀ πόλις, κύριο|ν ἔστω. τὸ δὲ
δικαστήριον τὸ ξενικὸν δικάζεν ἑξήκ|
25 οντα ἀμερᾶν· ὅσοι δ' ἂν ἰν ταῖς ἑξήκοντα ἀμέραις μὴ | διαδικάσωντοι, μὴ
ἦναι αὐτοῖς δικάσασθαι ἐπὲς τ|οῖς πάμασι ἰν τοῖ ξενικοῖ δικαστηρίοι, ἀλλ' ἰν
τοῖ | πολιτικοῖ ἆῖ· εἰ δ' ἂν τι ὕστερον ἐφευρίσκωνσι, ἰν ἀ||μέραις ἑξήκοντα ἀπὺ
τᾶι ἂν ἀμέραι τὸ δικαστήριο|
30 ν καθιστᾶ· εἰ δ' ἂν μηδ' ἰν ταῖνυ διαδικάσητοι, μηκέ|τι ἐξέστω αὐτῶι
δικάσασθαι· εἰ δ' ἄν τινες ὕστερον | κατ??νθωνσι, τῶ δικαστηρίω τῶ ξενικῶ
μηκέτ[ι] ἐόντ|ος, ἀπυγραφέσθω πὸς τὸς στραταγὸς τὰ πάματα ἰν ἀμ|έραις
ἑξήκοντα, καὶ εἰκ ἄν τι αὐτοῖς ἐ[π]απύλογον ἦ|
35 ι, δικαστήριον ἦναι Μαντινέαν· εἰ δ' [ἂν μὴ] διαδικάσ|ητοι ἰν ταινὶν ταῖς
ἀμέραις, μηκέτ[ι] ἦναι αὐτοῖ δι|κάσασθαι. ἐπὲς δὲ τοῖς ἱεροῖς χρήμασιν ὅλω[ς
σὺ]ν τ|οῖς ὀφειλήμασι, τὰ μὲμ πὸς τὰν θεὸν ἀ πόλις διωρθώ|σατυ, ὁ ἔχων τὸ
πᾶμα ἀπυδότω τῶι κατηνθηκότι τὸ ἥμ|
40 ισσον κατάπερ οἱ ἄλλοι· ὅσοι δὲ αὐτοὶ ὤφηλον τᾶι θ|εοῖ συνινγύας ἢ ἄλλως,
εἰ μὲν ἂν φαίνητοι ὁ ἔχων τὸ |πᾶμα διωρθωμένος τᾶι θεοῖ τὸ χρέος, ἀπυδότω

τὸ ἥμ|ισσον τῶι κατιόντι, κατάπερ οἱ ἄλλοι, μηδὲν παρέλ|[θ]ών· εἰ δ᾽ ἂν μὴ
φαίνητοι ἀπυδεδωκὼς τᾶι θεοῖ, ἀπυδό|

45 τω τοῖ κατιόντι τὸ ἥμισσον τῶ πάματος, ἐς δὲ τοῖ ἡμ|ίσσοι αὐτὸς τὸ χρέος
διαλυέτω· εἰ δ᾽ ἂν μὴ βόλητοι δ|ιαλῦσαι, ἀπυδότω τοῖ κατιόντι τὸ πᾶμα ὅλον,
ὁ δὲ κο|μισάμενος διαλυσάτω τὸ χρέος τᾶι θεοῖ πᾶν. ὅσαι δ|ὲ γυναῖκες τῶν
φυγάδων ἢ θυγατέρες οἴκοι μίνονσ|

50 αι ἐγά[μ]αντυ ἢ φυγόνσαι ὕστερον ἐγάμαντυ [ἰ]ν Τεγέ|αν κα[ὶ] ἐπίλυσιν
ὠνήσαντυ οἴκοι μίνονσαι, ταννὶ μ|ήτ᾽ ἀ[πυδοκ]ιμ<ά>ζεσθαι τὰ πατρῶια μήτε
τὰ ματρῶια μ|ηδὲ τὸς ἐσγόνος, ὅσοι μὴ ὕστερον ἔφυγον δι᾽ ἀνάγκα|ς καὶ ἰν
τοῖ νῦν ἐόντι καιρο͂ι καθέρπονσι ἢ αὐταὶ ἢ |

55 παῖδες, ταννὶ δοκιμάζεσθαι καὶ αὐτὰς καὶ τὸς ἐς τ||αιννὶ ἐσγόνος τὰ πατρῶια
καὶ τὰ ματρῶια κὰ τὸ διά|γραμμα. ὀμνύω Δία Ἀθάναν Ἀπόλλωνα Ποσειδᾶνα,
εὐν|οήσω τοῖς κατηνθηκόσι τοῖς ἔδοξε τᾶι πόλι κατυδ|έχεσθαι, καὶ οὐ
μνησικακήσω τῶννυ οὐδεν[ὶ] τ[ὰ] ἂν ἀμ||

60 π[ε]ίσῃ ἀπὺ τᾶι ἀμέραι τᾶι τὸν ὅρκον ὤμοσα, οὐδὲ δια|κωλύσω τὰν τῶν
κατηνθηκότων σωτηρίαν, οὔτε ἐν τᾶ|ι [– -9 – -] οὔτε ἰν τοῖ κοινοῖ τᾶς πόλιος
[– -6 – -]| [– -11 – -] διάγραμμα [– 5 –] πὸς τὸς κατηνθηκό|[τ]ας [– -13 – -]
τᾶ?? πόλι [– – 17 – –] |

65 [– -8 – -τ]ὰ ἰν τοῖ διαγρά[μμ]ατι γεγραμμένα τὰ ἐς| [– – – 19 – – -ο]ὐδὲ
βωλεύσω πὸς οὐδένα.

Map 7.1 Map of the Peloponnese and Arcadia drawn by E. Østby

8 Violating the security of the *oikia*

Thefts from houses in the Hellenistic and Roman imperial periods[1]

Nikolaos Giannakopoulos

Introduction

In many if not all historical societies based on private property the private residence has been perceived as enjoying a considerable degree of inviolability. For the Greeks and the Romans the home represented a private space where – as opposed to public space available for common use – the owner, protected from any violation and intrusion by the law, religion or common social beliefs, acted as a *dominus*.[2] In this sense the home may be considered as the most characteristic example of primary territory and personal space, providing security and privacy, demonstrating self-identity and allowing control of the flow of outsiders.[3] The present chapter deals with a very common form of violation of this private *territorium* in antiquity: thefts from houses. This topic has received considerable scholarly attention, as far as classical Athens, republican and imperial Rome and Hellenistic and Roman Egypt are concerned, mainly within the framework of various general or more specialised studies either on law and forensic oratory, or on political violence, criminality and self-help.[4] However, the evidence from Hellenistic and Roman Greece and the Greek East – being quantitatively restricted and considerably dispersed – has not been systematically treated, and it is precisely the period between the fourth century BCE and the third century CE that this chapter aims to examine. Needless to say, the conclusions reached both in the aforementioned studies on Athens, Rome and Egypt – and in the abundant modern research on another related topic, rural brigandage (see note 24) – will be frequently used as an interpretative framework.

It should be stressed in advance that the perspective presented here is not that of legal history, so the various judicial processes relating to theft lie outside the scope of this chapter. Furthermore, our purpose is not to provide a comprehensive account of thefts from houses, but only to present some remarks on certain aspects of this phenomenon. Hence, we attempt to assemble the rare evidence recording concrete instances of stealing from houses and to compare them with literary texts that have not been fully researched by previous scholars, so as to establish the significance of thefts from houses as a feature of everyday life in the Greek communities of the Hellenistic and imperial periods. Furthermore, based on this evidence, we examine the social background of thieves, the way the latter were perceived and the impact that this phenomenon had on views and discourses on civic life and on the civic community's self-image and identity.

Thefts from houses: a survey of the postclassical evidence

Surviving Greek laws of the Hellenistic period rarely focus on burglaries, thefts from houses or intrusions into private residences. A notable exception is the well-known judicial agreement between two Peloponnesian cities, Stymphalos and Sicyon-Demetrias, which contains a provision regarding the penalties inflicted on persons breaking into private dwellings and stealing (or attempting to steal) from houses;[5] since this clause was part of a detailed regulation also covering matters of judicial process, arbitration, fugitive slaves and damage caused by animals, we may safely conclude that the authorities of Stymphalos and Sicyon considered thefts from houses to be a significant problem which needed to be dealt with. In the legal output of the imperial period, as compiled in the *Digest*, thefts from houses appear more frequently,[6] as a problem affecting not only Rome but also the provinces.[7] In this respect it is significant that it was in a book on the duties of the provincial governor, the major source of the administration of justice in the Roman provinces, that the third-century CE Roman jurist Ulpian dealt with the proper punishment for burglars.[8]

But what about concrete instances of stealing from houses? It is true that ancient authors rarely refer to non-political everyday violence and crime. Furthermore, any record of criminal activities is by definition absent from the bulk of the available epigraphic evidence, such as treaties, decrees, official letters, honorary inscriptions, dedications and epitaphs. However, oracular questions, curse tablets *(defixiones)* and confession inscriptions, being the product of individuals seeking counsel, revenge or assistance in their private day-to-day affairs, may shed interesting light on our topic.[9] The relevant evidence is slight and very dispersed, both locally and chronologically. More importantly, it has never been evaluated with respect to our topic, at least as far as Greece and the Greek East is concerned.[10] Hence, our first task is to bring all this material together, so as to establish a list of texts recording real incidents of stealing from houses.

We may begin our survey with two tablets of the fourth or the third century BCE, containing questions addressed to the oracle of Zeus and Dione at Dodona. In the first one, a person named Agis asked the god to inform him if someone from the outside had stolen the blankets and pillows he had lost.[11] It is noteworthy that the formulation of the question implies that there had been no forced entry into Agis' residence. Suspicion fell on outsiders, probably acquaintances, friends and neighbours, who might have had access to the house under various circumstances, but the content of the question equally suggests that one of its aims was to rule out the possibility of insiders (relatives, workers or servants) having committed the theft.[12] In the second tablet pertaining to our topic the question also refers to the theft of household items (dry fleeces from a couch), but this time the suspect is identified by name. The victim wants to know if Pistos was the thief.[13] At least two other tablets from Dodone dated to the same period contain similar questions identifying by name suspects for stealing money and a cloth respectively; it is very likely that these thefts took place inside the house, perhaps after breaking and entering, although the possibility of the cloth having been removed from a bath, a rather frequent practice, cannot be ruled out.[14]

A first-century BCE Athenian curse tablet allows us to confirm and enlarge this picture. The dedicator pretends that he had been forced to resort to curses, since thieves had deprived him of household items such as spreads or blankets, tools, perhaps jewels, mastic and pepper. This surely concerned a burglary; the victim claimed not to know the identity of the thieves, but he was able to determine that they lived in a poor quarter of the city.[15] In another curse tablet from Asia Minor the owner of certain lost gold pieces asks the Mother of the Gods to punish those who illicitly possess them.[1617] A similar curse tablet from Delos, dated to the first century BCE or the first century CE, records the theft of a jewel or, more precisely, a necklace. Finally, a curse tablet from Kenchreai, dated to the imperial period, refers to the theft of a head garment and also identifies the suspected culprit by name.[18] Of course, in these three cases we have no means of confirming whether the stolen items were removed from houses or some public place (for example baths).[19] However, if the stolen κέρατα mentioned in a Knidian curse tablet were drinking-horns, they were probably removed from a private residence.[20]

A particularly interesting story relating the theft of valuable objects from a private residence is to be found in a frequently discussed confession inscription from Lydia, dated between 150 and 250 CE. A precious stone found by Syntyche's husband and kept into their house had been stolen. In her anxiety to recover it, Syntyche appealed to Men Axiottenos, and after one month the stone was finally restored to its original place, obviously by the thief, but in a ruined state. The culprit was a young girl named Apphia; although the details of the story are rather vague, it seems possible that Apphia wanted to use the magical qualities of the stone to avert problems related to (or caused by) her defloration. The girl's mother asked Syntyche not to allow this incident to be known, obviously fearing the disgrace which might fall on her family, but when Syntyche's own son fell ill, she interpreted this as a form of divine punishment for her unwillingness to publicly recognise the aid she had received, and revealed the whole episode by erecting a confession inscription.[21]

Admittedly, the sample is very small, only four or five inscriptions safely pertaining to thefts from houses. However, scattered references in contemporary Greek literary sources not only confirm that burglaries and thefts from houses were not unknown in Greek cities of the imperial period, but also permit us to investigate how the perpetrators of that kind of criminal activity were perceived. In Plutarch's *Moralia klope, toichôrychia* and nocturnal stealing of the neighbours' property appear within the context of discussions regarding the nature of justice.[22] In this context, theft from houses was associated not only with other crimes such as *lôpodysia* and adultery, but also with licentious and immoral behaviour in general. But it is a comment made by Dio Chrysostom in a rather similar context which presents greater interest. Dealing with the problem of virtue, the orator from Prusa remarked that it was the law and not genuine moral quality that prevented men from committing crimes such as beating each other, stealing the property of their neighbours or committing adultery; on the contrary, righteous men lived together with thieves, kidnappers and adulterers and shared with them the same citizenship rights. In this respect, the city – as a political community comprising not only men obedient to the laws, but also men keen to commit crimes – was conceptualised as resembling the world of animals.[23] Now, both the ancient sources and the modern bibliography dealing with crime in antiquity have placed a great deal of emphasis upon organised groups of rural and highway bandits, who could sometimes launch predatory raids on villages and cities. These groups represented an external danger; they were a threat emanating from the imperfectly controlled countryside to disrupt the normality of civilised city life.[24] On the other hand, urban theft, though acknowledged as a feature of everyday life, has not been equally highlighted.[25] Thus, it is useful to point out that the potential or actual criminals that Dio Chrysostom and Plutarch referred to were not perceived as a distinct marginalised section of the population living outside the city walls, but as part of the ordinary urban population which, though fully integrated into civic life, behaved like wild beasts. In this way a stereotypical perception of the rural bandits' lifestyle, i.e. bestiality,[26] was extended to apply to ordinary urban thieves as well.

It is in this light that we may approach Lucian's *The Dream or the Cock,* another important text of the imperial period dealing with the threat posed to the safety of private residences by potential intruders and burglars. The tone here is of course satirical: Simon, an upstart, hides 70 talents under his bed, but is still alarmed since he has also put 16 talents under the manger and has placed his cups in a rather unsafe place inside his dwelling. He constantly fears that his poorer neighbours and workers or servants may be plotting against him and attempting to break through the walls into his house. The fact that an acquaintance of his had bought a salt fish and an expensive earring for his wife makes him wonder if he had already been robbed without knowing it.[27] Simon is of course ridiculed by Lucian. His suspicions primarily serve Lucian's purpose of highlighting the misery and unhappiness of rich people. But what matters as far as our analysis is concerned is that, like Dio Chrysostom, Simon also believed that the threat to the safety of his rich house came mainly from his poor fellow citizens, from persons known to him by name, not from bandits from the mountains.[28] Already in the fourth century BCE, Aristotle, Theophrastos and Xenophon considered stealing as a small-scale crime committed by poor desperate men.[29] Even in literary contexts fairly sympathetic to the virtues of poverty, such as Dio Chrysostom's *Euboean Speech,* it was acknowledged that poor city dwellers having no work, no money and no access to basic commodities, such as food or clothes, were frequently compelled to turn to unworthy acts, i.e. crime.[30] In fact, Dio Chrysostom observed that unemployment left the poor no other choice but to become bandits, if they lived in the countryside, or *lôpodytai,* if they lived in the city.[31] These should be considered as just two indicative examples of criminal behaviour motivated by poverty; thefts from houses may be safely added to the list of choices available to poor city dwellers.

We could of course dismiss Simon's concerns, or Dio Chrysostom's comments, as a literary *topos* bearing no relevance at all to contemporary social reality. But the information derived from the epigraphic record presented previously rather confirms the picture drawn by the Greek authors of the imperial period. The objects stolen from houses included money, jewels, clothes and furniture items, while in most cases the suspected perpetrators were persons either of known abode or identified by name. Moreover, the fact that the thieves cursed in the aforementioned Athenian tablet clearly came from a poor urban environment is in accordance with Dio Chrysostom's comments on the relation between poverty and stealing and the coexistence of righteous men and criminals within the *polis*. It is against this background that we should evaluate Plutarch's interesting story about a notorious fourth-century BCE *toichôrychos,* who used to mock Demosthenes: the thief's criminal deeds were so well known to all his fellow-citizens that the Athenian orator could make use of them so as to respond to the attack.[32]

In fact, the story of Syntyche's precious stone indicates that a variety of motives and opportunities could incite neighbours and fellow villagers to attempt to appropriate alien property. In the milieu of a Lydian village the fact that a precious object was kept in someone's house could not remain a secret. Even if material gain was not the driving force for stealing, Syntyche's house did not provide the safety or the privacy that its owner might have hoped for. Dorotheos of Sidon's *Carmen Astrologicum,* written in the first century CE, but known to us only through an Arab translation, provides an interesting taxonomy of thefts from houses divided into three categories: those perpetrated by people belonging to the household (for example slaves), those perpetrated by persons known to the house owners who had visited the house, and those committed by strangers.[33] Besides the usual methods used by burglars (digging through walls, breaking locks, copying keys and entering through skylights), there are also thieves who benefit from their friendship with house owners and even thieves who enter houses without the intention of stealing, but end up taking advantage of an appropriate circumstance.[34] Hence, both Syntyche's story and Dorotheos of Sidon's comments demonstrate that fear of neighbours and fellow citizens, as presented by Lucian, was fairly widespread and not totally unfounded. According to Dorotheos of Sidon, stolen assets included money, gold, silver and luxurious clothes to be found only "in the treasures of the wealthy".[35] But this is not to suggest that only the houses of the rich fell victim to theft. Women's trinkets were frequently mentioned in the *Carmen Astrologicum*,[36] and neither the house of the Athenian curse tablet's author, nor Syntyche's residence, seem to have been luxurious.

In this respect a comparative approach may be extremely helpful. Studying the image of the nocturnal burglar in the biblical literature, Stanley has rightly emphasised the omnipresence of thefts from houses as a phenomenon affecting both rich and poor alike.[37] Egyptian papyri also constitute an historical source particularly rich on everyday social life.[38] It is there that we may find abundant information on our topic, deriving from petitions and complaints denouncing burglaries, thefts from houses and various sorts of attacks. Since theft in general is a topic well examined by specialists on Ptolemaic and Roman Egypt it will suffice here merely to emphasise two points important for our analysis. First, a great number of such incidents had to do with stealing household items, furniture, money and food, mainly from poor or modest private residences. Second, the alleged perpetrators were usually known to the victims, both being members of the same community.[39] The testimonies from Greece and Asia Minor surveyed above demonstrate that these two fundamental aspects of small-scale crimes such as thefts from houses cannot be treated as an Egyptian or a Jewish peculiarity. On the contrary, the papyrological and biblical evidence is in accordance with what the sources from Greece and Asia Minor presented above indicate.[40]

To sum up the conclusions reached so far: it could be legitimately argued that the paucity of evidence on concrete instances of thefts from houses rather reflects the nature of the available sources, not social reality as such. On the contrary, thefts from houses were a standard feature of everyday life in the Greek cities and communities of the Hellenistic and the imperial periods. Although the suspicions raised against specific individuals may not have been always justified, it was clearly understood that thieves and their victims lived side by side within the same community. In this respect poor city dwellers experiencing great difficulties in securing basic commodities for themselves were perceived as a kind of social pool from which burglars could emerge.

Admittedly, attempting to recapture the thieves' perception of their own acts is rather impossible. However, it is important to note that anonymity, a factor contributing to the increase in small-scale criminality in modern metropolises,[41] provided relatively little cover, at least in the majority of the face-to-face Greek communities of the Hellenistic and Roman world.[42] Fear of being recognised, arrested and punished – penalties ranging from death and forced labour to heavy fines – was far from negligible.[43] But the threat of a severe penalty did not always operate as a deterring factor. Clearly for many thieves what mattered most was the struggle for survival.[44]

The impact of burglaries on perceptions of civic identity

Reactions to burglaries were significantly manifold: the victims could resort either to the authorities (as the Egyptian petitions indicate), or to the supernatural (as oracular questions and curse tablets demonstrate). My purpose in the rest of this chapter is not to elaborate on the criteria defining which of these two alternatives a victim of burglary would pursue,[45] but to explore the impact of thefts from houses and the reactions they provoked on perceptions of civic identity, which aimed in principle at uniting the community. As Stanley has rightly emphasised, the New Testament amply demonstrates the feeling of fear caused by the threat of burglary in Israel.[46] The literary and epigraphic evidence surveyed above does not allow us to discern any level of widespread insecurity; however, it shows, as we have already emphasised, that feelings of fear, to which hatred, suspicion and distrust may be added, were focused mainly on poorer neighbours and fellow citizens.[47] The fact that the author of the first-century BCE Athenian tablet mentioned above felt the need to defend his appeal to the controversial practice of magic highlights the feelings of indignation provoked by the violation of one's private space.[48] Just like rural bandits, who were spatially located outside the community, urban thieves – persons living alongside their victims and thus easily identified by them – were also perceived as presenting a threat to the safety of the private residence and thus to the rules of city life and civilised society.[49] Although poverty was sometimes acknowledged as the driving force for stealing, the prevailing discourse – expressed in highly different contexts such as the philosophical and moral essays of Dio Chrysostom and Plutarch, and the curse tablets of ordinary men and women – insisted on the low moral standards and bestial behaviour of thieves. The latter were the enemy within the walls. At a conceptual level this created a dichotomy inside the civic community, separating not citizens from outsiders but, as Dio Chrysostom put it, the righteous members of the community from the vicious ones.

Above all, it was another alternative available to the victims of burglaries, i.e. the use of self-help, which reflected and reinforced this dichotomy. As is well known, the Athenian law allowed the killing of the nocturnal intruder.[50] The judicial agreement between Stymphalos and Sicyon-Demetrias was even more severe: anyone breaking into a house or attempting to steal from it could be legitimately killed by the residents.[51] In contrast to Athenian law, this clause concerned not only nocturnal but also daytime thieves and intruders. Admittedly, the judicial agreement between Stymphalos and Sicyon-Demetrias was a *symbolon* covering offences perpetrated by citizens and residents of one city in the territory of another, but the Athenian example suggests there is no reason to deny the existence of similar clauses in the law of each separate city as well. After all, the right of a house resident to kill an intruder was in one way or another fairly universal, though sometimes subject to important limitations. Thus, according to Ulpian, a nocturnal thief could be killed with impunity only in self-defence (if the thief used weapons and the victim was in danger).[52] In a slightly different manner, Paul remarked that those killing a nocturnal or daytime thief using weapons did not fall under the provisions of *Lex Cornelia de sicariis et veneficiis*.[53] So, despite considerable local and temporal differences, both Greek and Roman legal systems recognised and even formalised self-help as a reaction to burglary.[54]

How frequently and under what circumstances the victims of burglaries actually resorted to self-help cannot be determined, but it is by no means accidental that Simon's first reaction when he thought that someone was entering his house was to search for his sword, without stopping to think whether the intruder was armed. In fact, the Roman jurists' insistence on allowing self-help against burglars only in the case of self-defence may be seen as an indication that in everyday practice such distinctions were not always possible. It is worth pointing out that in Aulus Gellius' *Attic Nights* the killing of a nocturnal thief as prescribed in the Twelve Tables – i.e. without the limitation concerning the threat to the house owner's life and the use of arms on the part of the intruder – was considered by the jurist Sextus Caecilius as a legally obsolete, but socially proper reaction to theft, despite the philosopher Favorinus' objections.[55] We may thus detect a plurality of positions with regard to the proper circumstances of resorting to self-help against a burglar and, as Harries has remarked, these conflicting views reflected problems which still preoccupied the Roman jurists of the imperial period.[56]

After all, *latrones,* classified as such because of their violent disposition and intention to use arms in order to inflict physical damage or death, could be killed with impunity without any limitation. Although the term *latro* mainly referred to rural bandits, urban house-breakers carrying arms could also be viewed as falling into this category.[57] In this respect, a passage from Apuleius' *Metamorphoses* may be very helpful. On his way back to the house of Milo, his host at the Thessalian city of Hypata, Lucius, the novel's hero, observed three figures trying to break down the front door and storm into the house. He took them for thieves and his immediate reaction was to attack first and kill the three intruders (indicatively labelled as *latrones*) with his sword, again without bothering to find out if the latter were armed.[58] The next day he was charged with murder and brought to what would soon be revealed to be no more than a mock trial. The intruders had in fact been three "inflated wine-skins slit with various gashes" and the whole incident had been staged to celebrate a festival in honour of Laughter.[59] But the crucial point for our analysis is that before discovering the truth Lucius delivered an elaborate defence speech underlining that he was guiltless, since his actions had restored peace and protected both his host's house and the public safety.[60] This was his duty as a good citizen.[61] Admittedly, Lucius attempted to strengthen his case by pointing out the intruders' intention to kill all the residents, that is, by showing himself to be in complete compliance with the letter of the law;[62] but this was obviously a fabricated argument, since the description of the fight between him and the 'intruders' makes it clear that there had been no time to overhear the burglars' plan.[63] Of course, one could object that all this is no more than satire; but the comic result is achieved precisely because Lucius is presented as acting and speaking appropriately in an inappropriate situation. Though pure fiction, this episode is not at all unrealistic, at least as far as the reactions to a nocturnal burglary are concerned.[64] Lucius' defence line, and the contradiction between his arguments and what was supposed to have actually happened, highlight to what extent legal restrictions on the use of self-help could be overcome or manipulated by house residents.

Thus, it is clear that in everyday life self-help was always an option for house owners coming face to face with intruders, just as the use of arms was always an option for burglars.[65] This option actually meant that a respectable citizen could find himself in a position where he might hit or even kill one of his fellow citizens. But this could be conceptualised as a socially acceptable private violence, exercised by the victims, but sanctioned by the state and the law – at least as a reaction to the use of force by burglars. In Lucius' words we find an excellent illustration of how the victims of burglary resorting to self-help were perceived – or wanted to be perceived – as good citizens defending the values of private property and public safety and peace against an internal threat coming from what was perceived as the lowest sort of fellow citizens.[66] In this respect, Lucius' defence expressed a similar notion of dichotomy inside the civic community as the one found in Dio Chrysostom's previously mentioned passage.

But Lucius' speech also enables us to place this dichotomy within a wider context. By presenting an action of self-help against a burglar as an action securing peace, Lucius incorporated in his argumentation the important ideological symbol of *Pax Romana* and *Pax Augusta,* a major legitimising factor of Imperial power which had to do not only with stopping foreign and civil wars, but also – at least as far as Roman subjects' expectations were concerned – with suppressing criminal activity and any kind of arbitrary violence.[67] In fact, the peace which the Roman emperor guaranteed was sometimes explicitly associated with the security provided to city dwellers.[68] Despite the overall comic character of Lucius' speech, Apuleius' readers could easily recognise the essence of a simple realistic argument, which was nonetheless by no means incompatible with standard contemporary views: house-breakers were also breaking the imperial order; those who opposed them were supporting and consolidating that order.

Final remarks

Burglaries and thefts from houses are rather underrepresented in the literary and epigraphic sources of the Hellenistic and imperial periods. However, this does not mean that the cities and villages of Greece and Asia Minor were not exposed to this threat. Admittedly, estimating the frequency of thefts from houses is impossible in any period of ancient history (on the lack of data cf. the remarks made by Fisher in his contribution to this volume, p. 101). Nevertheless, scattered references to this phenomenon in authors like Plutarch, Dio Chrysostom and Lucian, combined with actual incidents of theft recorded in curse tablets, oracular questions and confession inscriptions, suggest that burglary was a danger that every house owner or resident had to take into consideration. Despite the tendency to recognise the social causes of this kind of small- scale criminality, the need to protect private property was inherently associated with the moral and social downgrading of those who threatened it. Hence, the prevailing views on housebreakers, their treatment by the law and in particular the potential or actual use of self-help against them – and of violence by them – tended to establish a particular – yet clearly defined – social boundary which, given the urban thieves' membership of the civic community, functioned inside the city. If violence may be seen as a factor creating divisions between insiders and outsiders (as Vlassopoulos and Xydopoulos point out in their introduction to this volume, p. 17), house-breakers, both in exercising unlawful violence and in being subject to legitimate violent self-help, became the outsiders inside the community, a sort of *atimoi* enjoying no protection at all (cf. Canevaro's contribution in this volume, p. 57). Thieves and their potential or actual victims constituted an example of 'pairs of complementary oppositions' which, as Lin Foxhall and others have showed, were so important for the way the Greeks constructed their identity.[69] In this way, not only the violent treatment of poor fellow citizens who acted as burglars could be justified, but space was also allowed for the emergence of a more elaborate form of civic identity, which embraced not all the citizens, but only those respectful of the private *oikia,* private property and ultimately the *Pax Augusta.* In a certain sense the violent self-help exercised on house-breakers may be seen as providing a way out of one of the paradoxes highlighted by the editors in their introduction to this volume (p. 6). Within the framework of a state which claimed to monopolise the legitimate use of violence, but for various reasons did not always enforce this claim, the citizens/subjects acted as agents who employed violence so as to implement the state laws and rules that regulated what was conceived as civilised life.

Notes

1 References to papyri are in accordance with the abbreviations of the Checklist of Editions of Greek, Latin, Demotic and Coptic Papyri, Ostraca and Tablets (http://www.lib. berkeley.edu/ARTH/ucblist.html). References to inscriptions are abbreviated according to *SEG*.

2 On these concepts see Saller 1994: 89–90 and Treggiari 2002: 108. Cf. also Christ 1998: 521 and Taubenschlag 1959b. On cultic activities inside private houses see Jameson 1990: 104–6.

3 On the validity of the concept of territoriality for domestic spaces – in particular personal occupancies – see Sanders 1990: 47–51. The papers included in Benjamin and Stea 1995 offer a very useful analysis of the perception of the home from an environmental-behavioural studies perspective.

4 In his recent study on criminality in antiquity Krause 2004: 150–5 examines thefts from houses based mainly on evidence from Egypt and Rome. On theft in classicalA-thens the basic study is Cohen 1983. Among the most recent works see Fisher 1999, with further bibliography. Stanley 2002 examines the figure of the nocturnal thief in biblical literature and focuses on the burglars' mode of operation and on the fear inspired in house owners. For thieves in Flavian Rome see Wolff 2011. On the use of self-help as a means of confronting (or generating) violence see the fundamental works by Lintott 1968: 8–34 (Rome) and 1982: 14–26 (Greece). More recent studies, bibliographically fully updated, are provided by Christ 1998 and Kloppenborg 2004 (who also surveys the evidence from ancient Israel). On thefts in Ptolemaic and Roman Egypt see the bibliography cited in note 39. For an examination of the way in which the Roman criminal law dealt with thefts see Schulz 1951: 575–83; Robinson 1995: 23–40 and Harries 2007: 43–58, with further bibliography.

5 *IPArk* 17 ll. 111–21.

6 *D.* 48.6.3.2.; 48.6.11. pr; 48.8.9.

7 As Wolff (2011: 76, 78 and 85) has pointed out, Rome, though notorious for thieves, was not an exceptional case compared with other ancient cities.

8 *D.* 47.17.1 and 47.18.1. On thieves prosecuted before the court of the provincial governor see also *D.* 47.2.57(56).1. In another passage from Ulpian's book on the duties of the provincial governor (*D.*1.18.13pr.) thieves (*fures*) are listed among the criminals that should be hunted down by the provincial authorities. Cf. Brélaz 2005: 35; 2007: 232; Wolff 2011: 76; Fuhrmann 2012: 150–1 and 182.

9 On a recent co-examination of oracular questions and curse tablets as evidence for ordinary people's concerns and anxieties see Eidinow 2007. The main corpus of curse tablets remains Audollent 1904. A survey of curse tablets not included in regional epigraphic corpora is provided by Jordan 1985. A distinctive category of curse tablets, usually termed judicial prayers, involved a provisional transfer of stolen objects to the god to which the injured party appealed. See Versnel 1991: 76–9. A corpus is provided by Gager 1992: 175–99. For a bibliography on this topic, see Faraone and Rife 2007: 141 no. 1. For a recent discussion of judicial prayers see Dreher 2009 and Vélissaropoulos-Karakostas 2009. Confession inscriptions, a particularity of Lydia, corresponded to a similar practice, as Versnel has pointed out. An injured party appealed to divine justice and initiated a process before the local temple by 'erecting a sceptre'. The accused party could either confess, or take an oath of innocence. Illness or other misfortunes suffered subsequently by the accused party could be considered as a form of divine

punishment and a proof of guilt. See also Ricl 1995: 69; Gordon 2004: 185–7. A corpus of relevant testimonies with extensive commentary is provided by Petzl 1994.

10 For the value of *defixiones* as evidence for criminal activity see Brélaz 2005: 51, n. 39.

11 See Lhôte 2006: no. 121; Eidinow 2007: 117, no. 4.

12 In fact Roman poets often mention thefts of household items perpetrated by guests for dinner, friends of the house owners or slaves. See Wolff 2011: 87, 81, 85–6. Cf. also what follows on Dorotheos of Sidon. Eidinow 2007: 132 has rightly pointed out that Agis seems to have had a specific suspect in mind.

13 See Daux 1960: 751; Eidinow 2007: 117–8, no. 7.

14 Lhôte 2006: nos. 119–20. Cf. Eidinow 2007: 117, nos. 3 and 6.

15 *SEG* XXX (1980), 326; Gager 1992: 180–3, no. 84; cf. Versnel 1991: 66.

16 The inscription was first published by Dunant 1978 with extensive commentary; cf. also Gager 1992: 190–1, no. 90. As Versnel 1991: 74–5 observed, the victim dedicated the stolen objects to the Mother of the Gods and demanded divine intervention.

17 The inscription was first published by Bruneau 1971: 650–5; cf. also Gager 1992: 188, no. 88. The inscription was republished with new readings by Jordan 2002. Unlike most *defixiones* the inscriber pinpoints the culprit's injustice and his own innocence using the verb ἐκδικέω, which denotes the 'prayer for justice'. On the reverse there are no curses at all, only an appeal to the Syrian gods to dispense justice. See on all this Versnel 1991: 66–7.

18 The inscription was published by Faraone and Rife 2007.

19 On this possibility cf. Faraone and Rife 2007: 152–3.

20 On this curse tablet see Audollent 1904: 18, no. 12.

21 The inscription was published with an extensive commentary by Petzl and Malay 1987; see further Pleket's remarks in *SEG* XXXVII (1987), 1001; the inscription was re-edited by Petzl 1994: 73–6, no. 59. See also Ricl 1995: 71–2; Paz de Hoz 1999: no. 39.9; Gordon 2004: 192.

22 See Plutarch, *Moralia* 585B: Ἔστιν οὖν τις, ὦ φίλε, καὶ δικαιοσύνη πρὸς φιλοπλουτίαν καὶ φιλαργυρίαν ἄσκησις, οὐ τὸ μὴ κλέπτειν ἐπίοντα νύκτωρ τὰ τῶν πέλας μηδὲ λωποδυτεῖν ... (For justice too, then, my dear friend, a mode of training exists, whereby we resist the appetite for riches and money. It does not lie in abstention from going about at night to steal our neighbours' goods, or strip men of their cloaks); *Moralia* 1076E: ὧν ἀνάγκη τὰ πλεῖστα πάσχειν τὸν θεόν, εἰ παρὰ τὴν βούλησιν αὐτοῦ μέρη ὄντες οἱ φαῦλοι ψεύδονται καὶ τοιχωρυχοῦσι καὶ ἀποκτιννύουσιν ἀλλήλους (But most of this must be what happens to god if, contrary to his will, the base, while being parts of him, deceive and cheat and rob and kill one another). Cf. also *Moralia,* 97F.

23 Dio Chrysostom, 69.9: Σημεῖον δὲ τῆς πονηρίας τῆς τῶν ἀνθρώπων· εἰ γὰρ ἀνέλοιεν τοὺς νόμους καὶ ἄδεια γένοιτο τοῦ τύπτειν ἀλλήλους καὶ ἁρπάζειν τὰ τῶν πέλας καὶ μοιχεύειν καὶ λωποδυτεῖν, τίνας ἔσεσθαι οἰητέον τοὺς ἀφεξομένους τούτων καὶ μὴ πάνυ ῥαδίως τε καὶ ἑτοίμως ἅπαντα ἐξαμαρτεῖν βουλομένους; ὡς τὸ νῦν γε οὐδὲν ἧττον λανθάνομεν μετὰ κλεπτῶν καὶ ἀνδραποδιστῶν καὶ μοιχῶν ζῶντες καὶ συμπολιτευόμενοι καὶ κατὰ τοῦτο οὐδὲν βελτίους τῶν θηρίων ἐσμέν (And here is an indication of the depravity of mankind. If men were to do away with the laws and licence were to be granted to strike one another, to commit murder, to steal the property of one's neighbours, to commit adultery, to be a footpad, then who must we suppose would be the persons who will refrain from those deeds and not, without the slightest scruple or hesitation, be willing to commit all manner of crimes? For even under present conditions we none the less are living unwittingly with thieves and kidnappers and adulterers and joining with them in the activities of citizenship, and in this respect we are no better than the wild beasts.)

24 On bandits in the Roman Empire see Shaw 1984, 1992; Riess 2001; Grünewald 2004. A thorough account of rural brigandage in the eastern part of the Roman Empire is provided by Wolff 2003. Apuleius in his *Metamorphoses* records several incidents of attacks on urban houses by rural bandits, of course fictional, but not alien to

contemporary social reality *(Met.* 2.32; 3.5; 3.28; 4.10; 4.12; 4.21). See on this point
Stanley 2002: 476; Wolff 2003: 44. An organised predatory raid upon an Egyptian vil-
lage carried out by an armed band is recorded in a series of petitions dating to 113 BCE
(P.Tebt. 1, 45–7 and *P.Tebt.* 4, 1095–6).

25 A notable exception is provided by Wolff 2011, who offers a detailed study of urban
theft in Flavian Rome, mainly based on the writings of Martial, Juvenal and Quintilian.

26 On this stereotype see Wolff 2003: 33.

27 Lucian, *The Dream or The Cock,* 28–9: ΑΛΕΚΤΡΥΩΝ: Ἐγώ σε ἰάσομαι, ὦ Μίκυλλε·
καὶ ἐπείπερ ἔτι νύξ ἐστιν, ἐξαναστὰς ἕπου μοι· ἀπάξω γάρ σε παρ'αὐτὸν ἐκεῖνον τὸν
Σίμωνα καὶ εἰς τὰς τῶν ἄλλων πλουσίων οἰκίας, ὡς ἴδοις οἷα τὰ παρ' αὐτοῖς ἐστι.
ΜΙΚΥΛΛΟΣ: Πῶς τοῦτο, κεκλεισμένων τῶν θυρῶν; εἰ μὴ καὶ τοιχωρυχεῖν γε σύ με
ἀναγκάσεις. . . . ΣΙΜΩΝ: Οὐκοῦν τάλαντα μὲν ἑβδομήκοντα ἐκεῖνα πάνυ ἀσφαλῶς ὑπὸ
τῇ κλίνῃ κατορώρυκται καὶ οὐδεὶς ἄλλος οἶδε, τὰ δὲ ἑκκαίδεκα εἶδεν, οἶμαι, Σωσύλος
ὁ ἱπποκόμος ὑπὸ τῇ φάτνῃ κατακρύπτοντά με· ὅλος γοῦν περὶ τὸν ἱππῶνά ἐστιν, οὐ
πάνυ ἐπιμελὴς ἄλλως οὐδὲ φιλόπονος ὤν. εἰκὸς δὲ ἡρπάσθαι πολλῷ πλείω τούτων, ἢ
πόθεν γὰρ ὁ Τίβειος τάριχος αὐτῷ οὕτω μέγα ὠψωνηκέναι χθὲς ἐλέγετο ἢ τῇ γυναικὶ
ἐλλόβιον ἐωνῆσθαι πέντε δραχμῶν ὅλων; τὰμὰ οὗτοι σπαθῶσι τοῦ κακοδαίμονος.
ἀλλ' οὐδὲ τὰ ἐκπώματα ἐν ἀσφαλεῖ μοι ἀπόκειται τοσαῦτα ὄντα. δέδια γοῦν μη τις
ὑπορύξας τὸν τοῖχον ὑφέληται αὐτά· πολλοὶ φθονοῦσι καὶ ἐπιβουλεύουσί μοι, καὶ
μάλιστα ὁ γείτων Μίκυλλος. . . . Ἄριστον γοῦν ἄγρυπνον αὐτὸν φυλάττειν· . . . ὁρῶ
σε γε, τοιχωρύχε. . . . ἰδοὺ πάλιν ἐψόφηκέ τις· ἐπ' ἐμὲ δηλαδή· πολιορκοῦμαι καὶ
ἐπιβουλεύομαι πρὸς ἁπάντων. ποῦ μοι τὸ ξιφίδιον; ἂν λάβω τινά. (COCK: I will cure
you, Mikyllos. As it is still night, get up and follow me; I will take you to visit Simon
and to the house of other rich men, so that you may see what their establishments are
like. MIKYLLOS: How can you do it when their doors are locked? You aren't going to
make me be a burglar? SIMON: Well, then, that seventy talents is quite safely buried
under the bed and no one else knows of it; but as for the sixteen, I think Sosylos the
groom saw me hiding them under the manger. At any rate he is all for hanging about
the stable, though he is not particularly attentive to business otherwise, or fond of
work. I have probably been robbed of much more than that, or else where did Tibeios
get the money for the big slice of salt fish they said he treated himself to yesterday, or
the earring they said he bought for his wife at a cost of five whole drachmas? It's my
money these fellows are squandering, worse luck! But my cups are not stored in a safe
place, and there are so many! I'm afraid someone may burrow under the wall and steal
them: many envy me and plot against me, and above all my neighbour Mikyllos. At
any rate it is best to stay awake myself and keep watch. I see you, burglar. There, now,
someone made a noise; he is after me; I am beleaguered and plotted against by all the
world. Where is my sword? If I find anyone.).

28 Krause 2004: 150 pinpoints the importance of this text as evidence for night-time burglaries, but does not associate it with other relevant references from contemporary
literary sources.

29 On Aristotle and Theophrastos see Fisher 1999: 65–6; on Xenophon see *Symp.* 4.36.

30 Dio Chrysostom, 7.104–9: Μήποτε σπάνια ἢ τὰ ἐν ταῖς πόλεσιν ἔργα τοῖς τοιούτοις
(πένησι), ἀφορμῆς τε ἔξωθεν προσδεόμενα, ὅταν οἰκεῖν τε μισθοῦ δέῃ καὶ τἄλλ' ἔχειν
ὠνουμένους, οὐ μόνον ἱμάτια καὶ σκεύη καὶ σῖτον, ἀλλὰ καὶ ξύλα, τῆς γε καθ' ἡμέραν
χρείας ἕνεκα τοῦ πυρός. . . . τάχα γὰρ ἂν φανεῖται χαλεπὸν τοιούτῳ βίῳ διαρκεῖν μηδὲν
ἄλλο κτῆμα ἔξω τοῦ σώματος κεκτημένους. . . . ἀλλὰ ἴδωμεν πόσα καὶ ἄττα πράττοντες
ἐπιεικῶς ἡμῖν διάξουσιν, ἵνα μὴ πολλάκις ἀναγκασθῶσιν ἀργοὶ καθήμενοι πρὸς τι τῶν
φαύλων τραπῆναι (For the poor of this type suitable work may perhaps be hard to find
in the cities, and will need to be supplemented by outside resources when they have to
pay house-rent and buy everything they get, not merely clothes, household belongings,
and food, but even the wood to supply the daily need for fire. It will perhaps seem hard
for men to subsist under such conditions who have no other possession than their own
bodies, but let us see what the variety and nature of occupations are which they are to

follow in order to live in what we believe is the proper way *and not be often compelled to turn to something unworthy because they are out of work).*

31 Dio Chrysostom, 7.40. In fact, the view that poverty led to crime and particularly to brigandage is not at all uncommon in the literary output of the imperial period. See the evidence assembled by Grassl 1982: 83–4; cf. Shaw 1992: 405–6. On poverty and hunger as causes of banditry see Riess 2001: 63–72 and 253. On the relation between poverty and urban theft in Quintilian see Wolff 2011: 81.

32 Plutarch, *Demosthenes,* 11.6; *Moralia,* 803 C-D.

33 Dorotheos of Sidon, *Carmen Astrologicum,* 5.35.75–8. The text is edited by Pingree 1976, who also provides an English translation. The value of *Carmen Astrologicum* for the study of thefts has been pointed out by Wolff 2011: 76 and 83–4, who rightly sees in it a confirmation of the omnipresence of the phenomenon.

34 Dorotheos of Sidon, *Carmen Astrologicum,* 5.35.134–8.

35 Dorotheos of Sidon, *Carmen Astrologicum,* 5.35.49.

36 Dorotheos of Sidon, *Carmen Astrologicum,* 5.35.53, 59 and 64.

37 Stanley 2002.

38 As Lewis 1983: 1 observes, papyri bring us closer to the private lives of ordinary men and women than inscriptions.

39 See Taubenschlag 1955: 452–8. Baldwin 1963 comments on several papyri recording thefts, assaults, smuggling, abductions, illegal seizure of agricultural land and inter-village feuds; Davies 1973: 199–212 focuses on the investigation of crimes by the Roman army. Lukaszewicz 1983: 107–19 provides a list of complaints of theft and robbery in Roman and Byzantine Egypt. This catalogue comprises all kinds of thefts and not just thefts from houses. As far as Ptolemaic Egypt is concerned, see indicatively: *P.Tebt.* III 1, 795 (early second century BCE); *P.Tebt.* III 1, 796 (185 BCE); *P.Heid.* IX, 423 + 425 Kol. II. (158 BCE); *P.Tebt.* III 1, 804 (112 BCE); *P. Dion,* 10 (109 BCE); *P. Würzb,* 5 (31 BCE). Cf. also Bauschatz 2013: 166, n. 13 (collection of petitions denouncing thefts). An exhaustive treatment of crimes against property in Roman Egypt is to be found in Drexhage 1989: 952–1004. Offences are classified according to the nature of the stolen assets (animals, food, textiles, money, jewels, wood, agricultural products, etc.). Grünewald 2004: 25–31 provides a very useful analysis of 29 petitions recording thefts. All these documents – dated between 28 and 42 CE – come from a single village, Euhemeria, and demonstrate that both the thieves and their victims came from the same social classes. Krause 2004: 150–3 reaches the same conclusion as well.

40 On the extent to which the rich information drawn by Egyptian papyri may be used as evidence for policing and criminality in other areas of the Roman Empire, see Yannakopoulos 2003: 872–3 and Brélaz 2005: 50–2 and 335–6. In this respect, it is worth pointing out that the stolen goods the Roman poets refer to (see Wolff 2011: 83–4 and 86–7) do not essentially differ from what is recorded in the few Greek inscriptions and the numerous Egyptian papyri.

41 See on this point Screvens 1981: 42–3; Tsitsoura 1981: 118.

42 The Egyptian papyri led Grünewald (2004: 29) to a similar conclusion. The literary and epigraphic evidence surveyed above shows that, in this respect too, Egypt did not differ from other parts of the Greek East.

43 According to Athenian law, thieves caught in the act were liable to *apagoge,* which was carried out by the victims and could lead to the summary execution of the burglars; pecuniary penalties were also inflicted on thieves not caught in the act (see on all this Cohen 1983: 72–4 and 92; Christ 1998: 522; Kloppenborg 2004: 510; on *apagoge* and other related judicial processes see Hansen 1976). The judicial agreement between Stymphalos and Sicyon prescribed that, if the perpetrator was arrested, the victim had the right to sue him for 500 drachmas, or even 1,000 drachmas in the case of damage caused in the house *(IPArk* 17 ll. 114–6). This clause apparently concerned only nocturnal burglars, since the next clause *(IPArk* 17 ll. 117–21) prescribed that daytime thieves stealing from houses (burglars) should pay a fine amounting to 50 drachmas

and double the value of the stolen property, but if they had stolen property worth more than 50 drachmas, they should pay a fine of 200 drachmas and double the value of the stolen property. In the imperial period penalties imposed by the courts ranged from death (if the thieves were armed) to scourging and forced labour. Paul, in his *De officio praefecti vigilum,* recorded that nocturnal burglars were scourged and sentenced to the mines, while daytime burglars were first whipped and then sentenced to forced labour, either for life or for a limited period of time (D. 47.18.2). This distinction between daytime and nocturnal thieves as a factor influencing the content and the gravity of sentences is also highlighted by Claudius Saturninus in his book on penalties imposed on civilians (D. 48.19.16.5). Of course, the *praefectus vigilum's* duties covered Rome, (Robinson 1995: 27), but in the Roman provinces too things were no different. Writing on the duties of the proconsul, Ulpian pointed out that the exact form of the punishment inflicted on burglars laid at the governor's discretion, but could not go beyond forced labour for the *humiliores* or banishment for the *honestiores* (D. 47. 18.1). However, burglars using violence were to be sentenced to the mines (D. 47.17.1), while Paul remarked that burglaries and attacks on houses perpetrated by armed groups carried the death penalty under the *Lex Iulia de vi publica* (D. 48.6.11.pr.; Paul used in this context the term *effrego,* which refers to burglars *[effractores]).* Furthermore, the use of arms with the intention of committing a theft fell under the *Lex Cornelia de sicariis et veneficiis,* which carried the death penalty (D. 48.8.1pr; cf. Berger 1953 s.v. sicarius; Wolff 2011: 75). Pecuniary penalties were perhaps also imposed. The Praetorian Edict prescribed actions for fourfold damage in the case of *furtum manifestum* and twofold damage in the case of *furtum non manifestum* (see *e.g. D.* 47.2.50.pr; Gaius, *Institutes,* 3.189–90; cf. Schulz 1951: 581–2). Thieves judged by the provincial governor could be sentenced to pay a fine (D. 47.2.57[56].1), but it is not certain if house-breakers were also treated in this way. It is worth pointing out that Roman jurists recognised the inability of a condemned poor man to pay a heavy fine and opted for penalties *extra ordinem.* It is thus clear that, if arrested, poor urban thieves and burglars could hardly avoid physical punishment or loss of freedom (see D. 48.19.1.3 with Harries 2007: 37–8 and 44). On theft treated within the framework of *cognitio extraordinaria,* which gave the judge considerable freedom to inflict any penalty he deemed proper, see D. 47.2.93; D. 48.19.1.3; D. 48.19.13. On penalties inflicted on burglars and thieves from houses see Robinson 1995: 10 and 27–8; Manfredini 1996: 515; Wolff 2003: 223; Harries 2007: 31, 37, and 58. On penalties in Egypt see M. Malouta in *P.Oxy.* 73.4960, p. 1640.

44 See on this point Stanley 2002: 476–7 and 479. The relatively high occurrence of easily identifiable house-breakers may be explained by the difficulty of entering and moving inside an average small urban house without being noticed. Once alarmed, the residents would immediately recognise the burglars as their fellow citizens. Stanley rightly points out that this kind of fear may have encouraged further acts of violence on the part of armed thieves willing, if necessary, to eliminate witnesses so as to avoid punishment.

45 It may be of course argued that one course of action (for example appeal to the authorities) did not exclude another (for example resort to magic). After all, the two strategies have a common point in that both curse tablets (intended to be known and not kept secret as Gager 1992: 176–7 has pointed out; cf. also Papakonstantinou's contribution in this volume, pp. 143–5) and petitions could be viewed as means of exercising pressure, so as to reach a private settlement (on this aspect of petitions see Kelly 2011: 261–5 and 276–85).

46 Stanley 2002: 476–81.

47 As it has been convincingly argued by Eidinow (2007: 228–37) oracular questions and in particular curse tablets allow us to grasp the manifold ways fear and distrust of fellow citizens, perceived as sources of danger and threat, constituted an important aspect of daily life and interpersonal relationships. In this respect, rumours and gossip also played a significant role.

48 See previous note 15. On the controversial character of binding practices see the contribution by Papakonstantinou in this volume (p. 143).

49 The brigand was as Brélaz (2005: 48) puts it, the anti-model of the good cultivated city dweller.

50 Cohen 1983: 72–4 and 92; Christ 1998: 522; Kloppenborg 2004: 510. As has been convincingly argued by Riess (2008: 53–7), self-help also played a key role in the process of *apagoge*.

51 *IPArk* 17 ll. 111–4.

52 *D.* 48.8.9. For a detailed study of self-defence against thieves and bandits in Roman law see Manfredini 1996, with full bibliography. Cf. also Brélaz 2007: 228 and 231. Fuhrmann 2012: 49, n. 49 collects the relevant sources and provides a survey of the modern bibliography.

53 Paul, *Sententiae*, 5.23.8–9. Cf. Manfredini 1996: 518–9 and Brélaz 2005: 227.

54 Cf. on this point Lintott 1968: 22. On self-help in Ptolemaic and Roman Egypt see Taubenschlag 1959a. Cf. also Bauschatz 2013: 173–5.

55 Aulus Gellius, *NA*, 20.1.7–10. The retaliatory violence exercised by the victims of crimes was met with a great deal of sympathy by the citizens of classical Athens, as Fisher remarks in his contribution to this volume (pp. 123–4). The Twelve Tables were considerably more severe than classical Roman law as they recognised the right to kill with impunity not only the nocturnal thief, but also the *fur diurnus,* if the latter used arms. See *XII Tab.* 8.12 and D. 9.2.4.1; cf. Lintott 1968: 13; Cantarella 2000: 306–7; Treggiari 2002: 85. Fuhrmann 2012: 49, n. 49 assembles the relevant sources and cites numerous references in the modern bibliography, but does not distinguish between the republican and imperial periods.

56 Harries 2007: 50–7.

57 On the various meanings of the word *latro* and on the right to kill *latrones* with impunity, see Manfredini 1996: 507 and 513–4; Wolff 2003: 10–20; Grünewald 2004: 15–7. On self-defence against bandits see also Wolff 2006, who analyses two Dacian inscriptions referring to private vengeance exercised against bandits by the relatives of their victims.

58 Apuleius, *Metamorphoses*, 2.32.

59 Apuleius, *Metamorphoses*, 3.2–9.

60 Apuleius, *Metamorphoses*, 3.6.

61 Apuleius, *Metamorphoses*, 3.5. Cf. on this point the remarks of Brélaz 2005: 227, n. 706.

62 Apuleius,*Metamorphoses*, 3.5. Riess 2001: 313 has pointed out that Lucius' strategy was to present his actions as a form of legitimate self-defence in accordance with what the XII Tables prescribed regarding the killing of a thief. However, in the XII Tables, as we have already noted (cf. previous note 55), a nocturnal thief could be killed with impunity, regardless of whether he was carrying arms. It was only the killing of the *fur diurnus* which was subject to this restriction. If indeed it was the XII Tables that Lucius and Apuleius had in mind, there would have been no need to prove the intruders' violent intentions. It was only the classical Roman law of the imperial period which established the use of arms by the nocturnal thief as a necessary condition for allowing the victims to resort to self-help. Thus, Lucius' defence strategy should rather be read against the background of the *Digest*, not the XII Tables.

63 On this inconsistency, see the sound remarks of Riess 2001: 289–90 and 313. Cf. also Gleason 1999: 296, who rightly points out that Lucius' defence speech in *Met.* 3.5–6 is a significant elaboration of the original account of the clash between Lucius and the 'intruders', as recorded in *Met.* 2.32.

64 On the realism of the 'world of the Golden Ass', see Millar 1981.

65 Studies on republican Rome and classical Athens have drawn attention to the fact that, given the lack of adequate policing systems, the victims of burglaries could primarily rely on self-help and the aid provided by their neighbours and fellow-citizens. See

Fisher 1999: 81–2 (Athens) and Lintott 1968: 13 and 24 (Rome). On the other hand, as Manfredini (1996: 514–8) has rightly pointed out, in the imperial period the prevailing tendency was to emphasise legitimate self-defence as a factor justifying the killing of an exclusively nocturnal thief. However, it would be methodologically unwise to suggest a considerable decrease in the use of self-help based only on legal regulations. What we rather need is to see how these restrictions were put into practice. In this respect, Simon's fictional response to a threat of burglary is not very different from a Knidian woman's actual reaction against an intruder who was not directly threatening her life (an episode known to us from *I.Knidos 34* recording a letter of Augustus to the Knidians). Both these cases indicate that violent self-help on the part of the victims was not uncommon.

66 See Apuleius,*Metamorphoses,* 3.6.

67 On the *Pax Romana/Augusta* as a political and ideological symbol and as a discourse legitimising the *Imperium Romanum,* see Weinstock 1960 and Woolf 1993. Though mainly denoting the end of civil and foreign wars, the *Pax Romana/Augusta* could also be used by Roman subjects as a concept associated with protection from any kind of violence, including crime. See on this point Yannakopulos 2003: 875–8; Grünewald 2004: 18; Kelly 2007: 158 and Fuhrmann 2012: 99–100 and 168–9. In this respect, particularly indicative is Epictetus' remark that a victim of arbitrary violence should appeal to Caesar's peace and resort to the judicial authority of the proconsul (Epictetus, 3.22.55). The association of imperial order with protection from arbitrary violence is also reflected in the concluding phrase of a petition addressed to an epistrategus by a victim of violence in Oxyrhynchus: 'let no violence occur in the so happy days of our lord Aurelius Antoninus Caesar' (*P.Oxy.* 31.2563).

68 *Pseudo-Aristides,* 35.36–7. Cf. on this passage the comments of Fuhrmann 2012: 89–90. Even in the late republic the notion of *pax* could be related to the eradication of brigandage and the reign of security both in the countryside and the cities of a Roman province, of course as a result of the efforts of the Roman governor. On this theme see Cicero, *Ad Quintum Fratrem,* 1.1.25. Cf. the comments of Brélaz 2005: 35.

69 Foxhall 1989: 23. Cf. also Garner 1987: 75.

Bibliography

Audollent, A. (1904) *Defixionum tabellae,* Paris.

Baldwin, B. (1963) 'Crime and criminals in Graeco-Roman Egypt', *Aegyptus* 43, 25663.

Bauschatz, J. (2013) *Law and Enforcement in Ptolemaic Egypt,* Cambridge, UK.

Benjamin, D. N. and Stea, D. (eds.) (1995) *The Home: Words, Interpretations, Meanings and Environments,* Aldershot, UK.

Berger, A. (1953) *An Encyclopedic Dictionary of Roman Law* (TAPS Vol. 43 Part 2), Philadelphia.

Brélaz, C. (2005) *La sécurité publique en Asie Mineure sous le Principat (Ier-IIIe s. ap. J.-C.),* Basel, Switzerland.

Brélaz, C. (2007) 'Lutter contre la violence à Rome: attributions étatiques et tâches privés' in C. Wolff (ed.), *Les exclus dans l'Antiquité,* Lyon, France, 219–39.

Bruneau, P. (1971) *Recherches sur les cultes de Délos à l'époque hellénistique et impériale,* Paris.

Cantarella, E. (2000) *Les peines de mort en Grèce et en Rome,* Paris.

Christ, M. (1998) 'Legal self-help on private property in classical Athens', *AJP* 119, 521–45.

Cohen, D. (1983) *Theft in Athenian Law,* Munich.

Daux, G. (1960) 'Chroniques des fouilles', *BCH* 84, 617–869.

Davies, R. W. (1973) 'The investigation of some crimes in Roman Egypt', *Ancient Society* 4, 199–212.

Dreher, M. (2009) 'Gerichtsverfahren vor den Göttern? – "judicial prayers" und die Kat-
egorisierung der defixionum tabellae' in G. Thür (ed.), *Symposion 2009: Vorträge zur
griechischen und hellenistichen Rechtsgeschichte*, Vienna, 30136.

Drexhage, H.-J. (1989) 'Eigentumsdelikte im römischen Ägypten (1. – 3. Jh. n. Chr.). Ein
Beitrag zur Wirtschaftsgeschichte' in *Aufstieg und Niedergang der Römischen Welt* II.
10.1, Berlin and New York, 952–1004.

Dunant, C. (1978) 'Sus aux voleurs!', *Museum Helveticum* 35, 241–4.

Eidinow, E. (2007) *Oracles, Curses and Risk among the Ancient Greeks*, Oxford, UK.

Faraone, C. A. and Rife, J. L. (2007) 'A Greek curse against a thief from the Koutsongila
cemetery at Roman Kenchreai', *ZPE* 160, 141–55.

Fisher, N. (1999) '"Workshops of villains": was there much organised crime in classical
Athens?' in K. Hopwood (ed.), *Organised Crime in Antiquity*, London, 53–96.

Foxhall, L. (1989) 'Household, gender and property in classical Athens', *CQ* 39, 22–44.

Fuhrmann, C. J. (2012) *Policing the Roman Empire: Soldiers, Administration and Public
Order*, Oxford, UK.

Gager, J. G. (1992) *Curse Tablets and Binding Spells from the Ancient World*, Oxford, UK.

Garner, R. (1987) *Law and Society in Classical Athens*, London and Sydney.

Garnsey, P. (1966) 'The *Lex Iulia* and appeal under the Empire', *JRS* 56, 167–89.

Gleason, M. (1999) 'Truth contests and talking corpses' in J. Porter (ed.), *Constructions of
the Classical Body*, Ann Arbor, MI, 287–309.

Gordon, R. (2004) 'Raising a sceptre: confession-narratives from Lydia and Phrygia', *JRA*
17, 177–96.

Grassl, H. (1982) *Sozialökonomische Vorstellungen in der Kaiserzeitlichen griechischen
Litteratur (1.- 3. Jh. n. Chr.)*, Wiesbaden, Germany.

Grünewald, T. (2004) *Bandits in the Roman Empire: Myth and Reality*, London and New York.

Hansen, M. H. (1976) *Apagoge, Endeixis and Ephegesis against Kakourgoi, Atimoi and
Pheugontes: A Study in Athenian Administration of Justice in the Fourth Century BC*,
Odense, Denmark.

Harries, J. (2007) *Law and Crime in the Roman World*, Cambridge, UK.

Herman, G. (2006) *Morality and Behaviour in Democratic Athens: A Social History*, Cambridge, UK.

Jameson, M. H. (1990) 'Space in the Greek city-state' in S. Kent (ed.), *Domestic Architecture and the Use of Space: An Interdisciplinary Cross-Cultural Study*, Cambridge, UK,
92–113.

Jordan, D. R. (1985) 'A survey of Greek defixiones not included in the special corpora',
GRBS 25, 151–97.

Jordan, D. R. (2002) 'Une prière de vengeance sur une tablette de plomb à Délos', *Revue
Archéologique* 55–60.

Kelly, B. (2007) 'Riot control and imperial ideology in the Roman Empire', *Phoenix* 61,
150–76.

Kelly, B. (2011) *Petitions, Litigation and Social Control in Roman Egypt*, Oxford, UK.

Kloppenborg, J. S. (2004) 'Self-help or "deus ex machina" in Mark 12.9?', *New Testament
Studies* 50, 495–518.

Krause, J.-U. (2004) *Kriminalgeschichte der Antike*, Munich.

Lewis, N. (1983) *Life in Egypt under Roman Rule*, Oxford, UK.

Lhôte, É. (2006) *Les lamelles oraculaires de Dodone*, Geneva.

Lintott, A. W. (1968) *Violence in Republican Rome*, Oxford, UK.

Lintott, A. W. (1982) *Violence, Civil Strife and Revolution in the Classical City*, Baltimore, MD.

Lukaszewicz, A. (1983) 'Petition concerning a theft: P. Berol. 7306*', *Journal of Juristic Papyrology* 19, 107–19.

Manfredini, A. D. (1996) 'Voleurs, brigands et légitime défense en droit romain', *Revue historique de droit francais et etranger* 74, 505–23.

Millar, F. (1981) 'The world of the Golden Ass', *JRS* 71, 63–75.

Paz de Hoz, M. (1999) *Die lydischen Kulte im Lichte der griechischen Inschriften*, Bonn, Germany.

Petzl, G. (1994) *Die Beichtinschriften Westkleinasiens*, Bonn, Germany.

Petzl, G. and Malay, H. (1987) 'A new confession-inscription from the Katakekaumene', *GRBS* 28, 459–72.

Pingree, D. (1976) *Dorothei Sidonii Carmen Astrologicum*, Leipzig, Germany.

Ricl, M. (1995) 'The appeal to divine justice in the Lydian confession inscriptions' in E. Schwertheim (ed.), *Forschungen in Lydien*, Bonn, Germany, 67–73.

Riess, W. (2001) *Apuleius und die Räuber: Ein Beitrag zur historischen Kriminalitäts-forschung*, Stuttgart.

Riess, W. (2008) 'Private violence and state control: the prosecution of homicide and its symbolical meanings in fourth-century BC Athens' in C. Brélaz and P. Ducrey (eds.), *Sécurité collective et ordre public dans les sociétés anciennes*, Geneva, 49–94.

Robinson, O. F. (1995) *The Criminal Law of Ancient Rome*, Baltimore, MD.

Saller, R. (1994) *Patriarchy, Property and Death in the Roman Family*, Cambridge, UK.

Sanders, D. (1990) 'Behavioral conventions and archaeology' in S. Kent (ed.), *Domestic Architecture and the Use of Space: An Interdisciplinary Cross-Cultural Study*, Cambridge, UK, 43–72.

Schulz, F. (1951) *Classical Roman Law*, Oxford, UK.

Screvens, R. (1981) 'Πόλη και εγκληματικότητα (κοινωνιολογική άποψη)' in *Tenth International Congress on Social Defence: General Reports*, Thessaloniki, Greece, 3348.

Shaw, B. D. (1984) 'Bandits in the Roman Empire', *P&P* 10, 3–52.

Shaw, B. D. (1992) 'Le bandit' in E. Giardina (ed.), *L'homme Romain*, Paris, 371–420.

Sherk, R. K. (1969) *Roman Documents from the Greek East*, Baltimore, MD.

Stanley, C. D. (2002) 'Who's afraid of a thief in the night?', *New Testament Studies* 48, 468–86.

Taubenschlag, R. (1955) *The Law of Greco-Roman Egypt in the Light of the Papyri*, 2nd ed., Warsaw.

Taubenschlag, R. (1959a) 'Self-help in Greco-Roman Egypt' in R. Taubenschlag, *Opera Minora II*, Warsaw, 135–41.

Taubenschlag, R. (1959b) 'The inviolability of domicile in Greco-Roman Egypt' in R. Taubenschlag, *Opera Minora II*, Warsaw, 143–50.

Treggiari, S. (2002) *Roman Social History*, London and New York.

Tsitsoura, A. (1981) 'Cities and criminality' in *Cities and Criminality. Tenth International Congress on Social Defence: General Reports and Synopses of National and Individual Reports*, Thessaloniki, Greece, 117–21.

Vélissaropoulos-Karakostas, J. (2009) 'Réponse à Martin Dreher' in G. Thür (ed.), *Symposion 2009: Vorträge zur griechischen und hellenistichen Rechtsgeschichte*, Vienna, 337–48.

Versnel, H. S. (1991) 'Beyond cursing: the appeal to justice in judicial prayers' in C. A. Faraone and D. Obbink (eds.), *Magika Hiera: Greek Magic and Religion*, Oxford, UK, 60–106.

Weinstock, S. (1960) 'Pax and the Ara Pacis', *JRS* 50, 44–58.

Welles, C. B. (1957) 'Complaint from a priest of Tebtunis concerning grain transportation charges', *Études de Papyrologie* 8, 103–11.

Wolff, C. (2003) *Les Brigands en Orient sous le Haut-Empire romain*, Rome.

Wolff, C. (2006) 'Le phénomène d'autodéfense sous le Haut-Empire romain à travers deux inscriptions de Dacie' in M. Molin (ed.), *Les régulations sociales dans l'Antiquité. Actes du colloque d'Angers 23 et 24 mai 2003*, Rennes France, 115–25.

Wolff, C. (2011) 'Voleurs et autres malfaiteurs urbains à l'époque des Flaviens' in M.-J. Kardos (ed.), *Habiter en ville au temps de Vespasien: Actes de la table ronde de Nancy 17 octobre 2008*, Nancy, France, 75–88.

Woolf, G. (1993) 'Roman peace' in J. Rich and G. Shipley (eds.), *War and Society in the Roman World*, London and New York, 171–94.

Yannakopulos, N. (2003) 'Preserving the Pax Romana: peace functionaries in Roman East', *Mediterraneo Antico* 6.2, 825–906.

Index

For Product Safety Concerns and Information please contact our EU
representative GPSR@taylorandfrancis.com Taylor & Francis Verlag GmbH,
Kaufingerstraße 24, 80331 München, Germany

Printed and bound by CPI Group (UK) Ltd, Croydon, CR0 4YY
01/05/2025
01858434-0001